Enterprise Project Portfolio Management

Building Competencies for R&D and IT Investment Success

Richard M. Bayney, Ph.D.
Ram Chakravarti

J.ROSS PUBLISHING

Copyright © 2012 by J. Ross Publishing

ISBN-13: 978-1-60427-060-0

Printed and bound in the U.S.A. Printed on acid-free paper.

10 9 8 7 6 5 4 3 2 1

Library of Congress Cataloging-in-Publication Data

Bayney, Richard M., 1956-
   Enterprise project portfolio management : building competencies for R&D
and IT investment success / by Richard M. Bayney and Ram Chakravarti.
      p. cm.
   Includes bibliographical references and index.
   ISBN 978-1-60427-060-0 (hardcover : alk. paper) 1. Project management.
2. Portfolio management. 3. Project management—Case studies. 4.
Portfolio management—Case studies. I. Chakravarti, Ram, 1972- II. Title.
   HD69.P75B39 2012
   658.4'04—dc23
                              2012016879

Phone: (954) 727-9333
Fax: (561) 892-0700
Web: www.jrosspub.com

Dedication

To the memory of Ma, who gave to me much more than ever she received, and to Pauls, Ma, and Zico for their unconditional love, patience, and encouragement.

Richard Bayney

To Su, my best friend and companion in the journey of life.

Ram Chakravarti

Contents

About the Authors

 **Richard Bayney** is President and Founder of Project & Portfolio Value Creation (PPVC), a consulting boutique that provides training, education, and guidance in project, program, portfolio, resource, and risk management, as well as business, strategic, portfolio, and scenario planning. He lectures at the University of Pennsylvania in Project Portfolio Management and Decision Modeling. Richard is a frequent speaker in portfolio and resource management, risk analysis and risk management, and strategic planning in drug development and an advisory board member to Cambridge Healthtech Institute. He is also a 23-year veteran of the pharmaceutical and biotechnology industries, having worked for Merck & Co., Bayer, Bristol-Myers Squibb, and Johnson & Johnson Pharmaceutical Research and Development. He has spent 11 years building and leading departments in strategic planning, decision analysis, and portfolio management, 2 years as an international project manager for a marketed cardiovascular drug, and 10 years in molecular biology research into gene expression in drug detoxification systems and Alzheimer's disease. Dr. Bayney obtained his M.Sc. and Ph.D. from the University of London, MBA from Columbia University, and PMP from the Project Management Institute.

 **Ram Chakravarti** is an information management professional, with demonstrated ability in enterprise strategy development, organization, facilitation, planning, execution, and value realization on large-scale programs and projects, from vision through delivery. Chakravarti's IT experience spans multiple industry verticals, encompassing the pharmaceutical, consumer goods, startup, telecommunication, financial services, and commercial aviation sectors. He has successfully delivered technology solutions, inclusive of ERP, CRM, e-commerce, BI & DW, SOA/BPM, and custom applications and has also encountered his share of failed IT initiatives. In his experience, the difference between the success and failure of IT initiatives can almost always be traced back to poor planning and misalignment of business and IT, with technology, rarely (if ever) the culprit. This multifaceted exposure has underscored the importance of IT portfolio management and influenced his career decision in becoming a practitioner of IT strategy, planning, enterprise architecture, and portfolio management for the last decade. Chakravarti has Master's degrees from the Indian Institute of Science and the University of Pennsylvania. He currently works for Oracle North American Enterprise Architecture, serving as a strategic technology advisor to Oracle customers.

Foreword

I have been thinking about project portfolio management in one way or another for a long time. When in business school, I studied how large organizations operated. I assumed that there was a thoughtful, fact-based process for deciding some of an organization's most important questions. I was quite surprised to learn that most organizations make decisions in sub-optimal ways.

In fact, I have seen up close that many organizations work on a "best story wins" principle, instead of making data-driven decisions. Examples are everywhere and take many shapes. One classic example is plain nepotism. When the boss's son is on a project, it gets selected more often than it would if he was just an employee. Also, if a manager has strong persuasive skills, then his or her project gets funded more often than it should. However, just because a person talks the loudest or the longest does not mean he or she is right.

Another difficult dynamic is the ability to end a project that is not meeting expectations. Also, linkages, conditions, and uncertainties are rarely accounted for in a systematic way. The most important thing is to get the "people side" of the organization correct. A framework like CREOPM™, which is described in this book, helps get the people side right by surfacing the best projects separate from the best communicators.

I have had a chance to work in two different but high-performing cultures: Oracle and Hyperion. At Hyperion, there was a highly decentralized collaboration culture. At Oracle, Larry Ellison is famous for his centralized command and control approach. CREOPM™ has a role in both structures. At Hyperion, CREOPM™ helped to facilitate the collaborative process. At Oracle, the framework helped to box in a strong personality and provided a systematic and rational project process.

I have been out of school for a long time and can tell you that this book is *not* just an academic exercise. The authors, Richard and Ram, have drawn on their years of experience and show how you can benefit from learning about how world-class organizations tackle tricky challenges. These lessons apply to a broad variety of companies and industries, primarily IT and pharmaceutical based, but the lessons can by utilized by new tech companies or anyone who is making decisions about capital or operations in light of uncertainty and trade-offs.

Business is about making money, but the more time I spend in business, the more I realize that business is *people*. In a resource allocation problem, the most difficult aspect to manage is the human factor. It is easy hypothetically to say that you will stop a failing project. In the real world, it is really hard to get people to stop doing things in the same way that they have been doing them every day for a long time. Even getting people to stop restarting things is hard. And here is a problem that has never been solved: How do you pay someone for successfully killing a bad project?

With CREOPM™, the role of flexibility in an uncertain environment is highlighted. Most managers tend to undervalue the role and value of flexibility. It is easy to minimize your cost or total cost of ownership, but in doing so, you trade off flexibility. For example, if you minimize unit cost by maximizing order size, you have *min'ed* your ability to hedge on your next transaction. Think of plant development: If you build one big plant, you will have the lowest cost per unit production, but have the least flexibility. So things can be great, until they are not. For example, when a hurricane disrupts your supply line to the one large facility, you are in big trouble. What is tricky is when you need the one big plant to get costs low enough to compete day to day; you are then subject to catastrophic risks, rare as they may be. What is the right answer? You won't find it in this foreword, but you will find it in this book.

When using math to evaluate a portfolio, you can measure the effect of sub-optimal portfolios. What is interesting about this is that if you measure the optimal portfolios and subtract the sub-optimal portfolio, you can quantify the cost of being sub-optimal. A classic case of sub-optimality is when the boss says, "I want to do Project 7," even if it is not part of a portfolio on the efficient frontier. If you can measure the sacred cow, you can kill it right there (even if it may be career limiting, from your perspective).

An important distinction to make is the difference between good decisions and good outcomes. When we make a decision and have a good outcome, we like to take credit for the link. However, there can often be a lot of uncertainty or luck in that link. Buying a lottery ticket and winning is not a good decision linked to a good outcome, but rather a bad decision coincidental with a good outcome. When we make a decision which is hopefully a good one but linked to a bad outcome, such as drilling a well in a promising location and then finding it dry, it was still a good decision. That's life! Sometimes we may want to make a decision that has negative net present value because the upside is so large that if it works, it may impact the entire portfolio. It is OK to expect failure as long as there is greatness in the aggregate.

Accounting for linked decisions is subtle and tricky, especially in a complex organization where decisions can cross departments and continents. Mapping links in decisions is an exercise unto itself. Because business is all about people, and people have biases, it is imperative to address the cognitive biases in any decision-making framework. In this book, the authors are systematic in their approach, which helps to alleviate the impact of well-known cognitive biases.

The devil of project portfolio management is in the details. Part of a robust analysis is to add uncertainty calculations. When you have uncertainty in the inputs, you can propagate that uncertainty through math and business logic and have uncertainty in the outputs. The interesting thing about that process is that you can then tell the probability or likelihood of a particular outcome. Whether it is measuring the downside or seeing the upside, it is much better to deal with reality than a "conservative" number. As a CEO, I do not want the conservative number; I want the right number with a sense for the upside and downside to that number.

However, project portfolio management is not a quick fix. Many projects, over a long time, have to be played out to discern a change from the status quo. You may make a long series of good decisions and still not have good outcomes.

Richard and Ram have put forth a rational and systematic approach with their CREOPM™ framework. PROACT.url is a great framework for thinking through decisions, and is just a sample of the deep content in this book. I especially like their focus on decision framing. Getting the right question is more than half the battle. When I first started doing Crystal Ball training, framing questions was—I thought—the most important part. It is more important to solve the right problem than to have an elegant solution to the wrong problem. So often in my business experience, I have either made that mistake or have seen others make it.

Also, real options are sometimes an academic exercise, but they are another key to management decision making. Richard and Ram have an approachable take on real options that can be understood by the student, as well as applied by the business executive. One example is the option to stop a project. Just getting this option right can save an organization a lot of expense.

This book is useful to a business reader, as well as a graduate student. The authors do an excellent job of blending the primer material with more advanced topics. The book is broad, but also deep. What I like best is that the CREOPM™ framework is not only rational, but systematic. So many books or frameworks tell you where to focus, but not what to do. This book dives deep into techniques such as stochastic optimization, and the result is what you *can* actually do. When you read, you will understand why we decide, "Do this and this and this, but not that or that." Better yet, they tell you the order to do those things. All organizations are doing project portfolio management, whether they realize it or not. By adding structure and math, we can have better decisions and, in the long run, better outcomes.

James Franklin
CEO of SendGrid
Former CEO Decisioneering, VP & GM Oracle Crystal Ball Global Business Unit

Preface

As a multitude of organizations spanning a spectrum of industries continue to restructure, the battle cry from within those organizations is: "To be successful, we need to do more with less." Of the ten words in that popular sentence, the following words are open to interpretation: *successful, more,* and *less.*

What is *successful?* Is it top line sales growth, gross margin, net present value of cash flows, return on investment, or a combination of financial metrics by which organizations routinely measure success? And, what do *more* and *less* refer to: more of one or another financial metric, and less resources such as budgets or people? By the way, there is no temporal reference in the sentence above, and in our experience, that sentence does not provide the necessary orientation for most employees, who are trying to help their organizations succeed.

Instead, a less ambiguous modification of that sentence may help to galvanize organization-wide support and could read as follows: "To be successful—as defined by increases in our primary financial measures (*e.g., top line sales growth and annual cash flows*)—over the next x (*e.g.,* 5, 10, 20) years, we need to maximize the value of our business (*as measured by financial metrics*) in accordance with limited resources (*e.g., budgetary and human*)." The clearer articulation of where an organization is heading, and how it will measure itself if/when it arrives, is the basis on which sound business practices such as portfolio management are built.

Value creation is another popular term in the lexicon of business and business schools alike, but where can the phrase *maximum value creation* be seen? On the assumption that "value" is appropriately defined, why would a rational decision maker wish to "create value" (presumably a good state of affairs) without knowing its optimal state, *create maximum value?* Whether for profit or not, should not the ultimate goal of every organization be to create maximum value? To skeptics of the term "business value," who posit that not all business value can be quantified in terms of financial value, we agree, albeit hesitantly.

So, let's do the sensible thing and mutually agree that all business value can be quantified in terms of benefit (i.e., utility, usefulness, or goodness) to the end user of a good (product, capability, service) created by another entity (e.g., an organization), in which case the phrase *create maximum value* is replaced, more palatably, by *create maximum benefit.* Whether a contributor or decision maker in an organization, if you are not in pursuit of the creation of maximum business value or benefit, but are instead satisfied by "good enough value or benefit," it is arguable that you are pursuing sub-optimal business value or benefit. If this all seems a tad harsh, it is because we are intent on creating an awareness of the lexicon of ambiguity that is tolerated at all levels in organizations—large and small, centralized and decentralized, autocratic and bureaucratic—that, if unchallenged or unchanged, will doubtless allow business value to be left on the proverbial table. In a nutshell, we have had a difficult time accepting that "good enough" should be *good enough*. Parenthetically, we do not find successful sports teams aspiring to be "good enough", so neither should other organizations contemplate attaining a sub-optimal business state.

For many years, we both worked for hugely successful organizations that created fabulous products, but which were forced, in one form or another, to alter their business model and value propositions to end customers. These changes were accompanied by various forms of local and global restructuring and, with it, a tidal wave of cost cutting that led to unabated job reductions. With more readily available access than ever before to skilled global labor, some jobs have shifted almost inevitably to emerging economies where cost efficiencies are bountiful. Despite this shift in the talent pool, how do organizations know that, subject to their constrained resources, they are maximizing (or not) the benefit or value that they are capable of creating? Perhaps if they did, the rationale for a greater number of investment decisions would become more transparent and, with healthier portfolios, there would be less need for restructuring, accompanied by fewer job losses.

In our experience, while one form or another of portfolio management is often practiced in organizations that have an R&D and/or IT function, there is tremendous room for improvement. To begin with, it is sometimes difficult to trace the decision roots of a project investment, that is, to understand *why* and *how* a project first becomes a component of an active portfolio. Although much has been written on the subject of risk, we find that in many organizations, risk quantification often lacks traceability and defensibility. Far too many project investments, in our opinion, are poorly evaluated, especially when data and information are uncertain, leading to the Pavlovian need to justify a point estimate to "make the evaluation more manageable."

When risk quantification and project evaluation are not well conducted, risk-adjusted valuations have limited importance to decision making. Project prioritization has become, to our surprise, synonymous with portfolio selection as the primary and, in most cases, sole framework for enabling portfolio management. While this methodology has served many organizations well for decades, we believe that, with the need for no additional data, better but far more underutilized techniques in portfolio optimization can be applied to create greater portfolio value. Finally, the management of project investments has been guided for decades by the frame of the triple constraint (scope, time, cost), but many projects in R&D and IT are completed late, over budget, and with altered scope. There is a glaring need to critically examine other factors that can impact the management of projects and therefore the portfolio.

Why Did We Write This Book?

The time has come for a greater appreciation of how portfolio management—as a *bona fide* discipline rather than a collection of annual or semi-annual organizational activities—can maximize business value on an ongoing basis, in consideration of constrained resources and other organizational prerequisites. In short, unless organizations learn how to embed active and prescriptive portfolio management into their DNA, while many may remain successful, they will leave untold value on the proverbial table and, in the process, create unnecessary restructuring that could lead to the loss of hard-working seasoned professionals and aspiring newcomers alike.

Before you begin to think about embracing project portfolio management and inculcating this discipline into your organization, please ask yourself the following question: "In less than 50 words, can I articulate to a layperson the temporal strategic and financial orientation of my organization?" In other words, do you know where your organization is heading, what it wants to look like when it gets there, and how it will measure its progress along the way, including its destination? If not, find someone who can describe this to you on the back of a small napkin and (hopefully) not in a PowerPoint presentation. With this level of clarity under your belt, you are ready to avoid the path of Alice in *Alice in Wonderland* and the dubious question that she famously asked: "Would you tell me, please, which way I ought to go from here?" Without knowing where "there" is, you will never know if project portfolio management can help you and your organization get there.

This book provides an orientation to strategic planning, which is a necessary prerequisite to successful project portfolio management and which we hope that you will share with others. Unlike the discipline of financial portfolio management, which has had a long and successful history in both academic and professional circles, project portfolio management has struggled to become recognized as a discipline in its own right. The concept of the efficient frontier (discussed in Chapter 7, Portfolio Optimization), as first introduced by Markovitz, defines the set of investments that maximizes financial return for any given level of risk. In other words, for a given level of risk, there exists a combination of investments that constitutes a portfolio whose return is the highest amongst all other possible portfolios, i.e., an optimal portfolio that, by definition, cannot be bettered when measured on the basis of financial return.

All other portfolios that lie below the efficient frontier are sub-optimal in that no matter how good their financial return, they are inferior to the optimal combinatorial set of investments. We apply the principle of the efficient frontier from financial portfolio management to project portfolio management in several chapters because we want you—irrespective of whether you are managing your own portfolio or helping the organization you work for—to ask yourself: "Do you want to be on the frontier, and if not, how far below the frontier can you afford to be?"

Over the past decade, we have found well-intentioned books that contain the term "project portfolio management" in their titles, only to engage in excellent discourses in project management. In an attempt to take the mystery out of project portfolio management and to prescribe a foundation for its use, we have defined a pragmatic framework called CREOPM™. CREOPM™ stands for Project Categorization, Risk Analysis, Integrated Evaluation, Portfolio Optimization, Project Prioritization, and Portfolio Management. When applied judiciously and with organizational and analytic discipline, this framework can lead to enhanced portfolio value creation across all types of businesses and industries.

To be sure, we do not expect nor recommend that every organization treat CREOPM™ as a panacea for project portfolio management. However, we expect that every organization would be able to apply some of its basic principles to enable project portfolio management to be successful. The basic principles include, but are not limited to: clear strategic thinking, disciplined decision making, robust technical and commercial analysis, and effective management and leadership. Every organization, we believe, currently employs one or more components of CREOPM™, but few appear to do this systematically or reproducibly. CREOPM™ can be considered as part of a project portfolio management capability maturity learning curve: first, apply the basic prerequisites, then build capabilities as ongoing training is provided to both portfolio management practitioners and decision makers. Without the correct capability building blocks, project portfolio management can quickly lose traction.

By the way, in the process of adopting the framework, we do not believe that glossy software tools are an effective substitute for training. In fact, we suspect the folks at IBM Research got it right when they stated: "A fool with a tool is still a fool." CREOPM™ allows you to examine an effective, prescribed framework for managing your portfolio of R&D and IT projects. If you wish to extract maximum value for what you are capable of investing in, its use is highly recommended.

Finally, we continue to encounter students and practitioners in academic and professional settings who appear to be resistant to implementing a formal project portfolio management framework, such as CREOPM™, to enable the successful management of a portfolio of R&D and IT investments. A plethora of reasons to avoid a new approach is generally offered, but the most disturbing reason is: "This other method of project portfolio management is the way it has always been done here." This implies one of two things—no need to change and/or fear of change, neither of which is likely to increase the chance of creating a sustainably successful business model in a rapidly changing global environment.

To these students and practitioners, we often ask the same question: "If this was your company, would you manage the portfolio the same way?" Without exception, the response is, "No, but…." Despite the "but," if you would not manage your own portfolio of project investments this way, why would you not help your company manage its portfolio of project investments differently? If you are a student or practitioner who has the inclination and patience to read this book, we hope that you will find the information sufficiently compelling to change your perspectives of project portfolio management.

Who Will Benefit from This Book?

The book is intended for the following audiences:

- Any stakeholder—a decision maker or other person—who participates in the active management of a portfolio of products, services, or capabilities in an organization. This category includes: (1) project portfolio management practitioners who are entering the discipline, (2) seasoned practitioners who are trying to improve their own capability maturity levels in project portfolio management, (3) financial managers whose main objective is to ensure transparency and defensibility regarding project investment estimates and spending patterns, and (4) resource managers whose primary goal is to ensure that projects receive timely budgetary and human support.

- Decision makers, who may or may not have a penchant for analysis, wishing to understand whether or not their project portfolio management functions are extracting maximum benefit or value from the use of their organization's constrained resources.

- Strategists who are responsible for advising CEOs, CFOs, CIOs, and R&D management about what it will take to integrate strategic plans, portfolio plans, and business plans in order to meet the organization's short-, medium-, and long-term goals.

- Entrepreneurs who are setting up their own businesses in traditional areas or embracing the uncertainties of changing business models by investing in innovative technologies and technology platforms.

- Graduate students with an interest in project portfolio management and decision making under conditions of risk and uncertainty, who are undertaking courses at the master's level (e.g., MBA, EMBA, EMTM, and MIS courses).

- Educators who are trying to blend hard-core operations research/management science with an organizational orientation to project portfolio management.

- Agnostics and naysayers who believe that project portfolio management can best be accomplished by a combination of experience and good judgment alone.

The Book's Organization

This book is organized into four sections with four accompanying appendices. In Section 1 and Chapter 1, we describe an R&D portfolio, from drug discovery to market, which is typical of the pharmaceutical and biotechnology industries, as well as an IT portfolio that can be disaggregated into distinct discovery, project, and asset phases. These cases provide an overview of the complexity of both types of project portfolios, R&D and IT, and an appreciation for the varying levels of risk and uncertainty that are embedded within them. CREOPM™, the project portfolio management foundation of this book, is used as a framework that is bound by both process and methodology, requiring stakeholder sponsorship and support at the highest levels of the organization to enable its success.

Section 2, Prerequisites for Enterprise Project Portfolio Management, is designed to provide the reader with an orientation to scenario analysis and strategic planning in Chapter 2, followed by an overview of decision making in Chapter 3. We are of the unshakeable belief that successful business models are founded on some form of strategic analysis and planning which, if clearly articulated and understood by stakeholders at all levels in an organization, can provide a beacon of directionality that fosters excellent leadership and followership practices. Without a clear understanding of the basis on which decisions will be made, organizations may tend to paralyze themselves with various forms of analysis (which, in turn, become the focal point of blame for not enabling decision making in the first place!) or tend to "cherry-pick" certain forms of analysis to either supplement judgment and heuristics or marginalize those forms altogether. Good decision making, especially under conditions of high risk and uncertainty, has its roots in clarity, transparency, traceability, and defensibility of argumentation, i.e., a combination of logically correct thinking, analysis, and judgment. Nevertheless, making good decisions under this umbrella of criteria does not guarantee successful outcomes to every decision. One of the realities of decision making is you have the opportunity to control the decision that you are about to make, but not necessarily the outcome of that decision.

Section 3, CREOPM™: A Framework for Enterprise Project Portfolio Management, is designed to approach project portfolio management in a holistic, sequential manner, with a foundation in robust process and methodology. Chapters 4-9 describe the CREOPM™ framework's individual components: Project Categorization, Risk Analysis, Integrated Evaluation, Portfolio Optimization, Project Prioritization, and Portfolio Management. We do not expect organizations to embrace the concept of CREOPM™ in its undiluted totality; rather, given an organization's level of maturity and commitment to excellence, we hope that it will adopt those aspects of the framework that are manageable to begin with and then progressively seek to create greater portfolio value.

An organization cannot enjoy sustainable success without high-level sponsorship and dedicated training and development in several functional areas of CREOPM™, most notably portfolio management. This is why we touch on a portfolio management capability maturity model in Chapter 9 that organizations can utilize to: (a) assess their level of competency in this discipline across multiple dimensions and (b) create transition plans to ameliorate their current state on a multi-year basis.

In Section 4, Case Studies, we provide two detailed project portfolio management cases in IT (Chapter 10) and R&D (Chapter 11), where portfolio selection based on project prioritization and portfolio optimization is described in depth. With a greater need for clarity and definition of strategic and financial business goals (a good thing), but without the need for additional data and information (also good), we demonstrate the "superiority"—defined as the creation of greater portfolio value—of one methodology (optimization) over another (prioritization).

We will let readers decide if the creation of greater portfolio value works best personally and/or for the organization. Note that no methodology should be applied without an appropriate framework, and this is why we introduce the framework of CREOPM™ before the case studies.

After the Epilogue in Chapter 12, there are four appendices. Appendix A, A Primer in Decision Analysis, and Appendix B, A Primer in Mathematical Programming, serve to further the interest of the reader in either or both disciplines. Appendix C, MODA Models for IT Investment Prioritization, and Appendix D, SIRC's Enterprise IT Portfolio, serve as complements to the IT case study that is found in Chapter 10.

Richard Bayney
Ram Chakravarti

Acknowledgments

The authors wish to thank several individuals without whom this book would not have seen the light of day. The inherent complexities and effort involved in writing a book are non-trivial, especially when there are multiple authors working in different time zones and with families to answer to. For starters, the collaborators have to be of a similar mindset and have the same passion toward the subject matter at hand. Luckily, we've been quite successful on that front. From the outset, our editor, Drew Gierman, has been a phenomenal source of support, and his nurturing approach in providing guidance at every juncture to two first-time authors has significantly enhanced the quality of this book. We would also like to thank Steve Buda of J. Ross Publishing for his diligent proofreading, refinement, and all the assistance rendered in taking this manuscript from draft to production.

We thank Jim Franklin for providing the foreword and, in essence, validating our work based on his extensive experience in the industry as well as on the topic of management science. We would be remiss if we failed to express our gratitude to the following individuals, who took time from their hectic schedules to provide insightful feedback and review of our compendium: Isabella Fugaccia, Frank Konings, Kevin Kuehm, Donald Pardew, Robert Prachar, Richard Sonnenblick, and Jonathan Woo.

From Richard Bayney:

To my wonderful wife, Pauls, who has been the bedrock of my existence and by my side each and every step of the way since Ma passed on, and to my precious children, Ma and Zico, for having brought so much joy and love to my life; try though I must, I can never fully express how fortunate I have been to have you all in my life. To my colleagues at Bayer (Kevin Kuehm, Samar Mehta, Christopher Seaton, Jeffrey Stonebraker), Bristol-Myers Squibb (Anthony Artuso, Kazuo Ezawa, Marc Goldring, Maureen Keegan, Jack Kloeber, Michael Miernicki, Steven Peterson, Che-Lin Su, Lotte Wang, Jonathan Woo), and Johnson & Johnson (Krishna Chepuri, Bennett Levitan, Vanessa Lum, Michele Pfund, Vish Viswanathan) for having contributed to my knowledge in portfolio management, I express my sincere gratitude. To the finest student I have met to date, my brilliant coauthor and friend, Ram Chakravarti, thank you for accepting my invitation to write this book. I trust that this is the first of many collaborations to follow. Finally, to my wonderful grandmother, Ma (Rajcoomarie Ramphaul), too poor to enjoy the value of a formal education but wiser than any human being I have met, I thank her every day for her boundless and unconditional love and for having instilled the right values in me.

From Ram Chakravarti:

To Su, my best friend and companion in the journey of life, I owe my personal motivation and discipline—your wisdom, values, humor, and belief in me have inspired my success at every turn. I have been fortunate for the whole-hearted love and support of my parents, Geethu and KK, in ensuring that my education and well-being were never compromised, regardless of economic constraints. I'm also grateful to my friends and family, who have been tremendous sources of support and encouragement during times of adversity, so thank you Anu Paul; Murali and Arjun Balaraman; Viji, Venkat and Vish Iyer; Greg Barnowsky; Mohan Kumar; Lisa Baum; Lee Jussim; Rich and Diane McGreal; Anjum Khan; Sajjad Ladiwalla; Jim and Judy Peiffer; Hita Durvasula; and Bill Muller. I'd like to thank Tim Stanley, Greg Barnowsky, Jay Gardner, Hima Patel, John Engelhart, Dr. Jean-Marc Choukroun, Dr. Larry Starr, Raj Agarwal, and Jay Chelur, who have been generous in sharing their wisdom at various stages in my career, from which I have benefited immensely. Finally, I'd like to express my gratitude to Dr. Bayney, whom I've known now for a few years, first as his student at the University of Pennsylvania and then as a good friend. I'm honored that he approached me with the idea of collaborating on this venture, which has truly been a humbling experience. I have learned a lot from him, not the least of which are his continued emphasis on precision of thought and pragmatic approach to decision making, which I hope to have assimilated personally, in some small measure.

At J. Ross Publishing we are committed to providing today's professional with practical, hands-on tools that enhance the learning experience and give readers an opportunity to apply what they have learned. That is why we offer free ancillary materials available for download on this book and all participating Web Added Value™ publications. These online resources may include interactive versions of material that appears in the book or supplemental templates, worksheets, models, plans, case studies, proposals, spreadsheets and assessment tools, among other things. Whenever you see the WAV™ symbol in any of our publications, it means bonus materials accompany the book and are available from the Web Added Value Download Resource Center at www.jrosspub.com.

Downloads for *Enterprise Project Portfolio Management* include:

- A slide presentation describing the utility of CREOPM™, a unique portfolio management process and methodology
- An Excel analytical setup template for the Innovations R Us Corporation case in Chapter 7 of the book with instructions for portfolio optimization
- An Excel analytical setup template for the Drugs R Us case in Appendix A of the book with instructions for decision analysis using TreePlan

Section 1

Introduction to Enterprise Project Portfolio Management

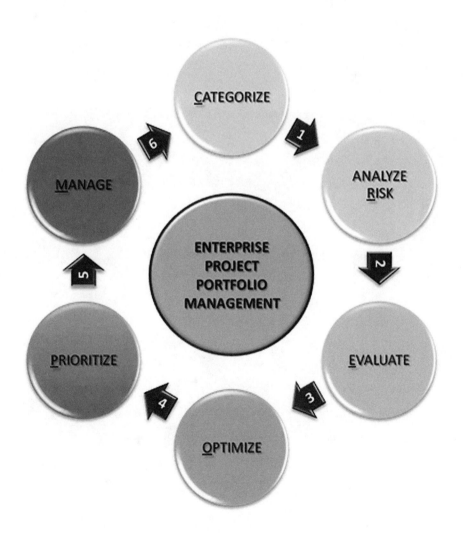

1

Basic Concepts of Enterprise Project Portfolio Management

Project portfolio management (PPM) is the active management of a collection of projects or investments (or programs), whose consolidated purpose is to aid in the attainment of an enterprise's ongoing strategic and financial goals under constrained resource conditions. In many organizations, this is referred to as *enterprise project portfolio management* (EPPM).

Although the management of a portfolio of assets (e.g., financial assets, research and development [R&D] assets, information technology [IT] assets) is a discipline that is several decades old, the term "portfolio management" has, for many reasons, become associated almost exclusively with the management of financial assets. In recent years, a plethora of publications targeting the management of projects—as opposed to financial instruments—has emerged. From this literature, the term "project portfolio management" has become an extension of the lexicon of project management. (Note that the abbreviations PPM and EPPM will be used interchangeably throughout this book.) Although portfolio management refers to the management of all types of organizational assets, it is easier to discuss the management of projects under the umbrella term "project portfolio management."

1.1 The R&D Portfolio

Since the start of the twenty-first century, the pharmaceutical and biotechnology industry has experienced an almost continuous wave of changes that have sparked an unprecedented transformation of the operating models of the most successful companies in this industry. One of the primary forces that spawned this ongoing transformation is the loss of patent protection for many blockbuster drugs, resulting in an inability to reproduce double-digit, top line growth experienced by many successful companies during the last half of the twentieth century.

In turn, this has led to heightened scrutiny of the proportion of sales revenues being reinvested in R&D engines, resulting in what may be described as draconian cost cutting, leading to ongoing fragmentation of the end-to-end business model that once served the industry with stellar results. An almost-perfect complement to the loss of patent exclusivity has been the inability of the industry to generate commercially successful drugs to replace those being genericized; in fact, when measured by the total number of new

3

drugs that have passed regulatory approval in any given year, the industry has failed to replicate the banner year of 1996 when more than 50 New Drug Applications (NDAs) were successfully approved by the U.S. Food and Drug Administration (FDA).

Despite the advent of many high-powered techniques that enable increasingly large numbers of chemical and genetic libraries to be screened for potential drugs at the front end of the R&D funnel, throughput of new drugs at the other end of the funnel has been largely abysmal. To counteract the scale of the lack of productivity of its R&D engines, the pharmaceutical and biotechnology industry has become engaged in a process of dismantling its internal discovery and development machinery, leading to massive outsourcing (and offshoring) and loss of internal employment that has reached staggering proportions. In an effort to bolster waning project pipelines, the industry has experienced an almost continuous wave of mergers and acquisitions that have resulted in further job losses from contraction in search of economies of scale and scope. Where will these changes take the drug discovery and development industry, and, of the multitude of players both large and small, who will be left standing?

While cost cutting and contraction are likely to improve the efficiency of R&D portfolios, it is unforeseen if these measures will improve the productivity of an industry that has matured in an era of high R&D and commercial investments. What is becoming more widely recognized is the need to better manage portfolios of opportunities in an industry that is renowned for its environment of high technical risk and commercial uncertainty. Portfolio management will require a better decision-making discipline than has been practiced hitherto, which is dependent on a combination of insightful strategic and analytic insights into what investments should be made, when, and why—the essence of successful portfolio management.

What are the main characteristics of an R&D portfolio, and how does it compare with an IT portfolio of projects and programs? To be sure, a portfolio is comprised of both projects (in various stages of research, development, or regulatory submission) and commercially available products. Within the pharmaceutical and biotechnology industries, a generic representation of the major phases of discovery, development, and commercialization of an R&D portfolio shows projects that actively enter and others that are terminated from the portfolio (often referred to as a "pipeline of projects"), while the products that survive the high risks of this industry environment emerge to become commercially viable (see Figure 1-1). At the end of each stage of research and development of the pipeline, projects (and programs) are reviewed to assess their pedigree and, consequently, to determine if they fulfill predetermined decision criteria for further investment. If not, they are subjected to one of several fates: termination, storage until a later date for reexamination, external exchange for another project, partnership, or sale.

Given the high risks of the pharmaceutical and biotechnology industry, based on industry attrition rates, it takes on average 36 discovery compounds or bona fide projects of chemical or biological origin (potential drugs) to achieve regulatory approval by the FDA of a single product. How many starting compounds are the result of earlier screening and structural optimization is a matter of definition and perspective and will not be dealt with in this book. Nevertheless, a multitude of projects emerge from the initial influx of compounds to the pipeline funnel, all requiring good portfolio management

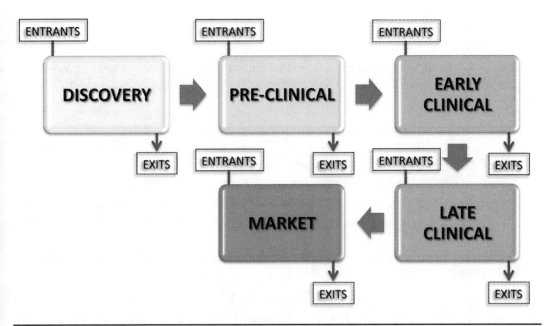

Figure 1-1   Generic representation of the stages of evolution of a portfolio in the pharmaceutical and biotechnology industry

processes and methodologies to enable an organization to maximize the value of its constrained resources in the hope of yielding successful marketable products.

During the drug discovery process, which can take 2-4 years, the following activities are conducted (Rang, 2006):

Target selection and validation—Conceptual and exploratory research aimed at identifying and validating a therapeutic target.

Lead identification—Applied research focused on developing assays for screening and evaluating compounds; screening for chemical and biological structures to create one or more lead compounds, and testing of such compounds to determine their target effect for structural optimization.

Lead optimization—Structural optimization and biological testing of the compound(s) intended for toxicology testing in animals; completion of all necessary *in vivo* studies, pharmacokinetic and pharmacodynamic tests, stability and solubility studies, and determination of surrogate markers for human studies, prior to first administration in humans.

Within pre-clinical development, a variety of objectives are targeted over an approximate 2-year period (Rang, 2006):

- Compound synthesis according to good manufacturing practices (GMP) and dose finding studies in animals.
- Stability tests, safety pharmacology, formulation, genotoxicity, toxicology, and analytic methods.

- Preparation of Investigational New Drug (IND) and investigator brochure for submission to the FDA.

Once FDA approval is gained to proceed to human clinical trials, a well laid-out approach to clinical development is expected to achieve information about the following during a 3- to 7-year period (Rang, 2006):

- Phase 1 trials—Exploratory safety, tolerability, and pharmacokinetics.
- Phase 2 trials—Exploratory safety and efficacy, preliminary evidence of proof of concept (POC); confirmatory dose selection based on statistical dose-response relationships and regimen for optimum safety, efficacy, and tolerability.
- Phase 3 trials—Confirmatory safety and efficacy, based on statistically rigorous measurements of the potential drug in comparison to placebo or existing therapies.
- Phase 4 trials—Obligatory post-marketing surveillance to monitor adverse events.

Once clinical trials and data analysis are completed, an NDA is submitted to the FDA, requiring 1-2 years before marketing approval can be gained. Over the entire drug discovery, development, and submission processes, the cost of getting a drug approved successfully by the FDA can range from approximately USD$900M to USD$1.7B (DiMasi et al., 2003; Gilbert et al., 2003). The costs include the cost of discovery and development of all projects that failed along the value creation chain (see Figure 1-2).

During the drug discovery and development process, as projects mature and others are terminated or stalled, many decisions within the portfolio need to be made under conditions of tremendous risk and high uncertainty. While the thrust of project management has largely been to do projects the "right" way, i.e., within the triple constraint of scope, cost, and time, the impetus for portfolio management is to do the right projects, i.e., those projects that are capable of providing the best strategic and financial value to the enterprise subject to its constrained budgetary, human, and other resources. Not surprisingly, the challenge of portfolio management evokes many critical questions about projects (and programs):

- Which projects should be worked on, and at what rate?
- How much information is necessary, and what criteria will be used for making informed decisions regarding the progression, delay, or termination of projects?
- What dependencies exist between projects in which decisions made on one project may impact the technical and/or commercial viability of other projects, and how should such dependencies be handled?
- Should all projects that have met their temporal objectives be automatically progressed to the next phase of their maturity, and if not, why not?
- Which projects should be allocated their full resources and which ones not, or which ones should be done "at risk"?
- When should the investment in a project, whether good or bad, be redirected to a potentially better internal or external asset?

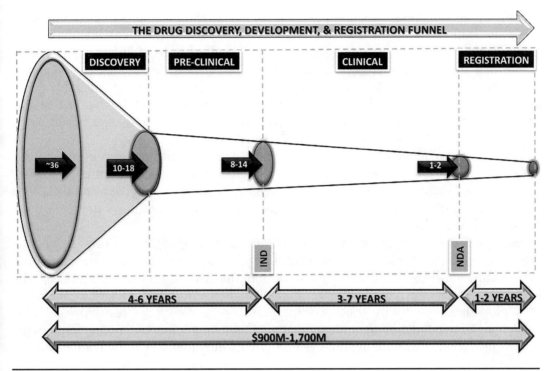

Figure 1-2   Chain of value creation of an R&D portfolio in the pharmaceutical and biotechnology industry

- In order to meet the enterprise's ongoing strategic and financial goals, how best should resources be allocated to projects, programs, and sub-portfolios?
- In a multi-business unit organization, how should resources be allocated to maximize overall value creation to the enterprise?

The aim of this book is to provide recommendations and answers to these questions.

1.2 The IT Portfolio

IT is a key enabler of success in many organizations, providing the requisite tools to the enterprise to respond with agility to changing market conditions and evolving business needs. Consequently, it is of no surprise that IT accounts for a significant portion of capital investment in many organizations, typically ranging from 1.5% to 7% of company revenues (Maizlish and Handler, 2005).

Similar to other capital investments, the scale of investment in IT necessitates rigor and discipline in investment planning and portfolio selection. However, the murky waters of the technical complexity that characterizes IT investments as well as the associated jargon and hype, coupled with the rapid changes in technology in the marketplace, result in considerable confusion, imposing significant challenges in making judicious choices in IT investments, with the net result being that wrong investment decisions are commonplace.

In many organizations over the past decade, executives have imposed considerable pressure on the IT division on account of its "poor performance" that can be traced to poor or wrong investment decisions by the IT leadership itself. It has, in fact, been noted than IT does not matter in terms of providing strategic advantage for organizations since, much like electric power or the railroad, it has become considerably commoditized (Carr, 2004). While this is debatable, it has no doubt further fueled the flames of microscopic scrutiny of IT investment decisions in companies, resulting in CIOs facing considerable pressure to significantly trim costs.

The active management of information technology is of utmost importance to the CIO, since organizations cannot afford the continued poor management of IT investments. Further, the treatment of IT investments as unchecked expenses, and their lack of alignment with organizational value creation, cause their continuity to be continually brought into question.

External factors that impose hurdles on IT include competitive offerings by unconventional entrants, increased governmental regulations on companies, changing customer demands, higher levels of personalization, the advent of cloud computing,[1] virtualization, services-oriented architecture, social computing, and a host of ephemeral technologies. Coupled with those external hurdles are even more restrictive internal challenges in the form of spending constraints, cost reduction initiatives, responsiveness improvements, and the loss of credibility that hurt many IT organizations on account of poor performance in the face of rampant spending on new techologies, with little to show by way of defined business results.

Despite the expansion of IT management's role into the formulation and development of strategic planning, a recent study by Hertz and Dowse (2009) indicates that 7 out of 10 CIOs are viewed with less respect than other C-level executives, and that 94% of IT executives are expected to change the way business works. The study also echoes what has been apparent to many IT professionals, which is that the definition of the IT-business relationship as a "partnership" is, in many organizations, a gross overstatement. Despite numerous attempts by IT organizations to demonstrate value and earn a seat at the table, IT leaders in many organizations have largely failed, and the relationship between IT and the business remains a contentious "us vs. them," as opposed to "we."

One of the primary reasons for IT's comparatively low position on the organizational totem pole is that decisions have been made rather injudiciously in many organizations, sometimes for the sake of technology, rather than making sound investment decisions based on aligning IT with business goals and objectives. Consequently, IT value has been consistently oversold while underdelivering. According to Maizlish and Handler (2005), the organizational prescriptions for improving IT's credibility are:

1. Adopting rational decision-making processes.
2. Making balanced investments across business units.

---

[1]"Cloud computing" is a general term for anything that involves delivering hosted services over the Internet. The services are broadly divided into three categories: Infrastructure-as-a-Service (IaaS), Platform-as-a-Service (PaaS), and Software-as-a-Service (SaaS). The name "cloud computing" was inspired by the cloud symbol that was often used to represent the Internet in flowcharts and diagrams.

3. Instituting pragmatic cost- and risk-control mechanisms.
4. Being flexible in reassessing and rebalancing priorities in a fluid environment.
5. Adherence to mandated compliance and regulatory requirements.

In other words, the prescription for success in IT organizations is the adoption of portfolio management as the basis for investment decision making—success being defined as IT becoming a trusted partner to deliver benefits in concordance with the business plan. A mature IT portfolio management discipline can be the change agent that could improve its performance considerably, help it evolve from a utility player to a trusted partner, and enable IT to earn an equal seat at the organization's management table.

In order to comprehend the nuances in IT portfolio management, it is imperative to understand the enterprise IT lifecycle, since an effective and efficient IT portfolio management practice is dependent on the foundational processes that constitute the IT lifecycle. The IT lifecycle is illustrated in Figure 1-3, which shows IT's linkage to the enterprise strategy and the three phases that constitute the IT lifecycle, as well as the inter-relationships between them.

The enterprise IT lifecycle includes three phases of activities: the discovery (or innovation) phase, project phase, and asset phase (Maizlish and Handler, 2005). From an IT organization's perspective, the three phases of the lifecycle receive input from IT strategy and planning, which in turn depends on the enterprise's strategic intent and business objectives. Additionally, linkages between each of the phases illustrate their interdependencies, where the output of the discovery phase can feed the project phase,

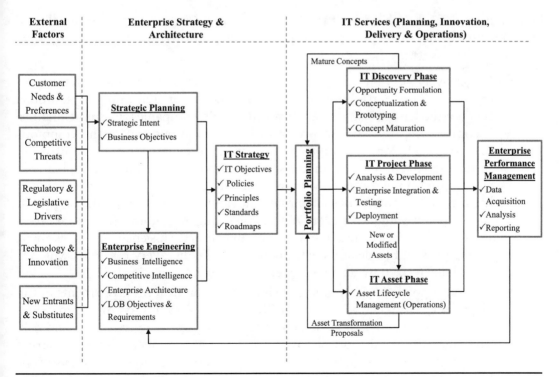

Figure 1-3   Enterprise IT lifecycle

which then initiates the asset phase for new or modified assets. The asset phase, in turn, can initiate activity in the discovery or the project phases, by feeding asset transformation proposals to the IT portfolio. Further, each phase provides input to enterprise performance management, which in turn is an internal factor that serves as an input to the organization's strategic planning:

- The discovery, or innovation, phase, also referred to as the "fuzzy front end," occurs during the concept and idea stages of basic research. This phase is comprised of potential growth and transformational IT investments that are typically longer, riskier, and more uncertain, such as emerging technologies, new business, geographic expansion opportunities, and mergers and acquisitions. This phase typically has a forward-looking view of 3-5 years.

- The project phase, sometimes characterized as new product development or project execution, pertains to the lifecycle of IT projects. Investments made in the IT project phase are typically short- to medium-term investments (1-3 months to 2 years) that companies use to grow and transform the business. Investments in this phase also include mandatory requirements brought about by legal, compliance, and safety regulations.

- The asset phase functions to replace, reposition, maintain, or redevelop existing IT systems and solutions. It is comprised of applications, infrastructure, human capital, processes, information, and data. Investments in this phase are used to help run the business, and this typically constitutes the bulk of IT investments. These serve the current needs of the enterprise.

In alignment with the phases of the IT lifecycle, organizations often classify the IT portfolio into the discovery portfolio, project portfolio, and asset portfolio, the aggregation of which constitutes the entire IT portfolio:

- IT discovery portfolio: Comprised of longer-term investments in the discovery phase. This portfolio comprises investments for innovative IT solutions that are the basis for strategic transformation in companies. This portfolio has become susceptible to cost pressures in organizations and to the commoditization of IT. Many IT organizations are focused primarily on short-term, sustaining, and low-risk initiatives, as opposed to experimental, higher-risk, and long-term investments. Moreover, the rapid pace of change in technology has resulted in enterprises acquiring innovative solutions in partnership with specialist software firms, as opposed to investing in in-house IT innovation, as was once done in the mid to late twentieth century. This change in investment strategy has all but dealt a death blow to the IT discovery portfolio, which is now characterized by its non-existence in most organizations.

- IT project portfolio: Comprised of short- to medium-term investments in the IT project phase. The IT project portfolio focuses on all the projects in development across a company and consolidates one view of overall value and risk. The objective of this portfolio is to serve as a gating mechanism for assuring that projects are in alignment with the organization's strategic intent, assumptions in the business case are adhered to, and decisions are based on accurate and timely data. It should be noted here that IT projects do not have a life of their own; they are primarily funded either by business units or as part of enterprise-wide initiatives, and are not funded by the IT organization. In many organizations, IT projects are rarely funded by the IT organization itself as financial control is not necessarily within the realm of the CIO; rather, it is the business that dictates the "go/no go" project decisions based on data provided by IT.

- IT asset portfolio: Comprised of existing investments in the IT asset phase. An IT asset is defined as anything in the operational phase (currently supporting the enterprise's needs) under IT's domain, such as applications, infrastructure, data and information, IT processes, and people. The IT asset portfolio provides a framework to catalogue and continuously monitor the performance of IT assets based on business alignment, value, cost, and risks to guide investment decisions. This portfolio represents the largest expenditure for an IT organization, and the investments in this portfolio are typically under the control of the CIO.

One main benefit of IT portfolio classification is that it provides an IT organization with an easy-to-use framework for the ongoing management of its diverse investments. From the perspective of selecting and funding investments (one of the most important functions of enterprise portfolio management), it could be argued that the diverse characteristics of each of the IT portfolios would merit the employment of separate evaluation criteria.

However, one should bear in mind that despite their different traits, the IT sub-portfolios generally compete for the same set of constrained resources within an organization, and hence should be examined under the same microscopic lens. Current and planned IT investments must be treated as part of a singular, all-encompassing IT portfolio for investment selection, rather than as separate sub-portfolios, in order to make defensible investment decisions that yield better, overarching business results. Developing an objective framework to logically and meaningfully group all IT investments in one portfolio for the purpose of portfolio selection (while keeping them separate from the perspective of ongoing IT investment management after the selection has been made) can represent a considerable challenge, especially if one considers the dearth of widely accepted, defensible techniques for IT portfolio valuation and selection.

For IT portfolios, the application of financial criteria alone for evaluation purposes is largely insufficient, since many IT investments cannot be justified purely in terms of their financial value. In an IT environment, operational and regulatory demands often overrule return on investment as the main determinant of project selection and continuation. Moreover, IT assets cannot be traded easily (if at all), have little to no salvage value, and often carry significant exit costs.

Another common shortcoming with IT initiatives is that resource allocation decisions are often made on a project-by-project or departmental budget-by-budget basis, rather than by looking at what is in the best strategic and financial interests of the enterprise. For multiple reasons (discussed later in this chapter), such an approach to resource allocation is sub-optimal and can result in the waste of IT assets as well as duplication of work. Consequently, any framework and methodology for evaluating IT investments should enforce discipline in identifying cash-needy projects or assets that may produce little to no direct financial value, but deliver indirect value in terms of improved productivity or cost avoidance. A significant portion of this book is devoted to providing the reader a set of processes, tools, and techniques for judicious decision making, enabling the alignment of IT with the organization's strategic and financial objectives and ultimately helping the CIO to earn a seat at the table.

A Question of Portfolio Management Practices

Why is it important for CIOs to elevate their portfolio management practices to have a greater say and stake in the enterprise's strategic and financial goals? In short, unless and until CIOs alter the pervasive perception of IT as a cost center rather than as a value creation discipline, they will continue to be asked to justify IT's relevance by implementing solutions with resources that are handed to them, rather than by demonstrating the value that could be delivered to the enterprise if they were appropriately resourced both in terms of people and budgetary allocation.

In discussions with executive students, who claim that a large part of their IT function is to "merely keep the lights on," the positive value created by such a function is exactly the same as the negative value that would be lost if "the lights were merely kept off." If, for example, an IT solution provides a search engine that better enables someone in R&D to scan the literature for successes and failures in a therapeutic endeavor, the indirect value gained is the difference between scanning with or without this search engine. All that remains is not a continued debate over whether value has been added, but rather, the challenge of quantifying the difference in value gained.

1.3 The CREOPM™ Framework

Over the past 15 years, the authors have encountered organizations that practice project portfolio management using a variety of processes and methodologies that range from informal autocratic decision making involving one or a few power brokers to formal consensual decision making, utilizing an executive governance committee. Therefore, some prescriptive project portfolio management is exercised, whether it involves the management of a single project, an assortment of projects and programs, or a collection of projects, programs, and sub-portfolios.

With these observations in mind, the seminal question of this book is not whether project portfolio management is employed in organizations of all shapes and sizes, but rather, *how well is it practiced, how much value does it create, and what value does it leave*, purposely or unknowingly? While great organizations practice good project portfolio management, it is worth asking how much greater they could become if they excelled in the discipline of project portfolio management. We have also seen organizations that are decidedly poor at this discipline, and yet seem to succeed in spite of their actions. Both sides of this coin tend to lead to a false sense of security, as it has not been uncommon to encounter myriad sentiments expressed by seemingly successful stakeholders in successful organizations, a handful of which are represented here:

- "How could we have been so successful if we were not good at project portfolio management?"
- "We call it 'experienced judgment,' and it has served us well for decades."
- "We don't need a formal discipline called 'project portfolio management'; things around here change too frequently."
- "Project portfolio management? That stuff is too theoretical and esoteric." (A favorite saying!)
- "How can you plan when there is so much risk and uncertainty? We need to be able to adapt as things change."
- "Our senior management would never understand it (project portfolio management). We need to keep it simple."
- "Information and data are only 'guesstimates' of the future. How can you use project portfolio management to make decisions when you're layering assumptions over other assumptions?"
- "That is the way it has always been around here. If project portfolio management isn't broken, there's nothing to fix."
- "Person X (or Function Y) makes all the portfolio decisions. We are the implementers."
- "It (project portfolio management) could threaten the way we do things here."

A primary observation made is that the greatest impediment to organizations in adopting a formal practice of project portfolio management is an inability to internalize how much better they could perform as opposed to what has traditionally been considered "overhead" in the form of a readily dispensable staffing function that does not appear to add immediate quantitative value to the bottom line. Perhaps worse still are organizations that have staffing functions that collect data and information, but do little to challenge and validate that data and information, and instead employ sexy software systems capable of generating colorful charts at the touch of a button.

Additionally, we have encountered portfolio management functions that are sometimes engaged in what appears to be unending analysis, which is eventually handed off to a select few executives who make decisions without much, if any, interaction with the heads of portfolio management. If naysayers are to be convinced and reluctance to project portfolio management overcome, a framework for this discipline must be advocated in such a manner that it captures the imagination of the volitional observers. In this regard, a multi-dimensional enterprise project portfolio management framework—CREOPM™—is proposed that captures the essence of the logical, sequential connectivity between six components (see Figure 1-4). The components of the CREOPM™ framework are: Project Categorization (Categorize), Risk Analysis (Analyze Risk), Integrated Evaluation (Evaluate), Portfolio Optimization (Optimize), Project Prioritization (Prioritize), and Portfolio Management (Manage).

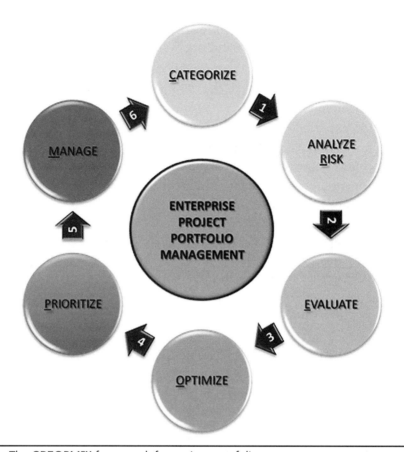

Figure 1-4   The CREOPM™ framework for project portfolio management

Categorize

All projects within a portfolio should be classified as Must Do, Won't Do, or May Do endeavors. "Must Do" projects include compliance and other mandates, as well as endeavors that are critical to the strategic and financial success of the organization; these are effectively non-discretionary projects. "Won't Do" projects represent investments that, for example, have been put on life support or remain active largely because of sunk cost or motivational bias, but which are no longer strategically or financially attractive to the enterprise. They also include "pet projects" that may have been questionable to begin with, but which are championed by one or more influential stakeholders. "May Do" projects are truly discretionary in nature and reflect the organization's ability to invest if sufficient resources become available.

As projects progress through the pipeline, and some of their risks and uncertainties are lowered, they may or may not remain in the same, previous categories; this dynamic interplay between categories of projects is fundamental to balancing the needs of an enterprise on an ongoing basis.

The discipline of transparent and defensible project categorization serves as a basis for understanding what degrees of freedom an organization possesses and enables justifiable project and program selection for project portfolio management.

Good project categorization also facilitates an open discussion regarding resource allocation, as it is seldom clear what proportion of resources should be allocated to each category. More importantly, as an organization's portfolio needs evolve, there is a requirement for a continual trade-off between these earmarked resources.

Analyze Risk

Although qualitative risk assessments are widely used across organizations, project and program risks are best analyzed quantitatively by using a systematic methodology of risk identification and decomposition by subject matter experts. Risk analysis should focus primarily on *technical risks* (e.g., drug efficacy, which cannot be mitigated or nullified through the provision of greater financial and human resources; the risk of obsolescence of a particular IT tool or technology) as opposed to *operational risks* (e.g., patient recruitment for clinical trials; risks associated with business continuity plans for IT infrastructure) that can be mitigated or nullified by the application of greater resources, perhaps requiring longer durations of time. However, if operational risks cannot be overcome during the timeline for which the risk analysis is conducted, they should be included in the overall risk assessment. Without a quantitative risk assessment, risk-adjusted valuations of projects, programs, and portfolios cannot be undertaken meaningfully.

Categorical assessments that yield low, medium, and high values are of little practical use to an organization as they lend themselves to far too much interpretation. Depending on its risk tolerance, an organization may choose not to pursue a project at its very inception because it appears to carry an unreasonably high risk load. On the other hand, if the risks to a project are understood and quantified well, an organization may choose to take a staged, options-based approach to its investment.

Evaluate

Portfolio valuations are dependent on project and program valuations, which, in turn, are dependent on the assessment of strategic alternatives available to pursue each project and program. Integrated evaluations account for the four value drivers—benefit, risk, cost, and time—and lead to the generation of risk-adjusted valuations; in the lexicon of decision analysis, risk-adjusted valuations are referred to as *expected valuations*, and therefore, "expected value" is the term used to represent "risk-adjusted value" throughout this book.

Evaluations are best conducted in an environment where uncertainty is accounted for by utilizing simulation techniques. The best integrated evaluations account for both risk (measured by a probability of success) and uncertainty (measured by a distribution of outcomes).

Optimize

Project portfolio optimization seeks to find that combination of projects (and programs) that best meets the goal(s) of an enterprise without violating its constraints (generally budgetary and human in nature). At the level of the enterprise, there is a global optimal portfolio, while at the level of separate business sectors or units, there are *local optimal portfolios*. Local portfolios may have their own budgetary and human resources, while global portfolios generally result from open competition for resources across all business sectors or units, subject to a minimum level of investment within each business sector or unit.

Optimization—in deterministic (non-probabilistic) or stochastic (probabilistic) form—enables an organization to understand what value can be gained by being on the *efficient frontier* and what is foregone as a result of pursuing a sub-optimal portfolio of projects. Although organizations rarely admit to pursuing sub-optimal portfolios, unless it can be shown by mathematical techniques that, for a given level of resource or risk, a portfolio of choice lies on the efficient frontier, this is by definition a sub-optimal portfolio. Unless an organization is a greenfield site, portfolio optimization is best conducted at the margin where the best combination of unfunded projects and programs is selected for incremental resource investment.

Optimization accommodates many logical conditions within a business unit or sector as well as across the enterprise, to be fulfilled. Such conditions can include: (a) selecting no more than one project or exactly one project from a group of similar or related projects and (b) selecting a project only if another project is chosen as well; this is an example of *project dependency*.

Once project categorization is in place, an organization may use as many requirements (e.g., selection of all mandates) and logical conditions as possible to enable maximization of value (and any other objectives) through the use of optimization techniques.

Prioritize

For operational reasons, project and program prioritization should be conducted with either quantitative decision criteria alone or a mixture of qualitative and quantitative decision criteria. A handful of good prioritization techniques such as multiple objective decision analysis (MODA) and analytic hierarchy process (AHP) exist; the challenge is to conduct each prioritization exercise with sufficient transparency and clarity, and without bias for one project or another.

Project prioritization rarely leads to an optimal portfolio, so the best form of prioritization takes place in the context of an already predetermined optimal portfolio. Project prioritization attains its highest value when there are operational reasons (e.g., manufacturing and production limitations) for determining the temporal order in which projects should be done. Marginal prioritization may be used instead of marginal optimization to select the next best unfunded projects to pursue once resources become available.

Manage

Projects and programs need to be managed creatively and adaptively in such a manner that new information is incorporated into ongoing decision making; tools and templates have their place, but can lead to flawed analysis and false recommendations unless there is good process and methodology.

Risk, resource, and stakeholder management form an important cornerstone of project portfolio management. Risk management enables organizations to manage controllable (e.g., operational) and to a lesser extent (if at all possible) uncontrollable (e.g., private or inherent) risks prescriptively; poor risk management is generally the result of reactive risk response. Resource management can be defined as the proactive allocation of budgetary and human resources to the right projects at the right time; ineffective resource management often results in unnecessary delays, compromised quality, and lost value to projects. Stakeholder management is critical not just to the betterment of projects and programs, but also to the viability of an ongoing project portfolio management function itself; weak stakeholder management can lead to uncoordinated and dysfunctional decision making.

Management of projects, programs, and portfolios requires the ongoing participation of all stakeholders in an organization; it is the result of their labors that enables decision making to be conducted by a handful of informed stakeholders. Project portfolio management is a continual process of managing changing and relevant information and data to enable good decision making in pursuit of the strategic and financial goals of the enterprise.

Since the turn of the twenty-first century, several industries, including pharmaceutical and biotechnology, have experienced less than stellar top line growth. Coupled with increasing fixed and variable costs, organizations have entered into an era of unprecedented cost cutting and contraction in an attempt to stem the tide of decreasing profit margins. Enter the accelerated epoch of outsourcing and offshoring with the intent of taking advantage of both economies of scope and scale, and organizations have "both eyes on the bottom line." The fundamental problem with this approach is that while it is certainly a means to an end (i.e., improvement of an organization's cost structure), there appears to be a broken or at best ineffective feedback loop to inform decision makers of the core of the problem that still remains: sub-optimal project portfolio management. Getting this framework right is not the domain of the smartest; it is the obligation of every stakeholder to treat organizational resources, both budgetary and human, as his or her own. Stated otherwise, if you treat your organization's budgetary and human resources as your own, wouldn't you want to know the best value you could create for those investments. Or, for example, would a sufficient return on investment be good enough?

If you take the position that CREOPM™ (or any other actionable project portfolio management framework) is a necessary prerequisite for creating sustainable portfolio value for your organization, you would begin by engaging not the smartest stakeholders in your organization, but those who were most committed to its implementation as an organizational discipline to be woven into the very fabric of the culture. To be sure, in the era of the "quick win" mindset, project portfolio management offers no such panacea. Rather, it professes to be a discipline which, if applied diligently and continuously and over the long term, is fully capable of yielding stellar strategic and financial results to any organization.

1.4 Organizational Dynamics Behind Enterprise Project Portfolio Management

A significant portion of the organizational challenge to excelling in project portfolio management is the willingness to invest in building this capability in terms that can be described as a capability maturity hierarchy (shown in Figure 1-5) with overarching responsibilities (shown in Figure 1-6) (Letavec, 2006). Irrespective of the level of the pyramid in an organization or whatever level the organization is striving to attain, effective project portfolio management is the product of: (a) good project and program management, (b) efficient financial management, and (c) defensible resource management. To be sure, efficient process management is necessary to ensure that there is interdependency and harmonization between those three primary elements.

At the base of the maturity hierarchy, a project and program office exists that represents the first semblance of project portfolio management. This function is primarily concerned with gathering project and program information and metrics. It is expected that senior management will make all decisions regarding the continuation or termination of assets, while the project and program office serves up the information and data. At this level, disproportionate emphasis is placed on data gathering, as opposed to data validation and decision making.

On the basis of the data gathered, senior management selects projects for the portfolio by any combination of single or multiple quantitative (e.g., sales, gross profit) and qualitative (e.g., customer satisfaction, unmet need) metrics. Unless there are dominant projects and programs within the portfolio, i.e., assets that are clearly superior in

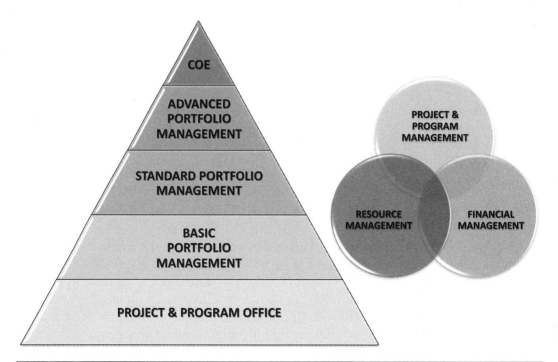

Figure 1-5 Project portfolio management capability maturity hierarchy (Note: COE = Center of Excellence). *Source*: Letavec (2006)

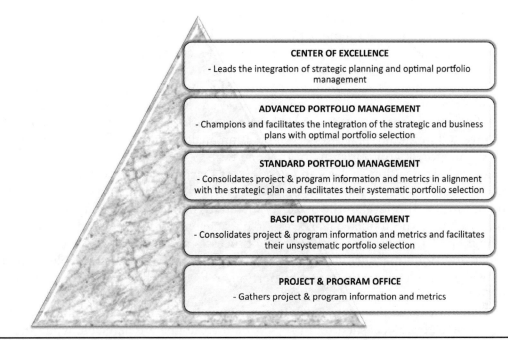

Figure 1-6 Overarching responsibilities across the project portfolio management maturity hierarchy

value, decision-making reproducibility on less than dominant projects and programs is, at best, tenuous. It is uncommon to find formal portfolio management reviews in organizations that only possess a project and program office.

As an organization's project portfolio management capability matures, a basic portfolio management office is formed. This function—not yet formally recognized as an organizational discipline—is concerned primarily with consolidation of project and program information and metrics. Although the basic portfolio management function is recognized as a body that is responsible for providing this knowledge to senior management for decision making, it provides little, if any, insight into the viability of the portfolio and almost no perspective on the ability of the portfolio to meet the organization's temporal strategic and financial goals.

Moreover, there is deep-seated organizational chaos regarding roles and responsibilities in terms of data ownership and validity for financial and human resource information. It may come as no surprise, therefore, to find different versions of the consolidated portfolio in the hands of portfolio management, financial management, and resource management functions, rendering decision making difficult. Portfolio reviews are conducted on an annual or semi-annual basis within the organization as monthly stage gate reviews enable decision making for projects and programs, but without an ongoing assessment in the context of the portfolio. At this level, the project portfolio management function may be comprised of personnel from different functional areas who undergo some form of training in decision analysis and portfolio management during their tenure.

As a standard portfolio management function, a key imperative is to utilize the strategic plan as a starting point against which portfolio consolidation derives its greatest value. Once the long-range strategic plan is provided in quantifiable terms to the standard portfolio management function, the shorter-term business plan assumes greater meaning and, in turn, the portfolio plan can be created along different strategic pathways.

Portfolio management now assumes a position of ownership for consolidated, validated information and data across the enterprise and is expected to create strategic options for senior management to consider before decisions are made. Considerable effort is invested in finding practitioners of decision analysis and portfolio management and in training them appropriately for the long term.

In cases where decision analysis and portfolio management talent cannot readily be found, it is necessary to build these capabilities into the discipline over a protracted period of time. At this level in the maturity hierarchy, portfolio management is seen as an equal partner to both financial and resource management, but is tasked with overall consolidation of the portfolio. Although the processes and methodologies utilized by a standard portfolio management function are far more robust and traceable than at either of the lower levels of the pyramid, portfolio selection is based almost exclusively on project prioritization.

Ultimately, financial management decides where to "draw the budgetary line" within the rank order of projects such that projects below the line are deferred, while those above the line are progressed into or through the pipeline. The standard portfolio management function invests well in ongoing training of its portfolio management personnel and helps to set process and methodology standards across the enterprise. Portfolio reviews are conducted on an annual or semi-annual basis within the organization, with greater credence given to monthly stage gate decision making for projects and programs in the context of the portfolio.

An advanced portfolio management function achieves not only the expectations of the standard portfolio management function, but takes portfolio management to its next logical level in that it seeks to optimize portfolio value to the enterprise. It does so not by passively interacting with its financial and human resource counterparts, but by championing and spearheading the integration of strategic and business plans with active portfolio management plans.

Rather than meander through various rounds of project prioritization and budgetary scenarios, portfolio management begins with a view of the optimal portfolio, subject to a robust portfolio management framework such as CREOPM™. Stated otherwise, once project categorization is performed, and risk analysis and integrated evaluations conducted, the portfolio is subjected to one or more optimization methodologies that provide a starting point for discussion regarding what projects and programs should or should not be included in the portfolio. Using various budgetary and, if necessary, human resource constraints, different optimal portfolios are created for each investment scenario. The organization can now confidently engage in a rigorous discussion on portfolio selection with the full knowledge that it has been presented with portfolio scenarios that lie on the efficient frontier, i.e., are optimal. The advanced portfolio management function invests heavily in ongoing training of its portfolio management personnel and sets process and methodology standards across the enterprise. Portfolio review is conducted on a quarterly basis within the organization as monthly stage gate reviews provide ongoing decision making for projects and programs in the context of the portfolio.

At the apex of the pyramid, the Center of Excellence (COE) represents the highest level of maturity that can be attained by a portfolio management function. The COE serves the role of leading the integration of strategic planning and optimal portfolio management, and the head of this COE is regarded as a peer to the heads of strategic planning, financial management, and resource management. Because strategic planning and portfolio management are so closely integrated, CREOPM™ is practiced seamlessly throughout the organization. The COE invests heavily in ongoing training of its portfolio management personnel and sets process and methodology standards across the enterprise. Individuals with a successful track record in the COE are sought out as leaders of strategic, project, program, and portfolio management staffing functions. As in the case of advanced portfolio management, at the COE level, portfolio reviews are conducted on a quarterly basis within the organization as monthly stage gate reviews provide ongoing decision making for projects and programs in the context of the portfolio.

Irrespective of the level of maturity, a highly discussed topic of project portfolio management revolves around an organization's reporting structure. By and large, since project management has evolved within the domain of R&D, most project management offices (PMOs) find themselves aligned with the technical or financial arms of organizations. On rare occasions, a PMO may be structured so that its natural home resides within the commercial domain of the organization. As the PMO assumes a higher-level role that is more closely tied to the project portfolio, a different series of questions need to be addressed:

- How best can a project portfolio management function maintain its objectivity in serving the needs of the organization's enterprise?
- Can bias for one organizational domain (e.g., R&D, commercial, manufacturing) cloud the judgment and, ultimately, performance of a project portfolio management discipline?
- What should the reward structure for a project portfolio management function be?
- To whom should a project portfolio management discipline look for guidance and pledge its obligations?

Because the authors have experienced what appears to be an unhealthy tension between organizational domains (i.e., R&D, commercial, finance, etc.) for control and ownership of project portfolio management, reporting directly to a *bona fide* strategic planning function might best serve the needs of the enterprise. If, as the authors assume, strategic planning is to be the responsibility of the strategic planning function, project portfolio management appears to be best positioned here to exercise its greatest degree of objectivity in ensuring alignment of the portfolio with the long-term strategic plan. Clearly, in organizations where the importance of the strategic plan is lessened by the impact of the shorter-term business plan, this reporting relationship is sub-optimal. But, if the short-term business plan takes precedence in importance and execution over the longer-term strategic plan, it is arguable that the organization is really not driven by its overall strategy and is instead reactive to short-term changes that may or may not impact its overarching strategy.

No matter where a project portfolio management function is positioned within an organization, there are fundamental barriers to its long-term success, which, if not addressed early in the life cycle of the function, can cause disruption and eventual marginalization of its overall impact. In centralized organizations where decision-making authority is concentrated, primary responsibility for decisions is largely known, and standards, processes, methodologies, and tools are easier to harmonize across the enterprise; project portfolio management has a less turbulent time in serving the needs of the enterprise.

Conversely, in decentralized companies where knowledge and power are distributed, primary responsibility for decision making may be unclear. Where standards, processes, methodologies, and tools tend to be idiosyncratic to the local company or business unit, it is inherently more difficult for project portfolio management to flourish as a cohesive function. In decentralized organizations, success lies not with any one individual or group of stakeholders, but with senior stakeholders across all business units, who share a common perspective and goal regarding the roles and responsibilities of project portfolio management. Nevertheless, standardization of project portfolio management practices across the enterprise can be a Herculean task. On the basis of its structure, therefore, the influence of culture and politics can help or hinder the successful implementation and longevity of project portfolio management (see Figure 1-7) (DuBrin, 2007; Gido & Clements, 2009).

Organizations that have strong functional units or departments generally have deep-seated expertise that is not easily shared across the enterprise. Likewise, once business units become territorially based, responsiveness to local conditions is paramount, but can result in a lack of overarching coordination at national and, more importantly, international levels. As the increasing trend toward virtual organizations continues, the problem of standardization of project portfolio management practices, processes, and methodologies becomes heightened. Where multiple structures exist in organizations and problems in coordinating policies exist, the difficulties experienced in attempting to standardize project portfolio management practices can become even more pronounced. Although project portfolio management should focus its efforts on influencing decision making from a position of power based on knowledge and expertise, it should be careful not to be blindsided by power brokers who may have greater decision-making impact as a result of other sources of power, as described by Lewis (2003) (see Figure 1-8).

As with all staffing functions, without the sponsorship of a high-level executive, project portfolio management can flounder or, at best, reinvent itself annually. This champion needs to be visible and act in the capacity of a mentor who helps the project portfolio management function: (a) avoid organizational minefields and (b) pay adequate attention to the politics and power brokers in the organization. The champion can assist in clarifying the needs and expectations of various stakeholders, some of whom may feel threatened by the function or who may need to be "walked around the square" by project portfolio management to ensure that their fears are understood

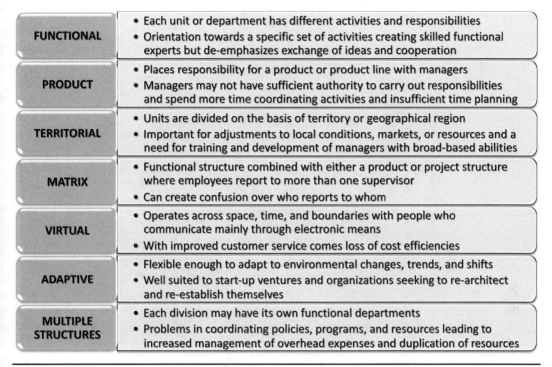

FUNCTIONAL	• Each unit or department has different activities and responsibilities • Orientation towards a specific set of activities creating skilled functional experts but de-emphasizes exchange of ideas and cooperation
PRODUCT	• Places responsibility for a product or product line with managers • Managers may not have sufficient authority to carry out responsibilities and spend more time coordinating activities and insufficient time planning
TERRITORIAL	• Units are divided on the basis of territory or geographical region • Important for adjustments to local conditions, markets, or resources and a need for training and development of managers with broad-based abilities
MATRIX	• Functional structure combined with either a product or project structure where employees report to more than one supervisor • Can create confusion over who reports to whom
VIRTUAL	• Operates across space, time, and boundaries with people who communicate mainly through electronic means • With improved customer service comes loss of cost efficiencies
ADAPTIVE	• Flexible enough to adapt to environmental changes, trends, and shifts • Well suited to start-up ventures and organizations seeking to re-architect and re-establish themselves
MULTIPLE STRUCTURES	• Each division may have its own functional departments • Problems in coordinating policies, programs, and resources leading to increased management of overhead expenses and duplication of resources

Figure 1-7   Types of organizational structure
Source: DuBrin (2007); Gido & Clements (2009)

and resolved. Just as important, the role of the champion is to help minimize duplication and redundancy of responsibility for the charter of enterprise project portfolio management.

Without actively opening up lines of communication within different functions, e.g., research, development, manufacturing, finance, resource management, and regulatory affairs, project portfolio management is likely to be un- or underinformed, making it difficult to ensure that there is consistency of its interpretation and understanding of issues across disciplines. Furthermore, it is critical that project portfolio management understand and internalize the risk tolerance of the organization in which it finds itself. Few engagements are as frustrating to a well-equipped project portfolio management function as those in which optimal strategic and analytic solutions are provided in support of the best possible portfolio management recommendations, only to find out after the fact that the organization will not act on such recommendations because of its risk attitude. To be sure, a risk-seeking organization may also create similar problems, but this is far more the exception than the rule of risk aversion. Classic symptoms of risk aversion manifest themselves in the following ways:

- Focusing overtly on negative outcomes to avoid the occurrence of bad consequences.
- Increasing judgmental estimations of outcomes with bad consequences.

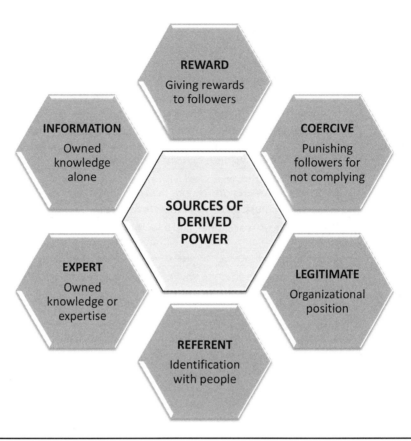

Figure 1-8   Sources of organizational power
Source: Lewis (2003)

- Ignoring significant uncertainty by focusing on the most likely scenario.
- Engaging in foolish optimism created by a lack of rational thinking.
- Avoiding complex decision making by doing nothing, delegating, or making arbitrary decisions.

1.5 The Future of Enterprise Project Portfolio Management

In summary, successful project portfolio management is as dependent on the acquisition and practice of knowledge and expertise for decision making as it is on the understanding of organizational dynamics that can enhance or marginalize its impact. The discipline of enterprise project portfolio management is not a function that is always readily capable of adding quantifiable value to the bottom line in the immediate term. Instead, it requires protracted sponsorship and support to build the appropriate level of organizational discipline necessary to yield value in the mid and long term.

So, what is the future of project portfolio management, and what does it hold in store for new and seasoned practitioners alike? First and foremost, there is a glaring need for portfolio management to be recognized as a discipline outside of the venue of the management of financial assets. It is incumbent, therefore, on schools of higher learning to foster the teaching of this discipline in a graduate environment—especially in MBA, EMBA, and EMTM programs—in order to prepare students for the practical world of process and methodology implementation in organizations.

Likewise, organizations would be wise to address how much better they could perform, strategically and financially, if they were to build and nurture such a discipline that is unique and integrates excellent strategic thinking with robust analytic mastery of decision analysis and various aspects of operations research. In order to develop the requisite expertise in enterprise portfolio management, it is necessary to have a thorough grasp of:

- Business, strategic, and technical skills as prerequisites for enterprise project portfolio management
- The CREOPM™ framework (or its equivalent)
- The application of real-world project portfolio management case studies

Section 2

Prerequisites for Enterprise Project Portfolio Management

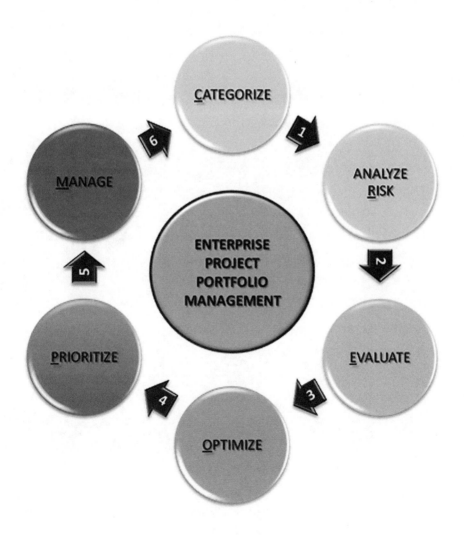

2

Scenario Analysis and Strategic Planning

- **Scenario analysis**—A process that prepares for a range of potential outcomes to a situation over which you may have little or no control, but, with good foresight, enables strategies that position you to take advantage of the positive or negative impact of such outcomes.
- **Strategic planning**—A process that develops approaches to attain one or more objectives, generally involving the definition of a desired state and "working backwards" to understand what steps need to be put in place to increase the likelihood of attaining the desired state.

2.1 Key Concepts of Strategic Planning

A fundamental skill acquired by the most successful organizations is the ability to consistently internalize and articulate their *raison d'être* in response to critical questions to their entire community of stakeholders:

- Who am I, and why do I exist?
- Where do I want to be at a specific point in time?
- What do I believe in, and what defines who I am?

The answers to these questions help to define an organization's overarching mission, vision, and values (see Figure 2-1), which, in turn, aid in the articulation of its desired state. Of what importance is a clearly articulated desired state to an enterprise?

It is the desired state that sets the stage for a multi-period strategy that shapes the generation of an evolving strategic plan. Effective strategic plans are first created by taking a longer view of where the organization is heading, both in the competitive space in which it is currently playing and for the foreseeable future plans to play. In other words, an organization must first envision what the future of its industry is likely to look like so that it may plan how to best position itself for sustainable success.

It is no more than foolish optimism or audacious mendacity to assume that the future is a linear extrapolation of the past and present and, worse still, that game-changing competitive strategies are the exclusive domain of the successful and powerful. Organizations that fail to reinvent themselves by adapting proactively to foreseeable environmental

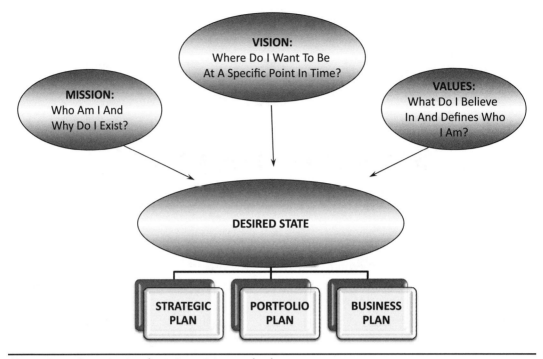

Figure 2-1   Organizational mission, vision, and values
Source: Hill & Jones (2010)

and competitive shifts run the significant risk of being ill prepared for uncontrollable elements, such as economic downturns. Sadly, under such circumstances, the Pavlovian response of many fine organizations is to contract their labor forces—invariably resulting in the shedding of highly talented individuals—in the name of "cost control."

The remarkable oddity, observed by the authors, is the temporal association between competitive pressures and labor contraction. Contraction, on one hand, helps to maintain many of the financial metrics by which organizations gauge their value creation, while on the other, it prolongs the pain and prevents an earlier emergence from poor competitive performance. To be sure, cost cutting can help maximize efficiency on an ongoing basis; however the issue becomes using it as a means of maintaining the attractiveness of financial performance metrics.

In the healthcare industry, for example, scenario analysis or scenario planning can involve the process of envisioning the extent to which personalized medicine is likely to impact: (a) the ways in which more targeted therapies are developed and delivered to a potential patient population and (b) the business model(s) of companies that are engaged in developing and commercializing diagnostics, drugs, and delivery devices to meet the needs of that patient population. While it is reasonable to anticipate that healthcare organizations and lobbyists can exert a large degree of control over the extent to which the therapeutic needs of patients are met, they have limited influence over the manner in which patients' expectations for more targeted therapeutic intervention evolve. The seminal difference, therefore, that distinguishes scenario analysis from strategic planning revolves around controllability and influence of future events.

It is arguable that all organizations engage in some form of scenario analysis, but it is the extent to which they do so (and take action on the basis of their findings) that differentiates the leaders from the laggards. Lagging organizations generally conduct the type of scenario analysis that follows the path of logical incrementalism of the question, "Given where we have come from, what do the lessons of the past and present lead us to conclude about what our business model should look like in the future?" This question looms largely in the minds of executives. On the other hand, leading organizations generally adopt an approach that challenges their beliefs of the future by asking this question: "Despite where we have come from, what critical uncertainties of the future are likely to impact our current business model, and how best should we be positioned to take advantage of the positive impact of these uncertainties, as well as minimize their negative consequences?"

A good scenario analysis begins with a multi-dimensional discussion of what the future could look like and what possible states may exist (see Figure 2-2). While it is likely that an organization can influence one or more possible states, it is far more often the case that it cannot control the materialization of those future states unless it finds itself in a monopolistic or oligopolistic market environment.

Black Swans notwithstanding (Taleb, 2007), it is highly unlikely that an organization can prepare for every possible future state, thus requiring that it focus its effort and investments on a comprehensive plan that best addresses a single future state. This should not imply that the plan be etched in stone to the point where the organization has few, if any, degrees of freedom in which to operate. Rather, it should serve as the

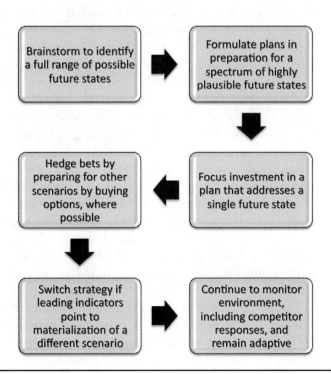

Figure 2-2 Scenario planning and analysis

focal point beyond which the organization makes investments in options to protect itself against unfavorable outcomes created by alternative future states, so that if leading indicators point to the materialization of a different scenario, the organization can respond with the highest level of preparedness. All successful learning organizations develop a proclivity for adapting to environmental changes in a manner that distinguishes them as leaders; a hallmark of this learning is their willingness and ability to monitor the environment continuously in order to predict competitor responses that may influence their own destinies.

Once scenario analysis has identified a future state on which the organization will focus, it is time to engage in good strategic planning. Although a good strategic plan is guided by an organization's mission, vision, and values, it is the organization's vision that should dictate what its strategic goals and objectives are. Consider the case of a hypothetical healthcare company whose vision is to be a Top 5 global player as defined by sales value in the pharmaceutical and biotechnology industry. Its strategic plan is predicated on the organization's vision that is encompassed by three primary strategic goals to: (a) become a stellar provider of integrated healthcare services, (b) be perceived as an upstanding and responsible corporate citizen, and (c) be valued as a caring employer (see Figure 2-3). Each goal is supported by multiple strategic objectives, which describe the means by which the organization intends to achieve that strategic goal.

The healthcare company in this example has made an expressed intent to become a premier provider of healthcare through its integrated suite of diagnostic, drug delivery, and therapeutic products. In pursuit of its goal to be seen as a highly responsible corporate citizen, the organization has outlined objectives that revolve around listening to its customers, volunteering its services, and adopting the highest standards of environmental friendliness. In addition, the company has articulated how it plans to achieve the goal of creating a safe and fulfilling work environment through hiring and retaining highly talented individuals, providing enriching work experiences, and continually providing opportunities for career growth. By definition therefore, scenario analysis and a strategic plan are interdependent while temporal precedence resides with scenario analysis. Alignment between scenario analysis and strategic planning is indicative both of a forward-thinking organization and good, prepared leadership.

If alignment between scenario analysis and strategic planning is a recipe for sustainable success, what is a good scenario plan, and how does an organization know when it has conducted a good analysis? Depending on cultural orientation, a scenario analysis of an organization may range from a group of senior executives engaged in an annual discussion of the future of their industry with recorded notes that are disseminated to no one beyond the group itself, to a carefully scripted analysis of a department whose task is to bring together the best internal and external minds, who are challenged with envisioning possible future states of the industry and the impact of each state to the organization. Although most scenario analyses have logical beginnings, the same cannot always be said of their endings, where, for example, debates regarding achieving closure can range from sentiments expressed as, "Haven't we squeezed this stone enough?" to "How can we be sure that we have accounted for every potential Black Swan?"

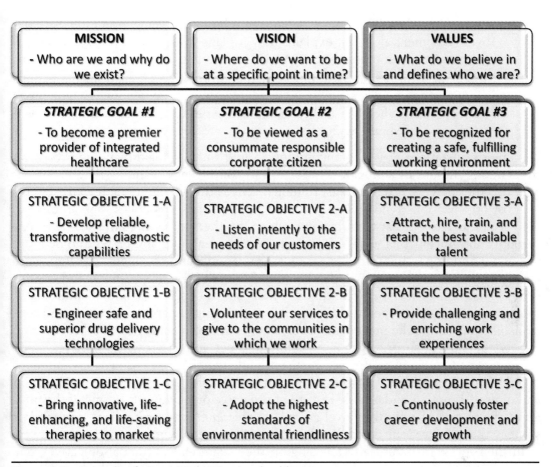

Figure 2-3 Example of strategic planning in a healthcare company

In reality, only a healthy combination of the understanding of an organization's orientation to risk, coupled with its propensity to pragmatic preparedness, will predicate when a scenario analysis should be concluded. As stated previously, an organization cannot prepare itself for every possible future state of nature, or it would paralyze itself into a position of perennial inaction; consequently, it should gauge when it has done a sufficient amount of research and analysis, after which it moves on to act on the basis of its most pressing deductions.

Similar questions can be asked of the strategic plan, such as "When do we know we have a plan that fulfills our strategic and financial goals in concert with the mission, vision, and values of our organization on a multi-period basis?" Strategic planning is the process by which an organization develops a strategy, i.e., what it does and what it intends to do in a tacit or explicit manner. A strategy itself is impacted by three major forces:

- Strategic thinking—A requirement for a thorough understanding of how markets and competitors may evolve and where new opportunities may lie; founded in the generation of strategic alternatives or business models that are oriented toward delivering renewed customer value.

- Business model—An explicit definition of how an organization intends to deliver customer value that explains how it plans to: (a) attain its objectives and (b) measure its success over a defined time period.
- Value proposition—A description of the cumulative set of resulting experiences that an organization causes its customers to have; a positive value proposition occurs when the utility of the net experience exceeds the price paid for the good (Abraham, 2006).

In some organizations, it is not uncommon to find that strategic planning involves a tremendous amount of annual, operational, and contingency planning that, in turn, is held together by very little strategic thinking. Why is this so? First, the reward systems of most organizations tend to be skewed in favor of those practices that promise to deliver immediate or near-term benefits which, by themselves, are antithetical to uncertainty and uncontrollability. While strategic and scenario planning tend to be more important and impactful in the longer term, operational and contingency planning are clearly more manageable over a shorter time horizon. Likewise, scenario and contingency planning are most impactful under conditions of uncertainty and uncontrollability. It is no wonder that operational planning, with its high degree of certainty and controllability, tends to take precedence over other forms of planning in the short term.

Second, and not surprisingly, in an effort to meet annual growth objectives, some organizations tend to focus on readily quantifiable metrics that enable the attainment of a desired end state, e.g., 10% compounded annual sales growth. While this focus, in and of itself, is not an undesirable feature of proactive organizations (if one of the morals of the tale of Alice in the novel *Alice in Wonderland* is to be heeded), any road or strategy that achieves the desired end state becomes a good one.

In the process of myopically focusing on the attainment of annual objectives, one should not be surprised if, in the long term, the core competence on which an organization is founded deteriorates almost predictably. For example, this can be the result of the prolonged act of trying to increase top line growth by creating a continuous stream of low-risk product line extensions, while at the same time failing to invest sufficiently in innovative platform technologies that could serve to revitalize the technical competencies on which the organization has built its reputation. Unfortunately, in some organizations, even when the discipline of good strategic planning is done well, it is delegated to a staff function that is not empowered to make many, if any, strategic decisions, resulting in the occurrence of a plethora of unintended consequences (Mintzberg et al., 1998) (see Figure 2-4).

Once a strategic planning function is not actively led by a visible, high-level champion, it can quickly degenerate into a process where the dominant theme becomes enabling the process itself, rather than enabling thinking associated with good strategy. Under these conditions, strategic planning has a remarkable tendency to focus on building the enterprise's portfolio by a variety of mechanisms that involve other parties (e.g., mergers and acquisitions) as opposed to further developing the core expertise of the business and, in the process, rendering many of its recommendations inactionable. For fear of being labeled an "ivory tower," strategic planning can be driven by a singular, deterministic view of the future, resulting in a paucity of creative and actionable options.

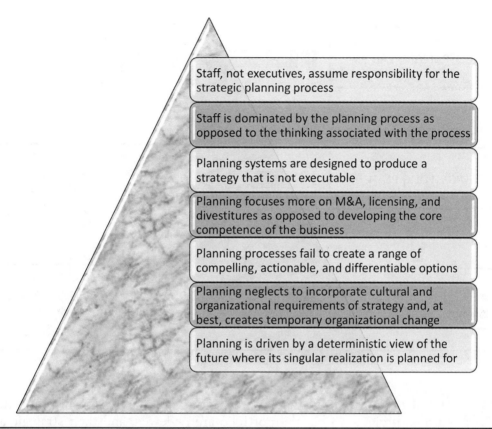

Staff, not executives, assume responsibility for the strategic planning process

Staff is dominated by the planning process as opposed to the thinking associated with the process

Planning systems are designed to produce a strategy that is not executable

Planning focuses more on M&A, licensing, and divestitures as opposed to developing the core competence of the business

Planning processes fail to create a range of compelling, actionable, and differentiable options

Planning neglects to incorporate cultural and organizational requirements of strategy and, at best, creates temporary organizational change

Planning is driven by a deterministic view of the future where its singular realization is planned for

Figure 2-4   The seven deadly sins of strategic planning
Source: Mintzberg et al. (1998)

Third, if the cultural predisposition of the organization is not well gauged, strategic planning may result in temporary organizational change where the comfort of the past and present eventually overrides the uncertainty and discomfort of the future.

A sign of a disciplined, mature, and proactive organization is evident when there is a clear articulation of the *raison d'être* of each of the major planning initiatives—strategic, portfolio, and business (see Figure 2-5). Without this, well-meaning stakeholders can get in each other's way in an effort to fulfill the needs of each major plan. Far worse is the tendency of different organizational functions (e.g., portfolio management, finance, resource management) to create their own versions of portfolio data that can inevitably lead to different strategic and analytic outputs, inferences, and conclusions. A good strategic plan should be oriented towards a period of several years; in the drug industry, it is not uncommon to find strategic plans that span 10- to 15-year periods.[1]

The primary objectives of a strategic plan are to determine: (a) the competitive space in which the organization plans to play and (b) the strategic and financial obligations

---

[1]In contrast, many IT departments do not participate in or contribute significantly to an enterprise's strategic planning process. Instead, as outlined in Chapter 1, IT departments are typically informed of the outcomes of such activities and get involved in the execution phase of the strategy, especially when it pertains to technology enablement in support of strategic initiatives.

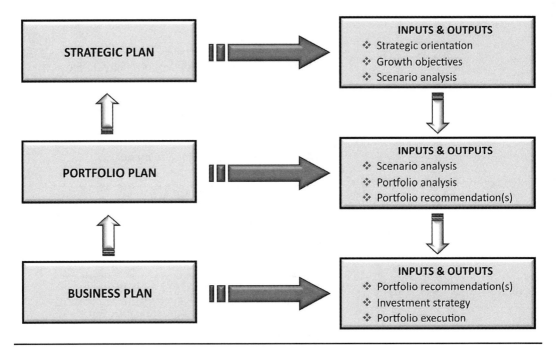

Figure 2-5   Temporal dependence between strategic, portfolio, and business plans

and priorities of the portfolio in the short, medium, and long terms. In preparation for its execution, projects within the portfolio are reviewed, and their strategic and financial values are updated. Based on the outcome of the strategic plan, the portfolio plan is charged with the enablement of the short-, mid-, and long-term objectives of the strategic plan. This involves not just an update and review of projects, but, more importantly, a robust optimization of the portfolio subject to potential budgetary and human resource constraints.

Within the context of the optimized portfolio, projects are subjected to a formal prioritization process that enables a resource management function to plan for the passage of projects in a temporal manner. Note that this form of prioritization is not strategic in nature; rather, it is an operational consequence of the need to allocate con-strained resources in as temporally efficient a manner as is possible.

Toward the end of the annual cycle, the business plan is positioned to inform the portfolio plan of what is most affordable and where the latter needs to make the neces-sary changes to either expand or contract its constellation of projects to best meet the objectives of the strategic plan. During the period of the business plan, data gathering for human resource management is generally intense, and project updates and data reviews become necessary. However, the appropriate temporal relationship between these plans should follow the order of strategic plan, portfolio plan, and business plan (see Figure 2-6), where the outputs of one plan serve as inputs to its successor plan. More importantly, the portfolio plan can serve as the pivotal link that translates stra-tegic and financial objectives into an understanding of what budgetary and human resource requirements are required to support the strategic plan.

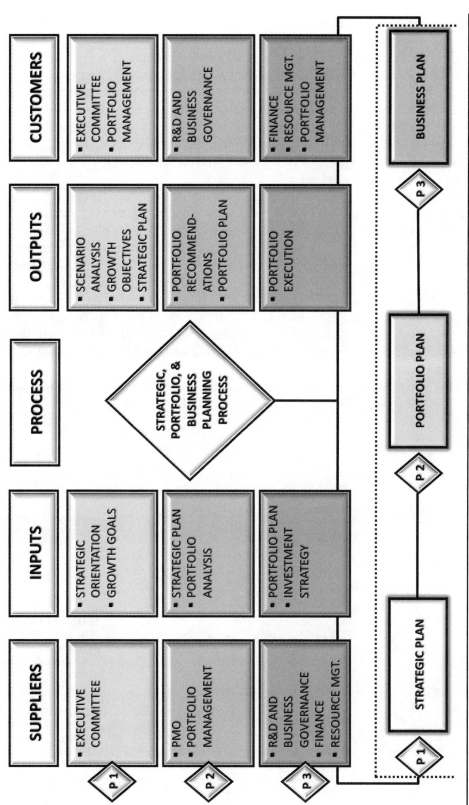

Figure 2-6   Temporal dependence between strategic, portfolio and business plans—Suppliers, Inputs, Process, Outputs, Customers (SIPOC)

Clearly, if the business plan cannot support the budgetary and human resource needs of the portfolio plan, the strategic plan should be immediately informed with one of these resulting outcomes: (a) the goals of the strategic plan are lowered or (b) the resource limitations of the business plan are reduced. Many successful organizations do not follow this temporal prescription and choose instead to insert the business plan ahead of the portfolio plan, but resource restrictions placed by the business plan often make it difficult, if not impossible, for the portfolio plan to generate the necessary value demanded by the strategic plan. When this occurs, an organization sets itself up for a continual cycle of missed targets that often results in its need to acquire or be acquired by another organization.

An alternative view is in the form of a hierarchy of dependencies where corporate goals and objectives set the overarching stage for what is expected from the portfolio strategy, which then dictates what is necessary from the business plan (see Figure 2-7).

If the business plan (which constitutes the R&D and business investment strategy) were to take precedence over either the portfolio strategy (and hence the portfolio plan) or corporate goals and objectives (which are driven by the strategic plan), it is highly unlikely that an organization will attain its goals and objectives on a multiperiod basis. Yet, it is our experience in several organizations that the annual budget from the business plan serves to shape the length and breadth of the portfolio plan, while the strategic plan remains largely unmodified and consequently outdated.

While having an intended or deliberate strategy is essential to good planning, a company's emergent or realized strategy may be the product of both planned and unplanned strategies (Mintzberg et al., 1998). According to Mintzberg's model, a number

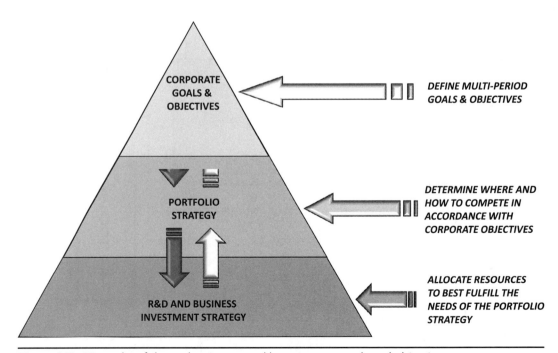

Figure 2-7   Hierarchy of dependencies created by corporate goals and objectives

of planned strategies are not realized because of unpredicted negative environmental changes, yet they often form the basis of continuous learning and imprinting so that future errors of the same type are avoided.

On the other hand, organizations with the right level of cultural proactivity and adaptability are often able to respond to positive environmental changes or to unplanned serendipity, which allow them to implement emergent strategies that were not the result of their original, planned intentions (Hill & Jones, 2010).

2.2 Summary

This chapter explained key concepts in scenario analysis and strategic planning—the fundamental prerequisites to the enterprise project portfolio management discipline. Scenario analysis and strategic planning provide the contextual and conceptual frameworks for an organization's business. Illustrations based on the healthcare industry underscored the salient features of scenario analysis and strategic planning. The linkages between a strategic plan, portfolio plan, and business plan were articulated using a SIPOC model to illustrate the interrelationships between organizational activities. The next chapter addresses another core prerequisite for enterprise project portfolio management practitioners: decision framing and data integrity.

3

Decision Framing and Data Integrity

- **Decision framing**—Identifying the appropriate problem to be solved, thereby focusing decision making on the relevant aspects of the problem.
- **Data and information integrity**—Inferential and judgmental data and information elicited from subject matter experts that are ideally devoid of cognitive and motivational bias and are logically consistent and defensible.

3.1 Key Concepts of Decision Framing and Data Integrity

Data, data, everywhere! But how much can you actually trust? While this bears the earmarks of a frivolous question, it is very much at the heart of what is referred to as "spinning wheels" in organizations, where as much data as possible is gathered at the beginning, partially sifted, and used for a preliminary analysis. More often than not, the results of that preliminary analysis set the expectations for what should be delivered in further refinements of subsequent analyses, and while this is not an unreasonable place to begin, both portfolio analyst and decision maker can quickly become anchored to the first set of data and inferences drawn therein.

Next, initial assumptions soon become lost in the maze of subsequent data gathering and analysis, expectations are reinforced, and (a) it becomes a difficult task for the portfolio analyst to admit that some of the initial assumptions on which the data were drawn may be flawed, and (b) decision makers become refractive to accepting valuations of projects in the portfolio that may be lower than initially forecasted. Yet, the reality of many portfolio assessments is that they are based on preliminary project evaluations that may not be grounded in reality. Stated otherwise, many project champions and sponsors often feel inclined to boost the attractiveness of their projects to ensure they are noticed and are given strong consideration for entry into and progression through the pipeline.

Before beginning data gathering, a reasonable place to start is by asking what the decision frame is: "What problem(s) are we trying to solve or what clarity are we striving to attain?" Without the appropriate decision frame, a great analysis can be lost on the wrong problem. Getting the decision frame right involves striking the appropriate balance between four primary elements, as shown in Figure 3-1 (Celona and McNamee, Strategic Decisions Group, 2005):

- Breadth—A broad frame leads to excessive data gathering and loss of focus on what is important; too narrow a frame can cause the importance of risks and uncertainties to be minimized or overlooked
- Complexity—A difficult frame creates a fear of failure leading to a propensity to "boil the ocean"; a simple frame can encourage unnecessary deliberation on trivial data and information
- Focus—A constrained frame can yield a solution to only a portion of the problem; a loose frame often results in either solving the wrong problem or solving a problem that has already been solved
- Involvement—Restrictive involvement of subjective matter experts (SMEs) often leads to a narrow view of the solution; unrestricted involvement can result in an inability to achieve consensus or an unintentional fostering of "group think." (Strategic Decisions Group, 2005)

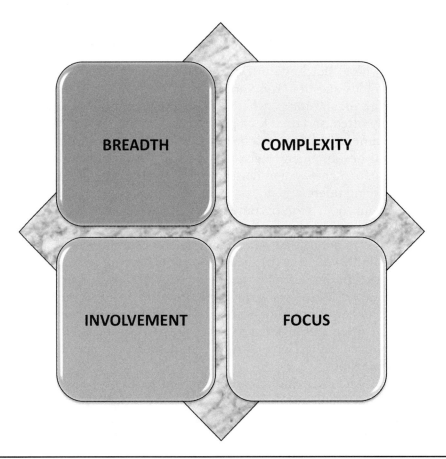

Figure 3-1 Key considerations in decision framing
Source: Strategic Decisions Group (2005)

Once the frame of a problem has been identified with sufficient clarity, it is helpful to place the decision to be taken in the context of other decisions in the organization, namely policy, strategic, and operational decisions (Strategic Decisions Group, 2005), as shown in Figure 3-2. In the example, an organization has a clearly stated policy decision, which sets the boundaries for lower-level decisions, to become a global market leader in first line solid tumor therapy. The frame of an example of a strategic decision relates to the conduct of global clinical trials in solid tumors and, once this decision is taken, sets the boundaries for a downstream operational decision that relates to the recruitment of patients in teaching hospitals.

A clear delineation of each type of decision aids good decision framing. Without this, well-intentioned stakeholders can commingle decisions, leading to unnecessarily protracted discussions and debates over how to solve problems, some of which may already be solved and others which may be beyond the boundaries of the decision rights of the participants.

In high-risk industries such as drug development, decisions need to be taken when information is often highly uncertain. Yet, the challenge of every decision maker is to understand the frame and scope of the problem, and to know what is required to make a good decision in the face of uncertainty, as opposed to deliberating until more

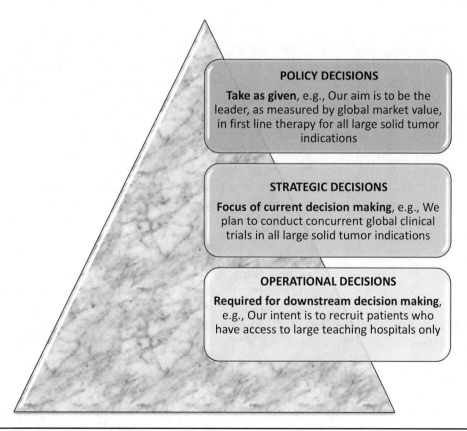

Figure 3-2   Hierarchy of policy, strategic, and operational decisions
Source: Strategic Decisions Group (2005)

information is gathered. A series of five questions (Strategic Decisions Group, 2005) is recommended before making a quality decision in response to the overarching questions, "What is important to me, and what do I need to know with what certainty to make a decision?" These questions should be asked:

- What problem(s) am I trying to solve? (frame)
- Are the boundaries of the investigation well established and understood? (scope)
- Are the relevant SMEs involved? (information credibility)
- What criteria will I use for decision making? (decision relevance)
- Am I willing to act on the best recommendation? (preparedness)

Whether at the project or portfolio level, it is important that an organization evaluate: (a) the range of strategic alternatives or options it has at its disposal and (b) its disposition to make trade-offs between competing quantitative and qualitative values. The best form of portfolio value maximization occurs when the optimal combination of projects is selected from a pool of strategies for each project. These strategies generally result from an integrated evaluation of different levels of the four value drivers—benefit, risk, cost, and time.

"Base case" strategies result from an assessment of a "middle of the road" strategy that represents a defensible, competitive approach to the discovery, development, and commercialization of a product. With the understanding that greater or fewer resources may be available to the organization at any given time, a project team can best prepare its defense to an investment committee by crafting two alternative strategy pathways, based on the organization's willingness and ability to invest more or fewer resources in a given project; these are often referred to as "buy up" and "buy down" strategies (Strategic Decisions Group, 2005). In the event that fewer resources are available for project investments, a project team may benefit from having a buy down strategy that gets the project into the pipeline, and if greater resources become available from other project terminations or an increase in resource capacity, the same project can be migrated to a more expensive strategy. Conversely, if more projects succeed than were planned initially, or if budgetary and human resources are contracted, a project with a base case or buy up strategy may be repositioned with a buy down option to continue.

Because of differing requirements for investments and time concomitant with differences in risk and forecasted benefit, the best portfolio optimization does not necessarily result from a selection of optimal project strategies (see Figure 3-3), as budgetary and human resource limitations often prevent an organization from pursuing what is best for each project or program; instead, its focus should be shifted to what is best for the portfolio by making trade-offs between projects and programs, and the level of affordable investments between these projects and programs. Depending on resource constraints, for two projects each with three R&D and commercialization strategies, any one of the nine portfolio optimization strategies could be selected, as shown in Figure 3-3.

How does a person ensure that the data and information used for the purposes of decision making are robust and therefore have the required degree of integrity? It is necessary to emphasize that the thrust of data gathering and validation should be

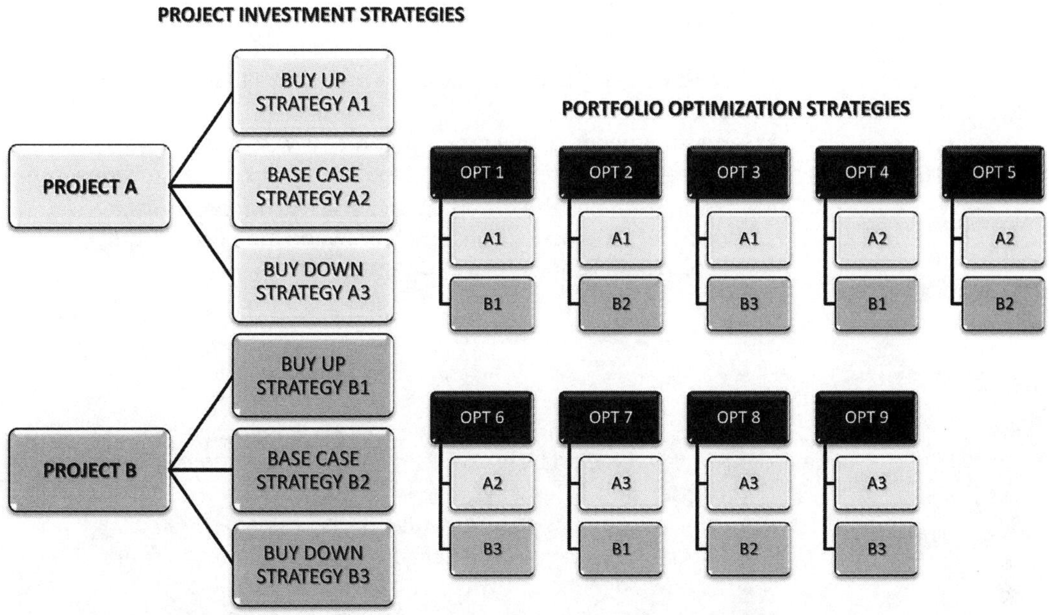

PROJECT INVESTMENT STRATEGIES

Figure 3-3 Portfolio decision making, based on optimization from project investment strategies

fueled by the need to acquire data that is traceable, logically consistent, and defensible in the knowledge that much of it is uncertain. The search for precise data, on the other hand, often leads to interminable investments in competitive intelligence and market research at considerable cost to the organization. The acquisition of good data rests with SMEs who are either internal or external to an organization. The challenge is to use effective elicitation techniques to extract information from SMEs, so that their expressed judgment becomes a faithful replication of their true, underlying knowledge. Unlike facilitation, which is geared toward designing and running a productive meeting impartially, *elicitation* is the process of capturing tacit knowledge, i.e., expressing knowledge that is present in the conscious or subconscious mind of an SME (see Figure 3-4).

A person skilled in elicitation is therefore tasked with minimizing cognitive and motivational biases that often cloud the judgment of SMEs (see Figure 3-5) (Strategic Decisions Group, 2005). Cognitive biases are often expressed through:

- Availability of information—Applying too much weight to information that is easy to recall as a result of its recency, impression created, and emotion generated.
- Representativeness of information—Basing judgments of the likelihood of events on the degree of similarity or resemblance to other events.
- Anchoring and adjustment—Focusing on heuristics or initial judgments and conveying false certainty.

Motivational biases can be expressed in several forms, including:

- Personal interest and commitment—Stakeholders, e.g., project managers and project champions, who identify themselves with the success of their projects

FACILITATION	• Process of designing and running a productive meeting impartially • Serves the needs of any group that meets with a common purpose, e.g. decision making, problem solving, idea exchange • A facilitator helps the group understand its common objectives and strives to enable a consensus between members of the group, including any areas of disagreement
ELICITATION	• Process of capturing tacit knowledge, i.e. knowledge that is a mixture of deliberations, subjective insight, intuitions, heuristics, and judgments • Techniques include direct or indirect elicitation (interviewing, storytelling, case study, role playing and simulation, concept and knowledge mapping, data flow analysis) and interaction with domain experts (observation, workspace analysis, work pattern analysis)

Figure 3-4   Facilitation and elicitation

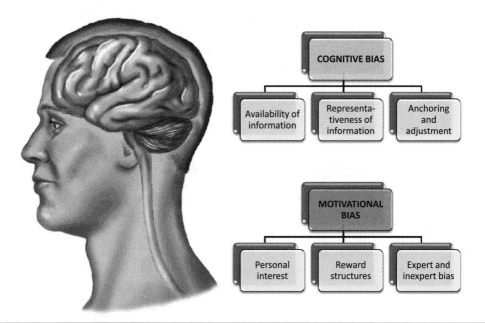

Figure 3-5   Cognitive and motivational biases
Source: Strategic Decisions Group (2005)

tend to underestimate project risks and overestimate project value and portfolio importance; project managers and champions tend to apply conservatism to their projects so as to avoid underperformance.

- Perceived reward structures—Adjustments of knowledge and beliefs due to a perceived system of rewards.
- Expert and inexpert bias—(a) Suppression of uncertainty to create the impression of being more knowledgeable and (b) exaggeration of uncertainty to avoid being wrong, respectively.

A detailed treatment of psychological traps in decision making is found in the excellent work of Hammond, Keeney, and Raiffa (2002).

Armed with valid information and data, decisions can now be taken in the context of the decision frame. Several types of decision-making models exist (Figure 3-6), the most popular of which is the *rational economic model*. Its characteristics can be described as follows:

- Rational economic—Based on the theoretical maximization of economic value(s).

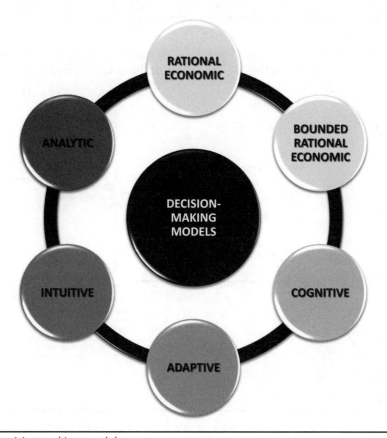

Figure 3-6   Decision-making models

- Bounded rational economic—Based on satisfactory, rather than optimal, decision making, resulting in the attainment of less than the theoretical maximization of economic value(s).
- Cognitive—Based on selectively sampling potential states of nature and building hypotheses based on short- and long-term experiences.
- Adaptive—Based on utilization of recent information to alter paradigms and beliefs.
- Intuitive—Based on abstract values and prior policy decisions.
- Analytic—Based on systematic structuring of problems by formal methodologies.

In portfolio management, it can be argued that unless decisions are based on value maximization derived from optimization methodologies, i.e., rational economic-based decisions, the best that one can achieve is sub-optimal economic value, resulting from bounded rational decision making. This can be depicted by examining the concept of the efficient frontier (Figure 3-7), described in detail in Chapter 7.

If the rate of return of different portfolios is compared to the standard deviation of their mean return (a measure of risk), portfolio C represents an optimal combination of projects in that it yields the highest return for the same level of risk borne by portfolio A, while portfolio B represents an optimal (but different) combination of projects that yields the same return as that of portfolio A with a much lower level of risk. Assuming that all three portfolios are actionable, rational economic decision making dictates that either portfolio B or C should be selected because they represent:

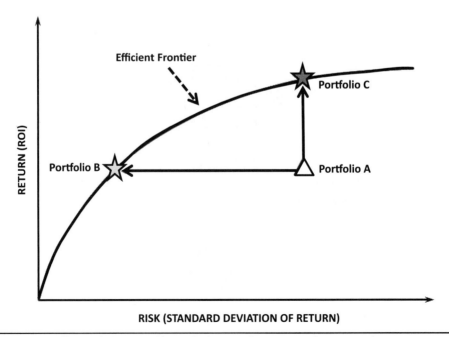

Figure 3-7   The efficient frontier and bounded rational economic decision making
Source: Cengage Learning Rights and Content Use (adapted with permission)

(a) the highest value one can obtain for a given level of risk and (b) the lowest risk one should undertake for a given level of value. Clearly, both portfolios B and C are superior to portfolio A, so a rational decision maker would not willingly choose portfolio A in favor of portfolio B or C unless he/she did not know of their possible existence. For a more detailed treatment of making trade-offs along the efficient frontier, the reader is advised to review the excellent work of Ragsdale (2008).

Why would a rational decision maker choose a portfolio other than B or C? In the absence of using an optimization frame to solve the problem of value maximization (attained by portfolio C) or risk minimization (attained by portfolio B), the best decision may emerge from one of the many portfolios that lie below the efficient frontier. Since these portfolios are all sub-optimal in the sense that they neither maximize value for a given level of risk nor minimize risk for a given level of value, they can be referred to as portfolios that are "good enough."

If "good enough" is the best decision taken, this is the equivalent of bounded rational economics as the decision maker is content to pursue a portfolio combination that meets the objective of less-than-value maximization and greater-than-risk minimization for a given level of return. If a decision is taken to pursue portfolio A, one would not immediately know how far away from the optimal solution this portfolio is. Stated otherwise, a decision maker could not easily quantify the value left on the table unless he/she were willing to at least understand the optimal solution represented by either portfolio B or C.

Hammond, Keeney, and Raiffa (2002) have articulated a process called *PROACT* that can be used for good decision making, a synopsis of which is shown in Figure 3-8. The PROACT process begins by identifying the frame of the problem, i.e., what decision needs to be taken. This is followed by establishing the scope (breadth and depth) that will serve as the boundaries of the investigation. Without the appropriate scope, it is often difficult to determine how much data and information need to be collected, which can easily lead to a costly and drawn out decision-making process.

Next, in order to attain the desired goals of the solution, there needs to be a way of measuring what is accomplished, and this can be achieved through the objectives of the solution. While it is often seductive to think that the strategy being pursued is the best for the solution to a problem, it is only after a close examination of alternative strategies, including creating hybrid strategies, that one can be certain superior alternatives do not exist. How one determines this is through an assessment of the consequences of each alternative solution, especially as they can be quantified in terms of their impact to the four value drivers—benefit (or value), risk, cost, and time. For many solutions, a situation seldom emerges when one strategy is dominant in each of these four dimensions, requiring trade-offs between alternative solutions (and conflicting objectives) to be made.

To the PROACT process, "url" can be added, based on the seminal work of Hammond, Keeney, and Raiffa. While it is tempting to utilize a single point estimate of any of the value drivers as a means of comparing alternative solutions, it is important to quantify the possible impact that uncertain data may have on a decision. For example, solutions with similar likelihoods of successful implementation (risk) may be highly differentiated when compared on the basis of the uncertainty of cost and time to

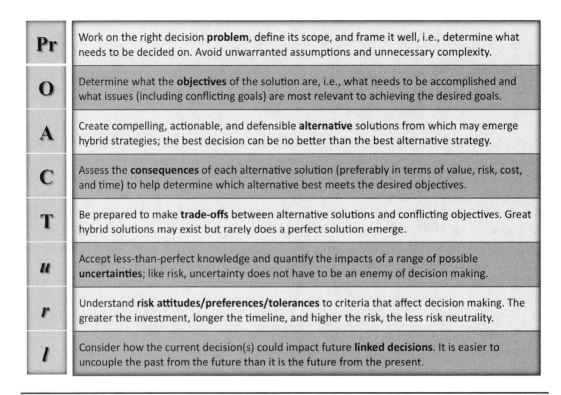

Pr	Work on the right decision **problem**, define its scope, and frame it well, i.e., determine what needs to be decided on. Avoid unwarranted assumptions and unnecessary complexity.
O	Determine what the **objectives** of the solution are, i.e., what needs to be accomplished and what issues (including conflicting goals) are most relevant to achieving the desired goals.
A	Create compelling, actionable, and defensible **alternative** solutions from which may emerge hybrid strategies; the best decision can be no better than the best alternative strategy.
C	Assess the **consequences** of each alternative solution (preferably in terms of value, risk, cost, and time) to help determine which alternative best meets the desired objectives.
T	Be prepared to make **trade-offs** between alternative solutions and conflicting objectives. Great hybrid solutions may exist but rarely does a perfect solution emerge.
u	Accept less-than-perfect knowledge and quantify the impacts of a range of possible **uncertainties**; like risk, uncertainty does not have to be an enemy of decision making.
r	Understand **risk attitudes/preferences/tolerances** to criteria that affect decision making. The greater the investment, longer the timeline, and higher the risk, the less risk neutrality.
l	Consider how the current decision(s) could impact future **linked decisions**. It is easier to uncouple the past from the future than it is the future from the present.

Figure 3-8　The PROACT.url method of decision making
Source: Harvard Business School Publishing (adapted with permission)

implement throughout their lifecycle. Given this, the risk preferences of the decision makers need to be understood, as risky solutions that require high investments over long periods of time tend to evoke different risk attitudes from those that take place over much shorter time periods.

Finally, before a decision is taken, it is good business practice to examine the impact on future linked decisions. For example, a highly defensible decision to build a manufacturing plant of a particular capacity may have adverse consequences on competing products if their commercial demand is excessive. This is particularly true for a program or portfolio of projects where there are linked technical dependencies, and a decision to continue a given project is contingent on incremental investments in one or another project.

The PROACT.url process is recommended for all types of decisions, including those that abound in the high-risk world of drug development as well as the lower-risk environment of IT. To be sure, one of the primary challenges for all decision makers is to recognize that while the ultimate objective is to make the right project or portfolio decision (i.e., one that leads to good outcomes), the best that one can do prescriptively is to make good decisions that will hopefully lead to good outcomes. Because most prospective information is, by definition, imperfect, good decisions can lead to bad outcomes. This is especially true in high-risk industries such as pharmaceuticals and biotechnology, where there is also high uncertainty, for example, in time to completion of development and forecasts of product value. In recognition of this, decision makers should strive to minimize both Type I (false positive) errors, which lead to expensive failures in a portfolio, and Type II (false negative) errors, which result in the termination of opportunities that would otherwise have been successful to a portfolio.

3.2 Summary

The success of any data-gathering effort is predicated on the fundamental soundness of the decision frame that drives that effort. Getting the decision frame right involves striking the appropriate balance between breadth, complexity, focus, and involvement. The next step is placing the decision in the appropriate organizational context, as well as asking key questions, in order to improve the quality of the decision, especially in the face of uncertainty. The heuristics encountered in decision making and their effects on project portfolio management were expounded upon. Decision-making models were introduced, and the concept of the efficient frontier and the implications on bounded rational decision making were illustrated. Best practices based on the PRO-ACT.url methodology were proposed as an aid to good decision making. This sets the stage for delving into the intricacies of the CREOPM™ framework, a methodology for successful project portfolio management, in Chapters 4-9.

Section 3

CREOPM™: A Framework for Enterprise Project Portfolio Management

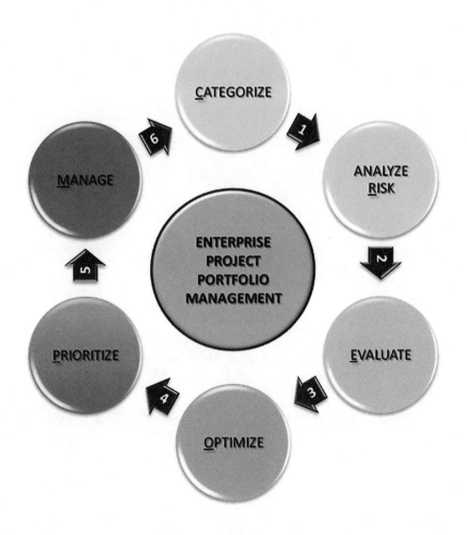

4

Project Categorization

- **Categorization**—The act of classifying, cataloging, or distributing projects (and programs) into a collectively exhaustive set of basic classes or categories. Each entity shares one or more particular properties within a class or category which, in turn, preserves those properties.

4.1 Key Concepts of Project Categorization

Just as scenario analysis, strategic planning, decision framing, and data integrity are the necessary prerequisites that enable an organization to best understand where it is heading and why, project categorization is a fundamental necessity for determining how the organization will achieve its objectives. If you were about to embark on a journey, you would most likely begin the task of preparing by considering the items that must accompany you (e.g., driver's license, evidence of car insurance, credit cards, cash, mobile phone, and so on) before giving consideration to the things that you may wish to take (e.g., types of clothing, favorite music, local maps, restaurant reviews). It is intuitive for the majority of people to decide on the articles to not take (e.g., less-than-favorite music, inappropriate footwear) while deciding on what must be taken. If this example seems trivial, why then do organizations have such a difficult time deciding on and making explicit those projects and programs that *must be* done, that *may be* done, or that *won't be* done? The Must Do, May Do, and Won't Do categories are discrete from each other. The Must Do category of endeavor is non-discretionary or mandatory, and the second and third categories are discretionary or optional.

Within the non-discretionary category of Must Do projects, are mandates such as FDA-imposed long-term carcinogenicity studies and post-marketing surveillance trials, IT initiatives in support of HIPAA compliance reporting in the healthcare industry, and business continuity plans in virtually every organization (see Figure 4-1). Mandated projects do not have to be pursued in accordance with regulatory timelines. Instead, an organization may choose to defer investing in or completing such projects while agreeing to pay a financial penalty for not doing so in a timely manner.

Projects deemed to be critical to the financial and/or strategic survival of the enterprise, along with those characterized as being within progressive phases or product life cycle extensions, may not be truly obligatory in nature. Yet, they represent a subcategory of projects for which there is little, if any, rationale to discontinue. In the case

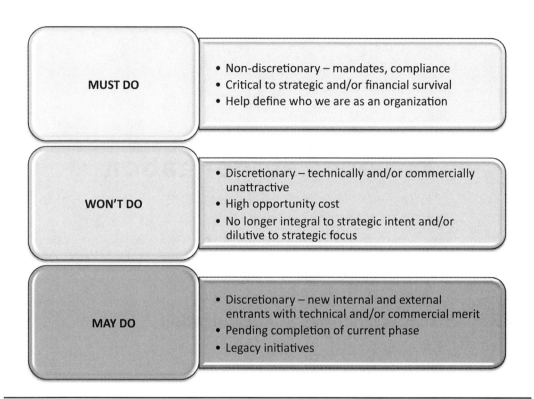

Figure 4-1 Project categorization

of projects that are in flight, unless dramatic internal forces (e.g., detection of highly unfavorable side effects) or external issues (e.g., adverse competitor information) impact the business case negatively and suggest that they be terminated, in-progress projects should be continued at least until the completion of their current phase of development or next decision point. In many instances, a cohort of projects exists that continues to define the very existence and values of an organization (e.g., an improved diagnostic kit for a chronic disease), rendering them non-discretionary.

Often, the temptation to justify the perceived strategic and financial value of projects in a portfolio results in overloading the Must Do category with an excessive list of truly discretionary projects. A sign of an undisciplined organization, therefore, is one in which far too many projects are assembled into a Must Do category, resulting in insufficient resources to undertake all of those projects or inadequate resources to pursue projects that lie outside of that category.

Must Do projects may have no strategic or financial priority per se; rather, they *must* simply be done within a defined time frame. To be sure, these projects have an operational or temporal priority where the fundamental question that needs to be addressed is not "Should these projects be done?" but rather "In what order should these projects be done?" Far too often, organizations create a list of rank-ordered projects after which a line that represents the budgetary constraint is drawn and below which it is expected that no further projects can be invested in. Invariably, in such a prioritization scheme, one or more Must Do projects (e.g., mandates), may find their way below the constraint line, prompting organizations to request one form or another of the unthinkable, but doable:

- Change the entire prioritization scoring methodology and rerun the prioritization until all mandates appear above the budgetary line.
- Apply a special "bump-up factor" to mandates that ensures they rise above the line.
- Override the rank order by invoking "other decision criteria" that are not embedded in the project prioritization methodology to get any number of projects sufficiently high on the priority list; this singular, but dangerous, act enables pet projects to be continued almost without open discussion.
- Disregard the prioritization altogether, and "pick the best projects" using "good management judgment."

Not surprisingly, although most organizations set out with the intent to prioritize projects with full objectivity using data, analysis, and logic, without the right level of discipline and an objective facilitator, decision making becomes overwhelmed by opinions, heuristics, politics, and advocacy. In the end, project sponsors with the loudest voice or proverbial "biggest stick" generally get their way to the detriment of the value of the portfolio. As shown in Chapter 7, Portfolio Optimization, under constrained resource conditions, every good project cannot always be a part of an optimal portfolio. However, as demonstrated in Chapter 8, Project Prioritization, the converse is also true, i.e., every good project can be a part of a sub-optimal portfolio.

In almost all organizations, a small proportion of the portfolio is populated by projects for which there is little, if any, rationale for ongoing budgetary and human resource investments. Yet, these projects consume resources that are much needed by other projects in that it would enable them to be initiated, continued, or used to enhance an existing strategic approach or project plan. Of particular note are projects that were once very good ideas, but which, despite protracted investments, fail to live up to their technical or commercial expectations. Despite the weakness of a business case, such projects continue to survive in many organizations primarily because a sponsor or project champion refuses to acknowledge that a previously good idea is no longer defensible or the lure of additional investments to justify those previously made (i.e., sunk costs) is far too emotionally compelling.

Why do organizations seem to have so much difficulty terminating projects in an effective and efficient manner? There are myriad reasons, including:

- Lack of clear decision criteria, threshold criteria for success, or decision-making discipline
- Ineffective stage gate review processes
- Politically powerful sponsors and other stakeholders
- Reluctance to revise and validate a project's business case
- Fear of acknowledgment of a bad idea or a once good idea turned bad
- The illusion of recouping sunk costs

- Emotional bias and organizational reward structures
- Fear of demoralizing a project team

In the same way that proactive organizations use scenario analysis and strategic planning to guide decisions about which projects should constitute their portfolios, it is equally important that transparent decisions are made on which projects will or will no longer become a part of their portfolios. While emotional detachment from previous investments can be a difficult undertaking, the value of doing so to a portfolio is self-evident: enhanced focus, revitalization of a project team, and better utilization of scarce resources.

Once the resource needs of Must Do projects have been attended to, and freed resources from Won't Do projects are recycled into the existing pool of available resources, it is time for an organization to focus its attention on the discretionary May Do category of projects within its portfolio. These projects represent the portion of the portfolio in which several combinations of projects can be investigated to best meet the goals, including adding the greatest value, of the organization. This category includes new internal and external entrants and projects that are due for an end-of-phase review.

It is the May Do category of projects that decision makers should spend the vast majority of their time deliberating over whether they should be done until successful completion or termination, as well as whether those projects warrant only a partial investment for the purposes of gaining information prior to committing to a full investment. As explained in Chapter 7, an organization is better positioned to meet its objectives by creating several degrees of freedom in its portfolio through the discretionary nature of its May Do projects. We will demonstrate both in Chapter 7 and in subsequent case studies that several portfolio strategies can be evaluated once a determination is made of what discretionary project decisions an organization has at its disposal. Far too many discretionary projects tend to be housed in the Must Do category, thereby reducing the amount of flexibility that the enterprise possesses; the Must Do overload can also serve as a smoke screen for investments that are really discretionary, but have been given the opposite designation by an interested stakeholder.

Two frequently asked questions about categorization are:

(a) How many projects should ideally be apportioned to Must Do and May Do project categories?

(b) What proportion of budgetary resources should be allocated to each of these two categories?

For both questions, the simple answer is, "It depends on the strategic and financial goals of the enterprise." Organizations that take a longer view of their portfolio needs are better able to defend their choices of discretionary investments in search of temporal value maximization, while those that create, defensibly or otherwise, a continual sense of urgency that may border on paranoia tend to focus myopically on the immediacy of their needs. In the latter case, far too many projects are thrown into the Must Do category as they are deemed to be absolutely essential to the survival of the enterprise, with the result that portfolio value can be destroyed.

Another relevant question to ask is: How can portfolio value be destroyed if a greater number of discretionary projects are simply made non-discretionary? The answer lies in a fundamental precept of portfolio optimization in that the greater the number of projects that *must* be pursued in a portfolio, the smaller the number of mathematically possible project combinations that lie close to the efficient frontier, making the creation of value for a defined resource constraint lower. To illustrate this principle, consider Must Do Project A costing $20M and yielding $100M in net present value (NPV), which destroys $10M in value when compared to two discretionary Projects B and C, costing $9M and $10M, respectively, and yielding $50M and $60M, respectively, in NPV. While it appears, *ceteris paribus*, that a rational decision maker would never choose Project A over the combination of Projects B and C, in a much larger portfolio, he/she would not readily know of the existence of a combination of projects that is better than one with the inclusion of Project A without an exhaustive manual search or aid of programming software. This topic of software use is further explored in Chapter 7 and in Appendix B, A Primer in Mathematical Programming. The resource allocation question is further addressed in Section 9.4, Resource Management.

4.2 Summary

The first component of the CREOPM™ framework, Project Categorization, involves the Must Do, Won't Do, May Do framework for categorizing projects in organizations. Organizational barriers to the termination of projects, including emotional attachments, were identified and their effects on the number of projects in each category were detailed. This introduction to the CREOPM™ framework sets the stage for related, more complex topics that follow in subsequent chapters.

5

Risk Analysis

- **Risk**—The likelihood of occurrence of an event, e.g., weather catastrophe or product recall (generally unfavorable in nature), measured by a discrete probability between 0 and 1. Risk may be subdivided into controllable or mitigatable by the allocation of greater time and resources (e.g., project completion) or uncontrollable insofar as increased time and resources have no impact (e.g., statistical drug efficacy).
- **Uncertainty**—The range of possible outcomes associated with the occurrence of an event; uncertain outcomes may be discrete (e.g., number of consumer deaths) or continuous (e.g., severity of rashes) in nature and can be measured by a probability (p) of occurrence.

5.1 Key Concepts of Risk Analysis

In R&D, risks generally represent obstacles to the successful progression of a project according to the timeline contained within the project plan. Within the IT industry, risks are generally associated more with successfully achieving the timeline of a project plan (i.e., temporal risk) than with creating a successful project. Many organizations, in both R&D and IT industries, are at a rudimentary stage with respect to portfolio risk analysis.

While companies have, in varying degrees, applied formal risk analysis and risk management successfully to individual projects and programs, they have been less successful in proactively analyzing and managing portfolio risk. Risks must be evaluated for both individual investments as well as the entire portfolio of investments, especially since failure to do so can lead to sub-optimal portfolio management practices. Therefore, a clear understanding of both project and portfolio risk is crucial for successful portfolio risk analysis within the R&D and IT communities.

Consider the ambiguity conveyed by the following statement: "This project is a sure bet and will most likely succeed." First, we know that there is no such thing as a sure, legitimate bet, and second, depending on your level of knowledge of and optimism about the project, the probability estimate may be high but not as high as 1.0. This is an important example of everyday usage of the language of *risk*, which, far too often, tends to be used interchangeably with the language of *uncertainty*. With sufficient discipline and application, risk can become a vehicle for understanding the frequency with which an event occurs, and uncertainty becomes a means of projecting how good or bad the outcome of the event may be.

Taken together, with a proactive assessment of risk and uncertainty, one may be able to put certain plans in place to benefit from the impact of the uncertainty once the risk occurs. This benefit may be the result of being positioned to take advantage of the upside of uncertainty (e.g., a competitor's loss of patent protection or market share) or minimize the impact of the downside of uncertainty (e.g., a new competitive entrant that impacts the organization's market share). This is also the basis on which scenario planning is conducted. Based on a project scenario (e.g., FDA approval of bio-similar drugs), generic drug companies may be able to make significant inroads on the prices of future biologic drugs.

While it is difficult to discuss financial portfolio risk without an understanding of the contributions of the individual assets to overall risk, it is equally difficult to engage in a treatment of R&D and IT portfolio risk without first identifying the contribution of each project to the overall risk load of the portfolio. Although we can now define project risk, how can it first be analyzed and quantified? To be sure, project risk is dependent on the strategy of choice to enable the objectives or deliverables of the project to be attained. Such objectives are usually captured in a target product profile (TPP) (shown in Figure 5-1). In this case, the TPP is a drug with specifications for target population(s), safety, efficacy, dosage and administration, and storage that are clearly documented.

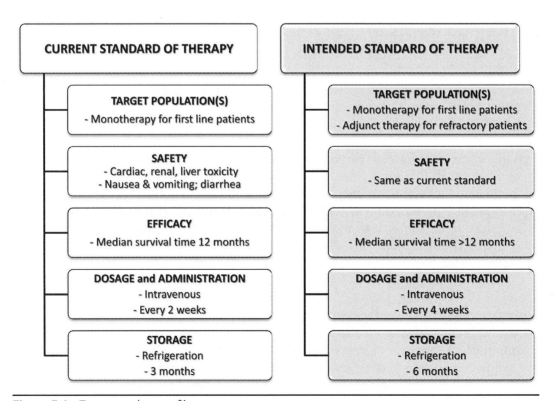

Figure 5-1 Target product profile

Depending on the strategy of choice, the overall risk of a project can be quantified in terms of the joint probability of success of attaining each of the individual elements within the dimensions of target population(s), safety, efficacy, dosage, and administration. Assuming probabilistic independence between the individual elements (i.e., the likelihood of achieving any of the TPP elements is not dependent on or affected by the attainment of any other element), it is not terribly difficult to envisage that the resulting overall probability of success can be quite low. However, this is the nature of business in high-risk, innovative industries, a classic example being the pharmaceutical and biotechnology drug development industry.

Not surprisingly, as the same project matures and more information is gained, the judgmental probability of success should increase. Without an explicit articulation of what objectives a project is aiming to achieve (as shown in the TPP example in Figure 5-1) and the quantification of each element of risk associated with those objectives, it is difficult to assess the overall risk of a project. While industry benchmarks may serve as a general guide for project success and failure, they tend to represent the average of both high- and low-risk projects and fail to capture idiosyncratic risk that may be present in any given project. A better, albeit tedious, approach is to assess the probability of success in attaining each individual risk element within the TPP, and then compute the joint probability after accounting for probabilistic dependencies, if any, between these elements.

Finally, a subjective judgment of a probability of success is really no more than a reflection of what would happen on the average (i.e., in the long term) if this exact project could be undertaken many times. Stated otherwise, for one roll of the die, the probability of success of a project may assume only one of two states, 0 or 1. In the long term, however, the probability of success of the same project will assume a non-integer state based on the average of both successes and failures.

How are defensible probability judgments generated? Elicitation methods that help minimize or overcome the cognitive and motivational biases, described in Chapter 3, are crucial to enabling subject matter experts (SMEs) to generate defensible risk estimates. Kirkwood (1997) and others have described a five-stage process that is applicable to the elicitation of probabilities for both discrete and continuous uncertainties. A synopsis of this process can be described as:

1. Motivating stage—This stage involves: (a) introducing the task at hand and (b) establishing a rapport with the SME(s) to determine potential areas of motivational bias, including expert and inexpert bias.
2. Structuring stage—The primary purposes of this stage are to define: (a) terms of use, e.g., the meaning of risk, success, and uncertainty, and (b) underlying assumptions used during the probability elicitation.
3. Conditioning stage—This stage is important in counteracting cognitive biases especially in the context of ensuring that all relevant information about the uncertain event or quantity is considered.
4. Encoding stage—This stage involves developing probability distributions for the event or uncertain quantity.
5. Verifying stage—This final stage is necessary to ensure that the SME can rationally defend his/her own judgments based on expert knowledge and beliefs.

5.1.1 Portfolio Risk Analysis

Let us build a thread between project risk and portfolio risk by first examining how project risk can be depicted in a simple decision tree (Figure 5-2).[1] Assuming the probability of success of a project in conveying specific benefits to patients with disease A is judged to be 0.15, its complement or probability of failure is 0.85. By "probability of success" we mean the probability that a project will become a product, i.e., the project will overcome all of the technical and regulatory hurdles in its path to become a commercial product. "Probability of success" does not address the probability that the product will be commercially successful, merely due to its launch in the market.

Now, consider a program consisting of three projects that are probabilistically dependent, i.e., if the project succeeds in becoming a product for disease A, there is a higher likelihood that it will be successful in disease B, and if successful in diseases A and B, there is an even higher likelihood that it will be successful in disease C (see Figure 5-3). This is not an uncommon facet of drug development, where, depending on its mechanism of action, a drug may convey therapeutic benefit in several related diseases.

In reviewing the complex decision tree in Figure 5-3, what is the risk—as measured by a probability of success—of the program? Without an explicit definition of what is meant by *risk*, the program may assume one of several values for the probability of success. For example, if risk is defined as the probability of success of Projects A and B and C, the joint probability of success (shown at the end of the top-most branch) is:

$$p = 0.15 * 0.45 * 0.75 = 0.05$$

As a further example, if the risk of the program is dependent on succeeding in at least disease A because it is the most commercially attractive disease, then any branch of the decision tree that carries a successful outcome to Project A (alone or in combination with other successes) would be defined as "success." In this case, the probability of success of the program can be calculated as

$$p = (0.05 + 0.02 + 0.01 + 0.07) = 0.15$$

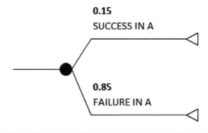

Figure 5-2 Project risk

---

[1]Those new to decision tree analysis are encouraged to review Appendix A, A Primer in Decision Analysis.

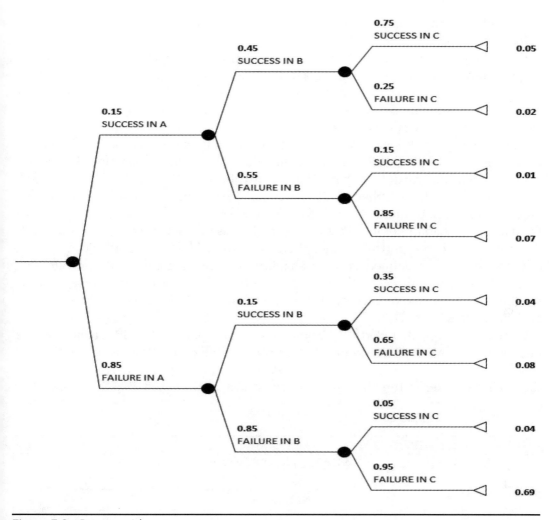

Figure 5-3   Program risk

This represents the following outcomes to the program, shown along the top four branches of the decision tree:

- Success in A, B, C (0.05)
- Success in A, B; failure in C (0.02)
- Success in A, C; failure in B (0.01)
- Success in A; failure in B, C (0.07)

Note that since all three projects in the program are being conducted, no outcome exists in which there is success in Project A alone; rather, the terminal calculations represent permutations of success or failure in Projects A, B, and C. In fact, of the eight mutually exclusive and collectively exhaustive outcomes, only one (bottom-most branch of failure in A and B and C) represents complete failure of the program, while any one of the other seven outcomes could be construed as an indicator of the success of the program, in the absence of explicitly defining the risk (e.g., success in at least Project A).

If a definition of risk is required before calculating the probability of success at the program level, it is also true at the portfolio level. Consider the case of two overlapping portfolios (portrayed by cumulative distribution functions) that have the same mean value of roughly $90M (shown in Figure 5-4). What is the risk of Portfolios A and B, and which one is riskier?

Ceteris paribus, a rational, expected value decision maker would be indifferent between these portfolio choices, as the mean value is the same. Upon close inspection, it can be seen that Portfolio A has a narrow distribution of values ($25M to $200M) with a relatively steep incline, while Portfolio B has a more gradual incline with a much wider distribution of values (–$100M to $300M). In this example, if risk is defined as the probability of loss, Portfolio B can lose as much as $100M, and is certainly the riskier of the two portfolios since there is no risk of loss with Portfolio A. On the other hand, if risk is defined as the probability of exceeding a defined portfolio goal, e.g., $120M (shown in Figure 5-5), Portfolio B becomes the superior choice, as it has roughly a 40% chance of exceeding this goal, while Portfolio A has a 20% chance of achieving better than $120M.

Notice, however, that Portfolio B also has an approximately 13% chance of loss, i.e., less than $0M. So, if we address the question of which portfolio is riskier, the best conclusion is that it depends on: (a) the stated goal(s) and (b) the risk tolerance of the decision maker. If the objective is to avoid loss, as discussed above, Portfolio A is

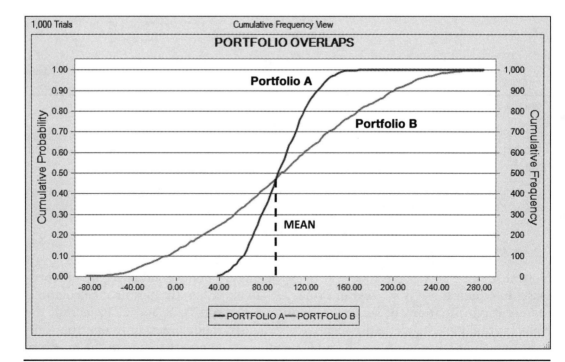

Figure 5-4 Portfolio risk undefined

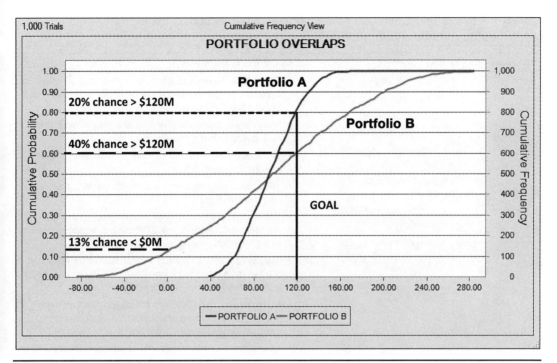

Figure 5-5 Portfolio risk defined

the better alternative; however, if the goal is to maximize upside potential, Portfolio B is the superior alternative. As will be discussed in Appendix A, A Primer in Decision Analysis, both Figures 5-4 and 5-5 are cumulative distribution functions (CDFs) that are the result of a simulation of the sum of the net present value distributions of all of the projects that constitute Portfolios A and B.

5.1.2 Modeling Risks Associated with Investments in a Portfolio

The previous section highlights the significant differences between portfolio risk and project risk. *Project risk analysis* pertains to the assessment of risks associated with each investment (project or program) in a portfolio and is predicated on (a) the development of a risk model, complete with the clear definition of the elements of risks associated with each investment, and (b) the measurement of the risks previously defined, to determine the relative risk of the investments in the portfolio.

A Model for Defining R&D Investment Risks

In the absence of a universally accepted framework for cataloguing the risks associated with R&D and IT investments, a hierarchical model defining such risks associated with *individual* investments in a portfolio can provide organizational decision makers a simple, yet objective framework for defining the risks. As illustrations, one such model (shown in Table 5-1) is proposed for clinical development risks in the pharmaceutical and biotechnology industry (Rang, 2006) and in the following section for IT risks.

Table 5-1 A model for defining R&D risks associated with clinical drug development in the pharmaceutical and biotechnology industry

Risk Type	Risk Sub-type	Definition/Explanation
Technical Risk	• Bioavailability • Pharmacokinetic profile • Pharmacodynamic profile • Pharmacogenomic profile • Antigenicity and antibody assays • Achievement of safety targets • Achievement of efficacy targets • Tolerability	• The rate and extent to which an active drug reaches the systemic circulation and is available at the targeted site of action in the body • The process by which a drug is absorbed, distributed, metabolized, and eliminated by the body • The biochemical and physiologic effects of a drug and its mechanism of action • The relationship between a person's genetic makeup and his/her response to a drug • The propensity of a drug to stimulate an antibody response in a person; the availability of a diagnostic test to an antibody response • Increased safety or patient acceptance at an accepted level of drug efficacy or increased efficacy at equivalent level of safety or patient acceptance • Ability of a drug to produce a desired effect as measured by one or more endpoints, e.g., increase in median survival time of a patient • Investigation of the symptoms of adverse effects over a range of doses of a drug
Technical Risk	• Drug-drug interactions • Food effects • Therapeutic index • Pharmacology • Benefit-risk assessment • Subject response variability • Clinical endpoints • Surrogate markers • Statistical methods • Formulation	• Modification of the effect of a drug when administered with another drug • The effect produced when a drug and certain foods and beverages are taken at the same time • The ratio between the dosage of a drug that causes a lethal effect and the dosage that causes a therapeutic effect • The body's reaction to an administered drug • The ratio of clinical benefits to risks from an administered drug • The degree to which subjects react differently in response to the same dosage and regimen of a drug • Occurrence of a disease, symptom, sign, or laboratory abnormality that constitutes one of the target outcomes of a clinical trial • Indicators of the presence and progression of a disease • Collection, analysis, and interpretation of data, including the planning of the collection of data • The development or preparation of a drug for its intended route of administration
Regulatory Risk	• Stability and heterogeneity of environment • Clarity of guidelines • Novelty of class labeling • Robustness of submission package • Preapproval inspection readiness	• Idiosyncrasies of regional authorities for local product approval • Clear guidelines for approvability and product labeling • Uniqueness of proposed product labeling • Acceptability of, e.g., statistical methods, cleanliness, and completeness of site data and information • Production and manufacturing readiness according to good manufacturing practices and standards

Risk Type	Risk Sub-type	Definition/Explanation
Operational Risk	• Achievement of patient enrollment targets • Acceptability of geographic data • Training of investigators • Manufacturing scale-up • Availability of clinical supplies	• Temporal risk associated with enrollment and dropout rates • Usability of country-specific data for regional and global submissions • Human risk due to incompleteness of training and understanding of standard practices • Ability to manufacture commercial quantities based on pilot batches for clinical use • Availability of clinical drug supplies to initiate and complete trials on time

A Model for Defining IT Investment Risks

Drawing on the authors' experience in the IT industry and the best practices outlined in the compendium titled *IT Portfolio Management Step by Step*[2] by Maizlish and Handler (2005), a hierarchical model for classifying and defining the risks associated with the individual investments in an IT portfolio is shown in Table 5-2. While this is not a "one-size-fits-all" model for classifying risks in a portfolio of IT investments, it can nevertheless be used either as is or tailored to suit the specific needs of an organization. At the highest level in the hierarchy, risks associated with IT investments can be classified under business risk, technical risk, and operational risk. Each risk type is comprised of sub-types, constituting a specific risk associated with an IT investment, as defined in Table 5-2.

5.1.3 Risk Measurement

Once the hierarchical project risk model has been developed, the next step is to quantify and measure the risks associated with the project investments in that portfolio. Risks can be quantified and measured in a number of ways, one example of which is a weighted scoring methodology. Using this method, an approach to scoring risks is to use traditional project risk management techniques whereby each risk attribute is measured in terms of its likelihood of occurrence and the magnitude of the impact (if it occurs) on the investment under consideration. Scoring ranges for risk assessment can be developed for both the likelihood of occurrence and its impact.

Each risk attribute is then assigned a combined score that corresponds to the likelihood and impact, with the product of these scores being the "risk score" of that risk attribute for the investment under consideration. Although this is a widely accepted approach to project risk measurement, a risk score does not lend itself well to the application of risk for the purposes of generating integrated, risk-adjusted evaluations of projects and portfolios. While it is clear that an understanding of the potential impact of risks to a project enables an organization to focus its efforts on mitigating such risks (if possible), it does not facilitate a quantification of overall portfolio risk. Consequently, risk analysis should be done primarily for the purposes of understanding the

---

[2]The book by Maizlish and Handler (2005) is a must-read for any practitioner of IT portfolio management.

Table 5-2 A model for defining risks associated with IT investments

Risk Type	Risk Sub-type	Definition/Explanation
Business Risk	Organizational Change Risk	The degree of organizational change management required for success, characterized by the level of management commitment, support and buy-in from the user community and the amount of extra effort required to implement the requisite change in the organization.
	Management Risk	What is the risk of change in management during the life of the investment, which would bring with it a change in corporate direction and potential cancellation of the initiative?
	External Risk	The risk of change in market conditions, current trends, actions by competitors, government agencies, etc. that may occur between inception and delivery of the investment, resulting in a decrease in the usefulness of the end solution or even rendering it obsolete.
	Strategic Risk	What level of risk is this investment likely to have on the organization's strategic goals and objectives?
Technical Risk	Complexity Risk	The degree of complexity of the IT investment under consideration; if new technology is introduced requiring hardware, software, network; and other infrastructure components that the organization does not currently support or if the level of customization is high (for packaged solutions), the complexity risk is high.
	Feasibility Risk	The risk that the proposed solution is not technically feasible; the degree of uncertainty is typically higher for IT investments that require more innovation.
	Scalability Risk	The underlying technology infrastructure and applications must be scalable in size, capacity, and functionality to meet changing business and technical requirements. This attribute measures the ability of an IT solution to be scalable enough to meet changes in requirements.
	Customization Risk	This risk measures the degree to which an existing IT solution has been customized, such that the higher the degree of customization, the lower the customization risk.
	Integration Risk	The level of integration required for the IT investment; generally, the higher the level of integration, the greater the level of integration risk.
	Lifecycle Stage Risk	What is the maturity level of the technology under consideration?
	Security Risk	The project meets the organization's standards for application and system security—data protection, authentication, authorization, encryption, system integrity management (non-intrusion). Utilize industry benchmarks to gauge (ISO, IEC, etc. where applicable).
Operational Risk	Business Continuity Plan Risk	The risk that the IT investment does not or likely will not meet operational requirements in terms of inadequacy of facilities, poor quality of delivered capability, or larger than expected number of defects.
	Project Risk	Scope changes, schedule overruns/under-runs, dependencies on other projects, etc. are captured as project execution risk for new investments.
	Supportability Risk	Supportability risk measures the degree of in-house support to an existing IT solution, with higher scores assigned to solutions that are completely supported in-house and lower scores for those whose support is contingent upon external service providers.
	Vendor Risk	The risk that a chosen vendor will fail to deliver needed products and/ or services in a usable state in a timely basis. This would also include the possibility that the vendor is acquired or otherwise ceases to exist.

contribution of individual risk elements to the overall likelihood of success of a project; in so doing, an organization is able to address where its greatest risks lie and what, if anything, can be done to mitigate the impact of such risks.

A recommended approach to risk analysis and measurement is the assignment of judgmental probabilities to represent the perceived likelihood of occurrence of unique risks. In the case of clinical drug development, one may utilize the checklist shown in Table 5-1 to determine what risk elements may affect the phased success of a project. Stated otherwise, once the hurdles for success are defined in each phase of clinical development, the risks that could affect each hurdle are quantified and a joint probability assigned to each phase of development. This is done for subsequent phases of clinical development, assuming success in each previous phase, and the overall risk of the project is assessed in terms of the joint probability across all phases of development.

While both approaches have merits, one cannot ignore the subjectivity that can arise in assigning risk scores and joint probabilities to risk assessments. Methods for minimizing bias in the elicitation of judgmental probabilities from SMEs exist, but are beyond the scope of this book; the reader is encouraged to review the work of Kirkwood (1997) for an excellent treatment of probability judgments.

Nevertheless, at the portfolio level, it is important to stress that risk assumes a very different connotation from that encountered at the project level. Whereas at the project level risk is generally associated with the likelihood of project completion within scope, budget, and time, the same cannot be stated of portfolio risk, which attunes itself to the likelihood of meeting goals (e.g., top line growth) and exceeding constraints (e.g., budget) along with a measure of the organization's risk exposure (e.g., variance around mean returns). If risk analysis is developed with sufficient rigor and discipline, it can provide a defensibly objective baseline by which all project investments can be compared and, in turn, serve to inform an organization of its chances of meeting stated goals.

Employment of sensitivity analysis to probabilities (treated in Appendix A) and comparison of investments in alternate scenarios (what-if analysis) can augment this approach to risk assessment and help with objective decision making. The importance of determining the organization's risk tolerance as a precursor to developing a risk assessment model cannot be overstated. Detailed risk measurement is illustrated in the case studies that appear in Chapters 10 and 11.

5.1.4 Key Considerations in Portfolio Risk Analysis

Organizational orientation to risk tolerance is the primary driver of portfolio risk management in enterprises. The use of portfolio risk analysis in organizations is heavily influenced by the need to seek a temporally balanced portfolio.

Balanced Portfolio

If beauty lies in the eyes of the beholder, so does the balance of a portfolio. To begin a discussion of a balanced portfolio requires, not surprisingly, a definition of what is meant by *balance* and the primary elements that need to be considered (see Figure 5-6). These elements include the temporal goals of the organization; the proportion of

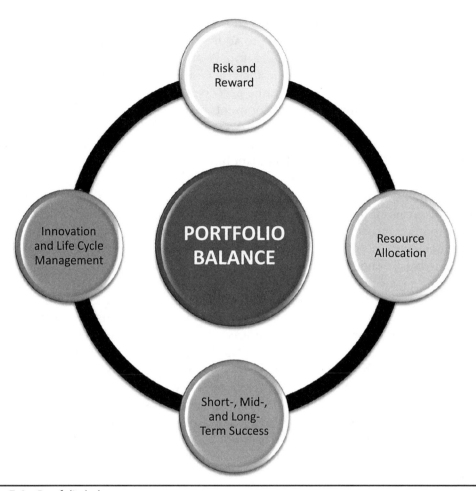

Figure 5-6   Portfolio balance

risky, innovative projects to less risky, life cycle extension projects; the mix of internal and external assets; and the level of budgetary and human resources allocated to each phase (e.g., concept, discovery, development) of the portfolio.

Why does an organization seek a balanced portfolio, and how important is it to attain short-term goals before striving to accomplish longer-term goals? In reference to the continual accomplishment of top line sales goals, a CEO of a Top 10 Pharmaceutical company once stated, "Without the short term, there is no long term."

While this statement is meritorious, taken to its logical extreme, a myopic focus on the attainment of short-term goals can impact negatively the fulfillment of long-term goals. Moreover, if the right incentives are not put in place to reward executives for creating sustainable portfolio value for the organization, the focus of portfolio management will, not surprisingly, be short term. Once the strategic and financial goals of an organization are clearly articulated, an actionable range of portfolio optimization strategies should be generated in response to a handful of scenarios. Once the results of project and program selection of each optimization are discussed, the organization can make an informed decision regarding the appropriate levels of resource allocation for different segments of the portfolio in order to attain a desired balance.

Many organizations tend to view portfolio balance as a function of a mixture of high- and low-risk projects, for which different levels of investment are necessary and that are capable of yielding a blend of high and low commercial value. A popular method of displaying such a portfolio involves the use of three-dimensional bubble charts that show the spread of projects in a portfolio through any three of four popular lenses—benefit, risk, cost, or time (Figure 5-7). In the example, although the portfolio appears to house relatively similar numbers of projects in each of the four quadrants, and thus conveys a sense of balance, unless it is tied to the goals of the organization, there is no simple way of knowing whether balance has been attained. Stated otherwise, if an organization is more focused on the attainment of its short-term growth goals (defined for this example as cumulative sales revenues over the next 1-3 years), its focus, not surprisingly, will be on those projects that are late in development and close to market launch, irrespective of how much it costs to get them to commercialization. On the other hand, with the same portfolio of projects, an organization that has a long-term view of its growth potential (defined for this example as cumulative sales revenues over the next 7-10 years) may be better served by nurturing projects that are in late discovery and early development.

In the absence of stated goals, therefore, an organization cannot assume that its portfolio is balanced even though graphical representations of its projects may appear to show otherwise. Perhaps it is better to discuss portfolio balance in the context of budgetary and human resource allocation over different time periods. The extent to which an organization nurtures its discovery portfolio is a reflection of how much value it expects to create from this segment of the portfolio over time.

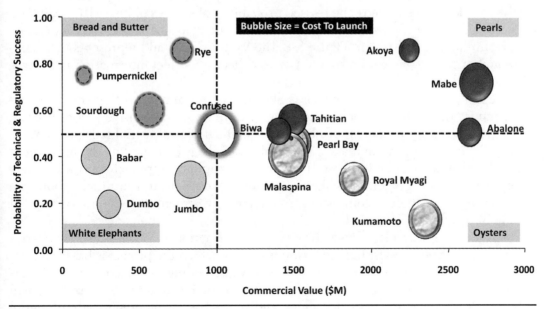

Figure 5-7 Graphical representation of assets in a portfolio

Value of Information

In many high-risk industries such as oil and gas exploration, or drug development, project investments in the tens or hundreds of millions of dollars are made over lengthy periods of time. It is common practice in high-risk industries to make phased investments and, as more information is gained, to use such information to make an informed decision regarding the progression of a project.

Information, which is largely imperfect but nevertheless valuable in nature, allows an organization to decide whether to continue investing in a project on the bases of (a) a revision of its belief in the probability of success of the project and (b) an assessment of competitive market forces and the evolving expectations of regulatory agencies. A good example of the use of imperfect information based on historical data to make a staged investment in drug development is depicted in Figure 5-8. Here, an organization is faced with the decision to conduct a relatively inexpensive Phase II clinical proof-of-concept (POC) trial before proceeding to the more expensive pivotal clinical trials (Phase III) or move directly to that latter phase of development. The following details are essential to understanding how value of investment (VOI) is measured in this example:

Cost of Phase II trial = $60M

Cost of Phase III trial = $600M

Commercial potential = $5,000M

Phase II and III probabilities of success = 0.38 and 0.20, respectively

Observed success of Phase II based on historical success of Phase III = 0.70

Observed failure of Phase II based on historical success of Phase III = 0.30

Based on Bayesian revision (discussed briefly in Appendix A, A Primer in Decision Analysis), if Phase II succeeds, the revised probability of success of Phase III = 0.36842; if Phase II fails, the revised probability of success of Phase III is 0.09677. As can be seen from the decision tree in Figure 5-8, the VOI is $72M and represents the maximum amount the organization should pay to collect imperfect information in a Phase II clinical trial.

Since the projected cost of the trial is $60M, it is recommended that the organization conduct this POC trial before moving on to the more expensive Phase III trials. Since the probability of success of Phase III is <10% if the POC trial fails (at a cost of $60M), the organization can make a more informed decision regarding the investment of $600M that is required in Phase III. This is a disciplined approach to risk management whereby an organization makes a judicious investment to learn more about the risks of the project before committing to a larger investment at sequential phases of the life of the project.

Since learning is rarely a linear process, as information is gained, disciplined risk management involves revisiting the business case on which the project is based to reaffirm that the next marginal investment is still value-adding in the context of the organization's portfolio objectives. Unfortunately, far too often, some organizations will invest in POC trials, test market surveys, and prototype development only to ignore

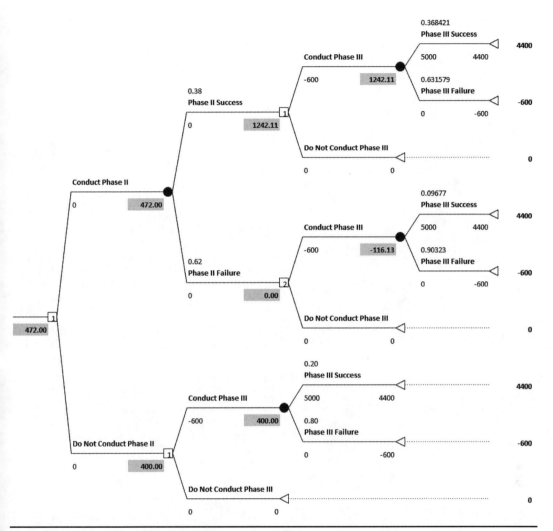

Figure 5-8 Value of information analysis

the results of such endeavors and proceed into full development of their projects. If the imperfect information gained from such studies or surveys is not used to inform decision making before committing to more expensive downstream investments, the VOI can be determined to be at a minimum zero or, in reality, negative.

Options Analysis

Few discussions on risk analysis and risk management would be complete without a discourse on options analysis, i.e. a staged investment in projects, to secure the right but not the obligation to make a further downstream investment. While options analysis has been widely used in the financial industry, this methodology, even in its current incarnation as "real options," has struggled to gain adequate traction within the R&D and IT communities. Rather than delve into the strengths and weaknesses of financial

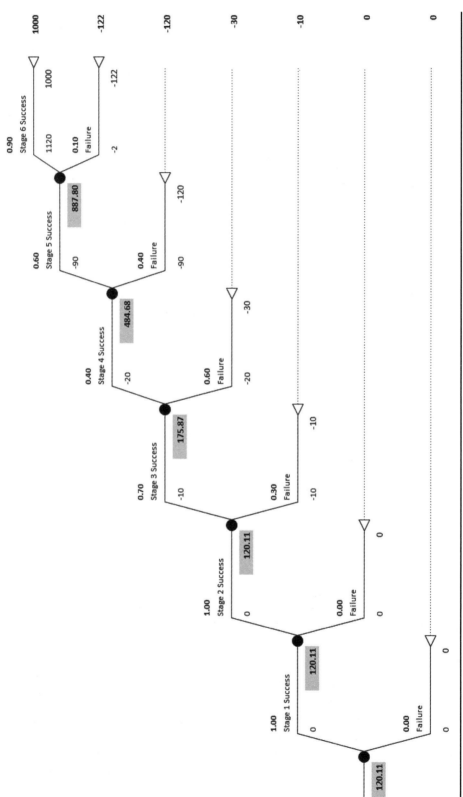

Figure 5-9 Staged options analysis

or real options analysis, a transparent and defensible methodology to model investment options in R&D and IT business sectors through the use of decision trees is presented (see Figure 5-9). In this method, a series of phased investments is shown for a project with an overall cost of $122M that has successfully completed the first two stages of a six-stage development process. If the project is successful in being introduced to the market, its forecasted commercial value (i.e., net of R&D costs) is $1,120M.

At the beginning of Stage 3, the company is faced with an investment of $10M and has determined that there is a 0.70 probability of successfully completing the stage. Notice that the rolled back, risk-adjusted value at the beginning of Stage 3 is $120.11M and increases to $175.87M if the investment of $10M is made. In risk-adjusted terms, therefore, if the $10M investment is made, the organization gains $55.76M in option value. Stated otherwise, the risk-adjusted productivity yield (or productivity index) of this investment is 5.576, but more importantly, if the organization makes the $10M investment and is successful in moving from the beginning of Stage 3 to the beginning of Stage 4, it will have secured the option (i.e., the right but not the obligation) to invest a further $20M during Stage 4.

An additional attraction of using decision trees to model R&D and IT project options lies in the flexibility to use range estimates of investments (payouts) and commercial values (payoffs), which, after simulation, yield a distribution or range of risk-adjusted values that can be much more informative than a deterministic risk-adjusted value. This is of particular importance if (a) phased cost, (b) commercial value, or (c) both are uncertain estimates and require a more detailed assessment of the rolled back, risk-adjusted value of a series of staged investments.

Perhaps the greatest utility of options analysis is in its assessment of the value of the incremental gain in knowledge and risk-adjusted value if staged investments in a project, program, or portfolio are made; it is the use of this knowledge to enable an organization to apply sufficient flexibility to continue or abandon a project or program in a staged manner that makes this method robust and attractive. Finally, options thinking should be an integral part of all high-risk R&D and IT portfolio investment decisions, so as to minimize the impact of the sunk cost principle where poor projects and programs are allowed to continue primarily on the basis of their sunken investments.

5.2 Summary

One of the most vital ingredients in ensuring successful enterprise portfolio management practices is a fundamentally sound risk analysis discipline. This core tenet of the CREOPM™ framework, risk analysis, was addressed. The distinctions between project and portfolio risk were highlighted, the lack of comprehension of which can be the bane of portfolio risk analysis. Models for defining and identifying risks associated with investments in the R&D and IT industries were explained as a precursor to risk measurement. Key factors influencing risk analysis are portfolio balance, value of information analysis, and options analysis.

6

Integrated Evaluation

- **Expected monetary value**—Defined the same as expected value or integrated value: A risk-adjusted value that is the combination of the probability of technical and regulatory success and the forecasted commercial value of a project. It is also the *rolled back value* in a decision tree in the lexicon of decision analysis. For a multi-phase project, it is not the multiple of its overall probability of success and forecasted commercial value. Rather, it is the rolled back earned value beginning with the terminal branches of a decision tree that accounts for phase-specific risks, payoffs (value inflows), and payouts (investments or value outflows).

- **Forecast**—A projection, not prediction, of the value of an uncertain quantity or metric (e.g., sales, net present value, cost, time) reflected by a distribution of outcomes with a defined confidence interval. If a forecast is known with certainty (e.g., manufacturing capacity), it can be predicted and, by definition, is a deterministic estimate. On the other hand, if a forecast is not known with certainty (e.g., sales), it cannot be predicted and, by definition, is a stochastic estimate.

6.1 Key Concepts of Integrated Evaluation

The net present value (NPV) of free, future cash flows is the standard metric by which the majority of organizations evaluate a portfolio's worth. Other financial metrics such as internal rate of return (IRR) and return on investment (ROI) are often used to track the health of a portfolio rather than to supplant the NPV metric. When project risk needs to be combined with commercial uncertainty, the expected net present value (ENPV) becomes the generally accepted metric for integrating benefit (measured by commercial value), risk (measured by a probability of success), cost to launch and commercialize, and time to launch. Not surprisingly, using probabilistic cash flows, both risk-adjusted IRR (EIRR) and ROI (EROI) can be calculated for a portfolio.

Parenthetically, the productivity index (PI)—defined as the NPV/Investment—as well as risk-adjusted PI (EPI; ENPV/EInvestment) are excellent metrics on which to make marginal portfolio investment decisions. In the previous chapter, as shown in Figure 5-9, the EPI was calculated as 5.576 in the example used to calculate the option value created by an incremental investment.

How is the ENPV generated first for a project and then for a portfolio? As shown in Figure 6-1, for a project that costs $9M and has a probability of success of 0.15, the NPV yields $75M. Since its probability of failure is 0.85, yielding an NPV of –$9M, the ENPV or rolled back value of this project can be calculated as

$$0.15 * (\$75) + 0.85 * (-\$9) = \$3.60M$$

But, can we be absolutely certain that the forecasted value (or payoff) of the project, if it becomes a commercially viable product, is exactly $75M? And, is there any uncertainty in the forecast of the cost (or payout) of development of the project as –$9M? If, for example, you were offered an opportunity to invest $10M in two products with the same mean sales of $20M, a rational investor would be indifferent between these two product choices. If, however, upon deeper inspection, the range of sales of Product A was forecasted with 95% confidence to be uniformly distributed between $10M and $30M, while that of Product B with the same level of confidence was uniformly distributed between $2M and $38M, depending on your level of risk tolerance, both alternatives would elicit differing choices from investors. Therefore, it is instructive to think of forecasted estimates not merely in the context of their historical values (if such data are available), but in the context of the uncertain impact of the future competitive environment.

For the purposes of this modeled project in Figure 6-1, let us assume that both forecasted estimates of payoff and payout are uncertain. Assuming asymmetric range estimates with 100% confidence of $50M and $90M for NPV of the project if it becomes commercially viable and –$11M and –$6M if it fails (Figure 6-2), what is the probability that the deterministic ENPV of $3.60M would be achieved?

This question can be answered by conducting a simulation of the rolled back ENPV from the decision tree, shown in Figure 6-2, which results in a range of ENPVs, shown in Figure 6-3a. What is the basis on which this occurs? For every trial in the simulation, a random number between 0 and 1 is selected, corresponding to a value between $50M and $90M for the payoff and a value between –$11M and –$6M for the payout. Both values are then automatically entered into their respective calculation cells in the decision tree from which the ENPV is generated. For a simulation consisting of 1,000 trials, this process of generating random numbers from each payoff and payout

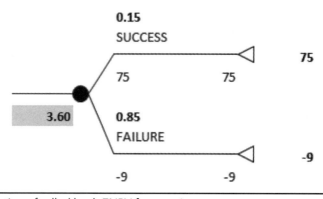

Figure 6-1   Calculation of rolled back ENPV for a project

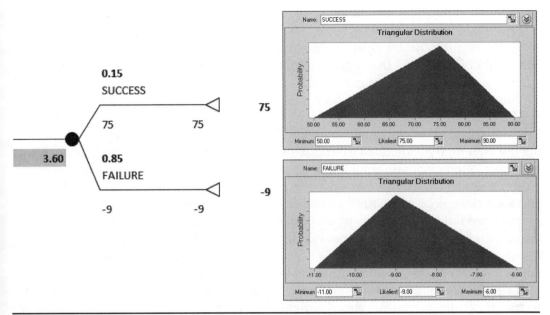

Figure 6-2   Incorporation of uncertainty in payoff and payout in a decision tree

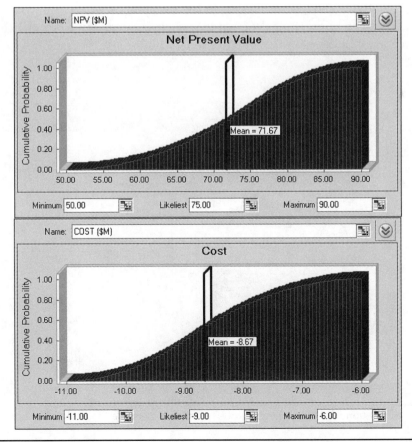

Figure 6-3a   Simulation of project payoffs and payouts to determine range of ENPVs

distribution is repeated 999 times and generates a distribution of ENPVs. The results of a simulation of 1000 trials (Figure 6-3b) show that there is 45.25% probability that the previous mean deterministic value of $3.60M will be exceeded. In fact, the distribution of ENPVs ranges from a minimum of −$0.35M to a maximum of $7.56M, with a mean of $3.38M and standard deviation of $1.53M.

Note that because there is skewness in the distributions of both payoff and payout, the ENPV of $3.38M displayed in Figure 6-3b is slightly different from the deterministic value of $3.60M shown in Figure 6-1. There is a simple message to readers regarding the asymmetry (or lack of it) of distributions of outcomes that represent uncertain forecasts: If forecasts are provided in a manner that represents +/− X% of the mean, a simulation will yield the same value as if the forecasts were all deterministic. In the previous example, if the distributions showed no skewness and were therefore symmetrical around the mean payoff and payout, the simulated ENPV would be $3.60M, the same value that could be generated from a decision tree that was devoid of uncertain payoffs and payouts. The value of symmetrical distributions is therefore limited, if one is trying to gauge potential upside gain and downside loss to the value of a project.

If all projects within a portfolio are independent of each other, i.e., they bear no technical or commercial dependencies between them, the ENPV of the portfolio becomes the simple aggregate of the ENPVs for all projects. If, on the other hand, technical or commercial (or both) dependencies exist between projects in a portfolio, careful decision tree analysis needs to be applied. In the case of a program or portfolio of three projects where there are technical dependencies, it is necessary to model them carefully with the aid of a decision tree (Figure 6-4).

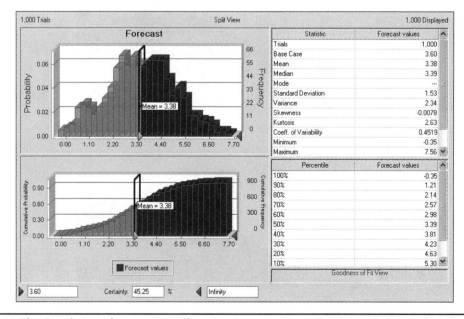

Figure 6-3b   Simulation of project payoffs and payouts to determine the probability of exceeding the mean ENPV

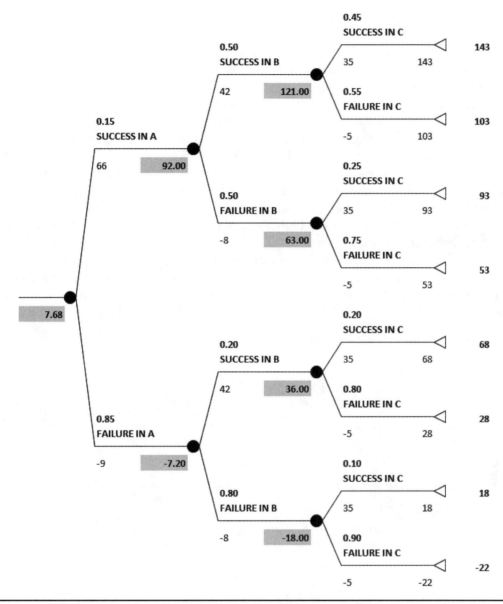

Figure 6-4   Deterministic integrated evaluation of a program or portfolio of three technically dependent projects

In the example in Figure 6-4, there is a higher probability of Project B succeeding if Project A succeeds and, conversely, a lower probability of Project B's success if Project A fails. The same logic can be applied to the probability of Project C succeeding, depending on whether Project A alone succeeds or Project B alone succeeds or whether both succeed or fail. Clearly, if commercial dependencies exist between these projects, one would expect the payouts associated with Project B to be different if Project A succeeds (e.g., the result of product cannibalization or bundled product usage) or fails (e.g., customer perception of product or organization). Likewise, the payouts associated with Project C would be different, depending on whether both Projects A and B succeed, either one of them succeeds, or both fail.

The rolled back ENPV displayed in the decision tree in Figure 6-4 is $11.76M and, at first blush, it appears as though the value of this program or portfolio should be much higher, given that each project is worth $66M, $42M, and $35M in NPV terms. However, it is clear that of the eight arms of the decision tree, the highest probability resides with failure of all three projects and is calculated at 61.2%. Conversely, the uppermost arm of the decision tree, which displays success in all three projects, shows a joint probability of success of 0.15 * 0.50 * 0.45 = 3.38%.

The results of this program or portfolio that display eight mutually exclusive and collectively exhaustive outcomes are shown in Figure 6-5. Note that the bubble with the highest likelihood of occurrence (failure in A + B + C) displays the lowest NPV of −$22M, while the bubble with the highest NPV (success in A + B + C) has one of the lowest probabilities of occurrence.

As described earlier in this chapter, to the extent that payoffs and payouts for each project are uncertain forecasts, one can incorporate range estimates in both commercial payoffs and development payouts to create a stochastic decision tree from which a range of rolled back ENPVs can be generated (Figure 6-6). As can be seen,

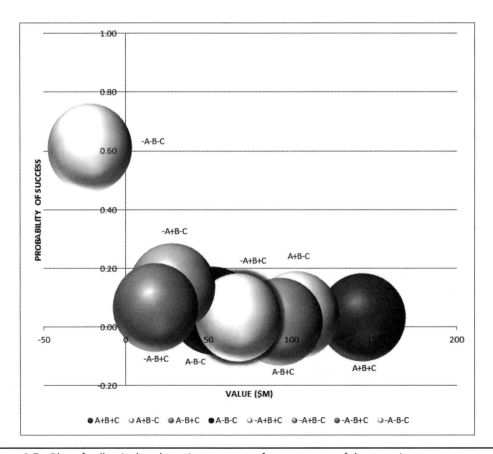

Figure 6-5 Plot of collectively exhaustive outcomes for a program of three projects

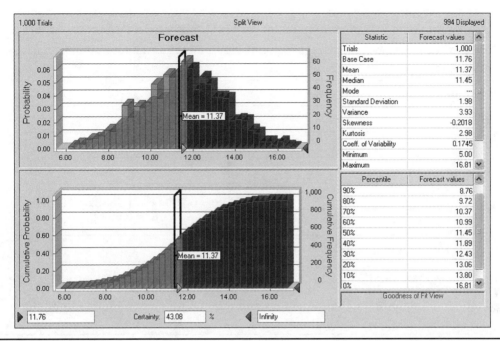

Figure 6-6 Stochastic integrated evaluation of a program or portfolio of three technically dependent projects with uncertain payoffs and payouts

the distribution of ENPVs resulting from 1,000 trials of a simulation ranges from a minimum of $5.00M to a maximum of $16.81M with a mean of $11.37M. Finally, the probability of exceeding the deterministic ENPV of $11.76M is roughly 43%.

Why is it important to use range estimates of forecasts when attempting to conduct an integrated evaluation of a project and, ultimately, of a portfolio? While it is much easier to generate a deterministic "base case" estimate of any forecast of benefit, cost, and time, it is difficult to tell what statistic (e.g., mean, median, mode, percentile) is represented by the estimate. Consequently, a comparison of two projects based solely on their potential base case sales can be quite misleading; without an explicit definition, the base case can assume any statistical value. Further, in a situation where historical sales for a product are available, one can conduct a typical regression analysis of this time series sales data, from which the R^2 statistic (coefficient of determination) and coefficient of the independent variable can be generated (Figure 6-7). In the example in Figure 6-7, one could compute the deterministic forecasted sales for any future time period using the formula:

$$y = 0.9094x^2 - 1.2688x + 100.93, \text{ where } y = \text{sales value and } x = \text{time period}$$

Using this regression formula, sales for periods 13-18 can be calculated as $229M, $245M, $260M, $276M, $291M, and $307M, respectively. Because of the very high R^2 statistic where the time period accounts for 99.72% of the variance of sales, it is expected that the regression formula will provide an accurate estimate of future sales.

Unfortunately, the "best fit" formula tells nothing about the uncertainty of sales in future time periods. To account for uncertainty, it is necessary to employ other

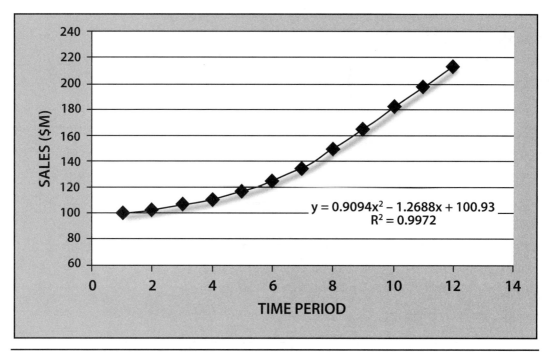

$$y = 0.9094x^2 - 1.2688x + 100.93$$
$$R^2 = 0.9972$$

Figure 6-7   Deterministic sales forecast of time series data using regression analysis

analytic methods to forecast the range of possible sales within a defined level of confidence. One such technique uses the Predictor feature within Oracle Corporation's Crystal Ball™, where it can be seen that as future periods increase, the uncertainty in sales grows (Figure 6-8a) within a fixed level of confidence of 95%. In period 13, for example, the range of sales is quite narrow ($224M–$235M), but this uncertainty increases steadily, so that by period 18, the range of sales with 95% confidence is $226M–$387M (Figure 6-8b). Clearly, broader distributions of possible outcomes are likely to have a meaningful impact on NPV calculations which, in turn, will affect integrated ENPV calculations. Just as important, as organizations create top line growth targets, it is important to understand how likely these targets are to be achieved and what proactive measures may need to be put in place to close growth gaps.

At the level of the portfolio, mean annual sales can be easily aggregated, but this does not inform decision makers of how high or low sales for any given year might possibly be. Using range estimates with a defined level of confidence, one can display the annual distribution of sales as depicted in Figure 6-9. In this example, the organization has forecast its annual sales of projects and products with 80% confidence to yield as much as $1B in periods 5 and 6 at the 90th percentile level. At the 10th percentile level, corresponding aggregate sales are shown to be as low as $220M. Given this degree of uncertainty, it is reasonable to ask what the mean of each annual distribution could be and this is revealed to be approximately $610M.

Although these aggregate estimates may be technically defensible, they assume that all projects will become products and contribute to sales over the time period under investigation. Clearly, this is not a valid assumption, so using the overall probability of

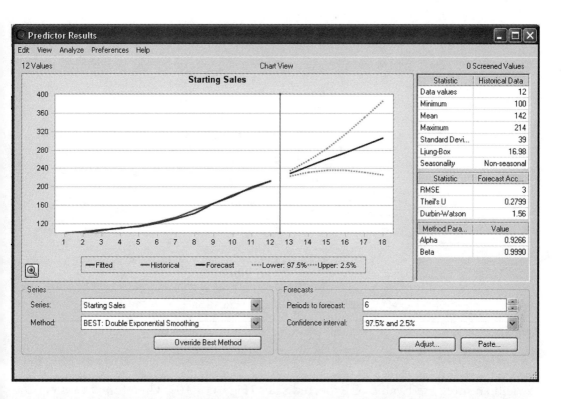

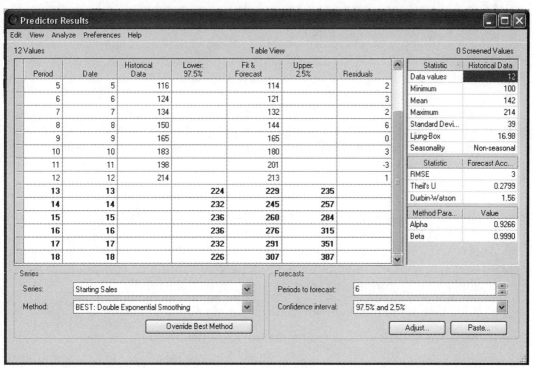

Figures 6-8a and 6-8b   Stochastic sales forecast of time series data using Crystal Ball™ Predictor

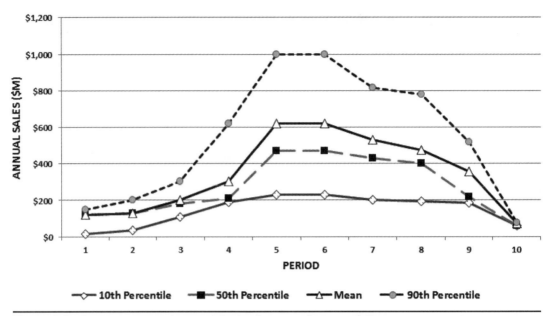

Figure 6-9 Aggregate annual potential sales forecasts for a portfolio

success of each project (as discussed in Chapter 5), potential sales can be risk-adjusted to yield an integrated value of expected sales (Figure 6-10). Therefore, to reflect the fact that not all projects eventually become launched products, it is recommended practice to use the mean sales forecast (generated by calculation or simulation) for each project and apply an elicited probability of success so that risk-adjusted or expected sales values can be determined. This is a more realistic representation of the sales value of the portfolio, given that there is both technical risk and commercial uncertainty for each potential product.

The dramatically lowered risk-adjusted sales across the 10 periods shown in Figure 6-10 are a more realistic representation of the sales value of the portfolio. Even though some organizations may find this practice of risk-adjusting sales to be unusual, the assumption of 100% success for every project in becoming a product leads to unattainable portfolio growth expectations.

Likewise, forecasts of time and cost can be seriously flawed if they do not take into account the impact of uncertainty. It is recommended that distributions of forecasts be created to reflect uncertainty, as shown in Figure 6-11.

In cases where there are insufficient data points to create a distribution, it is recommended that estimates of the minimum, mode, and maximum be created, from which one can apply a PERT formula to generate an estimated mean:

Estimated mean = (Minimum + 4 * Mode + Maximum)/6

Where there are sufficient data points to create a distribution, an estimated mean can again be derived from one of the following formulas used to convert continuous uncertain quantities to discrete uncertain quantities at three different possible levels:

Extended Swanson-McGill approximation

0.30 * (0.10 fractile) + 0.40 * (0.50 fractile) + 0.30 * (0.90 fractile)

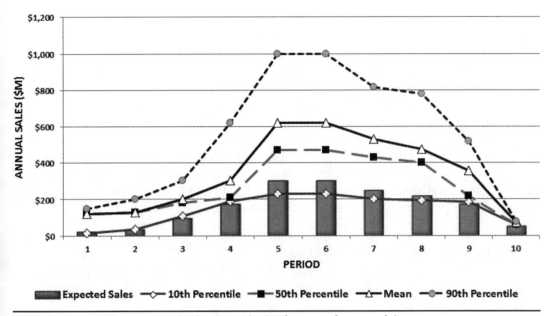

Figure 6-10   Aggregate annual risk-adjusted sales forecasts for a portfolio

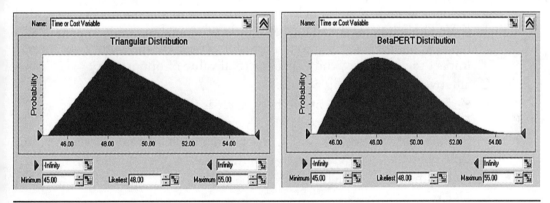

Figure 6-11   Forecast distributions of project time and cost

Extended Pearson-Tukey approximation

> 0.185 * (0.05 fractile) + 0.630 * (0.50 fractile) + 0.185 * (0.95 fractile)

For a comprehensive treatment of the calculation of mean values from continuous distributions, the reader is encouraged to review the work of Kirkwood (1997).

The concepts reviewed in this section have been applied extensively in the evaluation of investments in the R&D industry. However, they have been rarely used, if at all, in the evaluation of IT investments. As mentioned in Chapter 1, one of the primary challenges in IT portfolio management has been the dearth of widely accepted techniques for valuation of IT investments. Though IT portfolio management borrows many of its concepts from both the financial and R&D communities, there are fundamental differences in the manner in which IT portfolios are evaluated and managed when compared to financial and R&D portfolios. Notable among these, for IT portfolios, is that the application of financial criteria alone for evaluation purposes is insufficient, since many IT investments cannot be justified purely in terms of their financial value. In an IT environment, operational and regulatory demands often over-rule ROI considerations.

Consequently, a number of techniques have been applied in various organizations to evaluate IT investments, with no single one being universally accepted as the *de facto* choice. This is not to say that the techniques used for IT investment valuation are flawed. In fact, many of these techniques are based on rigorous quantitative and qualitative analysis of the investment in question. Rather, it is the seemingly esoteric nature of IT investments and the associated difficulty in benefits quantification that have been the primary barriers to the adoption of industry standards in investment valuation. IT investment valuation methods can be categorized as:

- Financial models, which include:
  - Traditional financial analysis using the widely accepted discounted cash flow method to determine financial metrics such as NPV, payback period, IRR, and ROI
  - Cost-oriented models such as total cost of ownership and earned value analysis
  - Value-oriented models, including Stern Stewart's economic value added (EVA®) analysis, and variants of cost-benefit analysis such as Microsoft's rapid economic justification, Forrester Research Inc.'s total economic impact methodology, and Gartner's total value of opportunity
- Qualitative models, which include:
  - Performance management methods, such as the balanced scorecard and IT Governance's IT scorecard
  - Scoring methods such as Intel Corporation's business value index and multiple objective decision analysis
- Advanced modeling, which include:
  - Decision tree analysis
  - Simulation (e.g., Monte Carlo, Latin hypercube)
  - Real options valuation
  - Applied information economics

Readers interested in learning more about these methods can do so by using the list of references provided at the back of the book. While the intent of this book is not to delve into the nuances of each analytical or valuation method, a brief description of each technique is provided here, along with a concise summary of strengths and weaknesses.

Discounted Cash Flow (DCF)

Traditional financial analysis based on the discounted cash flow (DCF) method is the most widely used technique to evaluate an organization's projects, assets, and investments. The DCF approach is based on the concept of time value of money to estimate and discount all future cash flows to their present value. The discount rate that is applied to determine the present value is usually the appropriate weighted average cost of capital (WACC) for the organization under consideration. A number of individual metrics can be determined using DCF, each of which basically provides insight into the payback from an investment under consideration. The most common metrics are payback period, NPV, ROI, and IRR.

Strengths of DCF: There is widespread acceptance and use of this method in the industry since it is based on standard definitions. Variables can be easily altered to enable "what-if" analysis. The method leverages existing accounting data and provides single numerical outputs. There is some rough degree of incorporation of risk—via the use of a higher WACC to recognize the riskiness of a project—in the computation.

Weaknesses of DCF: DCF takes a purely deterministic approach based on a single set of input values. It assumes a fixed path for the investment's outcome, which does not take into consideration management flexibility to change the course of the implementation and therefore is not well suited for multi-stage investments characterized by a high degree of uncertainty. In reality, the method accounts for downside risk while upside potential is unaccounted for; as a result, this method is inherently biased in favor of short-term investments. In addition, the evaluation is based solely on financial return and does not take into account intangible benefits, i.e., the qualitative aspects associated with the investment.

Total Cost of Ownership

The Gartner Group defines total cost of ownership (TCO) as the holistic view of costs across enterprise boundaries over time. TCO has evolved from an initial model that accounted for purely direct IT costs to one that includes non-IT costs (i.e., indirect costs) that have a relationship with IT. The non-IT costs include business support, facilities, and other enterprise costs that can be affected by IT initiatives such as mobility, process automation, outsourcing, and virtualization. Gartner has adopted a "chart of accounts" approach to developing TCO models, with costs categorized into direct (budgeted) and indirect (unbudgeted) costs at the highest level. This will be covered in detail in Chapter 10.

Strengths of TCO: TCO is one of the oldest IT valuation methods and is still widely used by IT managers. TCO has helped stakeholders consider the negative implications to business end users when IT investments are not optimized for value. TCO does an excellent job of providing a current cost benchmark, and it works well for analyzing a single IT asset or series of assets. When combined with best practices benchmarks, it can provide a good framework for assessing and controlling IT spending.

Weaknesses of TCO: TCO does not assess risk, nor does it provide a way to align technology with strategic and competitive business goals. TCO is not a comprehensive method for valuing IT investments on account of not considering risk, value, and flexibility; it should be considered more of an efficiency metric that works well when plugged into the financial perspective of a Balanced Scorecard or considered as one of the objectives in scoring methods.

Earned Value Analysis

Earned value (EV) analysis is a relatively straightforward technique for analyzing and tracking the progress and performance of a project. It encompasses cost, schedule, and technical performance in a manner that is informative to project stakeholders. EV is a structured method for determining project performance and producing defined deliverables for the actual vs. planned costs and schedules. EV uses continuous comparative analysis between estimated costs and actual costs or work performed for each project task, employing these monetary values as key performance indicators. By using labor costs as the metric, EV provides the project manager with the means to directly evaluate project performance against "planned" cost and schedule and to easily identify variances to provide project status reporting and forecasting.

Strengths of EV Analysis: The real value that EV analysis brings from an IT asset valuation perspective is in the evaluation of the performance of an investment. Basically, the derived EV metrics are excellent indicators of a project's performance at various gates in a Stage-Gate™ process for IT portfolio management to facilitate "go/no-go" decisions by the portfolio management team.

Weaknesses of EV Analysis: Key drawbacks of EV analysis from an investment/project selection perspective are that it does not provide a perspective on the value of the investment or the risks associated with the investment. It is a good indicator of the performance to date of a project, based on cost and schedule variances, and is limited to these facets of project management. Consequently, much like traditional financial metrics, while EV analysis provides useful metrics from project selection based on past performance, it does not provide a comprehensive framework to drive portfolio evaluation.

Economic Value Added

Economic value added (EVA®), a measure of economic profit, is a metric developed and successfully marketed by Stern Stewart & Company. It is calculated as the difference between the net operating profit after tax (NOPAT) and the opportunity cost of invested capital. This opportunity cost is determined by the WACC and the amount of capital invested. An EVA analysis demands that everything from initial cash outlays to maintenance and training—including any expenditure that is legitimately part of the initiative—is charged against profit. EVA is used as a key performance measure in organizations, based on the premise that capital deployed for any project or corporate strategy, including IT, is not free and that its cost must be discounted in the cost-benefit analysis of the particular investment. The economic argument is that unless a company earns a return beyond its cost of capital, it is destroying wealth for shareholders, not creating it (McClure, 2003).

Strengths of EVA: EVA approaches an IT investment as a value proposition, rather than as a cost. The advantage of EVA is that it produces a single financial index that can be used to characterize a diverse set of potentially contradictory directions. Approached as a trade-off between total investment cost and potential value, EVA is a good way to gauge the impact of any process such as a measure of overall profitability (Carnegie Mellon University, 2007).

Weaknesses of EVA: While EVA may be a good way to gauge the top-level impact of IT, it is difficult for many IT organizations to connect that high-end view with a lower-end perspective (e.g., the purchase of a new server) without using intermediate measures. EVA is better applied as one of several metrics that provide a perspective on the financial value of an investment in support of a more comprehensive valuation methodology. In addition, it does not account for project-specific risks.

Rapid Economic Justification

Microsoft Corporation proposed the rapid economic justification (REJ™) valuation methodology in 2005 to "optimize" IT investments, in alignment with business priorities. REJ focuses on balancing the economic performance of an IT investment against the resources and capital required to establish and operate it. The focus of that inquiry is on justifying business improvement; REJ involves tailoring a business assessment roadmap that identifies a project's key stakeholders, critical success factors, and key performance indicators in a systematic, six-step process (Carnegie Mellon University, 2007).

Strengths of REJ: REJ has been implemented in a number of global organizations since its inception. REJ's business assessment phase, TCO-like baseline, and inclusion of risk analysis are user friendly to analysts. REJ is best suited for developing business cases for managing single projects rather than an entire project portfolio.

Weaknesses of REJ: REJ is a good approach to develop a detailed business case—one investment at a time—the output of which is primarily financial in nature. This output can feed into one of the more comprehensive scoring methods that can be used subsequently to evaluate IT investments. A slightly negative perception that REJ suffers from is that it is a methodology proposed by an IT software vendor, so the inherent bias with which it is viewed by some may get in the way of leveraging its strengths.

Total Economic Impact

Total economic impact (TEI™), developed by Forrester Research, Inc., aims to quantifiably measure the business value of an IT investment or project. TEI is composed of four components: costs, benefits, flexibility, and risk. In evaluating potential IT investments, TEI assesses three key areas—cost, benefit, and flexibility—and determines the risk for each (Gliedman, 2008). Cost analysis takes a TCO-like approach in considering ongoing costs in addition to capital expenditures. Benefit assessments look at the project's business value and strategic contribution outside of IT. TEI calculates flexibility using a futures options methodology, such as real options valuation, using the Black-Scholes model. Once cost, benefits, and flexibility are quantified, the next step is to determine the risks associated with each of them. The risk assessment is expressed as a likelihood estimate that includes the potential economic impact of all major assumptions.

Strengths of TEI: TEI provides a good framework for determining a risk-adjusted estimate of an investment's costs, benefits, and flexibility. TEI is a good model for valuing a single assessment. Further, Forrester Research has published excellent white papers that provide guidelines and best practices for quantifying benefits associated with a multitude of IT investments.

Weaknesses of TEI: The end result of TEI is to basically provide a set of traditional financial metrics such as NPV, ROI, and PP for an investment, as well as the value of the real option under consideration. TEI does not provide a framework for evaluating a number of investments as part of a portfolio selection exercise. Additionally, TEI's treatment of flexibility is somewhat simplistic in that it uses the Black-Scholes model for options valuation, which has considerable limitations in its applicability. More importantly, all ROV calculations are based on heroic financial and comparator volatility assumptions. Facets of TEI can nevertheless be leveraged in valuing IT investments in qualitative methods for IT asset valuation.

Total Value of Opportunity

Total value of opportunity (TVO) is a methodology created by Gartner for determining the overall business value expected to be created by an IT-enabled business initiative. TVO uses the Gartner business performance framework as a standard methodology for measuring the business performance impact of an initiative being modeled. TVO is both a quantitative and qualitative methodology that centers on assessing risks and then quantifying the flexibility that a given option provides for dealing with each risk. TVO is built around cost-benefit analysis, organization diagnostics, future uncertainty, and best practices in measurement (Apfel & Smith, 2003).

Strengths of TVO: TVO is a fairly rigorous and comprehensive framework for valuing an IT investment. The net end result of the TVO analysis is a set of traditional financial metrics as well as the value of the real option under consideration. Additionally, a number of qualitative outputs such as value expectations, business impact, benefits realization, and a framework for monitoring the value delivered are also generated.

Weaknesses of TVO: TVO is best suited for providing useful metrics about a single investment. Additionally, TVO's treatment of flexibility is somewhat simplistic, much like TEI, in that it uses the Black-Scholes model for options valuation, which has considerable limitations in its applicability. The output of TVO can then be leveraged by scorecards or other qualitative methods to select and prioritize the set of investments in an IT portfolio.

Balanced Scorecard

The balanced scorecard (BSC)was originated by Robert Kaplan and David Norton as a performance measurement framework that added strategic non-financial performance measures to traditional financial metrics to give management a more "balanced" view of organizational performance. BSC is based on four perspectives of an organization: the Financial, Customer, Internal Business Processes, and Learning and Growth perspectives. Implementing the BSC includes: (a) translating the vision into operational goals, (b) communicating the vision and linking it to individual performance, (c) business planning and index setting, and (d) feedback, learning, and adjusting the strategy accordingly (Balanced Scorecard Institute, 2009).

Strengths of BSC: The BSC allows an organization to value all of its assets appropriately, if instituted with the support of the organization's senior executives. It provides an easy-to-understand (and implement) strategic management framework that can be used at all levels of an organization.

Weaknesses of BSC: As popular as the BSC is, one of its key limitations is that organizations find it challenging to map IT assets and activities to strategic goals. Moreover, while it provides a good framework for managing strategy, it is not suited for valuing IT assets with the purpose of comparing them to one another and then selecting the most appropriate ones to invest in. Other shortcomings of the BSC methodology are that the scores are not based on any proven economic or financial theory and therefore have no basis in decision sciences. The process is entirely subjective and makes no provision to assess quantities such as risk and value in a way that is economically sound.

The IT Scorecard

The IT scorecard (ITS) is a performance measurement system whose aim is to provide a strategic basis for evaluating the IT function that is independent of all other business or organizational considerations. The approach is therefore bottom up from the internal IT view (Carnegie Mellon University, 2007). ITS focuses its measurement activity on metrics that characterize what IT brings to the business. The measures used concentrate on capturing all of the leading indicators of value that support the achievement of the company's strategies; for example, how fast a help desk responds to a problem and how often that problem is fixed. The first step in the value assignment process is to precisely characterize what the business wants out of the IT function as well as what IT can feasibly bring to the business. That description is used to establish organization-wide consensus on the metrics that will be required to capture that value.

Strengths of ITS: Like the BSC, the ITS introduces the concept of external comparative measures and benchmarks in order to create meaningful IT performance metrics. The aim of the ITS is to determine how effectively current IT resources support the organization and to assess ways that IT can better respond to future needs.

Weaknesses of ITS: Effective measurement programs can only be customized to the strategies they support. That is the one main weakness in this approach. The ITS can never be used right out of the box, since it requires an organization to develop and then maintain a customized set of metrics. Of more relevance from a portfolio selection perspective is that, like the BSC, the ITS does not provide a framework for valuing IT elements from a perspective of choosing the right mix of components to invest in, since it is primarily a value measurement framework that ignores cost and risk, two other key pillars that should guide investment decisions.

Business Value Index

Intel Corporation developed a framework for comparing IT investments called the business value index (BVI), and has employed this methodology in IT portfolio management since 2001. Additionally, Intel has been successful in promoting this framework in a number of other companies as a thorough, yet simple IT portfolio evaluation technique.

The premise behind BVI is recognizing that IT investments serve a multitude of organizational needs, not all of which have direct financial value. BVI is a composite index of factors that impact the value of an IT investment. It evaluates IT investments along three vectors: business value (impact to the business), impact to IT efficiency, and the financial attractiveness of an investment (Intel Corporation, 2001). All three factors use a predetermined set of defining criteria. Each factor's criteria are weighted according to the ongoing business strategy and business environment; changes in business strategy could change how criteria are weighted for different factors. Key facets of BVI will be discussed in Chapter 10.

Strengths of BVI: A crucial aspect of BVI is its ability to account for the intangible benefits and strategic value of potential investments. It has a number of key characteristics that differentiate it from other prioritization methods. It provides a framework that is well-suited for the prioritization of IT investments. BVI also indicates how each investment might add value to the company and displays the results in a matrix that enhances comparative analysis of multiple investment opportunities. This approach supports options-based management of IT investments, helping decision making in a phase-dependent manner, including whether a project merits further funding.

Weaknesses of BVI: BVI has had its detractors, owing to the qualitative nature of its evaluation approach, whereby subjectivity can affect the scores assigned to the investments being evaluated. While BVI does not provide guidelines for the use of suitable elicitation techniques to validate subject matter expert judgment, one could nevertheless consider their employment in reducing subjectivity. Additionally, it is somewhat weak in incorporating the risks associated with investments. BVI can benefit from a more rigorous risk incorporation, which is probably the only real shortcoming of this technique, especially if this evaluation is supplemented by suitable portfolio optimization techniques.

Multiple Objective Decision Analysis

Multiple objective decision analysis (MODA) is a weighted, scoring-based methodology of quantitative and qualitative decision criteria that can guide decision making, specifically project prioritization. It is particularly useful in the absence of a dominant decision-making objective (e.g., benefit) and if there is an organizational requirement to incorporate multiple stakeholder decision-relevant concerns.

Much like the BVI, a MODA prioritization model is comprised of two structural components, one quantitative and the other qualitative. The qualitative component is the representation of the objectives of the exercise (i.e., the utility hierarchy), while the quantitative aspect is manifested in the measurable representation of the utility model. Once a MODA model is developed, investments can be evaluated on the basis of their assessed scores recorded for each of the measurable attributes, and once rolled up to the level of the objectives, an aggregate score can be generated for each investment. Graphical comparison of the weighted aggregate scores for the investments helps visually compare investments to select and prioritize them appropriately and select the portfolio of projects or assets to invest in. This method is explored in detail in Chapter 8, Project Prioritization.

Strengths of MODA: MODA incorporates decision-makers' objectives and preferences and subject matter expert judgment. MODA handles inputs in numerical and categorical forms, known and uncertain inputs, and is able to incorporate the risk tolerance of decision makers. MODA's ranking and insight are based on detailed characterization of the degree to which investments (or alternatives to a single investment) meet stated objectives and enable the following:

- Rigorous explanations of weighted scores
- Sensitivity analysis to attribute weights and impact to the rank order of projects
- Trade-offs between objectives
- Clarification and resolution of differences between multiple stakeholders

MODA is a framework that can be easily understood, modified, and updated as information changes, is relatively uncomplicated in its development, and is transparent in its use.

Weaknesses of MODA: By its nature, MODA evaluates IT investments using both quantitative and qualitative criteria and, without employing robust knowledge elicitation techniques, can become heavily dependent on subjective estimates pertaining to the scores of individual attributes for each investment. Moreover, there is no standard MODA model for an industry; instead, it needs to be developed from the ground up for an organization. This is both a strength and weakness: while MODA provides flexibility in tailoring its use specifically to suit the organization's needs, it requires an investment of time and effort as well as stakeholder sponsorship. In other words, it is not a plug-and-play solution. While some IT organizations have employed some form of multi-attribute value analysis, of which MODA is a specific adaptation, this has not yet become a widely accepted standard in the IT industry. MODA is not and probably will never be the method of choice for valuing IT projects alone. This is because a MODA valuation results in a measure of utilities, a concept that is not always fully understood by most executives. Nevertheless, it is a superior technique when used to value the relative attractiveness of projects to enable prioritization decisions at the portfolio level.

Decision Tree Analysis

As explained in Chapters 5 and 6, a decision tree is one of the most systematic tools of decision-making theory and practice. Decision trees are particularly helpful in situations of complex multi-stage decision problems. A decision-making tree is essentially a phase-dependent diagram that represents, in a sequentially organized manner, the decisions and main external or other events that introduce uncertainty, as well as possible outcomes of those decisions and events. Decision tree analysis (DTA) can be used to map out future events, their likelihood of occurrence, and associated consequences. In the IT industry, the introduction of new technologies often involves considerable uncertainties. Furthermore, past investment strategies and life cycle costing techniques have not adequately accounted for the value inherent in options to abandon, contract, modify, or expand a project as a result of future developments such as technology trends or requirement changes. Information about future events has rarely been incorporated into objective cost-benefit measures.

Strengths of DTA: DTA is an elegant solution because it accounts for contingent actions by assigning probabilities to outcomes instead of risk-adjusted discount rates. DTA is a powerful and elegant methodology that has considerable applicability in risky and long life cycle investments, such as pharmaceutical R&D. Decision trees provide an effective structure in which alternative decisions and the consequences of taking those decisions can be mapped out and evaluated. Overall, since decision trees allow for the general specification of the likelihood associated with outcomes, whenever a decision needs to be made on an investment where uncertain data is prevalent, their use appears to be readily justified. For example, decisions regarding the release of a novel software product or for determining when or if to proceed on multi-stage investments can be well modeled using decision trees.

Weaknesses of DTA: DTA accounts for risks by assigning a probability for each project outcome. Consequently, in the absence of robust knowledge elicitation techniques, it can suffer from biased expert subjectivity in assigning probabilities to potential outcomes. Also, it is not ideally suited for instances where the life span of an investment is fairly short or where there is little inherent risk, which, in fact, represents the state of most IT investments. IT decision analysts should therefore be wary of overusing decision trees as they can degenerate into overly complex models, thus defeating the purpose of their use in the first place as an easy-to-understand, yet elegant solution.

Simulation

Simulation methods (SIMs) are a class of computational algorithms that rely on repeated random sampling to generate their results and are often used when simulating physical and mathematical systems. They are intended for analysts who wish to construct stochastic or probabilistic financial models as opposed to the traditional static and deterministic models. Simulation for valuing projects or investments typically involves computing a project's NPV using the DCF method thousands of times, with different values for the input variables while keeping the discount rate constant. Whereas a single basic NPV calculation within the simulation can be viewed as deterministic by itself, the overall simulation is probabilistic, resulting in a probability distribution of the potential NPV.

Strengths of SIMs: Simulation can be used effectively in valuing IT investments and getting an estimate of the probability of a positive NPV of an investment to supplement or enhance the basic DCF technique. Simulation is preferred over other valuation techniques when there are several sources of uncertainty, such as those associated with future cash flows from the investment under consideration or the calculation of risk in business. Simulations have also been used to calculate the value of future options in cases where the Black-Scholes or the binomial lattice methods may be inherently limited in their applicability.

Weaknesses of SIMs: Although SIMs provide flexibility, and can handle multiple sources of uncertainty, the use of SIM techniques is nevertheless not always appropriate, since they are overkill for simpler cases of valuing IT investments where there are few uncertainties. In addition, if used to calculate NPV, which is the most popular use of this technique, it is just an extension of basic DCF and not a substitute for DCF. Though not as deterministic as DCF, all of the other limitations of DCF are applicable. Despite its technical appeal to analysts, the technique does require an investment in time and understanding by executives; consequently, it tends to be viewed as superfluous by many organizations that do not have a high tolerance for technical analysis.

Real Options Valuation

Real options valuation (ROV) aims to put a quantitative value on operational flexibility. It allows an organization to value any investment that will underwrite or create a more relevant and responsive operation. ROV accounts for a range of possible outcomes over the life of the project where uncertainty may increase over time. It does so by using stochastic processes and calculates a "composite" options value for a project, considering only those outcomes that are favorable (i.e., options are exercised) and ignoring those that are not (i.e., letting them expire). ROV is based on the assumption that decision makers will always take the value-maximizing decision at each decision point in the project life cycle (Kodukula & Papudesu, 2006).

Strengths of ROV: ROV is most valuable when there is high uncertainty with the underlying asset value, and decision makers have significant flexibility to change the outcome of the project in a favorable direction by exercising the appropriate option. In the case of IT investments, ROV provides value as an additional, useful financial tool to help with selecting suitable projects/assets from within the portfolio, especially when it involves a multi-stage investment with high uncertainty, as well as a high degree of managerial flexibility. An example of an investment for which ROV provides value is an enterprise data warehouse (EDW) implementation, followed by a customer relationship management initiative, whose implementation decision may hinge on the success of the EDW effort, specifically with regard to customer data integration.

Weaknesses of ROV: Although popular, ROV suffers from being labeled as somewhat academic. ROV by necessity is complex, so it works best in situations that are well defined or where experience with staged investment analysis already exists. It has not gained a large following in the IT industry or for valuing IT investments. Companies that use ROV usually utilize it as a building block along with more traditional financial tools. It can nevertheless be used as an attribute to compute financial value in scoring methods for valuing IT investments. Although options valuation has a firm basis in the financial industry, ROV has struggled in the non-financial community mainly because of the relative inability to securitize most non-financial assets. Stated otherwise, in a well-functioning capital market, there is almost always a buyer for a risky option (e.g., junk bond); the same cannot be stated for the R&D or IT industry, where if an asset displays its "warts," there are relatively few, if any, buyers willing to take on a risk that may not be controllable.

Applied Information Economics

Applied information economics (AIE) is the practical application of mathematical and scientific methods to the investment valuation process. AIE uses advanced methods from decision theory, portfolio optimization methods, operations research, statistics, and other areas to solve the most difficult IT valuation issues. AIE is a seven-step sequential process comprised of: (1) the definition of a decision model, (2) calibration of estimators, (3) population of a model with estimators, (4) conducting value of information analysis, (5) measuring value of information results and updating the model, (6) analyzing remaining risk, and (7) optimizing the decision (Chatterjee, 2008). The end result of AIE is an optimized IT investment decision established with considerable rigor, which is based on sound mathematical and financial theories.

Strengths of AIE: AIE is more precise than other methods of valuing an IT investment for a variety of reasons, including: (a) employment of a range of estimates as opposed to point estimates, (b) explicit modeling of uncertainty based on Monte Carlo simulation as a component of AIE, (c) calibration of probability assessments to reduce subjectivity on account of overconfidence and underconfidence biases; and (d) conversion of all values to economic terms that can be put through the rigor of powerful financial methods and optimization.

Weaknesses of AIE: AIE requires analysts trained in statistics, finance, and decision theory among other areas of expertise in order to be applied well. The level of skill, rigor, and discipline required for AIE does not justify its use unless the investment in question is considerably large. The cost of acquiring additional information, to the point of diminishing returns, is one concern that has continued to plague AIE. For small and medium investments, the amount of work required in determining additional information does not justify the use of AIE. Consequently, while this is an elegant scientific method for valuing an investment, it is not ideally suited for evaluating a set of IT investments from a portfolio selection perspective, owing to the amount of work that needs to be accomplished by this technique in order to guide portfolio decisions. Perhaps on account of the intimidation of the rigor, AIE has not gained widespread acceptance in the IT industry.

The purpose of the methodological comparison is to determine an appropriate valuation technique that can be leveraged for the purposes of IT portfolio selection. While each technique has its own applications and has been used with varying degrees of success in the IT industry, of primary concern is the selection of the best-suited technique to employ in IT portfolio selection, i.e., the one that offers the best choice between the level of effort required and level of comprehensiveness of the technique.

Consequently, the valuation techniques described above can be compared in terms of their comprehensiveness against the level of effort required for implementation, as shown in Figure 6-12. The *level of effort* takes into account not just the requisite level of technical skills required by analysts making this comparison, but also the support required in terms of senior management commitment, sponsorship, and participation. *Comprehensiveness* takes into consideration whether each technique incorporates value, cost, and risk and to what degree each of these is employed. The size of the bubble in Figure 6-12 indicates the degree of the quantitative nature of the method.

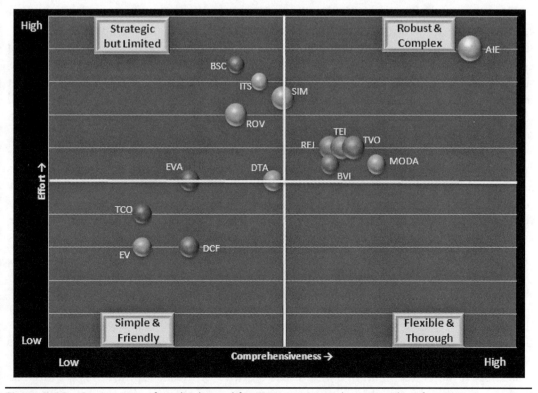

Figure 6-12   Comparison of methods used for IT investment valuation and performance measurement

The graph in Figure 6-12 is divided into four quadrants. The best-suited technique would be characterized as one that has a high degree of comprehensiveness and a relatively low degree of effort, one that would reside in the "Flexible & Thorough" quadrant. Practically, it is nearly impossible to envision a technique that would require a low degree of effort and yet be comprehensive, as is characterized by the fact that no technique falls in this quadrant.

In Figure 6-12, many of the techniques fall under the "Robust & Complex" quadrant, which is characterized by a high level of effort and high level of comprehensiveness. IT organizations would be well served by adopting one or more of the techniques from this quadrant based on the trade-off between the level of required effort and comprehensiveness. One could potentially consider the adoption of a valuation technique in this quadrant that has a relatively low effort level and a higher level of comprehensiveness when compared to the other techniques in this quadrant.

In the same vein, IT organizations would be well advised not to rely solely on the techniques in either the "Simple & Friendly" or the "Strategic but Limited" quadrants for valuing IT investments from a portfolio selection and prioritization perspective. This does not mean that these techniques are poor; in fact, many of them are used extensively in IT organizations. Techniques in the "Simple & Friendly" quadrant should not be used in isolation for IT investment prioritization. Instead, incorporating the outputs of these techniques as individual metrics is recommended, i.e., elements of some of the comprehensive techniques in the "Robust & Complex" quadrant. Such an integrated methodology could then be used for IT investment prioritization.

There is no single technique that is a panacea for making the correct investment choices. While the choice of the right methodology depends on the cultural predispositions of the organization, the chosen method should deliver value in a consistent and credible manner, with joint business and IT accountability for ownership, governance, stewardship, and judicious IT investment decisions. In the absence of a dominant methodology, perhaps a consolidation of the best features of some of the individual techniques into one unified approach could significantly enhance portfolio selection in mature IT organizations.

In order to consolidate the best features, the flexibility of existing techniques in accommodating and integrating the best practices and features from other techniques is a key consideration. This is all the more important if one considers that for a majority of IT investments, there is not one single dominant objective; instead, there are multiple objectives that need to be achieved, some of which compete with one another, requiring trade-offs among all objectives. Consequently, flexibility in existing methods is important when looking to adopt best practices from other techniques.

Existing methods that have a high degree of flexibility are the qualitative/contextual methods such as the BSC, ITS, BVI and MODA. Of these, the BSC and ITS are not ideally suited for portfolio selection and prioritization and are less attractive for this purpose than the scoring methods such as BVI and MODA. However, the quantitative aspects of a rigorous and compelling technique such as AIE are appealing as well, as are TVO, TEI, and others.

Perhaps a judicious blend of some of the features of these techniques is required so that a reasonable degree of flexibility coupled with the requisite level of due diligence may be applied to guide objective decision making in the selection of investments in an IT portfolio. The following chapters will look at ways to leverage facets of BVI, TVO, and TEI to build a MODA-based utility hierarchy for investments in an IT portfolio. Subsequently, mathematical programming techniques such as linear optimization and its variants will be used to select the best set of investments in a portfolio of investments.

6.2 Summary

At this stage of the book, the reader should have gained a basic understanding of commonly used techniques in investment evaluation. The distinction between deterministic and stochastic approaches to evaluation was made with examples and supplemented with recommended approaches to convert continuous uncertain quantities to discrete uncertain quantities. A wide spectrum of IT investment valuation techniques was reviewed, underscoring the absence of one single integrated valuation technique for the IT industry. The concepts learned in this chapter set the stage for perhaps the most important facet of the CREOPM™ framework, portfolio optimization, which is covered in the next chapter.

7

Portfolio Optimization

- **Optimization**—An act, process, or methodology that makes something as fully perfect, functional, or as effective as possible. "Optimization" can be defined more broadly as: (a) a system that makes the most effective use of an economic good; (b) a method to attain the highest degree of one or more objectives under implied or specified conditions. Generally utilized in the discipline of portfolio management as a methodology that is oriented toward finding the best combination of projects in a portfolio that fulfills specified objectives (e.g., maximization of value, balance of risk) without violating explicit constraints (e.g., budget, human resources). In addition to hard constraints such as manufacturing capacity, there may be certain requirements (e.g., launch of approximately 10 new products annually) that can be treated as soft constraints for a portfolio.

7.1 Key Concepts of Portfolio Optimization

Portfolio optimization is a robust methodology that has its roots in the field of management science/operations research, where it is more generally known as mathematical programming. It includes linear and non-linear programming, integer programming, goal programming, multiple objective linear programming, and stochastic programming. For decades, portfolio optimization has had widespread use in financial planning, logistics, sales force allocation, manufacturing, and project selection and is an excellent technique that accommodates both risk and uncertainty estimates. All optimization problems are characterized by three prerequisites:

1. Objective(s), such as: (a) maximization of growth that can be measured by sales revenues or net present value (NPV), and (b) minimization of risk that can be measured by standard deviation of mean return on investment (ROI).
2. Decision variables such as projects and financial instruments, i.e., which projects and financial instruments may be selected for investment purposes.
3. Constraints such as budget and human resources. On occasion, organizations may invoke requirements of the portfolio (e.g., launch of 10 new products annually) that, in effect, also serve as constraints. Constraints may also take the

form of obligatory business needs such as projects that are mandatory (e.g., compliance projects) and must therefore be included in any portfolio selection.

The goal of optimization, then, is to find the values of the decision variables (0 or 1) that maximize or minimize the objective, from which an objective function is derived, without violating the stated constraints. This methodology provides several advantages over other portfolio management techniques that include:

- Searches through a collectively exhaustive set of project combinations to find the optimal portfolio combination, which, by definition, best meets the organization's objectives without violating constraints and requirements.
- Allows calculation of value "left on the table" from selecting any other combination of projects, which, by definition, represents a sub-optimal portfolio.
- Accounts for project dependencies, such as where one project cannot be undertaken successfully without another project receiving investment.
- Facilitates the use of project selection logic, e.g., choosing one project from a sub-group of projects.
- Enables live scenario analysis to be conducted at portfolio management review meetings.

This methodology can quickly be considered technically burdensome if an organization does not make the investment of effort and time to educate stakeholders on its uses and merits on an ongoing basis.

To best appreciate the value of portfolio optimization, it is instructive to understand the concept of the *efficient frontier*, which can be described as a line of optimality on which reside portfolios that maximize return for given levels of risk. As shown in Figure 7-1, for a given level of risk (measured as the standard deviation of mean return), the optimal portfolio is represented by Portfolio C, which dominates Portfolio A in terms of return (as measured by ROI). Likewise, Portfolio A is dominated by Portfolio B because the latter portfolio minimizes risk for the same level of return provided by Portfolio A. All portfolios that lie along this frontier are termed *feasible, efficient,* or *optimal*, while those below the frontier are termed *feasible* but *inefficient* or *sub-optimal* (Ragsdale, 2008). In the case of project selection, the challenge of all optimization methodologies is to find that combination of projects which constitutes the optimal portfolio for any given level of measure, e.g., risk, budget, or human resources.

Let's examine the case of Innovations R Us Corporation, which has 10 projects in its portfolio, but does not have sufficient budgetary and human resources (simplified to reflect discoverers and developers only) to enable it to pursue all of these projects (see Table 7-1). To invest in all 10 projects and in pursuit of value maximization as measured here by NPV, the organization requires $2.555B in capital, along with 68 discovery and 60 development personnel. Unfortunately, all that is available to the organization is $1.5B in capital along with 45 discoverers and 40 developers. If it did have sufficient capital and human resources, the estimated NPV of the portfolio would be $6.245B. The challenge to Innovations R Us is to find the combination of projects that maximizes the availability of its constrained budget and human resources such that

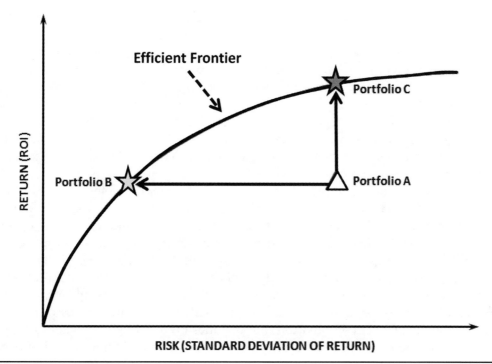

Figure 7-1 The efficient frontier
Source: Cengage Learning Rights and Content Use (adapted with permission)

Table 7-1 Project selection

Project	Decision Variables	Discoverers Required	Developers Required	Investment Required ($M)	Forecasted NPV ($M)
A	1	7	4	$250	$650
B	1	6	5	$175	$550
C	1	9	6	$300	$600
D	1	8	8	$400	$895
E	1	9	7	$500	$900
F	1	6	6	$150	$550
G	1	5	5	$150	$450
H	1	6	2	$145	$375
I	1	4	8	$160	$525
J	1	8	9	$325	$750
Total		68	60	$2,555	$6,245
Constraint		45	40	$1,500	

this project combination yields the highest possible NPV. In effect, Innovations R Us needs to determine which of the 10 projects constitutes its optimal portfolio.

Using the lexicon of portfolio optimization, the primary question now becomes: Which combination of Projects A-J best meets the portfolio objective of maximization of forecasted NPV, subject to the following constraints: (a) $1.5B in capital, (b) 45 discoverers, and (c) 40 developers? While one can manually check every possible permutation using a software program such as Excel, it is much easier to utilize an Excel add-in program such as Frontline Systems' Premium Solver or Oracle's Crystal Ball™ to achieve the same end in a matter of seconds. Using Premium Solver with Excel, the optimization solution is shown in Table 7-2.

The optimal portfolio, comprised of seven projects shown in Table 7-2, achieves a maximum NPV of $3.995B and utilizes $1.43B of its capital, along with 42 discoverers and 38 developers. However, Projects C, E, and J are excluded from the optimal portfolio. This may, at first blush, seem rather surprising since, on the basis of forecasted NPV alone, Projects C, E, and J represent three of the top five projects.

More importantly, the project with the highest NPV, E, is not selected as a part of the optimal portfolio. While this may seem counterintuitive at first glance, the optimal portfolio solution is comprised of projects that, for the same or lesser resource utilization as any project combination that includes Project E, yield higher NPV; this solution cannot be improved. Of course, Innovations R Us does not have to proceed with the optimal solution; rather, it may select any other combination of projects to pursue, as long as none of the constraints is exceeded. It is important to note that any combination of projects other than the seven projects selected previously will result in a sub-optimal portfolio, meaning that the aggregate NPV will be lower than the maximum it can achieve, i.e., $3.995B.

What would the portfolio be valued at if Project E, with the highest NPV, were forced into the portfolio? Let us, therefore, make Project E a requirement of any further optimal solution and in the process effectively add a constraint to portfolio selection. As demonstrated in Table 7-3, while Project E is forced into the portfolio by always being selected as a requirement, the maximum NPV attained is now $3.725B from a new combination of six projects. By having Project E in the solution set, a new optimal portfolio is found that is lower in value by $270M when compared to the previous solution, where Project E was not a requirement. Note that the second highest value-adding project, Project, D, is now deselected from the optimal solution. If Project E is a mandate or is critical to the survival of the corporation, and must therefore be included in the portfolio *ceteris paribus*, the best that the organization can realize from its projects, given stated constraints, is $3.725B.

This approach to project selection is highly recommended and can be envisaged as a series of sequential steps:

1. Given the organization's portfolio objectives, identify its budgetary and human resource constraints.
2. Delineate non-discretionary, Must Do projects from all others and ensure that they are always selected in the optimal portfolio (by constraining their binary selection logic to 1).

Project	Decision Variables	Discoverers Required	Developers Required	Investment Required ($M)	Forecasted NPV ($M)
A	1	7	4	$250	$650
B	1	6	5	$175	$550
C	0	9	6	$300	$600
D	1	8	8	$400	$895
E	0	9	7	$500	$900
F	1	6	6	$150	$550
G	1	5	5	$150	$450
H	1	6	2	$145	$375
I	1	4	8	$160	$525
J	0	8	9	$325	$750
Total		48	38	$1,430	$3,995
Constraint		45	40	$1,500	

Solver Parameters V10.0

```
□ Objective
   ...$G$15 (Max)
□ Variables
   □ Normal
      ...$C$5:$C$14
      ...Recourse
□ Constraints
   □ Normal
      ☑ $D$15:$F$15 <= $D$16:$F$16
      ...Chance
      ...Bound
      ...Conic
   □ Integers
      ...☑ $C$5:$C$14 = binary
   Uncertain Variables
```

Model | Standard LP/Quadratic | Solve
Add | Options
Change | Reset All
Delete | Help
Close

Table 7-3 Project selection using integer linear programming, version II

Project	Decision Variables	Discoverers Required	Developers Required	Investment Required ($M)	Forecasted NPV ($M)
A	0	7	4	$250	$650
B	1	6	5	$175	$550
C	0	9	6	$300	$600
D	0	8	8	$400	$895
E	1	9	7	$500	$900
F	1	6	6	$150	$550
G	1	5	5	$150	$450
H	0	6	2	$145	$375
I	1	4	8	$160	$525
J	1	8	9	$325	$750
Total	38	38	40	$1,460	$3,725
Constraint		45	40	$1,500	

Solver Parameters V10.0

```
□ Objective
   ...$G$15 (Max)
□ Variables
   □ Normal
      ...$C$5:$C$14
      ...Recourse
□ Constraints
   □ Normal
      ☑ $D$15:$F$15 <= $D$16:$F$16
      ...Chance
      ...Bound
      ☑ $C$9 = 1
      ...Conic
   □ Integers
```

Model | Standard LP/Quadratic | Solve
Add | Options
Change | Reset All
Delete | Help
Close

3. Optimize the portfolio, note the maximum value created, and review the lists of projects that are selected (List A) and those that are not (List B).
4. From the list of projects that are not selected, sequentially add project requirements to new rounds of optimization and calculate the value foregone as a result of forcing one or more projects from List B into the portfolio.

An alternative to a sequential approach is to account for the budgetary and human resources required of the category of Must Do projects and, after removing these resources from the overall pool, search for an optimal portfolio solution from discretionary May Do projects that maximizes value, subject to reduced budgetary and human resources.

Since many projects within a portfolio may have technical and/or commercial dependencies, how can one deal with such dependencies in an optimization frame? Going back to Table 7-2, assume that for Project D to be commercially successful, Project C needs to be commercially available, so if Project D is selected, Project C must also be a part of the optimal portfolio (however, the converse does not have to be true). Further, let's assume since Projects B and I compete in the same market segment, only one of these projects should be selected in the optimal portfolio. In effect, the optimal portfolio is now constrained by two requirements which can be accommodated in the optimization frame using the following binary integer logic:

$$\text{Project D} - \text{Project C} \le 0$$

$$\text{Project B} + \text{Project I} = 1$$

Resolving to fulfill these two additional requirements yields the optimal solution shown in Table 7-4.

Note again that the addition of two requirements creates an optimal portfolio valued at $3.900B, but results in the loss of $95M ($3.995B–$3.900B) when compared to the optimal portfolio in Table 7-2, which was devoid of project requirements. Not surprisingly, if these two project requirements were added to the requirement to have Project E in the optimal solution as shown in Table 7-4, one would expect the maximum achievable NPV to be less than $3.725B, as shown in Table 7-5.

Occasionally, instead of pursuing an objective to maximize NPV (or any other value metric), organizations may have an objective to attain a target NPV goal. This type of optimization problem, referred to as goal programming and multiple objective linear programming can be solved in a similar manner using a modified Excel model. Both will be elaborated on in Chapter 11, while Appendix B provides an overview of the core concepts behind these techniques.

The search for optimal portfolios using linear programming thus far can be described as *deterministic*, where all project data is portrayed with certainty as discrete or point estimates. But, as stated in Chapter 6, Integrated Evaluation, there is rarely a case when the data is known with absolute certainty. Clearly, one could transform the human and capital resources as well as forecasted NPVs into range estimates or variables, each of which can be represented by a distribution of outcomes. To keep the portfolio optimization problem relatively simple, the entire column of estimated NPVs in Table 7-5 could be converted into probability distributions and the optimization conducted

Table 7-4 Project selection using binary integer linear programming, version III

Project	Decision Variables	Discoverers Required	Developers Required	Investment Required ($M)	Forecasted NPV ($M)
A	1	7	4	$250	$650
B	0	6	5	$175	$550
C	1	9	6	$300	$600
D	0	8	8	$400	$895
E	0	9	7	$500	$900
F	1	6	6	$150	$550
G	1	5	5	$150	$450
H	1	6	2	$145	$375
I	1	4	8	$160	$525
J	1	8	9	$325	$750
Total		45	40	$1,480	$3,900
Constraint		45	40	$1,500	

Solver Parameters V10.0

- **Objective**
  - $G$15 (Max)
- **Variables**
  - Normal
    - $C$5:$C$14
    - Recourse
- **Constraints**
  - Normal
    - $C$18 <= 0
    - $C$19 = 1
    - $D$15:$F$15 <= $D$16:$F$16
    - Chance
    - Bound
    - Conic

Solve | Model | Options | Standard LP/Quadratic | Add | Reset All | Change | Help | Delete | Close

Table 7-5 Project selection using binary integer linear programming, version IV

Project	Decision Variables	Discoverers Required	Developers Required	Investment Required ($M)	Forecasted NPV ($M)
A	0	7	4	$250	$650
B	1	6	5	$175	$550
C	0	9	6	$300	$600
D	0	8	8	$400	$895
E	1	9	7	$500	$900
F	1	6	6	$150	$550
G	1	5	5	$150	$450
H	1	6	2	$145	$375
I	0	4	8	$160	$525
J	1	8	9	$325	$750
Total		40	34	$1,445	$3,575
Constraint		45	40	$1,500	

Solver Parameters V10.0

- **Objective**
  - $G$15 (Max)
- **Variables**
  - Normal
    - $C$5:$C$14
    - Recourse
- **Constraints**
  - Normal
    - $C$18 <= 0
    - $C$19 = 1
    - $D$15:$F$15 <= $D$16:$F$16
    - Chance
    - Bound
    - $C$9 = 1

Solve | Model | Options | Standard LP/Quadratic | Add | Reset All | Change | Help | Delete | Close

under uncertainty. This is no longer a deterministic environment, and the approach is now referred to as *stochastic optimization*.

Using Crystal Ball™ software, the search for the optimal portfolio can be conducted using simulation and optimization simultaneously. To begin with, even if there were adequate budgetary and human resources for every project in the portfolio to be invested in, the aggregate forecasted NPV of the portfolio would no longer be exactly $6.245B; instead, it would have a distribution of value around the deterministic value of $6.245B. Following a simulation of 1,000 trials, the range of NPVs is between $5.783B and $6.666B, with a 50% probability of exceeding the deterministic value of $6.245B (shown in Figure 7-2).

When the same logic is applied to the optimization problem under conditions of NPV uncertainty alone, the optimal portfolio yields the same solution in terms of project selection as shown previously in Table 7-2. A typical "stair step" is shown in Figure 7-3 as the optimizer searches for the best combination of projects while selecting random numbers between 0 and 1 from each of the project NPV distributions and computes the aggregate portfolio NPV.

To be sure, thousands of such project combinations are selected during the simulation and optimization process (Figure 7-4) until the best portfolio represented by the highest possible NPV of $4.006B is attained. Note that all of the project combinations below the maximum value of $4.006B represent feasible yet sub-optimal portfolios because they would all be valued at less than $4.006B. No infeasible portfolios, defined as exceeding budgetary and human resource constraints, are found during the search.

Finally, based on the distributions of project NPVs, once the optimal portfolio is found, one is able to assess the probability of meeting or exceeding the deterministic value of $3.995B, shown as 54% (see Figure 7-5). Perhaps more importantly, this optimal portfolio that excludes Projects C, E, and J can yield between $3.651B and $4.341B, with a standard deviation of $116M.

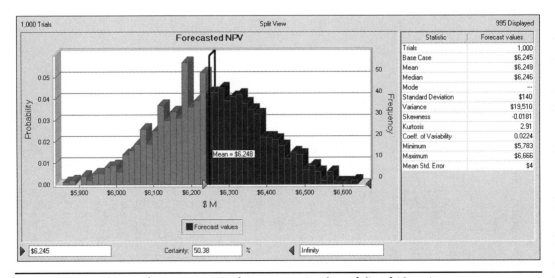

Figure 7-2   Simulation of aggregate NPV for unconstrained portfolio of 10 projects

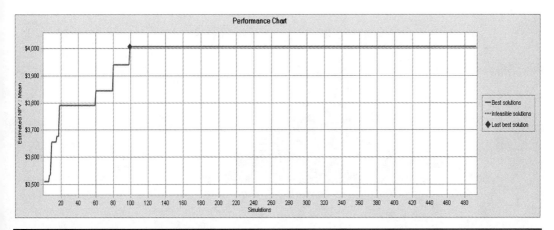

Figure 7-3 Simulation and aggregate NPV optimization of constrained portfolio of 10 projects I

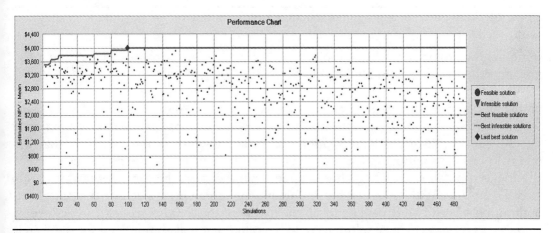

Figure 7-4 Simulation and aggregate NPV optimization of constrained portfolio of 10 projects II

Where there is reasonable uncertainty with project data for which high investments are necessary, the use of stochastic optimization rather than deterministic optimization is recommended to search for the optimal portfolio. Nevertheless, there is a fundamental assumption that underlies the manner in which all of the optimization searches thus far have been conducted: Once a project is selected as a part of the optimal portfolio, it succeeds and delivers all of its deterministic value or some portion of its uncertain value. This, however, is far from reality in many high-risk industries, e.g., natural reserves refining and drug discovery and development.

Therefore, project risk should be included in the analytic model since the selection of projects that constitute the optimal portfolio does not predicate that they will all be successful. This point can be demonstrated by the additional project data shown in Table 7-6, where risk—measured by a probability of success—is captured explicitly along with uncertainty in the forecasted NPV. In this case, although all projects may be pursued in an unconstrained portfolio, based on their probabilities of success,

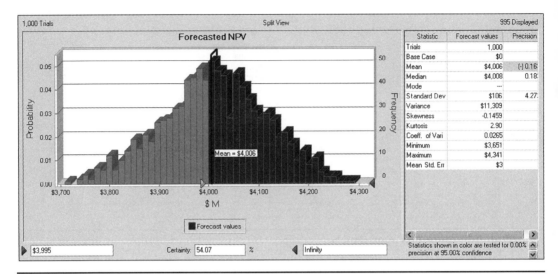

Figure 7-5   Distribution of aggregate NPV from optimized portfolio

some—shown hypothetically as Projects A, E, F, and I—are likely to fail, causing a significant drop in value from $6.245B to $3.620B.

When the risks of the 10 projects are modeled as yes/no distributions (where yes = probability of success) and estimated NPVs as beta distributions (alpha = 2; beta = 3), with a stochastic optimization run while simulating, the stepwise progression in the search for the global optimal portfolio solution occurs, as shown in Figure 7-6. Note that the optimal portfolio solution appears to occur at the plateau where the risk-adjusted NPV (ENPV) is approximately $2.7B after thousands of other portfolio combinations are evaluated (Figure 7-7). With stochastic optimizations, one cannot always be sure that the global optimum has been found; depending on the nature of the solution space (feasible region) being searched, a good, local solution could be found that makes it difficult for the search algorithms to move away from in pursuit of a better, global optimum.

An efficient frontier from the stochastic optimization is displayed in Figure 7-8. Note that as the standard deviation from the mean of the ENPV (a measure of risk) increases, optimal portfolios with increasing levels of mean ENPV (a measure of reward) are found. At a standard deviation of approximately $645M, an optimal portfolio is found with an approximate mean ENPV of $2.7B, and beyond this standard deviation from the mean ENPV, no further portfolios can be found. All that now remains to be found is the combination of projects that constitutes this optimal portfolio (Table 7-7). The results show that all projects with the exception of A, C, D, and H are selected to become a part of the optimal portfolio that contains a maximum ENPV of $2.679B and standard deviation of $643M. A simple spreadsheet calculation from Table 7-6 shows that when these four projects are deselected but the remaining six that are selected all succeed, the mean ENPV is $4.07B. It is clear, therefore, that of the six selected projects, more than one failed during the simulation and optimization exercise.

To get a better sense of the distribution of ENPVs from the optimal portfolio, a simulation was run of the portfolio of projects shown in Table 7-6 with Projects A,

Table 7-6 Incorporation of project risk and NPV uncertainty in stochastic portfolio optimization

Project	Decision Variables	Discoverers Required	Developers Required	Investment Required ($M)	p(Success)	Yes/No Probability Distribution	Forecasted NPV Distribution ($M)	ENPV ($M)
A	1	7	4	$250	0.65	0	$650	0
B	1	6	5	$175	0.70	1	$550	550
C	1	9	6	$300	0.60	1	$600	600
D	1	8	8	$400	0.50	1	$895	895
E	1	9	7	$500	0.75	0	$900	0
F	1	6	6	$150	0.65	0	$550	0
G	1	5	5	$150	0.55	1	$450	450
H	1	6	2	$145	0.35	1	$375	375
I	1	4	8	$160	0.75	0	$525	0
J	1	8	9	$325	0.90	1	$750	750
Total		68	60	$2,555			$6,245	$3,620
Constraint		45	40	**$1,500**				

C, D, and H deselected. The results of this simulation (Figure 7-9) reveal that there is a 52% probability that the mean ENPV of $2.679B would be exceeded. Further, the minimum and maximum values from the distribution of ENPVs are $0B and $3.813B, implying that during the simulation, on at least one occasion all of the projects failed (resulting in an ENPV of $0).

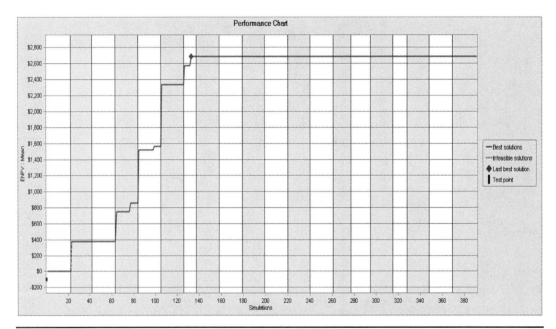

Figure 7-6 Stepwise search for the global optimal portfolio solution, version I

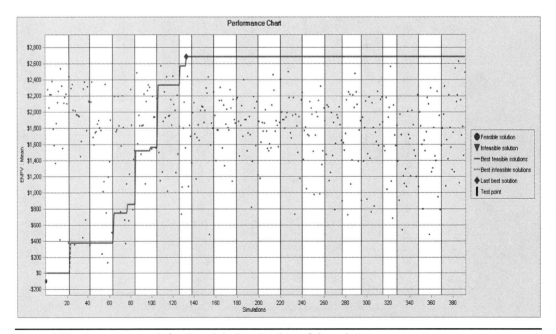

Figure 7-7 Stepwise search for the global optimal portfolio solution, version II

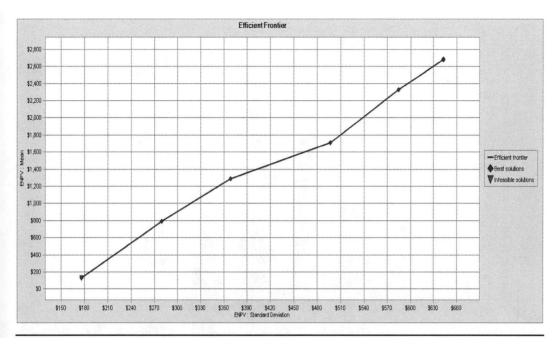

Figure 7-8   Efficient frontier of simulation and stochastic optimization

Table 7-7 Summary of project selection for stochastic portfolio optimization

Best Solution:	View test point: $2,000 ▾	
Objectives	**Value**	
Maximize the Mean of ENPV		$2,679

⊟ **Requirements**	**Value**	
** The Standard Deviation of ENPV must be between (inclusive) $100 and ...		$643

** - Testing efficient frontier

⊟ **Constraints**	**Left Side**		**Right Side**
'Proj.Select. W Risk & Uncertain'!D16 <= 'Proj.Select. W Risk & Uncertai...	38	<=	45
'Proj.Select. W Risk & Uncertain'!E16 <= 'Proj.Select. W Risk & Uncertai...	40	<=	40
'Proj.Select. W Risk & Uncertain'!F16 <= 'Proj.Select. W Risk & Uncertai...	1460	<=	1500

⊟ **Decision Variables**	**Value**
Project A	0.00
Project B	1.00
Project C	0.00
Project D	0.00
Project E	1.00
Project F	1.00
Project G	1.00
Project H	0.00
Project I	1.00
Project J	1.00

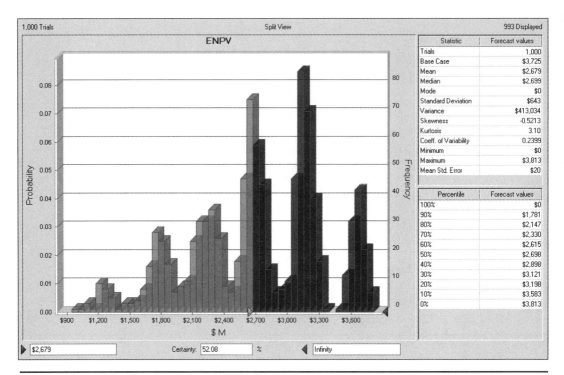

Figure 7-9 Simulation of portfolio with four deselected projects to show distribution of ENPVs

In some cases, an organization may wish to achieve several objectives at the same time, e.g., maximization of NPV, maximization of sales revenues, and minimization of risk. In this case, one would first employ deterministic goal programming (if approximate targets were set) or deterministic multiple objective linear programming (if objective functions were defined). In either case, the search for optimal portfolios is entirely dependent on the preferences of decision makers toward each objective and requires some judgment of the trade-offs between optimal portfolio solutions for each objective in search of a heuristic portfolio solution. These more advanced forms of portfolio optimization are explored in Chapter 11, Case Study in R&D Portfolio Management.

A question that is asked frequently of portfolio optimization is: How are project priorities accounted for? To be sure, *portfolio optimization does not address project prioritization*. Rather, optimization is dedicated to finding the combination of projects that best meets the organization's objective(s) without violating stated constraints. If, after the selection of projects that constitute the optimal portfolio is accomplished, an organization wishes to prioritize those projects for operational reasons, e.g., deciding which projects should be undertaken temporally as opposed to which projects should be undertaken at all, prioritization becomes an important consideration.

It is important to note that temporal-based project prioritization should take place in the context of the optimal portfolio that has *already been selected* by any of the optimization techniques detailed earlier in this chapter, as opposed to being done before the optimal portfolio has been found. Yet, this same practice has been so widespread within and across both high- and low-risk industries that it has generally become accepted that a portfolio of prioritized projects is as good a portfolio as anyone could select. The overarching fallacy of this argument stems from the fact that many decision makers are comfortable using heuristic judgments to determine which projects are "most important" (oftentimes judged by any metric possible) and therefore, should be undertaken first until resource constraints prohibit the pursuit of additional projects.

Because the vast majority of portfolios that are comprised of prioritized projects are sub-optimal, i.e., they do not best meet the organization's objective(s) without exceeding resource constraints, portfolio value is invariably destroyed. The problem with proving this in most organizations that are reluctant to use portfolio optimization as an alternative approach to project prioritization is that there is no defensible way of showing the value left on the table without searching for the composition of the optimal portfolio. In Table 7-2, the optimal portfolio solution generates an NPV of \$3.995B, and, as shown in Chapter 8, prioritization of the same projects by NPV creates a portfolio valued at \$3.195B, a staggering difference (loss in value) of \$800M!

Why would an organization not first seek its optimal portfolio and then, where necessary, prioritize the projects within this portfolio to meet one operational need or another? The authors have encountered several responses shown below to this question, all of which appear to have been stated in good faith:

- "No one will ever support a decision that comes directly from a software program." (Why not? We appear to be quite at ease trusting diagnostic data for life-saving conditions.)
- "Senior management prides itself on making the tough decisions, so we don't want them to feel disenfranchised." (How many complex decisions can most people really make without one analytic aid or another?)
- "The data changes far too frequently to be useful for optimization." (Data can and does change, but how much of this change is really decision relevant?)
- "The data is too imperfect to be of use to optimization." (Interestingly, it appears good enough, in almost all cases, to facilitate prioritization.)
- "We need to remain flexible to changing information and priorities, and this methodology constrains us far too much." (Do greater degrees of freedom really help us make better decisions? In his book *Predictably Irrational*, Ariely [2008] makes a strong case that it does not.)
- "We use a real options approach to decision making so that we can maximize upside potential and minimize downside risk." (If it were that easy, every major investment problem presented hitherto would probably have been solved!)
- "We simply do not have the discipline to make well-informed, logically consistent, defensible decisions." (A rare confession, if ever there was one!)

Far too many organizations are satisfied with making portfolio decisions that may yield sub-optimal or "good enough" outcomes (of course, these outcomes are rarely thought of as being sub-optimal). So, if "good enough" is indeed good enough, there is no compulsion for organizations to measure how much better they could have done in terms of selecting a better or optimal portfolio. In the high-risk world of many R&D industries, making good decisions regarding portfolio selection does not guarantee successful outcomes, as demonstrated in Table 7-6, yet most would agree that the more frequently that better decisions are made, the higher the likelihood that better outcomes will result.

In accordance with the Must/May/Won't Do categorization rules established in Chapter 4, portfolio optimization is best achieved when its focus is dedicated towards discretionary May Do projects once non-discretionary Must Do and discretionary Won't Do projects have been accounted for. As Figure 7-10 demonstrates, a good optimization process is predicated on first identifying Must Do projects and either (a) including them in the optimization selection after ensuring that they are "fixed" (i.e., equal to 1) in the optimal portfolio solution or (b) excluding them from the optimization selection but accounting for their resources, which must then be subtracted from the total pool of available resources.

Next, resources associated with Won't Do projects are added back to the available pool, and finally, optimization is conducted on the discretionary May Do projects

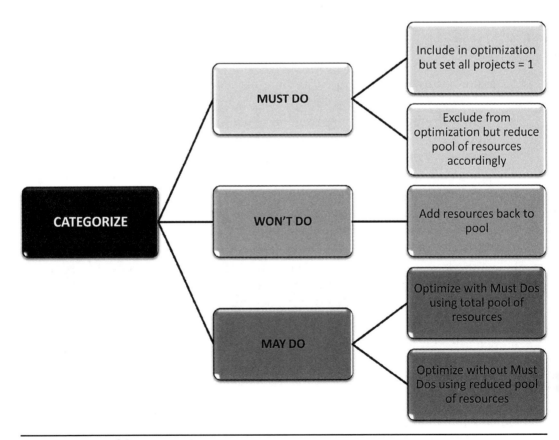

Figure 7-10   Portfolio optimization process

either with or without Must Do projects. The hallmark of a disciplined decision-making culture is exemplified by optimization at the margin, where decisions are taken on the best projects to allocate available resources, which become freed up as projects are completed or terminated.

7.2 Summary

Key concepts in portfolio optimization were explained in this chapter. Basic techniques in mathematical programming were used to optimize portfolios and highlight the subtleties of portfolio optimization. Despite overwhelming evidence of its technical soundness, optimization often fails to find a home in the portfolio management departments of many organizations. Some organizational factors that influence this lack of use were listed. The case studies in Section 4 of this book further illustrate the finer points of optimization wherein binary integer linear programming, goal programming, multiple objective linear programming, and stochastic optimization are leveraged in real-world portfolio selection in the R&D and IT sectors. In order to maximize the value of the case studies, the reader is encouraged to review Appendix B prior to reading Section 4.

8

Project Prioritization

- **Prioritization**—A system or method that determines the right to precedence; specifically, the right to have or do something before others. More broadly defined as a state of the level of urgency or importance of a project depicted by its rank order amongst a list of projects. Prioritization is generally utilized in the domain of portfolio management as a methodology that utilizes one or more quantitative or qualitative metrics to generate a rank order of projects.

8.1 Key Concepts of Project Prioritization

Few methodologies in the discipline of portfolio management are as well-known or widely utilized in one form or another as project prioritization. Mistakenly termed "portfolio prioritization" in many organizations (portfolios are seldom prioritized), this practice has metamorphosed into such an accepted surrogate for portfolio value maximization that the current state of its popularity is confounding.

Let us first examine why most—but luckily not all—organizations prioritize projects in their portfolios. It is an effort to determine the attractiveness of projects that are oriented toward the attainment of one or more goals, in the knowledge that because of resource limitations (better known as *constraints*), every project within the portfolio cannot be pursued. In its simplest manifestation, project prioritization uses a quantitative (e.g., sales revenues, risk-adjusted cost) or qualitative (e.g., customer satisfaction, strategic importance) attribute and facilitates an understanding of which projects will add the highest value to the objective, e.g., maximization of sales revenues or maximization of customer satisfaction. Not surprisingly, organizations often employ one of the following approaches to achieve project prioritization: quantitative attributes only, qualitative attributes only, or a combination of quantitative and qualitative attributes.

The simplest form of project prioritization involves a quantitative attribute, net present value (NPV) of future cash flows. In Chapter 7, in the case of Innovations R Us Corporation, the company had 10 projects within its portfolio, but had insufficient budgetary and human resources (simplified to reflect discoverers and developers only) to enable it to pursue all of its projects (see Table 8-1).

Assuming the objective of this company is to maximize NPV, one could simply rank order projects according to this attribute, as shown in Figure 8-1, and where, for example, there is insufficient budget, draw a line to segregate projects that should be

Table 8-1 Project selection

Project	Decision Variables	Discoverers Required	Developers Required	Investment Required ($M)	Forecasted NPV ($M)
A	1	7	4	$250	$650
B	1	6	5	$175	$550
C	1	9	6	$300	$600
D	1	8	8	$400	$895
E	1	9	7	$500	$900
F	1	6	6	$150	$550
G	1	5	5	$150	$450
H	1	6	2	$145	$375
I	1	4	8	$160	$525
J	1	8	9	$325	$750
Total		68	60	$2,555	$6,245
Constraint		45	40	$1,500	

invested in (above the line) from those that should not (below the line). According to this analysis, only Projects E, D, J, and A should be selected, as there are insufficient budgetary resources to invest in any of the remaining six projects. This is quite a feasible solution to the problem (making it a feasible portfolio); in fact, $1.475B in budget, 32 discoverers, and 28 developers are required for the four most value-adding projects, which create an aggregate NPV of $3.195B. But, how do we know that this is

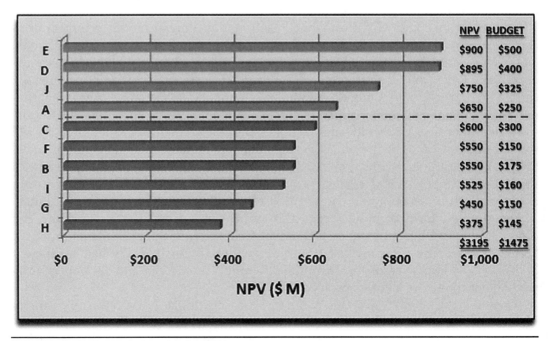

Figure 8-1 Project prioritization by NPV

the best portfolio (i.e., the one that maximizes NPV) for the organization to pursue? Stated otherwise, does this solution represent an optimal portfolio?

The optimal portfolio solution selected by linear programming, described in Chapter 7, Portfolio Optimization and in Table 7-2, creates an additional $800M in NPV and deselects Projects E, J, and C, while selecting all of the remaining seven projects in the portfolio! There appears to be very little relation in terms of project selection between the results of optimization (yielding an aggregate NPV of $3.995B) and those of prioritization (yielding an aggregate NPV of $3.195B). The portfolio selected by project prioritization is certainly feasible and is capable of delivering greater than $3B in NPV, but without searching for the best portfolio possible (i.e., the optimal portfolio) using linear programming, one would not know how much more value could have been created for the organization.

Using the same data in Table 8-1, portfolio value of $800M in NPV (or nearly 25% of the value of the portfolio) is destroyed by using an inferior project selection methodology! Consider the following question: If you were the CEO of Innovation R Us Corporation, would you knowingly and willingly walk away from $800M or 25% of your portfolio value?

The prioritization methodology shown in Figure 8-1 is a single objective technique, and in effect, either of the remaining two constraints (discoverers or developers) could be used instead of the budget as a constraint. More often than not, organizations make project selection decisions on the basis of multiple quantitative and qualitative criteria or attributes. This is accomplished through the use of *utility theory*, where all attributes that are used to directly measure objectives of a portfolio are converted to a common unit of currency—utils. *Utils* can be used to measure the level of attractiveness or usefulness of an initiative, endeavor, investment, or project. An appropriate methodology that accomplishes the aim of maximizing and/or minimizing multiple objectives through directly measurable quantitative and qualitative criteria using utility theory is multiple objective decision analysis (MODA).

MODA is generally employed to facilitate project prioritization when there is the lack of a dominant decision-making objective and confers several benefits:

- Accommodates decision-makers' objectives, preferences, and risk tolerances.
- Incorporates subject matter expert judgment for numerical and categorical inputs.
- Allows for uncertain inputs that can be discretized using the extended Swanson-McGill or extended Pearson-Tukey methods, for example (as discussed in Chapter 6).
- Provides a detailed understanding of the contribution of each project to the objectives of the portfolio.
- Enables trade-offs between weighted objectives.
- Facilitates sensitivity analyses to attribute weights to better understand their impact on prioritization.
- Clarifies and often resolves differences between multiple stakeholders.

- Can be easily understood and modified as necessary, thereby enabling its facile development and use.

A MODA methodology for project prioritization requires a good, transparent process, and one such procedure, Multiple Objective Project Prioritization (MOPP[SM]), depicted in Figure 8-2, can serve this important purpose. The MOPP[SM] process requires close interaction between a portfolio management function and a steering or governance committee of decision makers whose primary role is to guide the prioritization process. First and foremost, the purpose of the prioritization initiative needs to be clearly articulated, i.e., the reasons for project prioritization globally (across the enterprise) or locally (within sectors or business units) need to be understood by all. Generally, organizations prioritize projects because (a) there are insufficient budgetary and human resources to pursue every project in the portfolio and/or (b) there is a business need to place one project(s) ahead of another to avoid or minimize resource bottlenecks. Once this is understood, the objectives of the prioritization model (e.g., maximization of NPV or top line sales growth) are agreed to with senior decision makers, and weights or levels of importance are assigned to each objective.

Next, the portfolio management function needs to facilitate a close interaction between the steering or governance committee and appropriate subject matter experts to enable the relevant decision-making attributes to be used to measure the contribution

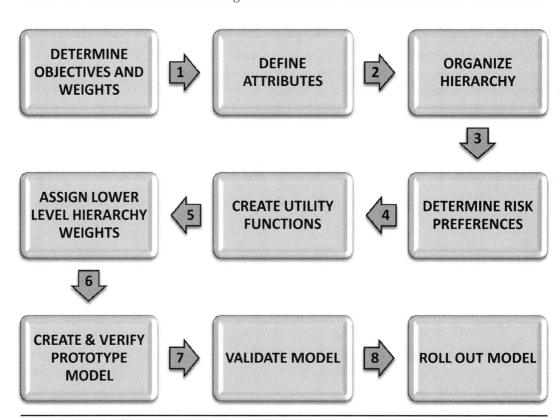

Figure 8-2 MOPP[SM] project prioritization process

of each project to the overall objectives of the organization. Without this in place at an early phase in the MOPP^SM process, prioritization meetings can quickly become untenable, as different stakeholders may invoke their own decision-making attributes on projects.

Once decision-relevant attributes are agreed upon, the MODA model hierarchy is organized in such a manner that directly measurable attributes (sometimes referred to as *secondary objectives*) are at the lower level of the hierarchy and serve to support the overarching objectives at the top of the hierarchy (sometimes referred to as *primary objectives*). Before utility functions can be created to measure each decision-relevant attribute in Step 5 (in Figure 8-2), the risk preferences of decision makers need to be established. As will be discussed shortly, risk preferences can be modeled in such a way that the attractiveness of increasing magnitude or score of an attribute represents either increasing or decreasing returns to scale. Once these utility functions are built, weights are assigned to each directly measurable attribute and a prototype of the prioritization model is ready to be tested.

The recommended approach is to select a handful of projects for which scores for each attribute are assigned and then perform a rank order of projects to determine the fidelity of the prioritization model. If inconsistencies arise during the validation phase (Step 8), the weights of the attributes and objectives in the model need to be revisited. As long as there is logical consistency between the relative rank of projects, the prioritization model is ready to be rolled out to accommodate weighted valuations of all projects in the portfolio.

Based on experience, where a dominant decision-making objective is absent, objectives will fall into four categories—benefits, risk, cost, and time (Figure 8-3). These objectives are directly measurable by attributes that feed each objective and, in this case, benefits are measured by five attributes: future market attractiveness, uniqueness of opportunity, product differentiation, contribution to strategic goals, and contribution to financial goals. While there is no rule of thumb to determine how many attributes should constitute a MODA hierarchy, a few guiding principles are:

- Attributes should be collectively exhaustive and mutually exclusive in that they (a) span the range of critical concerns for evaluation by decision makers and (b) display little or no redundancy due to overlap.
- Attributes should exhibit mutual preferential independence, i.e., preference for the level of an attribute should not depend on the level of another attribute.
- Attributes should be operable, i.e., understandable to stakeholders who may use the prioritization model.
- In general, the hierarchy itself should be populated in parsimonious fashion by attributes, as smaller hierarchies are not only easier to communicate and measure, but they possess meaningful weights that really impact prioritization.

As stated earlier, before creating utility functions, it is necessary to capture the risk preferences of decision makers toward each attribute. One such utility function, reflective of risk neutrality to product differentiation, is shown in Figure 8-4.

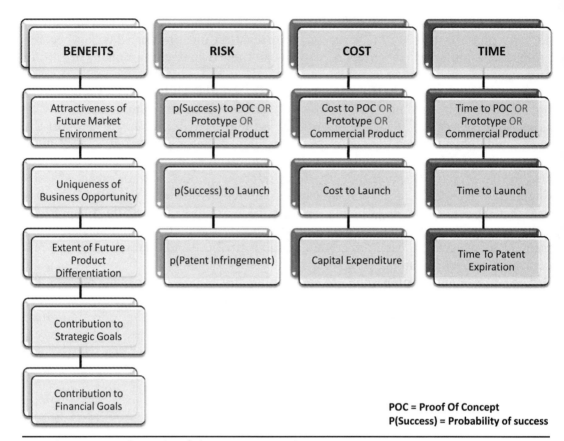

Figure 8-3   MODA hierarchy of objectives and attributes

In this case, low product differentiation, once defined, attains a fixed utility score, as do medium and high product differentiation, with constant returns to scale. Clearly, depending on the attribute being measured, a decision maker may exhibit (a) risk-averse preferences (concave, decreasing returns to scale), (b) risk-seeking preferences (convex, increasing returns to scale), (c) risk-neutral preferences (linear, constant returns to scale), and (d) both risk-averse and risk-seeking preferences (sigmoidal, increasing then decreasing returns to scale) (see Figure 8-5).

The assignment of hierarchy weights to both objectives and attributes is rarely without contention. How, for example, can one validate that a weight of 40% should be assigned to benefits and a corresponding weight of 30% to risk in the MODA model shown in Figure 8-6? Even if this appears to be in keeping with organizational objectives, should the assigned weights be exactly 40% and 30%? Perhaps not. Good practice dictates that weights should be assigned in a manner that reflect their relative importance to one another and, when necessary, altered sequentially to assess their sensitivity to the rank order of projects before finalization.

An alternative to this method of selecting weights for a MODA exercise is to conduct pair-wise comparisons of the relative importance of objectives (and attributes) using the analytic hierarchy process (AHP) methodology developed by T. L. Saaty (as

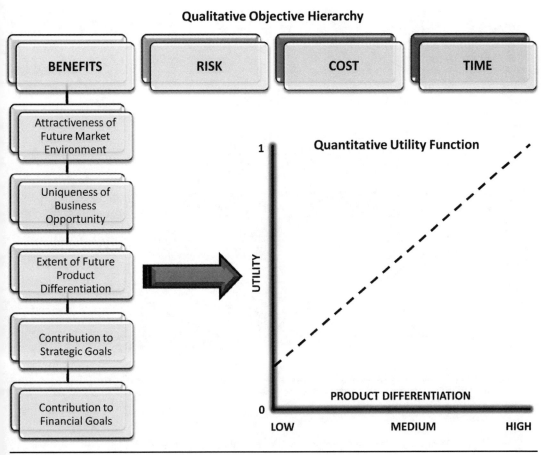

Figure 8-4   Risk-neutral utility function

cited in Ragsdale, 2008). First, using a scale to describe the decision-maker's preference for one objective (e.g., benefits) over another (Table 8-2), a matrix is created that shows the numerical preference of one objective when compared against every possible partner in a pair (itself, risk, cost, time) (see Table 8-3).

After weights are assigned to each objective, the process needs to be repeated so that weights can be assigned to each attribute (Figure 8-7). In concept, the entire process can be repeated again for each pair of projects, but this can quickly become an immensely time-consuming process for prioritization.

Apart from the issue of scalability (using AHP to prioritize seven projects on seven attributes requires that 168 pair-wise comparisons be made), it is well-known that the inclusion of new projects into an existing rank order of projects can lead to rank reversal of some projects and arises from the manner in which AHP normalizes the weights to sum to 1.0. Rather, it is recommended that, to the extent necessary, AHP should be utilized for the purpose of determining the weights of objectives (and, if required, attributes) while MODA should be used for the purpose of scoring every project against each attribute. Irrespective of which method is used to determine the weights of objectives and attributes, the utility score of each attribute for a project

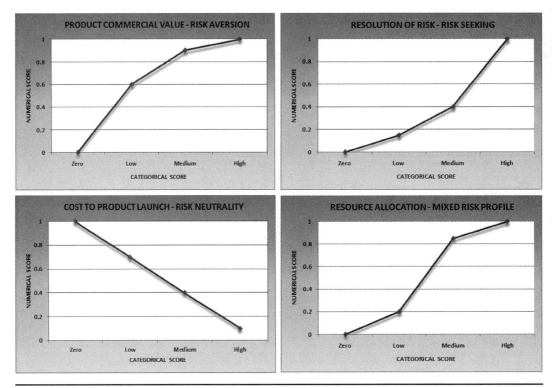

Figure 8-5   Utility functions with varying returns to scale

Table 8-2 Pair-wise preference-value scale used in the AHP

Value	Preference
1	Equally preferred
2	Equally to moderately preferred
3	Moderately preferred
4	Moderately to strongly preferred
5	Strongly preferred
6	Strongly to very strongly preferred
7	Very strongly preferred
8	Very strongly to extremely preferred
9	Extremely preferred

must be multiplied by its corresponding absolute weight to generate a weighted utility score; these scores are then aggregated to generate a weighted aggregate score for every project. For example, if the categorical score of a project on the "extent of future product differentiation" attribute is low and corresponds to a utility score of 0.15, this would be multiplied by 15% of 40% (i.e., 6%), resulting in a weighted utility score of 0.009. Once this is done for the remaining 13 attributes in the MODA model, the

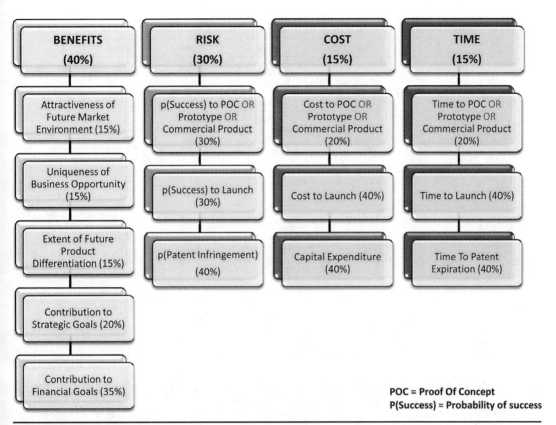

Figure 8-6   MODA hierarchy of weighted objectives and attributes

weighted aggregate score determines the rank order of this project amongst all other projects (Figure 8-8).

While several benefits can be attributed to the use of MODA methodologies, as with all other project prioritization techniques, the general approach suffers from some important drawbacks:

- MODA cannot account for project dependencies. For example, looking at Figure 8-8, if Project K (above the budget line) is dependent on Project E (below the budget line), both projects cannot be conducted without impacting any of the other projects that are above the budget line. This type of project dependency can be handled quite easily with binary integer logic, as described in Chapter 7, Portfolio Optimization.
- MODA does not allow for the use of project selection logic, e.g., choosing only one project from a sub-group of three projects (B, D, C) that may be competing within the same market segment.
- MODA does not reveal if a superior combination of projects exists that is better able to meet stated objectives without exceeding resource constraints. For example, prioritization does not reveal if some of the projects that lie below the budget line in Figure 8-8 could add greater value to the portfolio by displacing one or more projects that lie above the budget line.

Table 8-3 Matrix of objectives used to calculate weights in the AHP

	Benefits	Risk	Cost	Time
Benefits	1.000	2.000	3.000	4.000
Risk	0.500	1.000	2.000	2.000
Cost	0.333	0.500	1.000	1.000
Time	0.250	0.500	1.000	1.000
Total	**2.083**	**4.000**	**7.00**	**8.00**

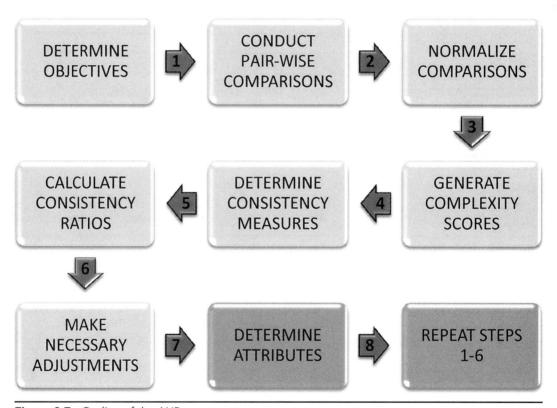

Figure 8-7 Outline of the AHP

Stated otherwise, prioritization does not guarantee that the selected combination of projects lies on the efficient frontier and hence makes it difficult to determine the value left on the table from the choice of a sub-optimal portfolio of projects. To place this within a graphical perspective, project selection via project prioritization will most likely yield one of the many feasible, sub-optimal portfolios shown under the horizontal line in Figure 7-7. The difference between any of these sub-optimal portfolios and the optimal portfolio itself represents the portfolio value destroyed by the use of a largely inferior methodology such as project prioritization.

Finally, many prioritization exercises seem to have natural beginnings without logical ends. This situation invariably leads to unnecessary organizational turmoil, resulting

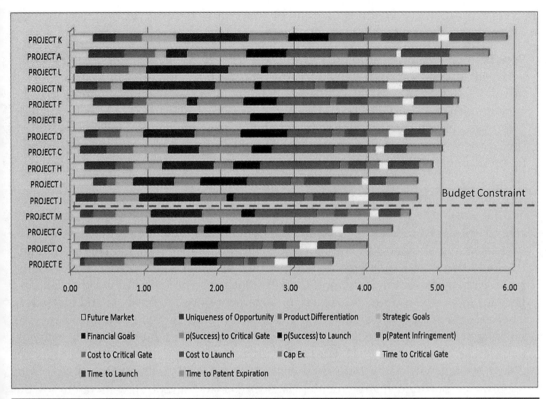

Figure 8-8 Project prioritization using MODA (note: read the legend left to right, top to bottom)

in tomorrow's prioritizations differing from those of today. While there is no doubt that project information is subject to change over time, such change is infrequently of the form and substance that revoke many existing prioritization decisions. The challenge of a disciplined organization is to make a sufficient number of prioritization decisions, and as resources become available from successfully completed or terminated projects, prioritization is conducted at the margin to ensure the best allocation of incremental resources.

8.2 Designing Prioritization Models—An Example

Some of the intricacies in developing models for project/investment prioritization in the R&D and IT industries are illustrated in the following example, with a step-by-step construction of models for prioritizing projects/investments in an IT portfolio. It is worth noting that while these real-world models for prioritizing IT investments leverage the MOPP^{SM} process, the emphasis here is to illustrate how facets of the AHP technique and the MOPP^{SM} process can be used to construct objective, defensible MODA models for project/investment prioritization.

In order to develop viable MODA models for IT investment prioritization, it is fundamental to understand the drivers of IT investment decisions. IT investment drivers are primarily benefits (also known as *value*), risk, and cost. Organizations must have a thorough comprehension of business and IT in terms of benefits (value), risk, and cost in order to make good decisions on IT investments:

Benefits (Value): In its simplest form, value is created when the benefits of an investment exceed its costs. However, this is a narrow view of value, since not all benefits are tangible. Many intangible benefits, while not being obvious, may be very important to certain key stakeholders. Examples of intangible benefits include improved customer satisfaction and knowledge gained by the organization's human resources, which are less straightforward to measure and quantify than traditional financial benefits. This is particularly true in the case of IT investments, many of which create relatively intangible benefits.

In order to maximize the value of an IT portfolio, it is imperative for business and IT leaders to agree and align on the definition of value and how both entities can contribute to establishing overall enterprise value. Value creation begins with an understanding of what is valued by the organization. Organizational factors affecting the definition of value drivers include personal and political agendas, organizational risk tolerance, current industry and market trends, interpretation of information, and perhaps most importantly, the degree of alignment between business and IT leaders. There are three types of value objectives: business value, IT value, and financial value. Drawing from many of the IT valuation techniques based on Intel's business value index (Intel Corporation, 2001), Gartner's® total value of opportunity (Apfel & Smith, 2003), Forrester Research Inc.'s total economic impact (Gliedman, 2008), and from texts on IT portfolio management (Maizlish & Handler, 2005), a hierarchy of the value objectives and their attributes is presented in Table 8-4.

Risk: Many organizations are at a rudimentary stage with respect to IT portfolio risk analysis. While companies have incorporated risk management in IT projects to varying degrees, they have not been as successful in proactively quantifying and managing portfolio risk. Risks can impact the cost of investments through dramatic changes in scope and unplanned funding requirements. Risks affect interdependent projects by delaying value, influencing schedules, and affecting performance, resulting in loss of trust, confidence, and ultimately competitive advantage. Risks must be evaluated for individual investments and assessed across the entire portfolio. There is a compelling need for the organization and IT to work together to define how portfolio risk will be managed. Failure to do so can lead to poor portfolio management practices. A hierarchy of the risk objectives and its underlying attributes was presented in Chapter 5, Risk Analysis, and will be used in this case study.

Cost: IT investments are constrained by limited financial capital, which necessitates effective cost management and a clear understanding of all the costs associated with IT investments. Poor estimation of the procurement, development, integration, and execution costs for a potential IT investment, as well as incorrectly forecasting the total cost of ownership for new and existing investments, can have debilitating consequences for the IT portfolio. Redundant investments, poor investment prioritization, and inherent biases that cloud retirement decisions or kill poor IT investments can drain IT costs, essentially suffocating IT investments that could add significant value and competitive advantage (Maizlish & Handler, 2005).

Table 8-4 Value objectives and attributes for IT investment prioritization

Value Objective	Value Attribute	Description/Explanation
Business Value	Strategic Fit	How does the IT investment's objectives align with the company's stated objectives and the customer's organization(s) stated objectives?
	Customer Need	What is the extent to which IT's customers are asking for this deliverable and what is the strength/influence of their request/demand?
	Compliance	Mandatory investments in IT solutions, required for compliance with regulatory obligations inclusive of government, legal, and tax regulatory practices.
	Revenue Impact	Directly related to protecting or enhancing revenue generation, not the magnitude of the impact (including: revenue, time to market, opening new markets, optimizing existing markets, up-selling and cross-selling).
	Performance Improvement	Customer user productivity, process efficiency, such as head count productivity, factory optimization, and yield improvement.
	Level of Innovation	Completely new, innovative solution to solve a business problem that creates competitive advantage or an enhancement/incremental improvement.
	Issues Resolution	To what level will this investment improve quality of service provided by IT in resolving top customer issues?
	Intangible Benefits	This includes benefits not captured above (for example: additional useful information on customers collected as a result of this initiative, even if it is not a primary objective of this initiative).
IT Value	Internal Demand	What is the extent to which internal demand exists, i.e., within IT organization what is the level of demand for this deliverable (volume, strength of demand)?
	IT Stated Objectives Alignment	Describe how the investment's objectives align with IT's stated objectives and goals.
	Time to Market	Does the investment increase the speed of IT products and services getting deployed to customers (company-wide) without impacting quality?
	Productivity Improvement	This is a measure of impact to IT employee productivity, i.e., efficiency, faster throughput, higher quality.
	Learning & Innovation	Is this a new technology approach/tool for IT internal usage?
	Unit Cost Reduction	What is the impact to the unit cost of IT's products and services (list the products and the type of costs affected)?
	Impact on Future Investments	Investments that provide a foundation or are necessary for future technologies, capabilities, or have a direct impact on strategic roadmaps.
	Quality & Reliability	Investments in maintaining required levels of quality of IT infrastructure, service delivery, operational efficiency, capacity, response rates, problem resolution.
	Component Reuse	Opportunities to reuse existing standard applicable capabilities and assets and/or opportunities to create new ones for future reuse.
	Architectural Fit	The level of fit with existing reference architectures and roadmaps, as well as the level of integration required in order to introduce into the IT environment.
	IT Employee Satisfaction	What is the level of improvement in IT employees' development and growth?
Financial Value	Net Present Value (NPV)	What is the NPV generated by the investment?
	Payback Period	What is the payback period for the investment?
	Internal Rate of Return (IRR)	What is the IRR for the investment?
	Return on Investment (ROI)	What is the ROI for the investment?
	Level of Initial Investment[1]	The level of initial investment as a percentage of the annual IT budget.

[1]Level of initial investment is typically an attribute of the "cost" objective. It is included in the "financial value" objective for consideration by IT organizations that do not want to utilize a separate "Cost" objective for reasons explained in the next section.

Trade-offs between fixed costs (in-house resources) and variable costs (outsourced or contractual resources) also affect cost efficiencies. *Fixed costs* are typically long-term expenditures that have an organizational commitment, such as hardware depreciation or lease payments, capitalized development expenses, maintenance, long-term software licenses, and salaried personnel. Variable costs are typically expenditures that change in the short-term based on immediate priorities, such as per-seat software licenses, training, incremental storage, and capacity required to support near-term growth, as well as on-demand IT solutions. Discipline in measuring and managing costs is crucial to the success of IT portfolio management and to the overall health of the organization. Gartner's total cost of ownership model (Apfel & Smith, 2003) is a comprehensive framework for capturing costs as the third investment driver in IT investment selection. The elements of the total cost of ownership framework are presented as a hierarchy of the cost objective and the underlying attributes. IT cost can be decomposed into two broad categories:

- **Direct costs:** This includes costs for staffing (labor), infrastructure (hardware, software, and network), administrative development (enhancements), and operations.
- **Indirect costs:** This includes costs for end users, outages (planned and unplanned downtime), and miscellaneous costs.

While a clear understanding of IT investment drivers is fundamental to developing a model for prioritizing investments in IT portfolios, it is equally important to take into consideration the differences between various types of IT investments. IT expenses can be classified broadly as capital expenditure (CAPEX) and operational expenditure (OPEX).

The CAPEX IT Portfolio

CAPEX refers to the money spent to acquire or upgrade physical assets such as technology, buildings, and machinery. From an IT perspective, it encompasses capital investments in new IT projects and programs to be implemented in support of business and IT initiatives. A CAPEX portfolio is also referred to as the *IT project portfolio*. Decisions on the approval of investments in a CAPEX IT portfolio are seldom under the jurisdiction of a CIO. Instead, it is usually a team of executives from the business units, led by the COO or the CFO, who determines the investments in a CAPEX portfolio that are to be funded, in pursuit of the fulfillment of an organization's objectives. Typically, the CIO is consulted by such a committee as a subject matter expert, who provides the details of the analyses to justify the selection of a set of CAPEX investments.

The OPEX IT Portfolio

An operational expense is an ongoing cost for a product, business, or system. In IT, these are ongoing investments necessary for the maintenance and operations of existing IT assets (applications, infrastructure, labor for maintenance, and so on). An OPEX portfolio comprises the entire set of investments required for the maintenance and operations functions provided by an IT organization in an enterprise. An OPEX portfolio is also referred to as the *IT asset portfolio*. Typically, the CIO is the final decision maker with respect to approving operational expenses, with input from IT senior management. The differences between the two portfolios are summarized in Table 8-5.

Owing to the differences in objectives and attributes between a CAPEX portfolio component and an OPEX portfolio component, it would be reasonable to create separate MODA models for a CAPEX portfolio and an OPEX portfolio. In summary, the CAPEX MODA model would use business value, IT value, financial value, and risk as the objectives in the utility hierarchy. The OPEX MODA model would be based on business value, IT value, cost, and risk as the underlying objectives. Once the objectives and underlying attributes have been identified, the next step is to create a utility hierarchy for the CAPEX and OPEX models, based on these value drivers.

8.2.1 Creating a Utility Hierarchy

As stated previously, owing to the differences in objectives and directly measurable attributes between a CAPEX investment and an OPEX investment, it would be reasonable to create separate MODA models for a CAPEX portfolio and an OPEX portfolio. Two such MODA models are presented below, one each for a CAPEX portfolio of investments and an OPEX portfolio of investments.

It should be noted that the MODA models presented here are not meant to represent a single set of all-encompassing decision models for prioritizing projects/investments in IT portfolios. While they have been designed to be as generic as possible to account for a broad spectrum of IT needs, they are also specific enough to be applicable to evaluating the portfolios of IT investments for the case study under consideration. IT organizations looking to adopt these models should tailor the models to suit the specific needs of their enterprise, in respect to changing objectives and attributes or in respect to adjusting attribute weights.

Table 8-5 Differences between CAPEX and OPEX

Feature	CAPEX Portfolio	OPEX Portfolio
Organizational Roles	• Decision maker—CFO/COO (responsible) • Accountable—CIO • Consulted—CIO, heads of business units • Informed—CEO, IT senior management	• Decision maker—CIO (responsible & accountable) • Consulted—IT senior management, heads of business units • Informed—CFO, COO
Financial Benefits	Future values of financial parameters can be computed by capital budgeting process based on discounted cash flow to determine NPV, IRR, payback period, etc.	Capital budgeting (discounted cash flow analysis) not applicable, since these are not expenses that are capitalized and hence cannot be depreciated.
Total Cost of Ownership	Cannot be determined accurately, since these are brand new investments, for which it is difficult to reasonably estimate certain types of ongoing expenses such as cost of outages, etc. Cost is captured under financial value.	Can be determined accurately. In fact, total cost of ownership is the primary basis for determining the monetary worth of ongoing IT investments that cannot be capitalized.
Business Value, IT Value, Risk	Applicable for analysis as objectives in CAPEX MODA model.	Applicable for analysis as objectives in OPEX MODA model.

MODA Model for the CAPEX IT Portfolio

A MODA model for the CAPEX IT portfolio is illustrated in Figure 8-9. The objectives of the CAPEX MODA model are business value, IT value, financial value, and risk. It is worth noting that the "cost" of a CAPEX project is captured as the attribute called "level of investment" in the financial value objective. Note also that this is a three-tier hierarchy, although illustrated for two tiers (to render the graphic readable), with the elements of the third tier (where applicable) captured under the second tier.

MODA Model for OPEX IT Portfolio

A MODA model for the OPEX IT portfolio in the case study is illustrated in Figure 8-10.

The next step is to employ a methodology that enables the assignment of weights to the objectives and attributes, which is addressed in the following section using the AHP.

8.2.2 Using AHP to Assign Weights to Objectives and Attributes

While the AHP technique has limited applicability in prioritizing large numbers of projects for reasons explained earlier, it can be used to determine the weights associated with the objectives and attributes used in a weighted scoring model, such as MODA, for investment prioritization. This is illustrated step by step for the CAPEX objectives and attributes.

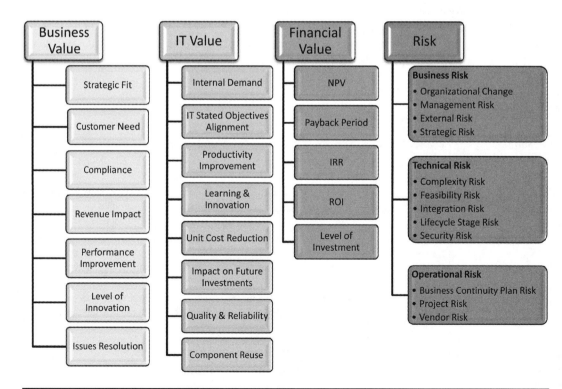

Figure 8-9   MODA model for CAPEX IT portfolio

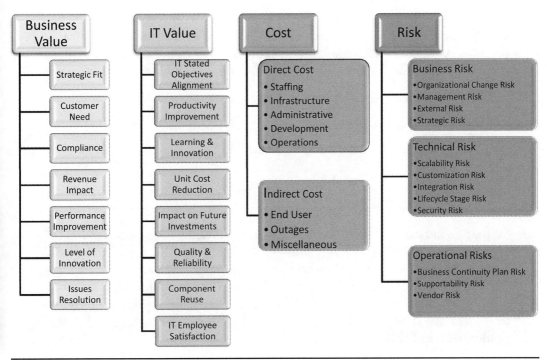

Figure 8-10 MODA model for OPEX IT portfolio

Step 1: Determine objectives. The objectives for a portfolio of CAPEX projects are business value, IT value, financial value, and risk.

Step 2: Conduct pair-wise comparisons between the objectives. This is illustrated in Table 8-6, where pair-wise comparisons have been made between the objectives. In developing this model for IT organizations, it has been determined through experience that the "business value" objective is twice as important as "IT value," which in turn is equally as important as "financial value" and "'risk," as reflected in the pair-wise comparison in Table 8-6. For example, since business value is considered to be twice as important as IT value, the second column in the first row has a value of 2.000, while the reverse pair-wise comparison (comparing IT value against business value), as reflected in the first column in the second row, has the reciprocal value of 2, i.e., 0.500. The last row in the table is the aggregate score of the pair-wise comparisons for each of the objectives.

Table 8-6 Pair-wise comparison of CAPEX model objectives

	Business Value	IT Value	Financial Value	Risk
Business Value	1.000	2.000	2.000	2.000
IT Value	0.500	1.000	1.000	1.000
Financial Value	0.500	1.000	1.000	1.000
Risk	0.500	1.000	1.000	1.000
Total	2.500	5.000	5.000	5.000

Step 3: Normalize the comparisons. The pair-wise comparisons are normalized by dividing the score of each cell in Table 8-6 by the total score for that objective, with the results displayed in Table 8-7. For example, the normalized score for the cell in the first row, third column is 2.000/5.000, or 0.400.

Table 8-7 Normalized comparison of CAPEX model objectives

	Business Value	IT Value	Financial Value	Risk
Business Value	0.400	0.400	0.400	0.400
IT Value	0.200	0.200	0.200	0.200
Financial Value	0.200	0.200	0.200	0.200
Risk	0.200	0.200	0.200	0.200

Step 4: Generate complexity scores. Complexity scores are calculated as the average score for each row in Table 8-7. This reflects the complexity score for the objective corresponding to the row in question, as outlined in Table 8-8. For example, the complexity score for the IT value objective is the average of the values in row 2, which is 0.200 (or 20%). Similarly, the complexity scores are determined for the other objectives and highlighted as the shaded cells in Table 8-8.

Table 8-8 Complexity scores for the CAPEX model objectives

	Business Value	IT Value	Financial Value	Risk	Criterion Weight (Complexity Score)	Consistency Measures
Business Value	0.400	0.400	0.400	0.400	40%	4.000
IT Value	0.200	0.200	0.200	0.200	20%	4.000
Financial Value	0.200	0.200	0.200	0.200	20%	4.000
Risk	0.200	0.200	0.200	0.200	20%	4.000

Step 5: Determine consistency measures. Consistency measures are determined for each row in the normalized comparison as a preliminary step in ensuring that the ambiguity in each of the pair-wise comparisons is minimized, as shown in Table 8-9. For each row in the normalized comparison (Table 8-7), the consistency measure is determined as the aggregate sum of the cross-product of each cell in the corresponding row in the pair-wise comparison (Table 8-6), with the corresponding cell in the complexity score column in the normalized comparison (Table 8-7) divided by the complexity score for that row. For example, the consistency measure for business value is the aggregate sum of the product of the cells in row 1 in Table 8-6 and the cells in the column titled Complexity Score in Table 8-8 divided by the complexity score for the business value objective in Table 8-8:

$$\text{Aggregate score for business value} = (1 \times 40\% + 2 \times 20\% + 2 \times 20\% + 2 \times 20\%) = 1.6$$

Consistency measure for business value = 1.6/40% = 4.00

Table 8-9 Consistency measures for CAPEX model objectives

	Business Value	IT Value	Financial Value	Risk	Criterion Weight (Complexity Score)	Consistency Measures
Business Value	0.400	0.400	0.400	0.400	40%	4.000
IT Value	0.200	0.200	0.200	0.200	20%	4.000
Financial Value	0.200	0.200	0.200	0.200	20%	4.000
Risk	0.200	0.200	0.200	0.200	20%	4.000

Consistency Index (CI)	$(\lambda - n/(n-1))$		0.000
Consistency Ratio (CR)	CI/RI		0.000

n – # alternatives
λ – Average consistency measure for all
RI – Random index (from sheet RI values)

Step 6: Calculate consistency ratios. The computation for the consistency ratio (CR) is based on the consistency index (CI) for the AHP model to ensure that it does not suffer from inconsistency of values chosen in the pair-wise comparisons by the decision makers. The random index (RI) was developed by Thomas Saaty in support of the AHP technique, to determine the CR. The RI is listed in Table 8-10. Basically, the RI is a fractional value based on the number of objectives under consideration. Since there are four objectives (alternatives) under consideration in this case, the RI (complexity score) is 0.90. These are computed as follows:

$$CI = (\lambda - n)/(n - 1)$$
$$CR = CI/RI$$

where

n = number of objectives or alternatives under consideration

λ = average consistency measure for all alternatives

Table 8-10 Random index for AHP

# Alternatives	Random Index (RI)
2	0.00
3	0.58
4	0.90
5	1.12
6	1.24
7	1.32
8	1.41

The rule of thumb suggested by AHP proponents is that an AHP model is fairly consistent if the value of the CR is less than or equal to 0.1, or else the AHP model might not yield meaningful results. Using this information, the values of CR and CI can be computed for this case as follows:

$$CI = (\lambda - n)/(n - 1) = 0$$
$$CR = CI/RI = 0$$

Therefore, our AHP model is extremely consistent with respect to the pair-wise comparisons of the alternatives.

Step 7: Make necessary adjustments. For the case study, the AHP-based determination of the relative weights for each of the objectives is:

Business value = 40%

IT value = 20%

Financial value = 20%

Risk = 20%

We do not need to make any further adjustments.

Step 8: Repeat Steps 2-7 for the attributes corresponding to each objective in order to determine the relative weights of the attributes. This is illustrated in Table 8-11 for the attributes corresponding to the business value objective. There are seven attributes, necessitating a 7 × 7 matrix and a multitude of pair-wise comparisons. Likewise, for the IT value objective, there are 8 attributes, which further increases the complexity of making consistent pair-wise comparisons. The weights assigned to the directly measurable IT value objective using AHP are shown in Table 8-12.

The effort associated with determining relative weights using AHP, illustrated in the above examples, further underscores the limitations of the use of AHP in project prioritization in the real world. In the example, a pair-wise comparison of 7 or 8 attributes required a reasonable effort, so one can imagine the amount of effort involved in ranking 25 alternatives, such as prioritizing 25 projects in a portfolio. For this reason, as well as for other reasons explained, AHP's role in project prioritization has been limited to determining the relative weights of the objectives and attributes used in a MODA model.

The relative weights of the attributes corresponding to each of the other objectives in the CAPEX model, as well as the OPEX model, can be generated in a similar manner. After incorporating minor adjustments to the relative weights of the attributes based on the preference of the subject matter experts and decision makers, the utility hierarchy (MODA models) for IT investment prioritization can be finalized with the appropriate weights assigned to the objectives and directly measurable attributes.

Table 8-11 AHP-based relative weight assignment for attributes of business value objective

Pair-wise Comparison of the Attributes of the "Business Value" Objective

	Strategic Fit	Customer Need	Compliance	Revenue Impact	Perf. Improvement	Innovation	Issues Resolution
Strategic Fit	1.000	1.000	1.000	1.000	1.000	2.000	1.000
Customer Need	1.000	1.000	1.000	1.000	1.000	2.000	1.000
Compliance	1.000	1.000	1.000	1.000	1.000	2.000	1.000
Revenue Impact	1.000	1.000	1.000	1.000	1.000	2.000	1.000
Perf. Improvement	1.000	1.000	1.000	1.000	1.000	2.000	1.000
Innovation	0.500	0.500	0.500	0.500	0.500	1.000	0.500
Issues Resolution	1.000	1.000	1.000	1.000	1.000	2.000	1.000
Total	6.500	6.500	6.500	6.500	6.500	13.000	6.500

Normalized Comparison

	Strategic Fit	Customer Need	Compliance	Revenue Impact	Perf. Improvement	Innovation	Issues Resolution	Criterion Weight	Consistency Measures
Strategic Fit	0.154	0.154	0.154	0.154	0.154	0.154	0.154	15.385%	7.000
Customer Need	0.154	0.154	0.154	0.154	0.154	0.154	0.154	15.385%	7.000
Compliance	0.154	0.154	0.154	0.154	0.154	0.154	0.154	15.385%	7.000
Revenue Impact	0.154	0.154	0.154	0.154	0.154	0.154	0.154	15.385%	7.000
Perf. Improvement	0.154	0.154	0.154	0.154	0.154	0.154	0.154	15.385%	7.000
Innovation	0.077	0.077	0.077	0.077	0.077	0.077	0.077	7.692%	7.000
Issues Resolution	0.154	0.154	0.154	0.154	0.154	0.154	0.154	15.385%	7.000

Consistency index (CI)	$(\lambda - n/(n - 1)$	0.000
Consistency ratio (CR)	CI/RI	0.000

Table 8-12 AHP based relative weight assignment for attributes of IT value objective

Pair-wise Comparison of the Attributes of the "Business Value" Objective

	Internal Demand	IT SO Alignment	Productivity Improvement	Learning & Innovation	Unit Cost Reduction	Impact on Future Investments	Quality & Reliability	Component Reuse
Internal Demand	1.000	0.500	1.000	3.000	1.000	2.000	2.000	2.000
IT SO Alignment	2.000	1.000	0.500	4.000	2.000	3.000	3.000	3.000
Productivity Improvement	1.000	0.500	1.000	3.000	1.000	2.000	2.000	2.000
Learning & Innovation	0.333	0.250	0.333	1.000	0.333	0.500	0.500	0.500
Unit Cost Reduction	1.000	0.500	1.000	3.000	1.000	2.000	2.000	2.000
Impact on Future Investments	0.500	0.333	0.500	2.000	0.500	1.000	1.000	1.000
Quality & Reliability	0.500	0.333	0.500	2.000	0.500	1.000	1.000	1.000
Component Reuse	0.500	0.333	0.500	2.000	0.500	1.000	1.000	1.000
Total	6.833	3.750	5.333	20.000	6.833	12.500	12.500	12.500

Normalized Comparison

	Internal Demand	IT SO Alignment	Productivity Improvement	Learning & Innovation	Unit Cost Reduction	Impact on Future Investments	Quality & Reliability	Component Reuse	Criterion Weight	Consistency
Internal Demand	0.146	0.133	0.188	0.150	0.146	0.160	0.160	0.160	15.544%	7.935
IT SO Alignment	0.293	0.267	0.094	0.200	0.293	0.240	0.240	0.240	23.322%	8.077
Productivity Improvement	0.146	0.133	0.188	0.150	0.146	0.160	0.160	0.160	15.544%	7.935
Learning & Innovation	0.049	0.067	0.063	0.050	0.049	0.040	0.040	0.040	4.959%	7.840
Unit Cost Reduction	0.146	0.133	0.188	0.150	0.146	0.160	0.160	0.160	15.544%	7.935
Impact on Future Investments	0.073	0.089	0.094	0.100	0.073	0.080	0.080	0.080	8.362%	7.904
Quality & Reliability	0.073	0.089	0.094	0.100	0.073	0.080	0.080	0.080	8.362%	7.904
Component Reuse	0.073	0.089	0.094	0.100	0.073	0.080	0.080	0.080	8.362%	7.904

Consistency index (CI)	$(\lambda - n/(n-1))$	-0.000
Consistency ratio (CR)	CI/RI	-0.000

SO = stated objectives

8.2.3 Finalizing the Utility Hierarchy

The finalized utility hierarchies (MODA models) with the appropriate weights assigned to the objectives and attributes are illustrated in Figures 8-11 and 8-12. Note that the weights for the attributes of the business value objective for both the CAPEX and OPEX models have been adjusted to reflect rounded values, with the "level of innovation" attribute being assigned 10% weight, which is slightly more than the AHP computed value of 7.692%. Such minor tweaks are commonplace in practice, where the results of the computed values are tweaked, based on decision makers' preferences, as long as the sum of the relative attribute weights for that objective adds up to 100%.

8.2.4 Finalizing Attribute Score Levels

The final step in the construction of the MODA models is to determine score levels for each attribute in the MODA models, so that the scores may be used for the prioritization of CAPEX and OPEX IT investments. The weights for each of the objectives and the associated attributes have been determined by using AHP (with minor tweaks to the AHP-generated values), as outlined in the aforementioned steps. The raw scores for the attributes are discrete values on a scale of 0 to 9,[1] corresponding to the definition and level for each score. The weighted score is computed as the product of the

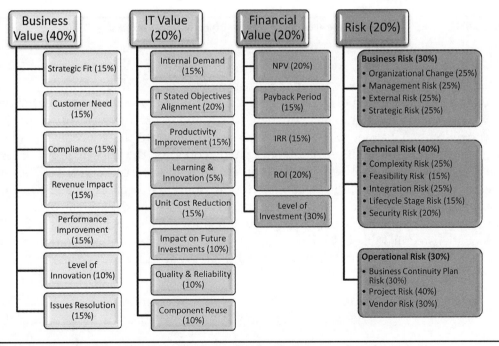

Figure 8-11 CAPEX IT MODA model with weights for objectives and attributes

---

[1]It should be noted that the choice of the scale used is typically at the discretion of the decision analyst who is creating the utility hierarchy. However, the same scale is recommended to be used for all the elements of the utility hierarchy to ensure consistency in measurement.

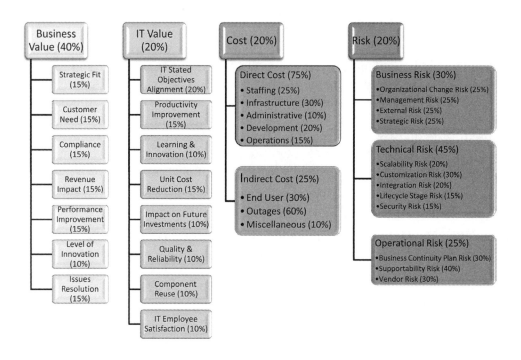

Figure 8-12   OPEX IT MODA model with weights for objectives and attributes

weights of the objective, attribute, sub-attribute, and the raw score divided by the maximum value of the raw score for an attribute (raw score value of 9).

A complete description of the score levels, raw scores, and weighted scores for every element in the utility hierarchies for the CAPEX and OPEX investments is provided in Appendix A, A Primer in Decision Analysis. To illustrate the concept, consider as an example the computation of the weighted scores for the sub-attribute "integration risk" under "technical risk," which is an attribute of the "risk" objective. The "risk" objective's weight is 20%; the "technical risk" attribute has been assigned a weight of 40%, and the "integration risk" sub-attribute has been assigned a weight of 25%. The score levels for determining the appropriate integration risk associated with a CAPEX project are listed in Table 8-13. For a project with a "high" level of integration risk, the raw score is 2 on a scale of 0 to 9. The weighted score for this level of integration risk is computed as:

$$\text{Weighted score for "high" level of integration risk}$$
$$= 100 \times (20\% \times 40\% \times 25\% \times 2/9) = 0.444$$

The weighted scores for each score level of every attribute/sub-attribute in the MODA models for CAPEX and OPEX investment prioritization are computed in a similar manner and listed in Appendix C, MODA Models for IT Investment Prioritization.

Table 8-13 Detailed representation of MODA model for CAPEX IT portfolio

Objective	Objective Weight	Attribute	Attribute Weight	Sub-Attribute	Sub-Attribute Weight	Score Description	Score Levels	Raw Score	Weighted Score
Risk	20%	Technical Risk	40%	Integration Risk	25%	Significant integration required necessitating architecture redesign; development of a number of new interfaces is required.	Very High	0	0.00
						Some degree of integration required, but does not require architecture redesign; however a number of new interfaces need to be developed.	High	2	0.44
						Low degree of integration, few new interfaces and/or modifications to existing interfaces.	Medium	5	1.11
						Minimal integration required; mostly minor tweaks to existing interfaces.	Low	9	2.00

At this stage, projects in CAPEX IT portfolios and operational investments in OPEX IT portfolios can be prioritized using the MODA models developed in this chapter. These will be utilized in the IT portfolio selection case study in Chapter 10.

8.3 Summary

Key concepts in project and investment prioritization were addressed in this chapter. Prioritization models such as MODA and the AHP were explained. Further, the MOPP^{SM} process for conducting an end-to-end prioritization exercise was outlined. As a mini-case study, a step-by-step approach to designing a MODA model for prioritizing IT investments was described. At this time, there should be no doubts about the superiority of optimization over prioritization as a portfolio selection technique, as illustrated with examples in this and the previous chapter.

9

Best Practices in Portfolio Management

- **Capability maturity model (CMM)**—A formal archetype of the evolutionary stages to enable a transition to a desired level of competency in a particular domain, such as software engineering. A brainchild of the Carnegie Mellon University and now owned by the Software Engineering Institute, CMM is a process improvement approach that provides organizations with the essential elements of effective processes that ultimately improve their performance.
- **Portfolio analysis**—The coordinated assessment of a collection of projects and programs whose overarching objective is to attain defined business goals.
- **Risk management**—The active identification, monitoring, and management of controllable risks, as well as the intentional mitigation of the impact of uncontrollable risks.
- **Resource management**—The allocation of constrained resources (e.g., budgetary, human, manufacturing) to business units or sectors across the portfolio, which in turn is based on the efficient allocation and reallocation of those resources as projects and programs succeed or fail in passing through stage gate reviews.
- **Stakeholder management**—The active management of individuals who are either directly or indirectly involved in a project, program, or portfolio and who are affected by the outcome of this endeavor. Such individuals may be internal or external to an organization, but their participation is nevertheless associated with the success or failure of the endeavor.

Projects and programs need to be managed creatively and adaptively in such a manner that new information is incorporated into ongoing decision making; tools and templates have their place, but are effectively marginalized unless there is good process and methodology. The active management of risks, resources, and stakeholders is critical not just to the betterment of projects and programs, but to the viability of an ongoing project portfolio management function itself.

Further, project portfolio management is a continual process of managing relevant information and data to enable good decision making. The objective of this chapter is to provide a set of best practices in the project portfolio management discipline for adoption by any organization that aspires to improve its portfolio management competencies.

This chapter comprises two parts. The first outlines a CMM in portfolio management, with the aim of providing a framework to enable organizations to determine their maturity level across a broad spectrum of portfolio management competencies. The maturity model can be used by organizations as a benchmark to determine the success of any organizational change management initiative aimed at attaining the requisite level of maturity and discipline required to employ these techniques to guide optimal investment decisions, not just from an R&D or IT perspective, but from a perspective that is applicable in the context of enterprise portfolio management. The second part of the chapter, which presents portfolio management best practices, provides guidelines on portfolio analysis, risk management, resource management, and stakeholder management, the key facets of successful enterprise portfolio management.

9.1 Capability Maturity Model

CMMs can be used to guide process improvement across a project, a division, or an entire organization. The models can help integrate traditionally separate organizational functions, set process improvement goals and priorities, provide guidance for quality processes, and provide a point of reference for appraising current processes, according to the Software Engineering Institute.

While the first application of the CMM was in software development, the framework itself has become an industry standard for process modeling and the assessment of an organization's maturity in a number of domains, including enterprise project portfolio management (EPPM). A CMM in portfolio management is proposed in this chapter, with the aim of providing a framework to enable organizations to determine their maturity level across a wide spectrum of portfolio management competencies.

9.1.1 Maturity Levels

As outlined in Chapter 1, Basic Concepts of Enterprise Project Portfolio Management, a significant portion of the organizational challenge to excelling in project portfolio management is the willingness to invest in building this capability in terms that can be described as a CMM, comprising five levels of maturity (Figure 9-1). Irrespective of the level of the pyramid in which an organization finds itself or is striving to attain, effective project portfolio management is the product of: (a) good project and program management, (b) efficient financial management, and (c) defensible resource management.

Level 1: Project and Program Office

At the base of the maturity hierarchy exists a project and program office that represents the first semblance of project portfolio management. This function is primarily concerned with gathering project and program information and metrics. It is expected

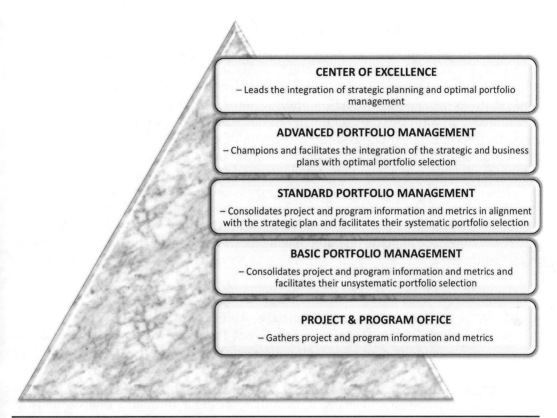

Figure 9-1   Project portfolio management CMM

that senior management will make all decisions regarding the continuation or termination of assets, while the project and program office serves up the information and data. It is rare to find formal portfolio management reviews in organizations that only possess a project and program office. An organization that is at this level of maturity is practicing EPPM in an ad hoc or informal manner, if at all.

Level 2: Basic Portfolio Management

As capability matures, a basic portfolio management office is formed. Here, this function—not yet formally recognized as an organizational discipline—is concerned primarily with consolidation of project and program information and metrics. Although the basic portfolio management function is recognized as a body that is responsible for providing this knowledge to senior management for decision making, it provides little, if any, insight into the viability of the portfolio and almost no perspective on the ability of the portfolio to meet the organization's temporal strategic and financial goals. Moreover, there is deep-seated organizational chaos regarding roles and responsibilities in terms of data ownership and validity for financial and human resource information. Portfolio reviews are conducted on a semi-annual or annual basis within the organization, but monthly stage gate reviews do not yet provide ongoing decision making for projects and programs in the context of the portfolio.

Level 3: Standard Portfolio Management

As a standard portfolio management function, a key imperative is to utilize the strategic plan as a starting point against which portfolio consolidation derives its greatest value. Once the long-range strategic plan is provided in quantifiable terms to the standard portfolio management function, the shorter-term business plan assumes greater meaning and, in turn, the portfolio plan can be created along different strategic pathways. Portfolio management assumes a position of ownership for consolidated, validated information and data across the enterprise and is expected to create strategic options for senior management to consider before decisions are made.

Considerable effort is invested in finding practitioners of decision analysis and portfolio management and in training them appropriately for the long term. Portfolio reviews are conducted on a semi-annual basis within the organization as monthly stage gate reviews provide ongoing decision making for projects and programs in the context of the portfolio.

Level 4: Advanced Portfolio Management

An advanced portfolio management function achieves not only the expectations of the standard portfolio management function, but takes portfolio management to its next logical step in that it seeks to optimize portfolio value to the enterprise. It does so not by passively interacting with its financial and human resource counterparts, but by championing and spearheading the integration of strategic and business plans with active portfolio management plans. Rather than meander through various rounds of project prioritization and budgetary scenarios, portfolio management begins with a view of the optimal portfolio, subject to the CREOPM™ framework (or an equivalent method). Stated otherwise, once project categorization is performed, and risk analysis and integrated evaluations conducted, the portfolio is subjected to one or more optimization methodologies that provide a starting point for discussion regarding what projects and programs should or should not be included in the portfolio.

Using various budgetary and, if necessary, human resource constraints, different optimal portfolios are created for each investment scenario. The organization can now confidently engage in a rigorous discussion on portfolio selection with the full knowledge that it has been presented with portfolio scenarios that all lie on the efficient frontier, i.e., scenarios that are optimal. The advanced portfolio management function invests heavily in ongoing training of its portfolio management personnel and sets process and methodology standards across the enterprise. Portfolio updates are conducted on a quarterly basis within the organization as monthly stage gate reviews provide ongoing decision making for projects and programs in the context of the portfolio.

Level 5: Center of Excellence

At the apex of the pyramid, the Center of Excellence (COE) represents the highest level of maturity that can be attained by a portfolio management function. The COE serves the role of leading the integration of strategic planning and optimal portfolio management. The head of the COE is regarded as a peer to the heads of strategic planning, financial management, and resource management.

Because strategic planning and portfolio management are so closely integrated, CREOPM™ (or its equivalent) is practiced seamlessly throughout the organization. The COE invests heavily in ongoing training of its portfolio management personnel and sets process and methodology standards across the enterprise. Individuals with a successful track record in the COE are sought out as leaders of strategic, project, program, and portfolio management staffing functions.

As in the case of advanced portfolio management, at the COE level, portfolio review is conducted on a quarterly basis within the organization as monthly stage gate reviews provide ongoing decision making for projects and programs in the context of the portfolio. Any organization that practices EPPM with this level of maturity is said to be doing so in an *optimized* manner.

9.1.2 Project Portfolio Management Competencies

While the five levels described above are real-world representations of what the authors have encountered, in order to develop a viable detailed CMM for EPPM and put together an action plan to improve an organization's EPPM capabilities, it is necessary to measure an organization's maturity level across a spectrum of EPPM competencies. The competencies range from a strategic understanding of an enterprise's assets to the underlying processes and people implications, as well as the fundamental technical capabilities associated with analysis, tools, and technologies.

An organization's readiness can then be assessed by determining the maturity level for each of the competencies and using these to effectively gauge the overall maturity level of the organization. There are four primary EPPM competency domains: Strategy, Process, People (Organization), and Technology. Individual sub-competencies in each domain should be measured to determine the maturity level for that competency. Key questions corresponding to every individual competency within the four domains are outlined below, the response to which will determine the appropriate level of maturity in that competency for an organization.

Strategy Competency Domain

- **Strategic alignment:** Are all the initiatives, projects, and capabilities undertaken by an organization assessed to ensure that they are aligned with the enterprise's strategic goals?
- **Business case development:** What is the organization's approach to developing business cases for projects/capabilities?
- **Business planning and strategic planning:** Are there functional linkages in place to organizational planning activities on which portfolio management depends for inputs and to which it generates outputs?
- **Value realization:** Do value realization results influence the strategy development process, i.e. is the value of project outcomes and its input to business strategy actively managed?
- **Collaboration:** How are inter-project dependencies and cross-functional initiatives across divisions managed?

Process Competency Domain

- **Project selection:** How are projects selected at an enterprise level to optimize the portfolio investment? Is selection done in order that only the most valuable projects are authorized? Are underperforming projects actively killed and resources reallocated?
- **Decision making:** What decision criteria are used to select projects? Are the criteria well established and aligned with strategic objectives? Does that process allow for challenging project data related to benefit, risk, cost, and time in order to ensure clarity and consistency for decision making?
- **Process standards:** Is the project portfolio management process integrated with the strategic planning process? Is the project portfolio management process continuous and distinct from the annual planning and budgeting process? Does the portfolio management process follow the industry's best practices, such as the Stage-Gate™ process, throughout the enterprise?
- **Portfolio review:** Does a portfolio review process exist in the organization? Is there a portfolio review board that manages the EPPM operations, policies, and procedures? Who comprises the portfolio review board? Are there periodic reviews of the projects in the portfolio, and are key decisions made during the review?
- **Portfolio metrics and process improvement:** Do portfolio metrics play a role in strategic planning, and how are they related to other organizational metrics? Is the portfolio management practice routinely reviewed and analyzed for continuous improvement? Is there a process improvement plan in place?

People Competency Domain

- **Organizational structure:** Is there an enterprise portfolio management office in place? What is its reporting level? Are there organizational structures in place in every division to ensure divisional portfolio management representation and responsibilities?
- **Organizational capabilities:** What are the competencies of employees in the organization with respect to portfolio management?
- **Executive support:** What is the level of recognition of portfolio management, and what is the associated sponsorship, support, or buy-in by the executive management team?
- **Resource management:** What is the organization's competency with respect to resource forecasting, planning, and allocation?
- **Communication and presentation:** Are the right stakeholders in place to enable decision making at the highest levels of the organization by communicating analyses in a manner that both fulfills and challenges strategic and financial objectives? Are decisions communicated throughout the organization?

Technology Competency Domain

- **Tools:** Is there an integrated suite of tools that support the portfolio management discipline, and are the tool capabilities improved as required?

- **Data quality:** What is the quality of the data used in the portfolio management process?
- **Reporting:** What are the reporting capabilities of the integrated portfolio management process?

9.1.3 Maturity Level Guidelines for Competency Domains

For each of the individual competencies in the Strategy, Process, People, and Technology domains, the organization's maturity level can be assessed, based on the guidelines provided in Tables 9-1 through 9-4.

The appropriate maturity level for each competency in a domain can be assigned using the model outlined, and the overall maturity level in a domain can be determined as the average score of the individual competencies. While there is a reasonable chance for some subjectivity in determining the maturity level, due to the somewhat qualitative nature of the CMM model, it nevertheless provides a framework for temporal self-assessment, an objective approach to which can best help organizations improve their overall EPPM competencies. Illustrative charts such as the ones outlined in Figures 9-2 and 9-3 can provide a visual reference which organizations can use to establish a baseline of their current capabilities.

9.1.4 Application of CMM for EPPM—Points to Ponder

Using this model as a benchmark, organizations can adopt the four-step approach outlined in Figure 9-4 to achieve a desired level of competency in EPPM.

To complete a thorough assessment of their current maturity level in EPPM, organizations can use the CMM framework outlined in this chapter. An assessment of the requisite level of maturity is not a one-time effort; rather, organizations must use the results of the first assessment as a baseline so that all initiatives aimed at enhancing their capabilities in EPPM can be measured. Periodic assessments using the CMM framework can help enterprises keep track of their progress in their march towards EPPM success.

Many organizations typically do not have a wide variance in maturity levels across competencies. In other words, it is unlikely that an organization that is at a Level 2 maturity in project selection, within the Process competency domain, will be at Level 5 maturity in collaboration or value realization within the Strategy competency domain. This is because each individual competency is intricately intertwined with the others.

For the same reasons, it is largely impractical for an organization to aspire to attain Level 5 maturity in one competency, while choosing to remain at Level 1 or Level 2 maturity in another competency. Attempting to do so can often nullify the benefit that can be obtained from reaching a certain maturity level in one competency. It is also unrealistic for an organization to aspire to achieve an overall maturity Level 5 within a short time period, say within 1-2 years of starting out from Level 1 or 2.

Table 9-1 EPPM maturity levels in the Strategy competency domain

Competency	Level 1 (Ad-hoc)	Level 2 (Basic)	Level 3 (Standard)	Level 4 (Advanced)	Level 5 (COE)
Strategic Alignment	Projects are not linked to enterprise's goals.	Some divisions understand that strategic alignment is necessary & comply.	Strategic alignment is a key driver for portfolio mix in all divisions.	Divisions leverage defined parameters to align portfolio & perform "what-if" portfolio scenarios.	All initiatives are continuously assessed & portfolio is optimized to ensure that they meet strategic goals.
Business Case Development	Projects are proposed and executed without a business case; new requirements can lead to new projects not officially authorized.	Business case development is cursory; the focus is primarily on project milestones.	There is a standard approach to business case development for each proposed project.	Standard business case development incorporates rigorous risk assessment as part of the process.	Risk management, target capability profile ranges, investment scenarios, & launch strategies are incorporated in business case development.
Business Planning & Strategic Planning	Non-existent.	Linkages established in some divisions between divisional portfolio and investment decisions.	Portfolio planning linked to business planning across enterprise; working towards seamless integration with strategic planning.	Effective bridges have been built between strategic planning & portfolio planning; as well as between portfolio planning & lower level business planning.	Portfolio planning is seamlessly connected to higher level corporate planning & lower level business planning, ensuring that any changes in corporate objectives are translated into a modified portfolio strategy that is, in turn, supported by an efficient investment strategy.
Value Realization	Value Realization is not understood.	Value realization is defined.	Divisions plan for value realization & sustainability for strategic projects.	Value realization is measured, tracked, and baselined across divisions.	Value realization results influence the strategy process.
Collaboration	Projects initiated based on division needs and without regard to impact on other divisions.	Divisions recognize that identification of cross-functional synergies is necessary to achieve an enterprise focus	Synergies, overlaps, & conflicts in each division's portfolio are discovered & resolved; cross-functional opportunities identified	Projects are proactively reviewed to identify synergies, overlaps, and conflicts; divisions collaborate to resolve.	Portfolio planning, execution, and review performed as a partnership.

Table 9-2 EPPM maturity levels in the Process competency domain

Competency	Level 1 (Ad-hoc)	Level 2 (Basic)	Level 3 (Standard)	Level 4 (Advanced)	Level 5 (COE)
Project Selection	Tactical and ad hoc management of incoming project requests within divisions.	Some prioritization at division level; standard processes or tools do not exist.	Standardized data & processes used to prioritize projects in each division; visibility into division project prioritization results.	Project selection is based on optimization and prioritization. Level setting is performed for projects competing for resources.	All projects are evaluated at the enterprise level to optimize and prioritize portfolios leveraging portfolio analysis (short & near term) & scenario analysis (near & long term) to achieve strategic & financial goals.
Decision Making	Projects are not selected according to well-defined and set criteria.	Criteria exist for making decisions on projects, but these are focused on the project rather than on what is required to achieve it successfully.	Projects are categorized by a set of common criteria which are established for making decisions for selecting projects.	Categories of portfolio components are established; techniques in decision analysis leveraged for quantifying the integrated value of ranges of discovery and development of projects.	Categories of portfolio components are established; decision analysis techniques leveraged for quantifying the integrated value of ranges of discovery and development of projects. Includes risk decomposition and analysis, value, time, cost range estimation, & decision tree analysis.
Process Standards	There are few if any processes or procedures available concerning portfolio management.	There is some effort underway to establish a portfolio management process at a divisional level; no standard PPM approach in the organization.	A process is in place to submit a proposal for consideration and enables costs, risks & benefits of projects to be evaluated.	EPPM is a separate process from the annual planning & budgeting process, so that it is done continuously, rather than once every year. Processes established for decision making & selection.	The EPPM process is integrated with the strategic planning process; investments, organizational capability, & capacity are optimized with programs & projects.
Portfolio Review	Non-existent.	No comprehensive portfolio review; project review process exists, but is cursory & milestone based.	An ongoing review is conducted of projects in the portfolio; projects may be deselected or terminated as appropriate. A formal portfolio review board comprising both portfolio management personnel and subject matter experts exists.	In addition to all the competencies for Level 3 portfolio review, the portfolio is continually reviewed & changed as needed to produce the highest returns; review examines projects' significance strategically & their value. Further, policies and procedures are established and periodically reviewed and modified.	In addition to the Level 4 portfolio review competencies, the portfolio management environment is continually reviewed & adjusted to ensure its alignment with corporate strategy.
Portfolio Metrics & Process Improvement	Project metrics are tracked by individuals and not shared within divisions.	Standard portfolio management metrics defined within divisions; some divisions capture project cost, risks, and benefits metrics.	Standard portfolio management metrics tracked across the organization.	Portfolio management metrics are baselined, benchmarked, and used to drive portfolio decisions.	Continuous improvement to PPM is the norm; portfolio metrics provide input to strategic planning; metrics used to evaluate the effectiveness of portfolio management & are related to other metrics in the organization.

Table 9-3 EPPM maturity levels in the People competency domain

Competency	Level 1 (Ad-hoc)	Level 2 (Basic)	Level 3 (Standard)	Level 4 (Advanced)	Level 5 (COE)
Organizational Structure	A portfolio management office (PMO) has not been established in the organization.	PMOs established in each division; overall PMO framework established for enterprise view.	PMOs work together to define a maturity model, share knowledge and best practices, and develop enterprise standards	Enterprise portfolio management office (EPMO) established. Cross-divisional training and collaboration occur among divisional PMOs; enterprise portfolio manager reports to executive team member i.e. COO/CFO/CSO.	EPMO established. Flexible, collaborative, mentoring culture; processes easily adapted to change; enterprise portfolio manager is a member of the executive team reporting to CEO.
Organizational Capabilities	A PMO has not been established in the organization. Few if any people have been trained in the concepts of portfolio management.	PMO members begin to understand their specific organization; a limited number of people have been trained in portfolio management.	PMO members provide suggestions to help manage the portfolio & increase the organization's maturity; each person understands the priority of the portfolio component they are assigned to.	PMO members measure performance and proactively provide analysis of portfolio data and suggestions for improvement; enterprise portfolio manager actively manages portfolio to meet changing business needs; prepares & issues process improvement plans for PPM.	PMO members provide analysis, enable maturity, and are looked to as subject matter experts in their divisions and across the company; people throughout the organization understand the portfolio management process followed and why it is being used.
Executive Support	There is basic awareness of portfolio management among the executives.	Some basic steps have been taken by executives to ramp up a portfolio management culture.	There is an executive sponsor or champion for portfolio management in the enterprise.	The organization's executives recognize the value of portfolio management & its components.	The enterprise portfolio manager is a member of the executive team. Divisions have portfolio managers reporting to the enterprise portfolio manager.
Resource Management	Tactical and ad hoc management of incoming resource requests within divisions.	Resource planning performed within each division; no standard tools for managing resources.	Resource planning performed within divisions using common tools and processes; optimized resource planning established for new initiatives within each division.	Divisions collaborate to allocate resources for maximum portfolio benefit; scenario ("what-if") analyses are performed based on changes to the portfolio.	Resource planning is performed; resource needs are forecasted in alignment with the strategy.
Communication & Presentation	Ineffective communication that may result in duplication of efforts across divisions. Decisions are not communicated effectively.	The need for a communications plan for portfolio management is recognized & the organization is working towards standardizing communication.	A communications management plan has been prepared and is used for portfolio management.	Decisions are communicated throughout the organization, with open communication being the norm.	The organization's culture is collaborative & communicative. People are encouraged at all levels to submit ideas to foster continuous improvement.

Table 9-4 EPPM maturity levels in the Technology competency domain

Competency	Level 1 (Ad-hoc)	Level 2 (Basic)	Level 3 (Standard)	Level 4 (Advanced)	Level 5 (COE)
Tools	Projects are tracked by individuals; no enterprise-wide visibility.	Projects are tracked in division-specific tool; no enterprise-wide visibility.	Project data integrated into a single tool across divisions for enterprise-wide visibility.	Uses standard tool; tool provides valuable and accurate view of overall portfolio, with the system set up to contain information across all business initiatives.	Tool suites are integrated & tool capabilities are continuously improved to meet the organization's needs. The portfolio management system interfaces with other tools in the organization.
Data Quality	Data is not captured formally. There is no inventory of all the current & past projects.	Division-level focus on data capture and data quality.	Standard data captured; data quality levels are defined and used to improve data.	Data quality meets reporting requirements and provides accurate view of portfolio.	Data quality is monitored; potential problems are proactively addressed.
Reporting	Basic reports are not available on the organization's projects.	Project reporting is standardized in some divisions.	There is a standardized approach to reporting on projects in the portfolio, across the enterprise.	Systems are available to support portfolio management with accurate & timely data to show performance across all projects as well as infrastructure investments; a digital dashboard is set up & maintained regularly.	Systems are available to support portfolio management with accurate & timely data to show performance across all projects as well as infrastructure investments; a digital dashboard is set up & maintained regularly. Reporting features include provisions for trend analyses & a balanced scorecard perspective.

Maturity Level in the Strategy Competency Domain

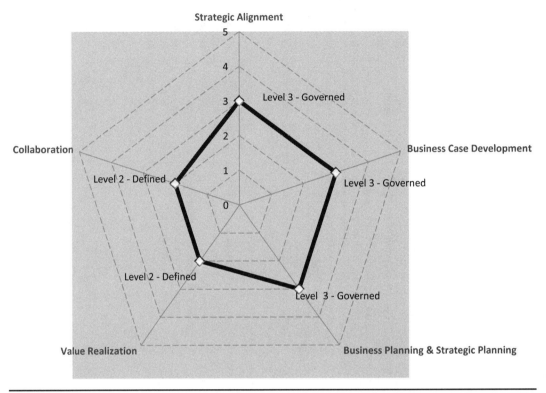

Figure 9-2   Illustration of maturity level in the Strategy competency domain

Even more important to note is that achieving Level 5 maturity may be an unrealistic goal for many organizations. Each enterprise should determine the requisite level of EPPM maturity that is practically achievable within the confines of its organizational and cultural predispositions, since the organizational change management effort in achieving the desired state can be non-trivial. Therefore, it is recommended that organizations should be realistic in their goal setting toward achieving a desired state and prioritize the competencies that they want to improve, working toward achieving goals in measurable and incremental steps, rather than employing a "big bang" approach.

Finally, many organizations fall prey to the notion that a tool can fix every problem for a variety reasons from lack of awareness to slick marketing by vendors. While tools can no doubt aid organizations in improving their capabilities, they are not the panacea for a successful EPPM discipline in an organization. A comprehensive approach to improving capabilities across all competency domains in iterative steps in a prioritized manner, with periodic measurements and assessments of progress, is the approach recommended for organizations seeking to improve their maturity level in EPPM. The remainder of this chapter outlines good portfolio management practices for achieving the desired state of EPPM maturity.

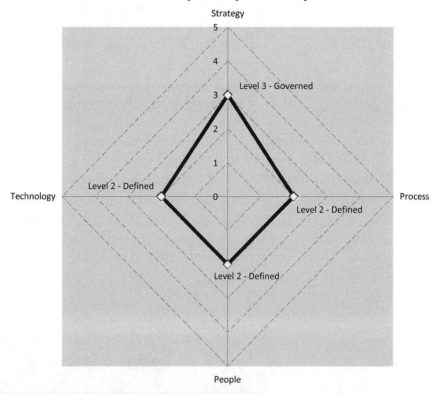

Figure 9-3 Illustration of overall capability maturity in EPPM

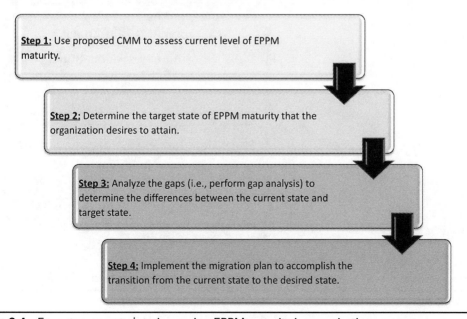

Figure 9-4 Four-step approach to improving EPPM maturity in organizations

9.2 Portfolio Analysis and Presentation

When conducted within the appropriate frame and scope, effective portfolio analysis can lead to the creation of tremendous insights that result in good decision making. Portfolio analysis generally fulfills the needs of three organizational imperatives (see Figure 9-5):

- Formal annual or semi-annual portfolio review—consolidated analysis of the viability and progress of the portfolio in the context of strategic and business plans.
- Marginal portfolio analysis to determine the best resource reallocation as projects are terminated or succeed into the marketplace.
- Portfolio impact analysis created by stage gate reviews as projects enter, progress, or are terminated from the pipeline.

Therefore, what distinguishes an effective portfolio analysis from an ineffective one? To be sure, what works for one organization may not be embraced by the culture of another. Nevertheless, common features of both types of portfolio analysis exist in all

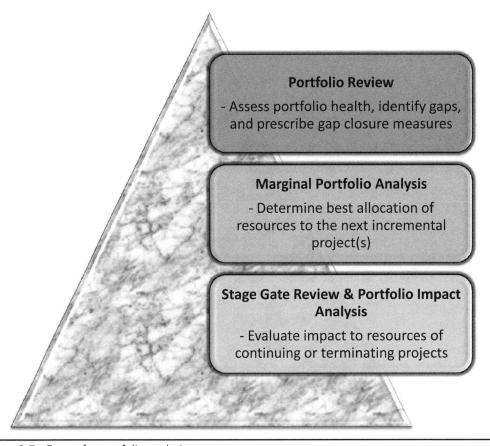

Figure 9-5 Frame for portfolio analysis

organizations (Figure 9-6). Once the decision frame is established, the primary tasks of portfolio management are to:

- Gather and validate necessary data and information from subject matter experts.
- Conduct a consolidated, integrated assessment of the current state of the enterprise portfolio on both a potential and risk-adjusted basis.
- Assess the future state of the portfolio in the context of strategic and business goals on both a potential and risk-adjusted basis.
- Determine the magnitude of the value creation gaps that exist on an annual basis.
- Generate insights from the analysis pertaining to portfolio strengths, weaknesses, opportunities, and threats, and make appropriate recommendations to senior management to fill identified gaps and to grow the enterprise business.

No portfolio analysis should begin or end without an affirmation of what the organization is trying to attain and why. This is necessary to ensure that the strategic imperatives of the organization are embedded within the composition of the portfolio (Figure 9-7). Similar to the Must Do, May Do, and Won't Do categorization of projects described in Chapter 4, the strategic intent of an organization can be reinforced by a clear articulation of its vision and reflected by both the composition of the portfolio and the resources necessary to support that vision.

It is strategic intent that sets the stage for effective portfolio management that is in alignment with who/what the organization wants to become within different segments

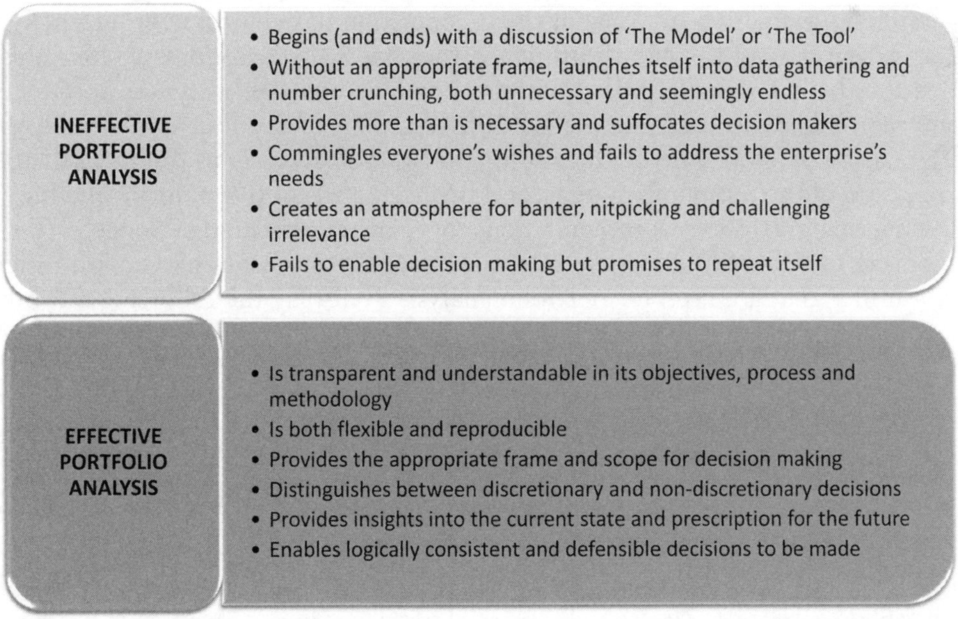

INEFFECTIVE PORTFOLIO ANALYSIS	• Begins (and ends) with a discussion of 'The Model' or 'The Tool' • Without an appropriate frame, launches itself into data gathering and number crunching, both unnecessary and seemingly endless • Provides more than is necessary and suffocates decision makers • Commingles everyone's wishes and fails to address the enterprise's needs • Creates an atmosphere for banter, nitpicking and challenging irrelevance • Fails to enable decision making but promises to repeat itself
EFFECTIVE PORTFOLIO ANALYSIS	• Is transparent and understandable in its objectives, process and methodology • Is both flexible and reproducible • Provides the appropriate frame and scope for decision making • Distinguishes between discretionary and non-discretionary decisions • Provides insights into the current state and prescription for the future • Enables logically consistent and defensible decisions to be made

Figure 9-6   Ineffective and effective portfolio analysis

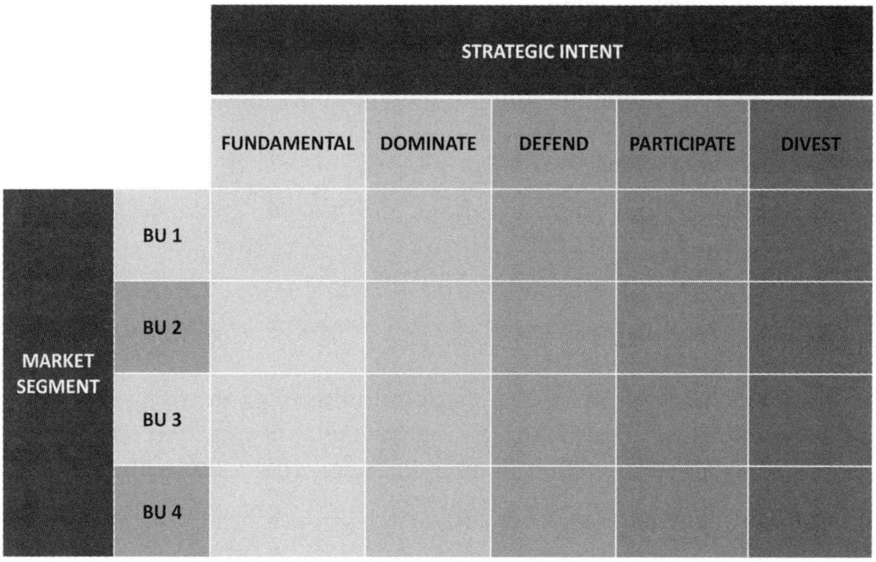

Figure 9-7   Strategic intent and market segmentation of the portfolio

of its business. Organizations that are hesitant to articulate this level of strategic intent—including those that pride themselves in being "opportunistic"—generally encounter tremendous internal resistance when disproportionate resource allocation decisions across business units (BUs) need to be made.

A good starting point for a portfolio review is to examine the strengths, weaknesses, opportunities, and threats (SWOT) faced by the portfolio (Figure 9-8). This provides an overarching strategic view of what the organization has control over internally and to what extent it may be able to influence the external environment. Once this assessment has been conducted, the frame for portfolio analysis becomes more focused in that recommendations can be placed in the context of the four dimensions of the SWOT analysis. A good rule of thumb for portfolio analysis is to orient itself to the bigger picture of the temporal strategic and financial goals of the strategic and business plans, rendering portfolio recommendations more meaningful and actionable.

According to Tufte (2001), there are four main categories of charts, with differing levels of utility, that are used for portfolio analysis to display the following attributes:

- Quantitative patterns and relationships (e.g., histograms, Pareto charts)
- Non-quantitative interrelationships (e.g., process flow, influence diagrams)
- Preciseness of information and ease of reference (e.g., spreadsheets, frequency charts)
- Conceptual and comparative relationships (e.g., business matrices, Venn diagrams)

While a wide spectrum of graphical analyses is available from within these categories with which to present portfolio information, it is important to secure from decision makers a clear sense of what types of analytic output they prefer and to understand

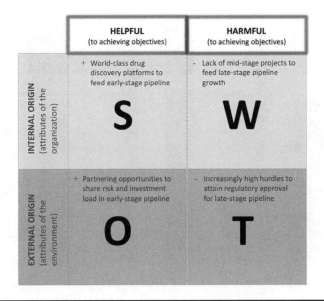

	HELPFUL (to achieving objectives)	**HARMFUL** (to achieving objectives)
INTERNAL ORIGIN (attributes of the organization)	+ World-class drug discovery platforms to feed early-stage pipeline **S**	– Lack of mid-stage projects to feed late-stage pipeline growth **W**
EXTERNAL ORIGIN (attributes of the environment)	+ Partnering opportunities to share risk and investment load in early-stage pipeline **O**	– Increasingly high hurdles to attain regulatory approval for late-stage pipeline **T**

Figure 9-8   SWOT analysis of portfolio

the types of graphical representations to which they are most attuned. Cooper, Edgett, and Kleinschmidt (2001) have described a wide number of graphical displays that are normally used for portfolio analysis. By far, the most popular charts are represented by risk and reward dimensions where risk is measured quantitatively or qualitatively as a probability of achieving technical or commercial success; reward is generally measured by several metrics including NPV, IRR, ROI, and peak sales. Where three-dimensional graphs are used, cost (defined as the cost to develop a product) is by far the most widely selected metric to complement the risk and reward dimensions.

At the heart of portfolio management is an understanding of the robustness of an organization's pipeline in meeting its temporal goals. The results of pipeline modeling (i.e., projecting how many projects are required to feed new product launches over time) can be displayed in tabular form, as shown in Figure 9-9, for a drug discovery and development organization. Armed with this information, an organization may be well positioned to understand which levers of risk and cost it can control to increase its throughput of products on an annual basis. In this case of a high-risk pharmaceutical and biotechnology portfolio, one is able to display the number of projects required in any given phase of discovery and development in order to create a single product launch.

Since a single product launch is unlikely to support the growth objectives of most organizations, Table 9-5 allows for comparisons of the number of projects required in every phase of discovery and development to support multiple product launches. Given the organization's annual goals of new product launches, one can document the probabilities of success of each project in the portfolio—derived from industry benchmarks or the organization's own history—to determine the gaps between goals and aggregate risk-adjusted launches.

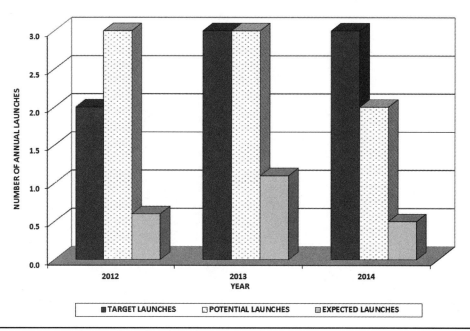

Figure 9-9 Potential annual product launches

Table 9-5 Pipeline modeling

Average of BUs	Discovery	Preclinical	Phase 1	Phase 2a	Phase 2b	Phase 3	FDA
p(Success to next phase)							
p(Success to launch)							
Average # of projects to achieve > = 1 launch							
Average p(Achieving > = 1 launch)							
Average # of projects for 80% probability of achieving > = 1 launch							
Average # of projects for 90% probability of achieving > = 1 launch							

From this chart, one can see that the risk load of the portfolio is such that there is a low likelihood of meeting the annual goal of new product launches from 2012 to 2014, therefore suggesting that the organization must make external investments (e.g., licensing, acquisition) in projects that are close to regulatory approval. Beginning in 2012 with a goal of launching two new products, the portfolio has three potential launches that will only materialize if all three projects succeed.

However, on a risk-adjusted basis, only 0.6 launches are expected. Clearly, partial launches will not occur as the range of potential launches is 0, 1, 2, or 3, but when the individual probabilities of success of each project are calculated, the aggregate risk-adjusted number of launches is 0.6. By 2014, the organization faces a real crisis in that it does not have a sufficient number of projects to meet the launch goal of three new products in that year. In fact, of the two projects that are capable of being launched as products in 2014, less than 0.5 will be launched on a risk-adjusted basis.

Although the number of risk-adjusted product launches can be calculated for a portfolio, the use of simulation techniques aids an understanding of the probability of meeting annual product launch goals (Figure 9-10). In this case, from a range of 0-3 potential new products, although the average number of risk-adjusted products launched in 2012 is 0.60, there is only a 48.7% probability that one or more product launches will take place.

A necessary next step in portfolio analysis is to evaluate the consolidated portfolio of products (often referred to as base business) and projects on both a potential and risk-adjusted basis as described in Chapter 6. To facilitate this analysis, sales forecasts of all products and projects are consolidated over the timeline defined by the strategic plan and in the context of the organization's overarching growth goals (Figures 9-11a and b).

Note that BUs 1 and 3 carry a low risk load as evidenced by the similarities in annual sales between the potential and risk-adjusted values, while the difference between potential and risk-adjusted sales is significant for BUs 2 and 4, suggesting a much higher risk load. More importantly, the annual sales growth goal is easily exceeded annually when viewed from a potential sales perspective; on the other hand, beginning in 2013, the target growth goal is underachieved by the current portfolio of products and projects on a risk-adjusted basis. As stated in Chapter 5, an analysis of risk-adjusted portfolio growth provides a far more realistic representation of portfolio viability than a simple view of potential growth, as it brings into question what options exist to fortify the portfolio over a multi-period basis.

Once different scenarios are envisaged and strategic options created, it is often helpful to examine the portfolio over three probabilistic dimensions: (a) exceeding a goal, (b) not underperforming against a low threshold goal, and (c) not exceeding a defined

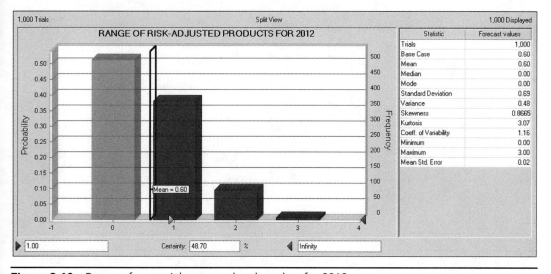

Figure 9-10 Range of potential new product launches for 2012

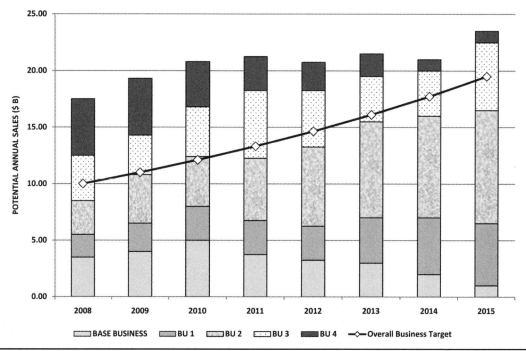

Figure 9-11a   Consolidated portfolio analysis with respect to strategic plan goals—potential growth

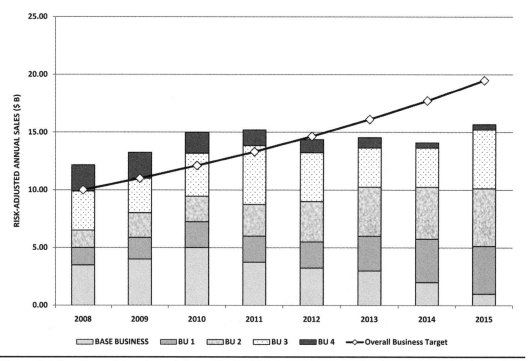

Figure 9-11b   Consolidated portfolio analysis with respect to strategic plan goals—risk-adjusted growth

budget (Figure 9-12). In this figure, while Portfolio A has the highest probability of exceeding $20B in value and the highest probability that it will not be lower than $15B, it has the highest chance of exceeding $5B in cost.

On the other hand, although Portfolio F has the lowest risk of exceeding a budget of $5B, it has the greatest chance of realizing less than $15B, as well as the lowest chance of exceeding $20B. As is often the case with portfolio analysis, few portfolio strategies result in an unambiguously dominant choice on all portfolio dimensions.

The full distribution of outcomes of a portfolio strategy can be obtained from a simulation of inputs and shown in a cumulative distribution function (Figure 9-13). Although the mean value of a strategy may be to exceed $20B in top line sales, this portfolio could earn as little as $17.76B or as much as $21.88B, with a likelihood of just greater than 21% of exceeding a stated goal of $20B. Especially in cases where no one portfolio strategy clearly dominates another (i.e., enhanced upside is tempered by greater downside), simulated portfolio cumulative distribution functions provide a full breadth of information regarding value and the probability of achieving any goal within that range of values.

An annual trend analysis of portfolio value can provide important insights regarding the sustainability of value creation from its BU segments (Figure 9-14). In this case, the growth potential of different BUs can be visualized over a typical short-term strategic plan. BU 2, for example, shows tremendous growth in risk-adjusted NPV over a five-year period, while BUs 3 and 4 require an influx of projects and resources to boost their value creation over the 2014-2015 time horizon.

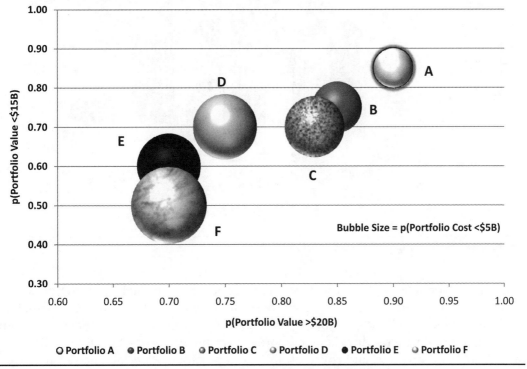

Figure 9-12 Analysis of portfolio strategies along three risk dimensions

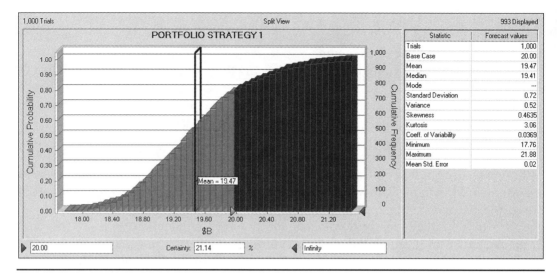

Figure 9-13   Simulation analysis of portfolio strategies

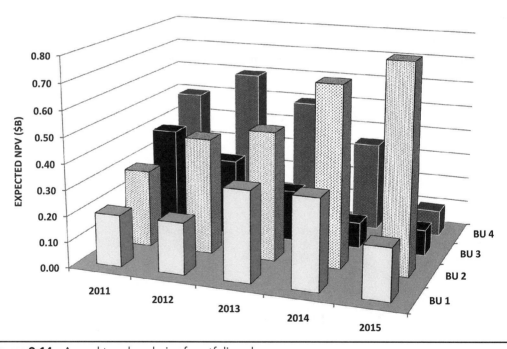

Figure 9-14   Annual trend analysis of portfolio value

Finally, a portfolio waterfall analysis represents a longitudinal overview of where value has been added and lost from the portfolio (Figure 9-15). Here, approximately $1.5B of risk-adjusted NPV has been added to the portfolio over a calendar year from a combination of new product launches, project terminations, assets that were licensed in and out, sold projects, and royalties. In fact, a portfolio waterfall analysis has been

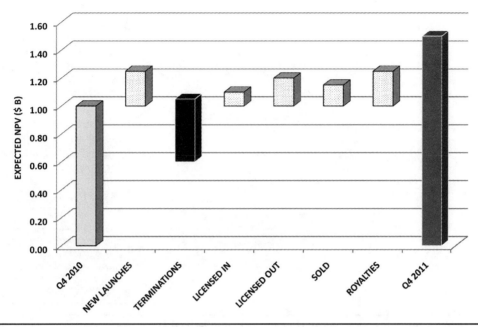

Figure 9-15 Portfolio waterfall analysis

used as a litmus test of the value added to the portfolio by a portfolio management discipline itself!

9.3 Risk Management

The term *risk management* should not imply that all risks can be managed. Rather, risks that are operational elements (e.g., completion of a project on time or within budget) are largely controllable in nature and can be managed. Some risks can be effectively nullified by adding greater resources or selecting a low-cost service provider. On the other hand, risks such as drug efficacy and drug safety are largely uncontrollable states of nature for which one may only be able to create plans to mitigate their impact, if these risks in fact do occur (Figure 9-16). What is really being managed, pertaining to the efficacy and safety of a drug, is not the risks themselves (they will occur whether we want them or not) but rather their impact. It is therefore essential to decouple the term *risk* from its impact or consequence.

As discussed in Chapter 5, the risk of an event happening can be measured by its probability of occurrence, while its impact or consequence can be measured by the uncertainty or range of possible outcomes. To take this one step further, the terms "positive and negative risk" are not embellished in this discussion. Rather, if risks occur, there can be positive and negative impacts or consequences.

As an example, the drug Viagra was developed by Pfizer for the treatment of hypertension and angina pectoris, but there was a risk that the drug would prove to be ineffective for the treatment of one or both diseases. In fact, the risk materialized and the drug was found to be inefficacious for the treatment of angina pectoris, although

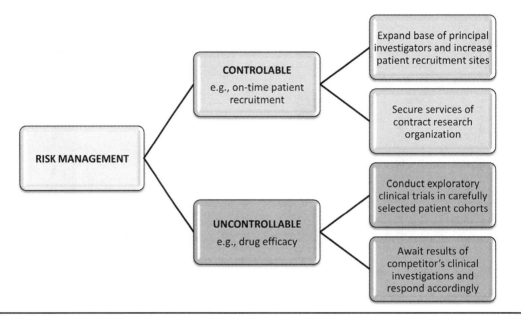

Figure 9-16   Management of controllable and uncontrollable risks

it later became successful for the treatment of pulmonary arterial hypertension (but not for general hypertension). During the conduct of clinical trials for both diseases, it was found that the drug had a noticeable side effect in that it induced penile erections. This impact to or consequence of taking the medication led to the successful development of the drug for erectile dysfunction. What would conventionally be viewed in this example as "positive risk" (penile erections) can be considered as a positive impact or consequence. To be sure, the positive impact of the drug in erectile dysfunction is not the result of the risk of its success or failure in hypertension or angina pectoris; it is simply a consequence of having taken the drug in the first place.

It is easy to find examples of impact or consequences that are tied directly to the occurrence of risks. One such example is the risk of the next major earthquake in the city of San Francisco. If or when this risk manifests itself, its impact or consequence could be devastating to the city, ranging anywhere from power outages, buckled streets, and loss of life to catastrophic loss of the magnitude experienced in 1906. Further, although widely used in the project management literature, the term *risk impact* is not used here to describe project, program, or portfolio risk.

Good project risk management is a necessary but insufficient prerequisite for effective program and portfolio risk management. Why is this so? In the pursuit of "the greater good for the greater number," portfolio risk management may sometimes require that resources be diverted from one or more successful projects within a program to a different program or sub-portfolio to enable the attainment of overall portfolio goals. At the portfolio level, therefore, risk management can be regarded as the deliberate attempt to balance the risks associated with enabling the portfolio to meet its temporal goals—short term, mid term, and long term.

To best understand the risks associated with achieving these goals, an organization needs to carefully evaluate potential opportunities available (Figure 9-17). These opportunities generally range from internal discovery concepts that provide value in the long term (and therefore at high risk) to wholesale external acquisitions in the short term (and therefore at comparatively low risk to the acquiring organization).

One of the difficulties in maintaining a balance of risk and value across the portfolio throughout time horizons resides with the perennial portfolio challenge of maximizing short-term value without compromising mid- and long-term value. Stated otherwise, to ensure that there is sufficient investment in mid- and long-term opportunities, an organization must be willing to forego short-term value, for example, by not pursuing one or more product line extensions (where there is relatively low risk) in favor of allocating those resources towards innovative projects (where there is comparatively higher risk) in the hope of generating competitive products in the long term (Figure 9-18).

So, what does a balanced portfolio look like, and how does an organization know when its portfolio is balanced? To answer this question, it is perhaps better to first address what a balanced portfolio is *not* (Figure 9-19). Far too often, and in the absence of explicit goals, portfolios are deemed to have attained a state of balance if one or more of the following occurs in a matrix of risk and return (or value):

- The portfolio is populated more or less equally by high- and low-risk and high- and low-value projects.

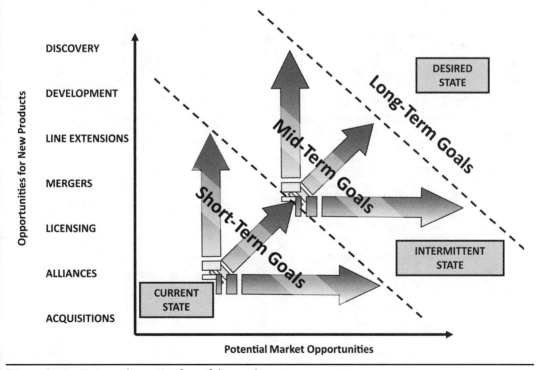

Figure 9-17   Temporal pursuit of portfolio goals

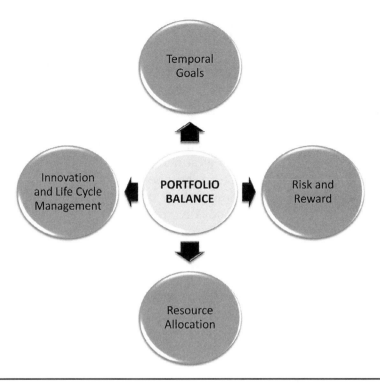

Figure 9-18   Common elements of portfolio balance

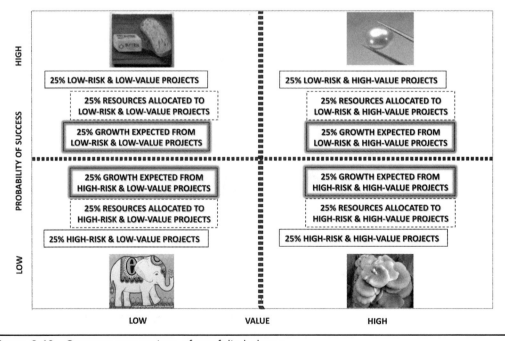

Figure 9-19   Common perceptions of portfolio balance

- Equal resources are allocated across high- and low-risk and high- and low-value projects.
- Growth is expected to be generated, more or less equally, from each of the segments of high- and low-risk and high- and low-value projects.

Portfolio risk management requires continual, diligent attention to the progress of all projects and programs so that informed judgments can be made regarding how best the constellation of assets in the portfolio is likely to meet its temporal goals. As stated earlier, what is particularly important is an organization's discipline in conducting marginal portfolio decision making, where freed-up resources are best allocated to new or ongoing projects and programs. Once this is done, the ultimate risk management question becomes: What is the probability that the portfolio will meet the goal(s) of the enterprise?

Not surprisingly, several graphical techniques exist for displaying the status of a portfolio along many dimensions, the most popular being a combination of data pertaining to risk, value, and cost previously described in Chapter 5 (see Figure 9-20).

While it is tempting to argue that each quadrant displayed in Figure 9-20 should be populated by more or less equal numbers of projects, in the absence of clearly stated portfolio goals, this line of argumentation could be seriously flawed. Consider the situation being experienced by an organization that is concerned about its mid-term viability. In an effort to best position itself to meet its mid-term goals, it has investigated the relative contributions of each of its four BUs to specific value creation metrics (NPs=new products, LEs=line extensions, NPV=net present value, ENPV=risk-adjusted NPV) and usage of different resources (DC=direct cost, FTE A/B/C=full time equivalent by Function A, B, and C) (see Figure 9-21).

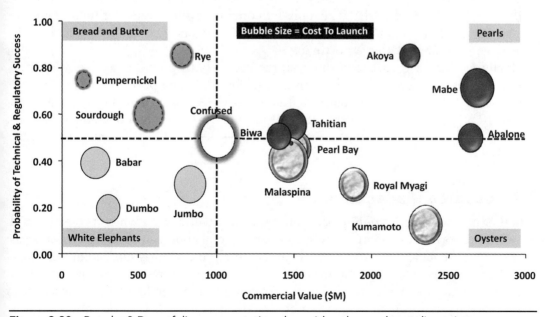

Figure 9-20   Popular 3-D portfolio representation along risk, value, and cost dimensions

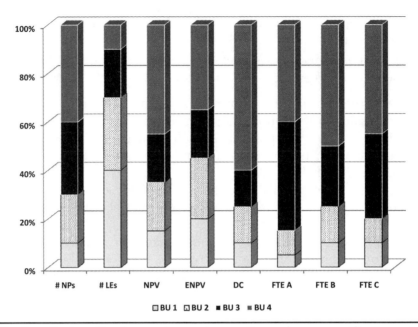

Figure 9-21   Contribution of business units to value creation and resource utilization metrics

From Figure 9-21, one can see the contributions of each of the BUs to NPV and ENPV and their corresponding consumption of budgetary and human resources over an aggregate period. Although BU 4 contributes significantly to NPV, its high risk load is reflected in the relatively smaller contribution to ENPV, while its consumption of DC is disproportionately high. On the other hand, BU 2 utilizes moderate levels of DC and FTEs A, B, and C while carrying a low risk load, as evidenced by its contributions to both NPV and ENPV. It is only by comparing these types of metrics to the contributions of an organization's BUs or sectors that one can determine if there is, indeed, good balance within a portfolio.

Finally, as discussed earlier in this chapter, use of both potential and risk-adjusted sales revenues as metrics to guide decision making regarding portfolio balance is recommended. Although the annual potential portfolio sales exceed the target growth rate of 10% (Figure 9-22a), a very different picture emerges when one adjusts potential sales revenues on the basis of the risk load of the portfolio in different years (Figure 9-22b).

9.4 Resource Management

Whether or not systems are in place to track who is working on which project(s) and for what proportion of an employee's time, the general consensus is that in most organizations, FTE data appears to be largely judgmental, suspiciously misleading, and subject to continuous revision. What makes FTE forecasting and resource management, in general, difficult undertakings? To begin with, resources generally come in two varieties—budgetary and human, which can be described as *fungible* (can be converted to a

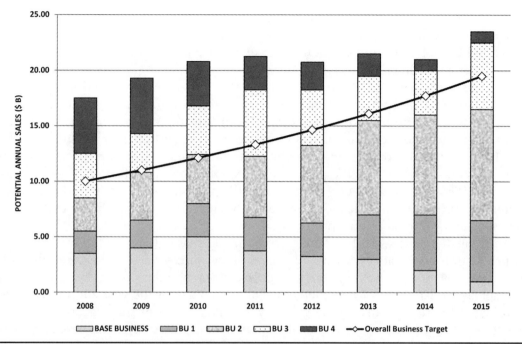

Figure 9-22a   Annual potential portfolio sales revenues

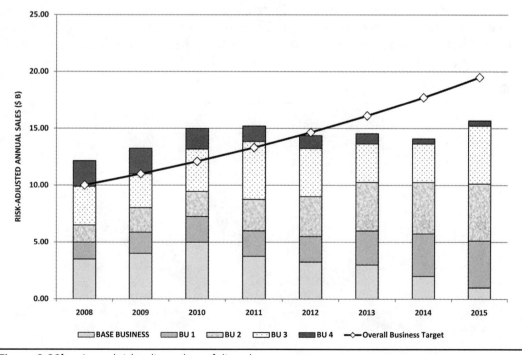

Figure 9-22b   Annual risk-adjusted portfolio sales revenues

common financial unit and could be moved from one project or program to another) and *non-fungible* (cannot be converted to a common unit, e.g., chemists cannot be converted to biologists, or a COBOL programmer cannot be used instead of a UNIX administrator), as described in Figure 9-23.

A primary challenge to all organizations in the area of resource management is to understand what proportions of budgetary and human resources, by functional specialty, are already committed to projects and programs that are in progress; only then can a clear assessment of available resources be made regarding their potential allocation to incremental projects and programs. Resource management is impacted by several factors that include: (a) the proportion of stable internal and constantly changing external FTEs, (b) the budget, (c) risks that affect whether or not an individual remains on a project for the planned duration of his/her time, and (d) timing that affects how long an FTE remains on a project.

Additionally, since several resources are normally shared (e.g., central services such as production and manufacturing), partial FTE resources need to be carefully estimated to prevent real and phantom bottlenecks from emerging along the value chain. Further, as unplanned projects emerge during the course of the year and projects are terminated for reasons that are largely beyond the control of the organization (e.g., uncontrollable risks), the ongoing challenge is to continue to find the best combination of incremental projects to invest in. Armed with the knowledge of what resources are available, it is healthy practice to re-optimize the portfolio at the margin, i.e., to address the question of what is the most efficient use of remaining available resources. Although most organizations tend to allocate marginal resources to projects that are next in the rank order, the discussion in Chapter 8 shows this to be a good but suboptimal practice. As the organization strives to balance its portfolio, attaining balanced resource management remains a full time preoccupation.

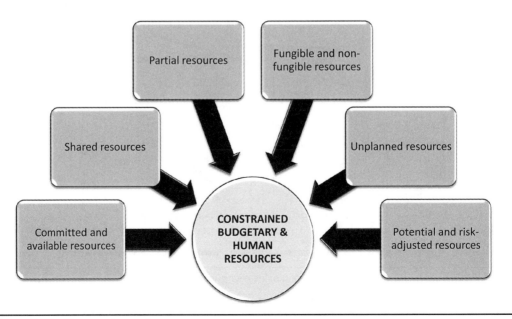

Figure 9-23 The spectrum of resource management issues

It is noteworthy that, for multi-phase or risky projects, human resources should be risk adjusted by functional specialty in the same way as budgetary dollars are. Otherwise, as resource plans are made for a calendar year, one can create the perception of resource bottlenecks and therefore undertake fewer projects and programs early on in the year. In the project example shown in Table 9-6, without risk adjustment, a total of 287 FTEs is required, whereas when phase-dependent risks are accounted for, a much lower number of 76.2 FTEs is required. As portfolios become populated by larger numbers of risky projects, it becomes increasingly important to plan for resource allocation on a risk-adjusted basis.

Resource demand and supply estimation is not an exacting science, but if not done well can lead to several problems that may include the following:

- Imagined resource constraints leading to unwarranted shelving of opportunities as well as faulty deployment in undertaking too many projects that compromise quality and increase operational risk.
- Unnecessary bottlenecks that can result in increased development and production cycles.
- Gaps between planned resource allocation and actual resource utilization.
- Lack of transparency in dealing with project attrition, project dependencies, and operational uncertainty (scope, time, cost).
- Inefficient resource utilization resulting in lower returns on opportunity investments.

On the other hand, when conducted well, resource management can yield several benefits that include:

- Efficient resource deployment and resource utilization.
- Effective planning of anticipated resource bottlenecks.
- Seamless updating of resource estimates as (a) milestones are passed, (b) new milestones are undertaken, and (c) significant events occur, e.g., unanticipated project reviews that warrant a formal resource revision.
- Obviating the necessity for major overhauls of project resource estimates that are often reflected in (a) annual business plan events and (b) continuous "organizational churn."

Table 9-6 Risk-adjustment of functional FTEs in a multi-phase project

Phase	Preclinical	Phase 1	Phase 2a	Phase 2b	Phase 3	Registration	Aggregate
p(Success) by phase	0.66	0.74	0.62	0.62	0.55	0.74	0.08
p(Success to next phase)		0.66	0.49	0.30	0.19	0.10	
Potential phase FTEs	6	12	25	40	200	4	287
Risk-adjusted phase FTEs	6.00	7.92	12.21	12.11	37.55	0.41	76.20

Despite rigorous resource demand and supply estimation, a plethora of events can occur during a calendar year, making the discipline a frustrating undertaking:

- "Too much success"—A seemingly great problem to have but which often leads to a continuous stream of project prioritizations, reprioritizations, and recategorization of projects in the portfolio. In addition, in an effort to undertake more projects than really can be afforded, resources are spread thinly to cover a larger spectrum of project investments
- "Too much failure"—Budgetary surpluses result that are generally not allowed to be carried over into the next year. Further, projects that could have been better resourced or included in the portfolio were not.
- Acquisition of external assets—Acquisitions may have been planned strategically but not operationally, resulting in forced delays or terminations of internal projects. It is here that the impact of constrained non-fungible resources is felt most.

Balanced resource management across the portfolio, therefore, is a combination of several elements (Figure 9-24). How should an organization optimally manage its constrained resources to ensure that it invests in the best combination of projects within its portfolio? Beginning with an understanding of the magnitude of the budgetary constraint along with a clear catalogue of functional roles, it is recommended that any of the optimization approaches described in Chapter 6 be adopted.

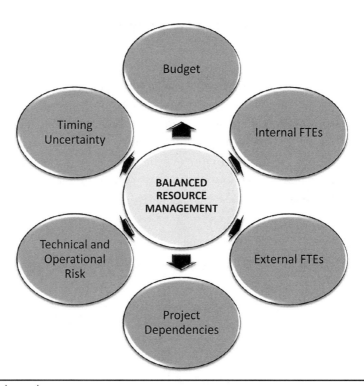

Figure 9-24   Balanced resource management

To this end, optimization can be performed in such a manner that it facilitates an examination of the impact to the organization's objectives of utilizing different combinations of internal and external FTEs under specified budgetary constraints, as shown in Table 9-7.

At a budgetary constraint of $1,000M, 8 of the 10 projects in the portfolio, which constitute the optimal portfolio that yields $10.0B, can be afforded with a requirement for 100, 125, and 150 FTEs belonging to Functions A, B, and C, respectively. If the organization wishes to pursue this optimal portfolio, it needs to address how many of each FTE function will need to be sourced externally, given its internal FTE constraints. Alternatively, if the cost of sourcing external FTEs is prohibitive, a tighter budget constraint of, say $900M may allow the organization to pursue 6 of its 10 projects (omitting Projects A, B, G, J) because these maximize the ENPV objective while allowing sufficient funds to hire external FTEs.

Clearly, any or all of the three FTE functions can be used as constraints in searching for the optimal portfolio solution, but since the feasible region is progressively narrowed by the inclusion of additional constraints, it is often easier to treat the budget as a hard constraint while allowing for the possibility of increasing FTE availability by the use of excess budgetary resources to invest in the necessary external resources. The template shown in Table 9-7 can also be used to track different metrics (e.g., sales revenues, gross profit, NPV, etc.) at varying constraint levels if they are not a part of the portfolio objective(s). If they are, then a more complex optimization solution such as goal programming can be used.

Finally, depending on the choice of portfolio strategy, it is possible to estimate the likelihood of exceeding one or more FTE constraints where the external supply of such functional specialization may be severely limited. As demonstrated in Figure

Table 9-7 Resource management optimization template

ENPV OBJECTIVE	$7.7 B	$8.0 B	$8.3 B	$9.0 B	$9.3 B	$10.0 B
BUDGET CONSTRAINT	$750 M	$800 M	$850 M	$900 M	$950 M	$1,000 M
UNUSED BUDGET	$1 M	$4 M	$2 M	$11 M	$7 M	$5 M
REQUIRED FTEs FUNCTION A	83	87	90	94	98	100
REQUIRED FTEs FUNCTION B	111	117	119	120	124	125
REQUIRED FTEs FUNCTION C	142	143	147	148	148	150
PROJECT A						
PROJECT B						
PROJECT C						
PROJECT D						
PROJECT E						
PROJECT F						
PROJECT G						
PROJECT H						
PROJECT I						
PROJECT J						

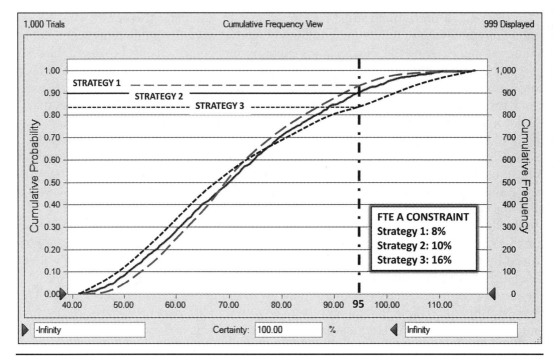

Figure 9-25   Portfolio optimization and functional resource management

9-25, different portfolio strategies lead to differences in the probability of exceeding a given functional FTE constraint.

In the example in Figure 9-25, assuming an internal constraint of 95 FTEs for Function A, Strategy 1 represents the lowest likelihood of exceeding this FTE constraint, while Strategy 3 is twice as likely to exceed this critical constraint. Depending on the risk tolerance of the organization, a portfolio strategy that yields the lowest likelihood of exceeding one or more functional constraints may be chosen even though this portfolio may yield less value than another in which one or more functional constraints are exceeded.

9.5 Stakeholder Management

During the conduct of clinical trials, a plethora of stakeholders, both internal and external, and each with their own contributions, needs, and expectations, will exist (Figure 9-26). Who are these individuals, and how concerned should we be about their roles, responsibilities, needs, and expectations with respect to project portfolio management? In pondering this overarching question, several key questions emerge:

- What are stakeholders' primary responsibilities, and how are they impacted by project portfolio management?
- What strategic, financial, and emotional interests do stakeholders have in the success or failure of portfolio management?
- What conflicting interests may stakeholders have regarding the success or failure of project portfolio management?

Figure 9-26   Key stakeholders in clinical trial management

- What motivates stakeholders to be engaged in and participate in the portfolio management process?
- How do stakeholders benefit from being involved in portfolio management, and how may they be threatened by the existence of this discipline?
- What information do stakeholders require of you, when do they want it, and how do they want it communicated to them?
- What are stakeholders' current opinions of the roles and responsibilities of the portfolio management function?
- Who influences stakeholders' opinions, who may be influenced by their opinions, and how likely is it that you can influence their opinions?
- Who are the dominant stakeholders, and what are the consequences of not managing their relationships well?
- Which stakeholders have direct control over resources that could impact the success of project portfolio management?

Although the term *stakeholder management* is well used in the project management literature in particular, it should be more accurately portrayed as *stakeholder relationship management*. However, for the purposes of this discussion, the more generally accepted term "stakeholder management" will be applied. What does the process of stakeholder management entail? To begin with, a portfolio management function needs to identify who its primary stakeholders currently are and, perhaps just as important, who they are likely to be in the future (Figure 9-27).

The identification of primary stakeholders to a portfolio management endeavor is far from a trivial process. When one considers the definition used at the beginning of this chapter that invokes "individuals internal or external to the organization who are either directly or indirectly involved, are affected by the outcome of this endeavor, and whose participation is associated with its success or failure," the catalogue of primary stakeholders can quickly become lengthy. Nevertheless, once identified, the immediate task is to clearly articulate the intentions of the portfolio management process that should include but not be restricted to the following themes:

- The current and desired states of project portfolio management in the organization
- The organizational benefits, including how they will be measured, of an improved project portfolio management practice, with a synopsis of the accompanying processes (e.g., data elicitation), methodologies (e.g., risk analysis), and toolsets (e.g., resource management consolidation system)
- The benefits, including how they will be measured, to their functions
- The short-term drawbacks of altering the current *modus operandi* and the future benefits of change management

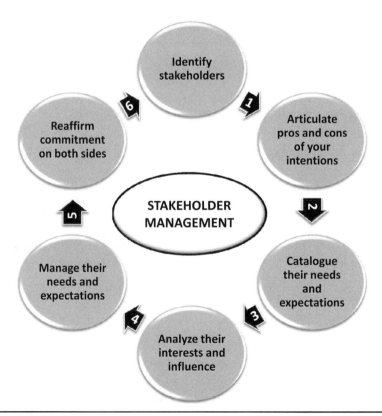

Figure 9-27   Stakeholder management process

- The critical importance of stakeholders' visible engagement, enablement, and participation

The next step in the stakeholder analysis process is to catalogue their needs and expectations and to understand how these may differ amongst stakeholders. In particular, to gain initial endorsement for the function, it is critical to understand if their needs take precedence over the needs of the overall organization, in which case the challenge becomes far more acute.

The task of analyzing the interests and levels of impact of stakeholders to the success of the project portfolio management function is of such significance that it should not be undertaken without the advice and close guidance of the primary sponsor of the function. This individual should be used as a guide to help avoid some of the less obvious political minefields that lie along the path to portfolio management success, and includes stakeholders whose domain may be threatened by a successful portfolio management discipline. The penultimate step in the stakeholder management process is to manage the needs and expectations of stakeholders through effective relationship building. In fact, every bridge built with a stakeholder's function may be an avenue to secure that individual's ongoing support if or when there is doubt cast on the value of the portfolio management function itself.

Finally, gaining commitment from a stakeholder at the beginning of the change management process for portfolio management implementation should not be taken as a permanent state of affairs. Rather, it is imperative that, as part of the ongoing dialogue with stakeholders, the portfolio management function seeks to reaffirm its commitment to creating the highest value possible for the enterprise and in the process of doing so secure the enduring assurance of visible engagement, endorsement, and support from each stakeholder.

During the stakeholder management cycle, Step 5 is a continuous cycle in and of itself, as managing relations with stakeholders requires continual interaction in order to assess their degree of satisfaction with implementation of a project portfolio management function. Two dimensions have been used traditionally to assist in focusing on the different types of stakeholders within the internal and external communities: (a) their level of engagement and interest and (b) their degree of influence and impact on the success of project portfolio management. Stakeholders with relatively low interest in and low influence on project portfolio management are generally regarded as passive and are required to be kept informed on a timely basis of the progress of the change management initiative relating to project portfolio management. Those key stakeholders at the other end of the spectrum (i.e., with relatively high interest in and high impact on the success of project portfolio management) need to have their buy-in and support of the initiative reaffirmed on an almost continual basis.

Without a stakeholder analysis process in place, project portfolio management can lose organizational traction, flounder, and eventually become marginalized. Between key and passive stakeholders are those that are interested and important, requiring a combination of activities to maintain their interest and active consultation to nurture their level of support. Clearly, the lines of demarcation between these two categories of stakeholders are blurred, and it requires good judgment on the part of those in the portfolio management function to determine how much interaction and relationship building are necessary. It is not recommended that the same levels of interaction and information be afforded to all categories of stakeholders, as some can quickly become overwhelmed with detail that inadvertently conveys the mistaken impression of how complex and burdensome the institutionalization of project portfolio management can become. Rather, it is expected that a proactive portfolio management function that excels in stakeholder management will aid in the migration of stakeholders who find themselves in the low to medium quadrants of engagement and interest to areas where they display the highest levels of engagement and interest possible.

Despite active stakeholder relationship management, not all stakeholders will be convinced of the benefits being promised by project portfolio management; especially if current practices have yielded lengthy success, they will remain resistant to change (Figure 9-28). Those who are most resistant to change but also most important to the success of the endeavor need to be the focal point of attention, and protracted efforts should be made to try to convince them of the way ahead in search of greater portfolio value creation. Stakeholders who display high resistance but who are low in importance to the successful implementation of project portfolio management need to be monitored frequently. This is primarily because they may be able to influence others who are less resistant to the implementation of portfolio management and who may be quite important to the success of the endeavor. This applies, in particular, to the category of stakeholders described as "involve."

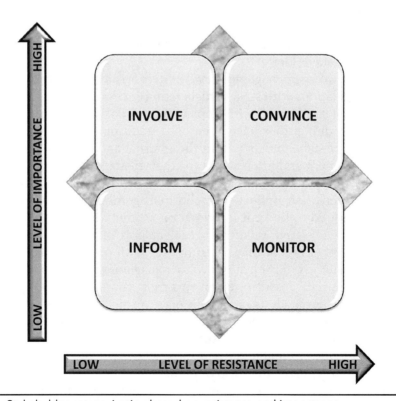

Figure 9-28   Stakeholder categorization based on resistance and importance

At different points in time in the life cycle of a project, some stakeholders assume a role of greater importance than at other stages of the project. Likewise, at the portfolio level, different stakeholders assume varying levels of influence and control over the process, analysis, recommendations, and decisions rendered in portfolio management. At the beginning of the portfolio management process, guidance is provided by the steering or executive committee, while during the process, a multitude of stakeholders are required to participate. At the end of the portfolio management process, the steering or executive committee again closes the cycle by making the necessary decisions (Figure 9-29).

It is important to obtain the necessary guidance from the steering committee as to what its goals and objectives are and what constitutes a successful outcome to the portfolio review. Without this, most portfolio reviews quickly degenerate into aimless bantering over data that is not decision relevant, leading to a lack of decision making by members of the steering committee. The most labor-intensive portion of the portfolio management process takes place during the phase of data gathering. It is here that a portfolio management function spends most of its time trying to validate data inputs that will be used for analysis and recommendations, and it is also where stakeholder management involves a spectrum of activities that are geared toward building coalitions with important functions, such as resource management and finance, and enlisting functional representatives to provide robust and defensible data and information in the face of uncertainty. Stated otherwise, unless stakeholders understand their role in and importance to the success of the endeavor, data gathering is likely to be characterized by the population of data templates with information for which there is little defensibility. To achieve credibility at this stage of the process, portfolio management is challenged with acquiring data from several functions, which, despite its inherent

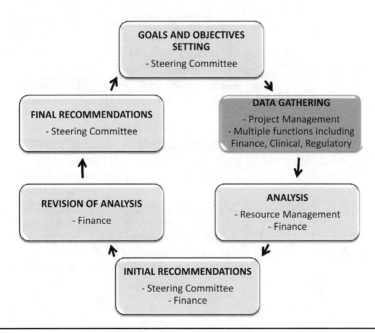

Figure 9-29   Stakeholder involvement during the portfolio management process

uncertainty, is logically consistent and defensible. Preselling the importance of each function to the value generated by a portfolio review is an important step in gaining alignment across the breadth of an organization.

Although analysis of the data is largely a responsibility of the portfolio management function, it is important that other functions, especially resource management and finance, be kept informed of the potential implications of preliminary insights that could shape future recommendations to the governing steering committee. Once the results of the preliminary insights and conclusions are discussed with the steering committee, it is expected that further guidance will be provided to the portfolio management function, after which a revised analysis is conducted, preferably in close collaboration with the finance function. Before final recommendations are made to the steering committee, it is critical that the finance function understand and endorse the budgetary implications of the portfolio recommendations, which are finally presented to the governing body for decision making.

As portfolio management becomes a more mature discipline in an organization, it is expected that the level of sophistication necessary to manage stakeholder relationships successfully will increase (Figure 9-30). From Levels 1 and 2, where the portfolio is driven bottom up by projects and programs and stakeholder management is largely focused on data and information collection and aggregation, to Levels 3-5, where the

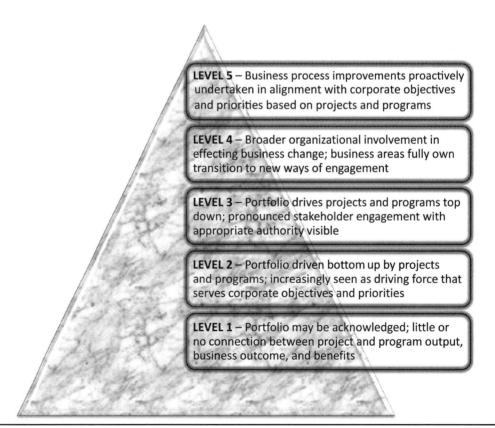

Figure 9-30   Stakeholder management maturity model

portfolio is driven top down by business imperatives (Office of Government Commerce, 2008), there is a much higher degree of organizational involvement, sponsorship, and ownership for the success of portfolio management. Therefore, a continual challenge for a portfolio management function is to determine the current level of its maturity, and as it works to improve its competencies and capabilities, to ensure that it pays the requisite attention to the growing interests and expectations of its stakeholders.

9.6 A Practical Approach to Improving Portfolio Management Competencies

The previous sections addressed key competencies that must be mastered by any enterprise seeking to improve its competency in portfolio management. Any action plan geared towards achieving a higher capability maturity level in portfolio management can be difficult and time consuming. In order to be successful, it is necessary for an organization to adopt a realistic and practical approach toward achieving a higher level of maturity in portfolio management. One such approach is illustrated in Figure 9-31. Each step of achieving a higher level of maturity is described below.

1. Implement Organizational Change Management in Support of Portfolio Management Vision

The implementation of an enterprise-wide project portfolio management discipline geared toward attaining a higher level of maturity is likely to encounter a number of growing pains and obstacles on account of existing organizational barriers to success. Barriers can be overcome only by instituting a formal organizational change management effort aimed at changing the enterprise's mindset, such that project portfolio

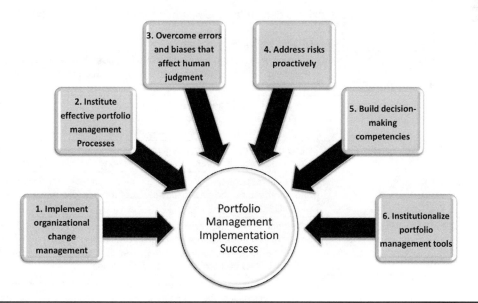

Figure 9-31   Approach to improving EPPM competencies

management becomes an integral part of the organization's culture. Such an enterprise-wide change management effort requires these actions:

- **Secure executive support.** Perhaps the most important factor influencing successful implementation of improved capabilities in portfolio management is securing appropriate executive support, in the absence of which failure can almost always be guaranteed. Securing the right level of top-level, cross-functional executive support from finance, operations, IT, human resources, and other BUs is a fundamental prerequisite of any effort aimed at instituting an enterprise-wide portfolio management discipline. The reader is encouraged to follow the best practices on stakeholder management provided earlier in this chapter.

- **Build organizational design by establishing the right governance structure.** Establishing the right governance structure is crucial to ensuring the success of the implementation plan. While effective governance starts with executive support, appropriate organizational structures have to be defined with a clear understanding of roles and responsibilities for the stakeholders in portfolio management. While organization design for portfolio management success varies from one enterprise to another, the roles and responsibilities of the stakeholders are fairly standard across organizations. Based on Merkhofer (2008), an example of a typical set of roles and responsibilities for stakeholders is shown in Table 9-8.

- **Train staff in portfolio management based on their roles and responsibilities.** The portfolio management team needs to be adequately trained in portfolio management competencies. Specific focus areas in training, especially if the requisite level of expertise is lacking, must include fundamental concepts

Table 9-8 Portfolio management stakeholders' roles and responsibilities (Merkhofer, 2008)

Role	Responsibilities
Executive Team	Decision-making and oversight group composed of senior executives. The group sets portfolio funding levels, approves project recommendations, and provides policy guidance.
Enterprise Portfolio Management Office	The portfolio management and competency center composed of the portfolio manager, portfolio administrator and divisional portfolio managers. Responsible for the portfolio management process.
Enterprise Portfolio Manager	Head of the portfolio management team. Responsibilities include making project recommendations and reporting to the executive team.
Portfolio Administrator	Individual responsible for collecting project information, applying tools, and coordinating the day-to-day steps of the portfolio management process.
Divisional Portfolio Managers	Divisional representatives responsible for coordinating all portfolio management functions for their respective divisions and serving as a liaison with the EPMO, in order to ensure that each division is in alignment with the EPMO charter, standards, and policies.
Project Managers	Persons responsible for day-to-day management of individual projects. Responsibilities include providing project proposal data and communicating project status to their divisional portfolio manager and enterprise portfolio manager.

and techniques in decision analysis, portfolio analysis, scenario analysis, data elicitation, risk management, and other technical skills required for portfolio management. Additionally, a number of personnel in the organization who are either directly or indirectly impacted by portfolio management require basic training and awareness building, so that the benefits of EPPM are clearly understood across the organization. The value of the new approach should be clearly communicated and sufficient time allocated within the budget cycle to allow necessary training and familiarity with new processes. Staff expectations should be set and roles should be defined. The types of changes to be expected should be clearly signaled, along with communicating the value to be gained from achieving those changes. The organization should be made aware that challenges are to be expected, especially early on; however, working on change should be balanced against the anticipated payoff.

- **Embrace portfolio management principles.** A key factor in ensuring the success of organizational change management is the adoption of portfolio management principles. Securing clarity on basic principles is important for two reasons. First, the principles promote understanding and agreement on the contextual (why) and conceptual (how) reasons for improving portfolio management capabilities in organizations. Second, the principles provide the foundation for creating the structure, supporting processes, and tools that will enable putting the principles into practice.

  One set of principles based on ISACA's Val IT framework (ISACA, 2006) for portfolio management is outlined below:

  o Projects will be managed as a portfolio of investments.

  o The goal is to create the greatest possible value considering the resources available and accounting for risk and organizational risk tolerance.

  o For the purpose of decision making, projects will be defined to include the full scope of activities necessary to generate value.

  o Value delivery practices will recognize that there are different types of projects that will be evaluated and managed differently.

  o Value delivery will be managed throughout the project life cycle and the life cycle of any products, services, or assets created by the project.

  o Value delivery practices will engage all stakeholders and assign appropriate accountability for the delivery of capabilities and the realization of value.

  o Value delivery practices will be continually monitored, evaluated, and improved.

2. Institute Effective Portfolio Management Processes

Instituting effective portfolio management processes is critical from the perspective of portfolio management operations. The Stage-Gate™ process (Cooper, Edgett, & Kleinschmidt, 2001) is an excellent framework that can be adopted by organizations for improving the operational processes associated with portfolio management. While each organization needs to tailor the Stage-Gate™ or a similar process to suit its specific needs, one such flavor is presented in Figure 9-32 (based on Cooper, Edgett, & Kleinschmidt, 2001), which illustrates the adoption of a five-step Stage-Gate™ process based on the portfolio review approach,[1] wherein portfolio review and decision making occur at Gate 3.

Organizations that adopt the Stage-Gate™ model should conduct a review of the entire portfolio of investments more than once a year. There are two go-kill decision points defined in Gates 3 and 4 to provide for the termination of under-performing projects, whose resources can be reallocated to other projects. During the portfolio review, all the investments in the enterprise portfolios should be reviewed and selected, as illustrated in Figure 9-33.

The portfolio review process outlined here is an integrated approach that performs optimization first, followed by prioritization. Portfolio optimization as the first step would result in an optimal selection of projects to pursue, which can then be prioritized based on their forced ranking for operational purposes, e.g., resource allocation. Project prioritization should be based on well-defined criteria, which can reduce the number of "pet" projects that many organizations harbor in their portfolios on account of existing biases among key stakeholders. The adoption of such a portfolio

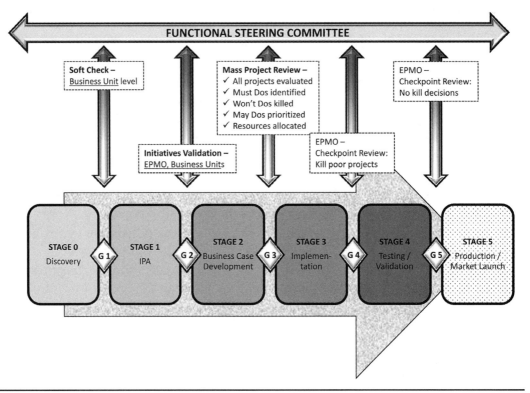

Figure 9-32   The Stage-Gate™ process for project portfolio management

---

[1]The reader is encouraged to review the book titled *Portfolio Management for New Products* by Cooper, Edgett, and Kleinschmidt in which the Stage-Gate™ is introduced and discussed in detail.

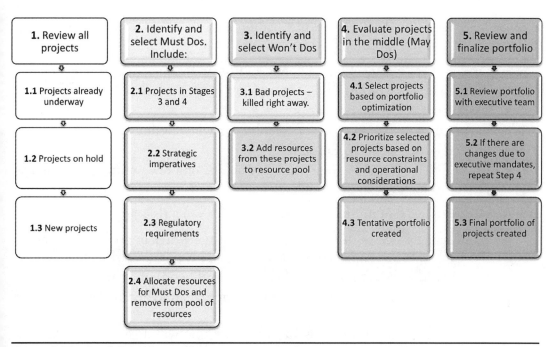

Figure 9-33   Portfolio review process

management process will significantly improve an organization's portfolio management capabilities, provided there is requisite executive support for the new process, coupled with the required cultural change in the organization.

3. Overcome Errors and Biases That Affect Human Judgment

Decision makers in many organizations are often afflicted by psychological traps, biases, and pitfalls that cloud objective decision making. Bias invariably leads to poor decisions, resulting in severe and systematic errors in project selection. Errors in judgment when making portfolio selection decisions typically fall in two categories of biases: cognitive and motivational biases. Understanding these unconscious shortcuts, termed *heuristics*, is of utmost importance in objective decision making, which is fundamental to portfolio management. Once these are understood and acknowledged, suitable techniques can help overcome the heuristic-based errors and biases that affect human judgment, as given in Chapter 3, Decision Framing and Data Integrity.

4. Address Risks Proactively

While risk management at the project level has been incorporated to varying degrees in organizations by addressing risks in terms of effects on the cost and schedule of projects, most organizations lack sophistication when it comes to addressing risks within the context of project portfolio management. Portfolio risk analysis and risk management competencies need to be developed concomitantly in organizations and incorporated into the project selection process, so that the optimal set of projects can be selected for investment. As discussed in Chapter 5, portfolio risk can be expressed in terms of:

- Likelihood of not meeting economic and/or strategic goals
- Likelihood of exceeding budget constraints
- Variance of value and returns
- Downside potential in terms of creation of negative value
- Innovation and other technical risk
- Lack of diversification and dependency on one or a few products or technical platforms

The keys to creating a culture that is proactive in addressing risks are:

- Establishing processes for creating and identifying risks in project risk categories, such as technical risk, operational risk, and regulatory risk
- Quantifying risks in terms of probabilities (likelihood) of occurrence
- Leveraging techniques such as decision tree analysis for making informed choices
- Incorporating risk in the decision framework that will drive project selection via optimization and prioritization
- Comparing competing projects in terms of risk vs. reward profiles
- Training project teams in computing risk-adjusted commercial values, as opposed to potential commercial values for initiatives
- Determining organizational risk tolerance to guide decision making

To be sure, challenges arise in introducing risk assessments in portfolio management because of inherent biases and errors in judgment about the occurrence of an event and the magnitude of its impact. Additionally, expressing risk in terms of probabilities is an unnatural skill for most people. However, with adequate training in techniques for addressing biases and errors, risk management can become an integral part of any organization's portfolio management discipline. The reader should master core concepts in Chapter 5 and the best practices in risk management given in this chapter.

5. Build Decision Making Competencies

Building competencies in decision making in any organization is a fairly challenging task. The key to improved decision making in project selection (via optimization and prioritization) is in leveraging a framework that incorporates both the qualitative and quantitative values of initiatives. One of the primary areas of weakness in portfolio management in organizations is objective decision making, since subjectivity often undermines the credibility of the portfolio management process.

Selection of projects competing for the same resources can be considerably improved by following the tenets of the CREOPM™ framework, inclusive of developing and employing a Multiple Objective Project Prioritization (MOPP[SM]) process to create multiple objective decision analysis (MODA) models for prioritization, as discussed in Chapter 8. The institution of such practices as a follow-up to portfolio optimization

(Chapter 7), coupled with the guidelines presented in Chapter 2 on decision framing, can go a long way in improving organizational competency in decision making. Further, organizations can benefit immensely by adding management science competencies to the EPMO and to BUs, as well as support divisions such as IT, finance, HR, etc., so that investments can be optimized at the divisional, cross-divisional, and enterprise levels.

6. Institutionalize Portfolio Management Tools

Tools can help in improving the effectiveness of portfolio management competencies in an organization. The implementation of a portfolio management information system (PMIS) has the potential to address specific gaps in resource management, tools, data quality, reporting, and analysis. Key features and functionality that the integrated tool suite should include are decision aids, optimization, prioritization, financial analysis, risk analysis, project valuation, data management, governance and security, displays, reporting, project planning, workflow management, project data and status reporting, integration with financial management (A/P, billing, etc.), resource management, demand management, resource assignment, resource utilization analysis, and time tracking (Merkhofer, 2008).[2] The implementation of a PMIS should be based on these key principles:

- **Accuracy:** The tool should enable accuracy, since the value of the tool depends on its ability to create reproducibly sound analyses.
- **Logical soundness:** Since portfolio management tools play an important role in aiding decision making on the portfolio of projects/capabilities, it is imperative that the tool is based on logically sound theories, in the absence of which such tools will be exposed when subject to technical review.
- **Completeness:** The tool must be complete, accounting for all significant and relevant considerations to aid decision analysis, scenario analysis, and portfolio analysis.
- **Effectiveness:** In order for the integrated tool suite to be effective, it needs to be sensitive to considerations in timing, decision process, project management, and performance monitoring.
- **Acceptability:** The tool must be acceptable to stakeholders and compatible with an organization's processes and culture.

The deployment of an integrated PMIS should be based on a roadmap for implementation, as provided by Merkhofer (2008), which is outlined in Figure 9-34.

While there are specific considerations that vary from one organization to another, the adoption of these recommendations can go a long way in ensuring that an organization can achieve a desired level of portfolio management maturity in order to significantly improve enterprise value creation.

---

[2]The reader is encouraged to visit the web site for Priority System, a source for a number of illuminating articles and white papers on project portfolio management by Dr. Lee Merkhofer.

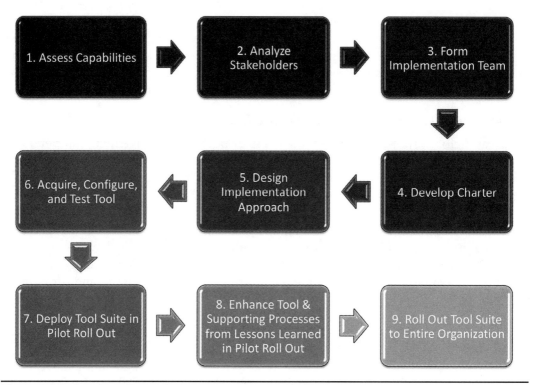

Figure 9-34   Roadmap for implementing a PMIS (Merkhofer, 2008)

9.7 Summary

A CMM in portfolio management was proposed to serve as a framework for organizations to determine their maturity level across a spectrum of portfolio management competencies. The maturity model can be used by organizations as a benchmark to determine the success of any organizational change management initiative aimed at attaining the requisite level of maturity and discipline required to employ these techniques, with the goal of guiding optimal investment decisions in organizations. Best practices were outlined for adoption by any organization that aspires to improve its portfolio management competencies. The maturity model and best practices are applicable to the whole enterprise, not just for an R&D or IT department that is aspiring to improve its portfolio management competencies.

Section 4

Case Studies in Enterprise Portfolio Management

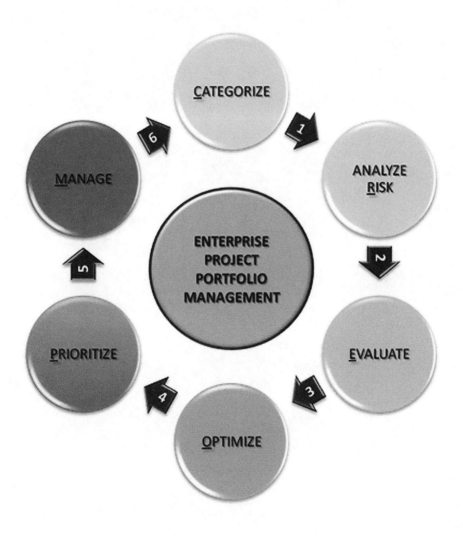

10

Case Study in IT Portfolio Management

The following case study outlines an enterprise IT portfolio selection problem for SIRC Corporation, a fictional organization, which has a diversified product portfolio. SIRC's strategic goals, and objective and business requirements driving the enterprise IT portfolio selection, are presented first to provide the context and framework for selecting the optimal set of IT investments to pursue. Techniques in portfolio selection such as integer linear programming and multiple objective decision analysis (MODA) are utilized in detail for this case study, as their application reflects portfolio selection choices that are typically faced by IT decision makers.

The case study will show how portfolio selection is typically done in many organizations today, i.e., by prioritization of the projects/investments in the portfolio. Next, portfolio selection by optimization using integer linear programming will be accomplished. The sequencing of these activities may seem counter to the CRE-OPM™ framework. However, the reason for doing so is to illustrate the superiority of optimization over prioritization and how sub-optimal portfolios are generally created as a result of prioritization (as opposed to the optimal portfolio created by optimization). This case study should encourage practitioners of portfolio prioritization to adopt superior portfolio selection techniques and thereby not unwittingly discard value in the portfolio.

10.1 Case Study Outline: SIRC Corporation

This section introduces the fictional organization under consideration for the case study, providing a brief overview of the company's product and service offerings, its recent financial performance, the stated goals, objectives, and the enterprise IT portfolio for the organization. All of the existing and new investments under consideration in the enterprise IT portfolio are identified for the company. The company strategy and performance, and their resulting impact on the enterprise IT portfolio, are also highlighted in order to establish the context for IT portfolio selection and optimization in the following sections.

10.1.1 Overview of SIRC Corporation

SIRC Corporation, referred to as SIRC, is a (fictional) multinational company that was founded in 1979 in the United States and has its corporate headquarters in Somerset, NJ. SIRC has a diverse product portfolio that spans consumer and specialty healthcare products and services, ranging from skin care, oral hygiene, and inexpensive cosmetics to select consumer electronics in personal care such as hair dryers and electric razors.

The corporation experienced steady growth over the years to evolve into a global organization with operations in North and South America, Asia-Pacific, and Europe, employing nearly 18,000 people. SIRC became renowned for the reliable consumer products that it introduced into the marketplace by virtue of protracted innovative R&D. SIRC's first-mover advantage, complemented by aggressive marketing of new products, had been its particular strengths in contributing significantly to top-line growth.

Recently, however, the company's performance has been less than stellar. Specifically, the company's annual revenue in 2009 was $7.4B, down by more than 12% from its initial forecast of $8.5B. Profits have fallen dramatically as a result, since operating costs have remained more or less unchanged. The company faces considerable pressure in the marketplace from its competitors, and the global economic downturn has also contributed significantly to its revenue shortfall.

Based on a strategic planning effort, SIRC's executive management has drawn up a plan of action in response to the $1.1B revenue shortfall and in anticipation of turbulent times ahead in the marketplace. This case study identified that SIRC's product pipeline is strong and that its core strengths are R&D innovation and marketing in traditional channels. Further, the company has streamlined some of its operations by automating components of the supply chain. However, there exist significant areas for improvement. The dénouement of the strategic planning effort is the identification of the following strategic objectives for SIRC, to respond to its recent financial woes:

- Improve operational efficiencies and reduce costs across the board to increase profit margins.
- Increase revenue by exploiting new online marketing channels that leverage social computing.[1]
- Improve collaboration with strategic suppliers and distributors (customers) to increase speed and efficiency across the value chain.
- Improve margins by lowering working capital required for business operations in cost centers. Improve quality of customer service to increase brand loyalty and provide opportunities for more up-selling and cross-selling of products.

10.1.2 Overview of SIRC's IT Division

SIRC's IT division has been a key enabler of the company's strategic initiatives, and has successfully delivered IT solutions for large-scale initiatives. The CIO has been at the helm for four years and has carried on the predecessor's policy of investing in

---

[1]One of SIRC's competitors successfully exploited online social media to improve sales in 2009.

commercial off-the-shelf solutions for key IT capabilities. In fact, IT aspires to slowly phase out custom software development efforts within the organization. Accordingly, key investments in enterprise resource planning (ERP), supply chain management (SCM), supplier relationship management (SRM), and facets of customer relationship management (CRM) have been implemented as packaged solutions.

However, there exist custom-developed IT solutions in the product lifecycle management (PLM) domain, as well as in key areas of the CRM domain. A recent success story was the completion of the global SAP ERP and SCM implementation, a seven-year program that cost $180M and was delivered successfully only after going through a number of hiccups over the first three years. The CIO has established a Global Infrastructure department within IT, as a single distributed organization responsible for managing all of the infrastructure needs of SIRC. Furthermore, investments have been made in IT Service Management in the last two years to improve the level and quality of service that IT provides to business units.

The IT division defines a set of objectives every year with the aim of improving the division's performance in support of the organization's goals. These objectives are in addition to the company's stated strategic objectives:

- Improve customer service, i.e., improve the level of service provided by IT to business units.
- Reduce the cost of IT to business units.
- Leverage IT for strategic business advantage with better alignment between IT and business priorities.
- Institute new technologies, standards, policies, and practices that will deliver innovative capabilities to the business.

10.1.3 SIRC's Enterprise IT Portfolio

The CIO, with the CEO's endorsement, has had an almost free reign in capital expenditure (CAPEX) investment projects until recently, in an effort to transform IT from a traditional role as a utility player to a trusted partner of the business. The recent financial performance of the organization has changed this status quo. Information on the proposed IT spend as a percentage of forecasts and actual revenue, as well as the revised expectations based on the board's mandates for cost cutting are provided in Tables 10-1, 10-2, and 10-3.

The portfolio of IT investments to be considered for the financial year 2010 for SIRC called for a proposed total budget of $516.6M, around 6.08% of the revenue forecast in 2009. The proposed operational budget was $340M, approximately 4.0% of the revenue forecast. The proposed IT CAPEX was $176.6M, equivalent to 52% of the operational expenditure (OPEX). Given IT's past performance, if the company had met its revenue targets, the proposed IT budget would likely have been approved. However, given SIRC's revenue shortfall, the executive team mandated that IT and other divisions in the company reduce costs significantly.

Specifically, the CIO was asked to reduce the IT budget to less than 5.7% of the actual annual revenue from the current amount of 6.98% of the actual revenue. This

Table 10-1 SIRC IT division's 2010 proposed budget in terms of revenue forecast

#	Description	Value
1	SIRC Corporation's Forecasted Annual Revenues (2009)	$8,500,000,000
2	IT Proposed Operational Budget as % of Forecasted Annual Revenue	4.00%
3	IT Proposed Operational Budget (2010)	$340,000,000
4	IT Proposed Capital Budget as % of Operational Budget	51.95%
5	IT Proposed Capital Budget (2010)	$176,616,000
6	IT Proposed Total Annual Budget (2010)	$516,616,000
7	IT Proposed Total Annual Budget (2010) as % of Forecasted Revenue	6.08%

Table 10-2 SIRC IT division's 2010 proposed budget in terms of actual revenue

#	Description	Value
1	SIRC Corporation's Actual Annual Revenue (2009)	$7,400,000,000
2	IT Proposed Operational Budget as % of Actual Annual Revenue	4.70%
3	IT Proposed Operational Budget (2010)	$340,000,000
4	IT Proposed Capital Budget as % of Operational Budget	51.95%
5	IT Proposed Capital Budget (2010)	$176,616,000
6	IT Proposed Total Annual Budget	$516,616,000
7	IT Proposed Total Annual Budget (2010) as % of Actual Revenue	6.98%

Table 10-3 SIRC IT division's revised budget limits based on leadership mandates

#	Description	Value
1	Board-Desired IT Operational Budget as % of Annual Revenue	4.00%
2	Board-Mandated IT Capital Budget as % of IT Operational Budget	40.00%
3	Board-Mandated IT Operational Budget (2010)	$296,000,000
4	Board-Mandated IT Capital Budget (2010)	$118,400,000
5	Mandated IT Annual Budget (2010) as % of Actual Revenue	5.60%
6	Board-Mandated IT Total Budget (2010)	$414,400,000
7	Difference between Proposed and Mandated Budgets	$102,216,000

equates to a maximum approvable IT spend of $414.4M, with the operational budget accounting for $296M and capital investment accounting for $118.4M. It is noteworthy that the IT division has been requested to keep the capital expense limited to 40% of the operational expense, a reduction by about one-third (33%) from the proposed capital expense. The CIO, with the help of direct reports, therefore has to institute appropriate reductions in the budgets for operational expense initiatives across the board.

10.1.3.1 SIRC IT OPEX *Portfolio*

There are a total of 40 investments that constitute the proposed IT operational budget. The proposed operational spending for these investments amounts to $340M, while the executive mandate is to reduce this to $296M. The challenge in this OPEX category, which encompasses the Application Preservation, Technology Preservation, and Service Management portfolio groups, is to institute cost reductions in existing IT investments without compromising the quality or level of service provided by IT. Each of the operational IT investments is listed in Table 10-4, with detailed descriptions provided in Appendix D, SIRC's Enterprise IT Portfolio.

10.1.3.2 SIRC's CAPEX IT *Portfolio*

There are a total of 25 investments that constitute the proposed IT CAPEX budget, with a total proposed investment of $176.6M, from which SIRC's executives have earmarked only $118.4M for capital IT investments. Based on the project prioritization and portfolio optimization, the CIO will provide the EOC a list of CAPEX investments that are to be approved for funding. The final decision on the new IT initiatives to be funded rests with the EOC and will be made in alignment with the organization's strategic business objectives. The new investments are listed in Table 10-5, with detailed descriptions provided in Appendix D.

10.1.4 Decision Criteria for SIRC IT Portfolio Selection

SIRC IT senior management has outlined the following criteria to guide IT portfolio selection:

- All IT investments, whether CAPEX or OPEX, should reflect their degree of alignment with the company's strategic objectives and with IT's stated objectives.
- Every IT investment should include a risk profile as part of its assessment criteria.
- In addition to their business value, all CAPEX investments must be evaluated on the basis of their forecasted financial value, IT value, and the risk associated with each investment.
- All OPEX investments must be evaluated on the basis of the cost of the investment.
  - The ceiling for 2010 OPEX initiatives is $296M, and all approved OPEX initiatives will be fully funded. Every OPEX initiative that is not selected as a result of IT portfolio valuation will be subject to a 50% reduction in operations. The 50% funding for each unapproved OPEX investment is the cost of maintaining the minimally required operations for that functional area, inclusive of existing contractual agreements for license and maintenance, as well as existing service level agreements that can be supported at the bare minimum level by the IT organization.

Table 10-4 SIRC's proposed IT OPEX investments

ID	Investment Name	Asset Class	IT Domain	IT Segment	Requested Funding ($)
PFM-2010-001	PeopleSoft HCM OpEx	Application	ERP	Human Capital Management	$15,402,000
PFM-2010-002	SAP ERP FI OpEx	Application	ERP	Financials	$11,492,000
PFM-2010-003	SAP ERP EAM OpEx	Application	ERP	Enterprise Asset Management	$6,052,000
PFM-2010-004	SAP ERP DP OpEx	Application	ERP	Direct Procurement	$3,672,000
PFM-2010-005	SAP ERP XFO OpEx	Application	ERP	Cross-Functional Operations	$6,732,000
PFM-2010-006	Ariba SRM SBM OpEx	Application	SRM	Supply Base Management	$3,672,000
PFM-2010-007	Ariba SRM SC OpEx	Application	SRM	Supplier Collaboration	$4,012,000
PFM-2010-008	Ariba SRM PG OpEx	Application	SRM	Purchasing Governance	$3,502,000
PFM-2010-009	Ariba SRM IP OpEx	Application	SRM	Indirect Procurement	$6,222,000
PFM-2010-010	Ariba SRM CM OpEx	Application	SRM	Contract Management	$5,882,000
PFM-2010-011	SAP SCM WH OpEx	Application	SCM	Warehousing	$4,352,000
PFM-2010-012	SAP SCM TP OpEx	Application	SCM	Transportation	$4,352,000
PFM-2010-013	SAP SCM SNC OpEx	Application	SCM	Supply Network Collaboration	$3,672,000
PFM-2010-014	SAP SCM SCV OpEx	Application	SCM	Supply Chain Visibility	$4,692,000
PFM-2010-015	SAP SCM PR OpEx	Application	SCM	Procurement	$4,012,000
PFM-2010-016	SAP SCM OF OpEx	Application	SCM	Order Fulfillment	$7,922,000
PFM-2010-017	SAP SCM MF OpEx	Application	SCM	Manufacturing	$8,092,000
PFM-2010-018	SAP SCM DSP OpEx	Application	SCM	Demand & Supply Planning	$4,692,000
PFM-2010-019	Siebel Sales OpEx	Application	CRM	Sales	$8,262,000
PFM-2010-020	Legacy Marketing OpEx	Application	CRM	Marketing	$10,132,000
PFM-2010-021	Siebel Call Center OpEx	Application	CRM	Customer Service	$6,392,000
PFM-2010-022	Legacy PLM PM OpEx	Application	PLM	Product Management	$3,672,000
PFM-2010-023	Legacy PLM PDC OpEx	Application	PLM	Product Development & Collaboration	$2,992,000
PFM-2010-024	Legacy PLM PDM OpEx	Application	PLM	Product Data Management	$4,182,000
PFM-2010-025	Legacy PLM FC OpEx	Application	PLM	Foundational Components	$3,162,000
PFM-2010-026	ITSM ST OpEx	Technology	ITSM	Service Transition	$2,210,000
PFM-2010-027	ITSM SO OpEx	Technology	ITSM	Service Operation	$7,820,000

PFM-2010-028	ITSM SMT OpEx	Technology	ITSM	Service Management Tools	$2,210,000
PFM-2010-029	ITSM SD OpEx	Technology	ITSM	Service Design	$10,880,000
PFM-2010-030	INFR UDM OpEx	Technology	INFR	Unstructured Data Management	$3,910,000
PFM-2010-031	INFR SDM OpEx	Technology	INFR	Structured Data Management	$8,160,000
PFM-2010-032	INFR SM OpEx	Technology	INFR	Security Management	$11,560,000
PFM-2010-033	INFR PM OpEx	Technology	INFR	Platform Management	$66,640,000
PFM-2010-034	INFR NM OpEx	Technology	INFR	Network Management	$28,560,000
PFM-2010-035	INFR DC OpEx	Technology	INFR	Data Center & Facilities Management	$19,040,000
PFM-2010-036	INFR DAM OpEx	Technology	INFR	Data Access Management	$11,900,000
PFM-2010-037	INFR AM OpEx	Technology	INFR	Application Middleware	$6,630,000
PFM-2010-038	IT LCM SDLC OpEx	Technology	IT LCM	Systems Development Lifecycle	$2,890,000
PFM-2010-039	IT LCM RP OpEx	Technology	IT LCM	IT Resource Planning	$6,800,000
PFM-2010-040	IT LCM EA OpEx	Technology	IT LCM	Enterprise Architecture (EA)	$3,570,000

Table 10-5 SIRC's proposed IT CAPEX investments

ID	Investment Name	Asset Class	IT Domain	IT Segment	Requested Funding ($)	Portfolio Sub-Group
PFM-2010-041	ERP HCM - e-Learning	Application	ERP	Human Capital Management	$7,500,000	Informational
PFM-2010-042	ERP EAM - RFID Asset Tagging	Application	ERP	Enterprise Asset Management	$6,250,000	Transactional
PFM-2010-043	SRM SC - Supplier Collaboration	Application	SRM	Supplier Collaboration	$3,755,000	Strategic
PFM-2010-044	SRM SC - Sourcing	Application	SRM	Sourcing	$6,752,500	Strategic
PFM-2010-045	SRM SC - Spend Analytics	Application	SRM	Purchasing Governance	$3,126,000	Informational
PFM-2010-046	SCM SCV - SAP Supply Chain Design & Analytics	Application	SCM	Supply Chain Visibility	$3,950,000	Informational
PFM-2010-047	SCM OF - Service Parts Order Fulfillment	Application	SCM	Order Fulfillment	$3,452,500	Transactional
PFM-2010-048	SCM DSP - Service Parts Planning	Application	SCM	Demand & Supply Planning	$2,650,000	Strategic
PFM-2010-049	CRM Sales - Contracts & Pricing Management	Application	CRM	Sales	$22,500,000	Transactional
PFM-2010-050	CRM Marketing - Siebel Marketing and Analytics	Application	CRM	Marketing	$17,000,000	Strategic
PFM-2010-051	CRM CS - Service Contracts Integration	Application	CRM	Customer Service	$4,500,000	Transactional
PFM-2010-052	PLM - Oracle Product Management	Application	PLM	Product Management	$4,500,000	Transactional
PFM-2010-053	PLM - Oracle Product Management Integration	Application	PLM	Product Development & Collaboration	$2,500,000	Transactional
PFM-2010-054	PLM - Oracle Product Data Management	Application	PLM	Product Data Management	$12,500,000	Transactional
PFM-2010-055	PLM - Oracle Product Analytics	Application	PLM	PLM Foundational Components	$3,000,000	Informational
PFM-2010-056	INFR SDM - Trillium Data Cleansing	Technology	INFR	Structured Data Management	$2,500,000	Transactional
PFM-2010-057	INFR SM - Risk Monitoring Tools	Technology	INFR	Security Management	$5,430,000	Infrastructure
PFM-2010-058	INFR PM - Thin Computing Wyse & VMWare	Technology	INFR	Platform Management	$8,500,000	Infrastructure
PFM-2010-059	INFR NM - Unified Messaging System	Technology	INFR	Network Management	$11,000,000	Infrastructure
PFM-2010-060	INFR NM - Corp. HQ Wireless	Technology	INFR	Network Management	$7,500,000	Infrastructure
PFM-2010-061	INFR DC - Data Center Consolidation	Technology	INFR	Data Center	$24,750,000	Infrastructure
PFM-2010-062	INFR DAM - Reporting Tools Consolidation	Technology	INFR	Data Access Management	$3,500,000	Infrastructure
PFM-2010-063	INFR AM - WPS Upgrade	Technology	INFR	Application Middleware	$2,000,000	Infrastructure
PFM-2010-064	IT LCM - EA Reference Models	Technology	IT LCM	Enterprise Architecture (EA)	$2,000,000	Infrastructure
PFM-2010-065	IT LCM - Service Design Implementation	Technology	ITSM	Service Design	$5,500,000	Infrastructure

o Certain OPEX investments are of vital importance from the IT division's perspective of being able to effectively serve the critical aspects of SIRC's business needs. These are effectively non-discretionary investments and will be funded to the full amount requested. The mission-critical IT OPEX investments amount to 12 of the total of 40 IT OPEX investments:

Application Preservation → SCM → Transportation Management (PFM-2010-012)

Application Preservation → SCM → Order Fulfillment (PFM-2010-016)

Application Preservation → SCM → Manufacturing (PFM-2010-017)

Application Preservation → SCM → Demand and Supply Planning (PFM-2010-018)

Application Preservation → CRM → Siebel Call Center Operations (PFM-2010-021)

Service Management → ITSM → Service Operation (PFM-2010-027)

Service Management → ITSM → Service Design (i.e., Business Continuity Plan and Disaster Recovery) (PFM-2010-029)

Technology Preservation → INFR → Security Management (PFM-2010-032)

Technology Preservation → INFR → Platform Management (PFM-2010-033)

Technology Preservation → INFR → Network Management (PFM-2010-034)

Technology Preservation → INFR → Data Center and Facilities Management (PFM-2010-035)

Technology Preservation → IT LCM → IT Resource Planning (PFM-2010-039)

- Optimization of the IT portfolios should take into consideration dependencies not only within individual investments within the same portfolio, but should also account for cross-portfolio dependencies between investments. These are as follows:

o Dependencies between OPEX investments, i.e., within the OPEX IT portfolio:

ERP: Enterprise Asset Management Operations (PFM-2010-003) may be fully funded only if Financial Operations (PFM-2010-002) is fully funded.

ERP: Cross-Functional Operations (PFM-2010-005) may be fully funded only if Financial Operations (PFM-2010-002) is fully funded.

SRM: Purchasing Governance Operations (PFM-2010-008) may be fully funded only if Indirect Procurement Operations (PFM-2010-009) is fully funded.

○ Dependencies between CAPEX investments, i.e., within the CAPEX IT portfolio:

PLM Program Inter-Project Dependencies: The PLM program comprises four capital initiatives: the Oracle Product Management (PFM-2010-052), Oracle Product Management Integration (PFM-2010-053), Oracle Product Data Management (PFM-2010-054), and Oracle Product Hub (PFM-2010-055) projects within the program. Of these, the Oracle Product Data Management Project (PFM-2010-054) is the primary initiative and can be implemented independently from the other initiatives within the program, albeit based on integration with the existing legacy PLM operational investments. More importantly, PFM-2010-052, PFM-2010-053, and PFM-2010-055 are dependent on PFM-2010-054 and can be approved (launched/started) only if PFM-2010-054 is approved.

Service Parts Project Dependencies: The Service Parts Planning Project (PFM-2010-048) cannot be approved (launched/started) unless the Service Parts Order Fulfillment Project (PFM-2010-047) is approved.

○ Cross-Portfolio Dependencies, i.e., dependencies between investments across CAPEX and OPEX IT portfolios due to technical and functional constraints between investments:

CAPEX RFID Asset Tagging Project (PFM-2010-042) cannot be approved unless OPEX Enterprise Asset Management Operations (PFM-2010-003) is fully funded.

CAPEX RFID Asset Tagging Project (PFM-2010-042) cannot be approved unless OPEX ERP Cross-Functional Operations (PFM-2010-005) is fully funded.

CAPEX Siebel Marketing and Analytics Project (PFM-2010-050) cannot be approved unless OPEX Legacy Marketing Operations (PFM-2010-020) is fully funded.

CAPEX Siebel Marketing and Analytics Project (PFM-2010-050) cannot be approved unless OPEX INFR Structured Data Management Operations (PFM-2010-031) is fully funded.

CAPEX Siebel Marketing and Analytics Project (PFM-2010-050) cannot be approved unless OPEX INFR Application Middleware (PFM-2010-037) is fully funded.

CAPEX ITSM Service Design Implementation Project (PFM-2010-065) cannot be approved unless OPEX ITSM Service Management Tools Operations (PFM-2010-028) is fully funded.

○ Optimization of the IT portfolios should take into consideration resource constraints within and across various teams within the IT division. OPEX resource constraints include:

PLM: At most, only Product Management (PFM-2010-022), Product Development and Collaboration (PFM-2010-023), or Foundational Components Operations (PFM-2010-025) can be fully funded.

ITSM: At most, only Service Transition (PFM-2010-026) or Service Management Tools Operations (PFM-2010-028) can be fully funded.

INFR: At most, only Unstructured Data Management (PFM-2010-030), Data Access Management (PFM-2010-036), or Application Middleware Operations (PFM-2010-037) can be fully funded.

IT LCM: At most, only Systems Development Lifecycle (PFM-2010-038) or Enterprise Architecture Operations (PFM-2010-040) can be fully funded.

○ Cross-Portfolio Resource Constraints (mutual exclusivity): The organization can only support either the OPEX PLM Operations (PFM-2010-022, PFM-2010-023, PFM-2010-024, and PFM-2010-025) or the CAPEX PLM program (PFM-2010-052, PFM-2010-053, PFM-2010-054, and PFM-2010-055), owing to resource constraints and limited subject matter expertise in the organization. Consequently, exactly one of each of the corresponding initiatives within each set must be fully funded. Additionally, one set of corresponding investments within each portfolio must be funded in order that the IT division meets its obligations to SIRC's business units. Therefore:

Either OPEX Legacy PLM Product Management Operations (PFM-2010-022) or CAPEX Oracle Product Management (PFM-2010-052) must be approved (i.e., fully funded).

Either OPEX Legacy PLM Product Development and Collaboration (PFM-2010-023) or CAPEX Oracle Product Management Integration (PFM-2010-053) must be approved (i.e., fully funded).

Either OPEX Legacy PLM Product Data Management Operations (PFM-2010-024) or CAPEX Oracle Product Data Management ((PFM-2010-054) must be approved (i.e., fully funded).

Either OPEX Legacy PLM Foundational Components (PFM-2010-025) or CAPEX Oracle Product Analytics (PFM-2010-055) must be approved (i.e., fully funded).

- All approved CAPEX investments will be fully funded, subject to the approval of the EOC. All unapproved CAPEX investments will not be funded at all.
- The portfolio of investments should be evaluated by taking into consideration the dependencies between various investments in the CAPEX and OPEX portfolios, so that funding decisions are not made in isolation. The CAPEX portfolio of investments has to be balanced, such that a judicious mix of CAPEX investments is made across IT investment categories such as infrastructure, transactional, informational, and strategic, within a 2% tolerance, as illustrated in Figure 10-1. Basically, this indicates that new CAPEX investments are not to exceed the proportions specified in Figure 10-1, within the acceptable tolerance limits.

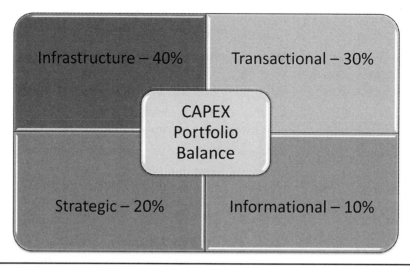

Figure 10-1   SIRC IT CAPEX investments portfolio balance

To recap, the case study calls for the IT CAPEX budget for 2010 to be reduced from the proposed $176.6M to $118.4M and for the IT OPEX budget for 2010 to be reduced from $340M to $296M, with the aim of selecting the best set of investments for full funding, based on a set of decision criteria set by IT senior management, headed by the CIO.

10.2 SIRC IT Portfolio Selection

As mentioned in Chapter 1, IT portfolios may not be evaluated on the basis of financial criteria alone, since many IT investments cannot be justified purely in terms of their financial value. However, utility theory provides an excellent alternative in evaluating a portfolio of IT investments for the purpose of selecting the best-suited set of investments for the organization to pursue under constrained budgetary and human resource conditions.

Portfolio selection by project prioritization using MODA will be accomplished first, followed by portfolio selection using optimization. This is done deliberately (counter to the CREOPM™ sequence of processes) to illustrate why optimization needs to precede prioritization as the primary portfolio selection technique. The portfolio of investments selected, using both approaches, will be compared subsequently to illustrate the superiority of one method over the other. In either method, the prerequisites are the same:

- **Step 1:** Develop MODA model(s) for the portfolio of IT projects/investments.
- **Step 2:** Compute the utility value of each investment in the portfolio using the MODA model(s) developed in the previous step.

Once the utility values have been computed for each investment in the portfolio, one has a choice of either prioritization or optimization as the primary methodology for portfolio selection. The intricacies in computing the utility value of the IT investments are addressed in the following section before portfolio selection is performed.

10.2.1 MODA Models for IT Investments

The development of MODA models for IT investments was explained in Chapter 8. The reader may recall that two MODA models, one for CAPEX investments and another for OPEX investments, were developed. Chapter 8 and Appendix A describe the objectives and underlying attributes of the utility hierarchy for the CAPEX and OPEX MODA models in detail, which are illustrated in Figures 10-2 and 10-3.

10.2.2 Computation of Utility Values for IT Investments

10.2.2.1 CAPEX Utility Value Computation

A step-by-step process for computing the utility values for the MODA models is illustrated for the CAPEX IT investment PFM-2010-049, i.e., SIRC Contracts Management Project.[2] The steps involved in determining the utility value of this investment are as follows:

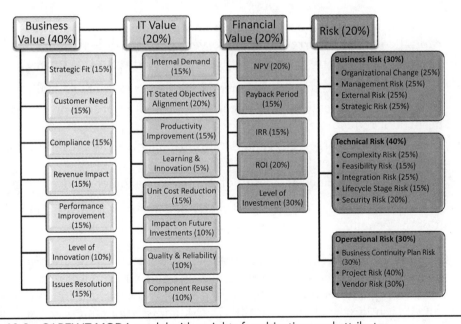

Figure 10-2   CAPEX IT MODA model with weights for objectives and attributes

---

[2]Project Description (PFM-2010-049): SIRC Corp.'s current contract and pricing management business processes and underlying supporting systems are unable to adequately support the dynamic needs of the business in rebates management and up-front discount sales schemes driven by complex marketing innovations, with potential contractual violations resulting in fines or overpayment. Also, the underlying infrastructure and procedures are unable to support informed decision making and reporting requirements. This initiative aims to implement a new commercial-off-the-shelf contract management system which will integrate with ERP and SCM systems and considerably reduce profit leakage, loss of financial controls, and channel conflicts and improve customer service.

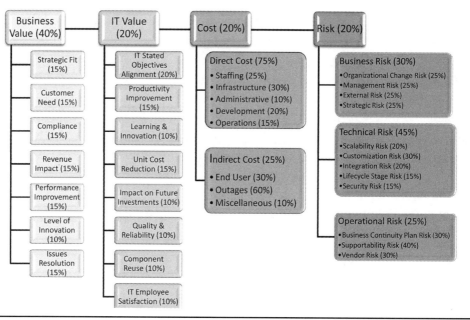

Figure 10-3 OPEX IT MODA model with weights for objectives and attributes

Step 1. Evaluate project/program proposal to determine costs/benefits. For this project, capital costs are incurred over a five-year period, while benefits need to be quantified in monetary terms. The key benefits expected from this project include:

- Additional revenue, due to incremental sales as a result of optimal pricing
- Cost savings in revenue management, as a result of improved productivity and headcount reductions
- Cost savings in charge-backs and rebates management, as a result of improved productivity and headcount reductions
- Indirect cost avoidance as a result of improved customer service

The estimated capital costs and monetized yearly benefits for this investment, derived as a result of the benefits quantification, are listed in Table 10-6.

Step 2. Compute absolute values for financial value attributes. These are primarily the financial value parameters such as net present value (NPV), payback period, internal rate of return (IRR), and return on investment (ROI), whose values are computed using discounted cash flow analysis, with SIRC's risk-adjusted discount rate of 25% and straight-line depreciation, as shown in Table 10-7.

Table 10-6 Costs and benefits from PFM-2010-049 CAPEX investment

Parameter Description	Year 1	Year 2	Year 3	Year 4	Year 5
Total Costs Estimated	$22,500,000	$6,000,000	$2,500,000	$2,000,000	$1,500,000
Total Benefits Estimated	$0	$11,023,545	$14,084,700	$19,709,754	$19,622,626

Table 10-7 Computation of financial value based on discounted cash flow

Parameter Description	Year 1	Year 2	Year 3	Year 4	Year 5	Total	Present Value
Total Benefits Estimated	$0	$11,023,545	$14,084,700	$19,709,754	$19,622,626	$64,440,625	$28,769,493
Total Costs Estimated	$22,500,000	$6,000,000	$2,500,000	$2,000,000	$1,500,000	$34,500,000	$24,430,720
Net Cash Flow	–$22,500,000	$5,023,545	$11,584,700	$17,709,754	$18,122,626	$29,940,625	$4,338,773
Cumulative Cash Flow	–$22,500,000	–$17,476,455	–$5,891,755	$11,817,999	$29,940,625		

Financial Value Attributes	
NPV	$4,338,773
Payback Period	3-4 years
IRR	35.53%
ROI	17.76%

Step 3. Estimate MODA values for every attribute and objective in the CAPEX MODA model. For this particular CAPEX project, the estimated MODA values for each attribute in the utility hierarchy are:

- Business Value
  - Strategic fit: Medium—directly impacts business unit's strategic objectives.
  - Customer need: High—multiple business units clamoring for this capability.
  - Compliance: Required for the medium term (1-2 years).
  - Revenue impact: Directly generates revenue for the company.
  - Performance improvement: >10%.
  - Level of innovation: Moderate enhancement in competitive advantage.
  - Issues resolution: Moderate improvement in resolving customer issues.
- IT Value
  - Internal demand: Medium—IT senior management request.
  - IT stated objectives (SOs) alignment: Medium—directly aligned with IT business unit's strategic objectives.
  - Productivity improvement: <5%.
  - Learning and innovation: Low—departmental level.
  - Unit cost reduction: <5%.
  - Impact on future investments: Potential impact or optional building block.
  - Quality and reliability: Necessary to maintain current level of service.
  - Component reuse: Minor opportunities to create or consume assets.
- Financial Value
  - NPV: ≥$1M, but <$5M.
  - Payback period: ≥3 years but <5 years.
  - IRR: ≥25% but <40%.

- ○ ROI: ≥10% but <25%.
- ○ Level of initial investment: ≤10% but >5% of overall IT budget.
- Risk
  - ○ Business Risk

    Organizational change risk: Medium; two of the following are true: (1) executive management commitment is lukewarm at best, and/or (2) end-user community is skeptical about this initiative, and/or (3) business and IT need to invest more effort.

    Management risk: Medium (organizational redesign anticipated—some likelihood of management change).

    External risk: Low (fairly stable external environment or little impact of external changes on this IT investment).

    Strategic risk: Low (little to no impact on organization's strategic goals and objectives).

  - ○ Technical Risk

    Complexity risk: Medium (hardware exists but is not operations tested, software requires significant advance, or some amount of specialized expertise required in technical competencies).

    Feasibility risk: Medium (step change in capabilities requiring some innovation; there is a reasonable chance that the desired solution may be infeasible).

    Integration risk: High (significant integration required necessitating architecture redesign; development of a number of new interfaces is required).

    Lifecycle stage/maturity risk: Medium (niche or special use technology).

    Security risk: Medium (security model in alignment with organization's security standards, practices, and policies).

  - ○ Operational Risk

    Business continuity plan risk: Medium (Class B plan—disaster recovery within two business days).

    Project risk: High; two of the following are true: (1) project may encounter slippage in cost, schedule, and/or (2) project is dependent on the success of other initiatives, and/or (3) project scope change is likely during implementation).

    Vendor risk: Medium (vendor with international presence, excellent product strategy, multiple channels of sales and implementation support, products have >100 customers with live implementations).

Step 4. Translate the raw scores into weighted scores. Translation of raw scores into weighted scores is illustrated in Table 10-8, in which the raw score for each attribute is assigned a value on a scale of 0 to 9; in other words, the minimum assignable raw score for an attribute is 0 and the maximum assignable raw score is 9. The weighted score for an attribute[3] is computed as:

Weighted score of attribute = (Objective weight) * (Attribute weight) * (Sub-attribute weight) * (Raw score)/(Maximum raw score for attribute)

Step 5. Compute the utility value of the investment. The aggregate MODA score (or utility value) of an investment is computed for this CAPEX investment as the sum of the weighted scores of Business Value, IT Value, Financial Value, and Risk, each of which in turn is the sum of the weighted scores of each of the underlying attributes comprising each objective. These are listed in Table 10-9.

It is worth noting here that the computation of the Risk score is inversely proportional to the risk carried by an investment; in other words, the greater the risk of an investment, the lower its risk score and vice versa. Utility values have been computed for each of the 25 newly proposed investments in the CAPEX IT portfolio by following the process outlined above. The resulting portfolio with the computed utility value for each of the 25 CAPEX IT investments is in Table 10-10.

10.2.2.2 OPEX *Utility Value Computation*

The computation of utility values for each OPEX investment follows a similar procedure to the one above for investments in the CAPEX portfolio, with the following variation:

- Financial Value is not one of the objectives for an OPEX investment for reasons specified in Chapter 6. Instead, each OPEX investment is characterized by the computation of the total cost of ownership, as one of the objectives. A sample total cost of ownership computation is listed in Table 10-11 for OPEX investment PFM-2010-019 (i.e., CRM Siebel Sales OPEX).

Raw scores, weighted scores, and the overall MODA utility are computed for all the objectives and attributes in the OPEX utility hierarchy, for all 40 OPEX investments, in a manner similar to that outlined for the CAPEX IT investment, while accounting for the slight variations in attributes constituting an objective as applicable. Appendix A, A Primer in Decision Analysis, provides the details of the objectives and the underlying attributes of the OPEX MODA model. The resulting portfolio with the utility values is given in Table 10-12.

10.2.3 Portfolio Selection by Prioritization

This section will illustrate how portfolio selection is typically accomplished today in numerous organizations via prioritization. As stated previously, MODA is the

---

[3]The maximum raw score for an attribute in the CAPEX and OPEX MODA models used in the case study is 9. This can easily be tailored to suit each organization's preference.

Table 10-8 MODA score computation for CAPEX IT investment PFM-2010-049[1]

Objective	Objective Weight	Attribute	Attribute Weight	Sub-Attribute	Sub-Attribute Weight	Score Description	Raw Score	Weighted Score
Business Value	40%	Strategic Fit	15%	N/A	100%	Medium — Directly impacts BU SOs	5	3.33
		Customer Need	15%	N/A	100%	High — Multiple BUs clamoring for this capability	9	6.00
		Compliance	15%	N/A	100%	Required for the medium term (1-2 years)	5	3.33
		Revenue Impact	15%	N/A	100%	Directly generates revenue for the company	9	6.00
		Performance Improvement	15%	N/A	100%	>10%	9	6.00
		Level of Innovation	10%	N/A	100%	Moderate enhancement in competitive advantage	5	2.22
		Issues Resolution	15%	N/A	100%	Moderate improvement in resolving customer issues	5	3.33
IT Value	20%	Internal Demand	15%	N/A	100%	Medium — IT sr. management request	5	1.67
		IT Stated Objectives Alignment	20%	N/A	100%	Medium — Directly aligned with IT BU's SOs	5	2.22
		Productivity Improvement	15%	N/A	100%	<5%	2	0.67
		Learning & Innovation	5%	N/A	100%	Low — Departmental Level	2	0.22
		Unit Cost Reduction	15%	N/A	100%	<5%	2	0.67
		Impact on Future Investments	10%	N/A	100%	Potential impact or optional building block	2	0.44
		Quality and Reliability	10%	N/A	100%	Necessary to maintain current level of service	5	1.11
		Component Reuse	10%	N/A	100%	Minor opportunities to create or consume assets	2	0.44

Category	Weight	Attribute / Subcategory	Weight	Sub-Attribute	Weight	Value	Score	Weighted Value
Financial Value	20%	NPV	20%	N/A	100%	≥$1M but <$5M	5	2.22
		Payback Period	15%	N/A	100%	≥3 years but <5 years	2	0.67
		IRR	15%	N/A	100%	≥25% but <40%	5	1.67
		ROI	20%	N/A	100%	≥10% but <25%	5	2.22
		Level of Initial Investment	30%	N/A	100%	≤10% but >5% of overall IT budget	2	1.33
Risk	20%	Business Risk	30%	Organizational Change Risk	25%	Medium	2	0.33
				Management Risk	25%	Medium	5	0.83
				External Risk	25%	Low	9	1.50
				Strategic Risk	25%	Low	9	1.50
		Technical Risk	40%	Complexity Risk	25%	Medium	5	1.11
				Feasibility Risk	15%	Medium	5	0.67
				Integration Risk	25%	High	2	0.44
				Lifecycle Stage/Maturity Risk	15%	Medium	5	0.89
				Security Risk	20%	Medium	5	0.89
		Operational Risk	30%	BCP Risk	30%	Medium	5	1.00
				Project Risk	40%	High	2	0.53
				Vendor Risk	30%	Medium	5	1.00

[1] Excel spreadsheets for each investment have been built to limit the choice of attribute score selection to the list of values described in Appendices A and B, so that errors in computation are minimized.

Table 10-9 Utility value for CAPEX investment PFM-2010-049

Utility Objective	Score
Business Value	30.22
IT Value	7.44
Financial Value	8.11
Risk	10.70
Utility Value	56.48

Table 10-10 SIRC IT CAPEX portfolio with computed utility values

ID	Investment Name	Portfolio Type	Portfolio Sub-Group	Utility Value	Requested Funding ($)
PFM-2010-041	ERP HCM - e-Learning	CAPEX	Informational	42.84	$7,500,000
PFM-2010-042	ERP EAM - RFID Asset Tagging	CAPEX	Transactional	42.82	$6,250,000
PFM-2010-043	SRM SC - Supplier Collaboration	CAPEX	Strategic	58.82	$3,755,000
PFM-2010-044	SRM SC – Sourcing	CAPEX	Strategic	47.98	$6,752,500
PFM-2010-045	SRM SC - Spend Analytics	CAPEX	Informational	40.20	$3,126,000
PFM-2010-046	SCM SCV - SAP Supply Chain Design & Analytics	CAPEX	Informational	62.20	$3,950,000
PFM-2010-047	SCM OF - Service Parts Order Fulfillment	CAPEX	Transactional	56.89	$3,452,500
PFM-2010-048	SCM DSP - Service Parts Planning	CAPEX	Strategic	61.22	$2,650,000
PFM-2010-049	CRM Sales - Contracts & Pricing Management	CAPEX	Transactional	56.59	$22,500,000
PFM-2010-050	CRM Marketing - Siebel Marketing and Analytics	CAPEX	Strategic	72.92	$17,000,000
PFM-2010-051	CRM CS - Service Contracts Integration	CAPEX	Transactional	42.89	$4,500,000
PFM-2010-052	PLM - Oracle Product Management	CAPEX	Transactional	42.56	$4,500,000
PFM-2010-053	PLM - Oracle Product Management Integration	CAPEX	Transactional	44.22	$2,500,000
PFM-2010-054	PLM - Oracle Product Data Management	CAPEX	Transactional	45.28	$12,500,000
PFM-2010-055	PLM - Oracle Product Hub	CAPEX	Informational	48.17	$3,000,000
PFM-2010-056	INFR SDM - Trillium Data Cleansing	CAPEX	Transactional	43.44	$2,500,000
PFM-2010-057	INFR SM - Risk Monitoring Tools	CAPEX	Infrastructure	45.40	$5,430,000
PFM-2010-058	INFR PM - Thin Computing Wyse & VMWare	CAPEX	Infrastructure	43.09	$8,500,000
PFM-2010-059	INFR NM - Unified Messaging System	CAPEX	Infrastructure	40.62	$11,000,000
PFM-2010-060	INFR NM - Corp. HQ Wireless	CAPEX	Infrastructure	41.91	$7,500,000
PFM-2010-061	INFR DC - Data Center Consolidation	CAPEX	Infrastructure	46.79	$24,750,000
PFM-2010-062	INFR DAM - Reporting Tools Consolidation	CAPEX	Informational	49.31	$3,500,000
PFM-2010-063	INFR AM - WPS Upgrade	CAPEX	Infrastructure	45.98	$2,000,000
PFM-2010-064	IT LCM - EA Reference Models	CAPEX	Infrastructure	61.81	$2,000,000
PFM-2010-065	IT LCM - Service Design Implementation	CAPEX	Infrastructure	54.92	$5,500,000

Table 10-11 Total cost of ownership for OPEX investment PFM-2010-019

Cost Component	Total Annual Cost ($)	% Total Annual Cost
Direct Costs		
Staffing Costs[1]		
Employees	$2,025,000	25%
Contractors	$1,215,000	15%
Consultants	$0	0%
Total Staffing Costs	$3,240,000	39%
Infrastructure Costs		
Hardware Costs		
Servers	$200,000	2%
Client Computers	$250,000	3%
Peripherals	$50,000	1%
Maintenance Fees	$0	0%
Other Hardware Costs	$50,000	1%
Total Hardware Costs	$550,000	7%
Software Costs		
License Fees	$807,000	10%
Maintenance Fees	$0	0%
Other Software Costs	$0	0%
Total Software Costs	$807,000	10%
Network Costs		
Network Components	$50,000	1%
Storage	$150,000	2%
Local Area Network	$50,000	1%
Wide Area Network	$50,000	1%
Remote Access	$50,000	1%
Other Network Costs	$50,000	1%
Total Network Costs	$400,000	5%
Total Infrastructure Costs	$1,757,000	21%
Administrative Costs		
Travel	$100,000	1%
Support Contracts	$0	0%
Overhead/Labor	$0	0%
Other Administrative Costs	$450,000	5%
Total Administrative Costs	$550,000	7%
Development Costs		
Analysis	$25,000	0%
Design	$50,000	1%
Engineering (Install, Coding, Configuration)	$50,000	1%

(continues)

[1]Total # of full-time equivalents (FTEs) for this OPEX investment = 24, based on the assumption that the fully loaded cost of 1 FTE is $135,000 per year, inclusive of salary, benefits, etc. The total # FTEs is computed in a similar manner for every OPEX investment.

Table 10-11 *(Continued)*

Cost Component	Total Annual Cost ($)	% Total Annual Cost
Integration	$75,000	1%
Training	$10,000	0%
Testing	$50,000	1%
Deployment	$10,000	0%
All Other Development Costs	$100,000	1%
Total Development Costs	$370,000	4%
Operations Costs (Maintenance)		
Analysis	$75,000	1%
Design	$75,000	1%
Engineering (Install, Coding, Configuration)	$150,000	2%
Integration	$150,000	2%
Training	$5,000	0%
Testing	$75,000	1%
Deployment	$15,000	0%
All Other Operations Costs	$500,000	6%
Total Operations Costs	$1,045,000	13%
Total Direct Costs	$6,962,000	84%
Indirect Costs		
End-User Costs		
Formal End-User Training	$50,000	1%
Informal End-User Training	$0	0%
End-User Operations	$800,000	10%
Other Training Expenses	$0	0%
Total End-User Costs	$850,000	10%
Outages		
Planned Downtime	$150,000	2%
Unplanned Downtime	$250,000	3%
Total Cost of Outages	$400,000	5%
Miscellaneous		
All Other costs	$50,000	1%
Total Indirect Costs	$1,300,000	16%
Total Cost of Ownership	$8,262,000	100%

Table 10-12 SIRC IT OPEX portfolio with computed utility values

ID	Investment Name	Portfolio Type	Portfolio Sub-Group	Utility Value	Requested Funding ($)
PFM-2010-001	PeopleSoft HCM OpEx	OPEX	Application Preservation	45.57	$15,402,000
PFM-2010-002	SAP ERP FI OpEx	OPEX	Application Preservation	61.64	$11,492,000
PFM-2010-003	SAP ERP EAM OpEx	OPEX	Application Preservation	46.48	$6,052,000
PFM-2010-004	SAP ERP DP OpEx	OPEX	Application Preservation	46.62	$3,672,000
PFM-2010-005	SAP ERP XFO OpEx	OPEX	Application Preservation	53.33	$6,732,000
PFM-2010-006	Ariba SRM SBM OpEx	OPEX	Application Preservation	47.18	$3,672,000
PFM-2010-007	Ariba SRM SC OpEx	OPEX	Application Preservation	66.28	$4,012,000
PFM-2010-008	Ariba SRM PG OpEx	OPEX	Application Preservation	43.04	$3,502,000
PFM-2010-009	Ariba SRM IP OpEx	OPEX	Application Preservation	46.01	$6,222,000
PFM-2010-010	Ariba SRM CM OpEx	OPEX	Application Preservation	49.16	$5,882,000
PFM-2010-011	SAP SCM WH OpEx	OPEX	Application Preservation	49.53	$4,352,000
PFM-2010-012	SAP SCM TP OpEx	OPEX	Application Preservation	52.42	$4,352,000
PFM-2010-013	SAP SCM SNC OpEx	OPEX	Application Preservation	57.03	$3,672,000
PFM-2010-014	SAP SCM SCV OpEx	OPEX	Application Preservation	66.01	$4,692,000
PFM-2010-015	SAP SCM PR OpEx	OPEX	Application Preservation	41.67	$4,012,000
PFM-2010-016	SAP SCM OF OpEx	OPEX	Application Preservation	64.66	$7,922,000
PFM-2010-017	SAP SCM MF OpEx	OPEX	Application Preservation	63.32	$8,092,000
PFM-2010-018	SAP SCM DSP OpEx	OPEX	Application Preservation	58.91	$4,692,000
PFM-2010-019	Siebel Sales OpEx	OPEX	Application Preservation	62.54	$8,262,000
PFM-2010-020	Legacy Marketing OpEx	OPEX	Application Preservation	39.56	$10,132,000
PFM-2010-021	Siebel Call Center OpEx	OPEX	Application Preservation	67.07	$6,392,000
PFM-2010-022	Legacy PLM PM OpEx	OPEX	Application Preservation	50.12	$3,672,000
PFM-2010-023	Legacy PLM PDC OpEx	OPEX	Application Preservation	51.01	$2,992,000
PFM-2010-024	Legacy PLM PDM OpEx	OPEX	Application Preservation	51.57	$4,182,000
PFM-2010-025	Legacy PLM FC OpEx	OPEX	Application Preservation	45.01	$3,162,000
PFM-2010-026	ITSM ST OpEx	OPEX	Service Management	57.07	$2,210,000
PFM-2010-027	ITSM SO OpEx	OPEX	Service Management	56.16	$7,820,000
PFM-2010-028	ITSM SMT OpEx	OPEX	Service Management	55.73	$2,210,000
PFM-2010-029	ITSM SD OpEx	OPEX	Service Management	59.97	$10,880,000
PFM-2010-030	INFR UDM OpEx	OPEX	Technology Preservation	48.60	$3,910,000
PFM-2010-031	INFR SDM OpEx	OPEX	Technology Preservation	56.01	$8,160,000
PFM-2010-032	INFR SM OpEx	OPEX	Technology Preservation	57.36	$11,560,000
PFM-2010-033	INFR PM OpEx	OPEX	Technology Preservation	54.69	$66,640,000
PFM-2010-034	INFR NM OpEx	OPEX	Technology Preservation	53.65	$28,560,000
PFM-2010-035	INFR DC OpEx	OPEX	Technology Preservation	51.34	$19,040,000
PFM-2010-036	INFR DAM OpEx	OPEX	Technology Preservation	51.02	$11,900,000
PFM-2010-037	INFR AM OpEx	OPEX	Technology Preservation	53.36	$6,630,000
PFM-2010-038	IT LCM SDLC OpEx	OPEX	Technology Preservation	51.33	$2,890,000
PFM-2010-039	IT LCM RP OpEx	OPEX	Technology Preservation	59.46	$6,800,000
PFM-2010-040	IT LCM EA OpEx	OPEX	Technology Preservation	60.50	$3,570,000

technique chosen for prioritization for reasons discussed in Chapter 8. Using the computed weighted aggregate utility values of the investments, project investments can be prioritized with a simple data sorting tool such as an Excel spreadsheet. It is worth noting here that two separate prioritizations have to be performed, one each for the CAPEX projects and the OPEX investments. SIRC's 40 OPEX investments are evaluated using the OPEX MODA utility hierarchy (where the OPEX MODA objectives are Business Value, IT Value, Cost, and Risk) and assigned appropriate values.

Likewise, the 25 CAPEX investments are evaluated using the CAPEX MODA utility hierarchy (comprised of Business Value, IT Value, Financial Value, and Risk as the objectives). The determination of the raw values, conversion to the appropriate utility value, and the subsequent computation of the weighted scores was accomplished using Microsoft Excel.

10.2.3.1 *Prioritization of CAPEX Projects*

The utility values for each of the CAPEX IT investments have been consolidated in a single spreadsheet to facilitate the prioritization of the CAPEX investments. The spreadsheet showing the investments is illustrated in Table 10-13, which shows all the CAPEX investments that have been ranked and selected on the basis of their MODA scores. These correspond to the rows for which the column labeled "Selected (Y/N)" has a value of "Y," and the available CAPEX IT funding for 2010 (i.e., $118.4M).

The MODA-based prioritization has resulted in the selection of 14 new investments for funding approval. These are ranked 1 to 14 in Table 10-13 and have the 14 highest aggregate MODA scores. The investment cutoff occurs at the 15th project, based on the fact that the inclusion of this project in the category of approved investments would set the total CAPEX funding at $118.74M, higher than the funding cutoff limit of $118.40M. Hence this investment and all investments ranked below it are not selected. Any CAPEX investment that has been selected by prioritization is funded at the requested funding amount (i.e., allocated funding = requested funding in Table 10-13), while unselected investments are not funded (i.e., allocated funding = $0 in Table 10-13). A graphical illustration of investment selection based on MODA prioritization is shown in Figures 10-4 and 10-5. The selection of these investments results in the portfolio balance listed in Table 10-14.

The portfolio selection by prioritization of CAPEX investments fulfills the objective that the total cost of the funded CAPEX portfolio should be limited to a maximum of $118.4M. Fourteen investments have been selected, while 11 investments were not chosen to be a part of the CAPEX portfolio. Every CAPEX investment that has been selected is to be recommended to be fully funded, while every investment that has not been selected will not receive any funding, i.e., for such investments, the funding allocation is $0.

MODA-based prioritization, however, fails to meet the decision criteria imposed by IT senior management in terms of achieving a balanced portfolio of CAPEX investments, even within the desired tolerance limits of ±2%.[4] Additionally, the limitation of prioritization is that it cannot incorporate inter-project dependencies into the selection of investments for funding. The end result is that while prioritization can help

---

[4]Note that ±2% is not a magic threshold range, but has been used in the case study simply to illustrate that practical considerations do not impose a rigid adherence to the portfolio balance criteria.

Table 10-13 MODA-based prioritization of SIRC CAPEX IT investments

ID	Portfolio Sub-Group	Business Value	IT Value	Financial Value	Risk	Total Score	Rank	Requested Funding ($)	Cumulative Amount ($)	Selected (Y/N)	Allocated Funding ($)
PFM-2010-041	Informational	10.89	6.67	6.56	18.73	42.84	20	$7,500,000	$149,990,000	N	$0
PFM-2010-042	Transactional	13.56	7.11	4.67	17.49	42.82	17	$6,250,000	$129,490,000	N	$0
PFM-2010-043	Strategic	18.89	8.33	16.89	14.71	58.82	6	$3,755,000	$51,855,000	Y	$3,755,000
PFM-2010-044	Strategic	16.22	10.33	7.44	13.98	47.98	9	$6,752,500	$67,560,000	Y	$6,752,500
PFM-2010-045	Informational	6.89	6.00	6.67	20.64	40.20	25	$3,126,000	$176,616,000	N	$0
PFM-2010-046	Informational	14.89	9.78	16.89	20.64	62.20	2	$3,950,000	$20,950,000	Y	$3,950,000
PFM-2010-047	Transactional	19.56	8.44	10.11	18.78	56.89	7	$3,452,500	$55,307,500	Y	$3,452,500
PFM-2010-048	Strategic	21.56	9.44	11.44	18.78	61.22	3	$2,650,000	$23,600,000	Y	$2,650,000
PFM-2010-049	Transactional	30.22	7.44	8.11	10.81	56.59	5	$22,500,000	$48,100,000	Y	$22,500,000
PFM-2010-050	Strategic	32.22	12.22	15.00	13.48	72.92	1	$17,000,000	$17,000,000	Y	$17,000,000
PFM-2010-051	Transactional	13.56	6.44	6.56	16.33	42.89	16	$4,500,000	$123,240,000	N	$0
PFM-2010-052	Transactional	13.56	9.11	4.67	15.22	42.56	18	$4,500,000	$133,990,000	N	$0
PFM-2010-053	Transactional	11.56	8.78	6.00	17.89	44.22	22	$2,500,000	$159,990,000	N	$0
PFM-2010-054	Transactional	14.89	9.11	7.44	13.83	45.28	13	$12,500,000	$111,310,000	Y	$12,500,000
PFM-2010-055	Informational	13.56	9.11	8.22	17.28	48.17	12	$3,000,000	$98,810,000	Y	$3,000,000
PFM-2010-056	Transactional	12.89	4.44	7.33	18.78	43.44	24	$2,500,000	$173,490,000	N	$0
PFM-2010-057	Infrastructure	9.56	8.56	6.56	20.73	45.40	14	$5,430,000	$116,740,000	Y	$5,430,000
PFM-2010-058	Infrastructure	10.22	8.78	7.44	16.64	43.09	19	$8,500,000	$142,490,000	N	$0
PFM-2010-059	Infrastructure	5.56	11.89	4.67	18.51	40.62	23	$11,000,000	$170,990,000	N	$0
PFM-2010-060	Infrastructure	5.56	11.89	4.00	20.47	41.91	21	$7,500,000	$157,490,000	N	$0
PFM-2010-061	Infrastructure	12.89	15.56	7.44	10.90	46.79	10	$24,750,000	$92,310,000	Y	$24,750,000
PFM-2010-062	Informational	6.89	14.22	7.33	20.87	49.31	11	$3,500,000	$95,810,000	Y	$3,500,000
PFM-2010-063	Infrastructure	6.89	9.11	7.33	22.64	45.98	15	$2,000,000	$118,740,000	N	$0
PFM-2010-064	Infrastructure	13.56	13.22	16.89	18.14	61.81	4	$2,000,000	$25,600,000	Y	$2,000,000
PFM-2010-065	Infrastructure	14.22	16.89	7.44	16.37	54.92	8	$5,500,000	$60,807,500	Y	$5,500,000

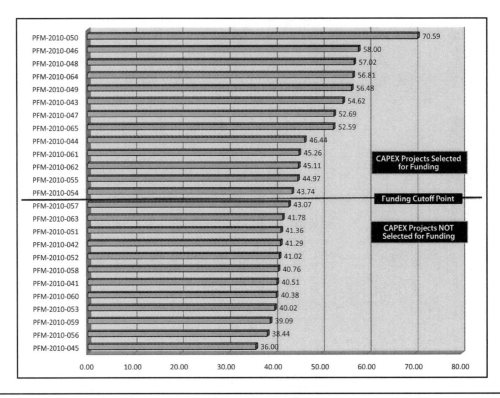

Figure 10-4 MODA-based prioritization of CAPEX portfolio—summary scores

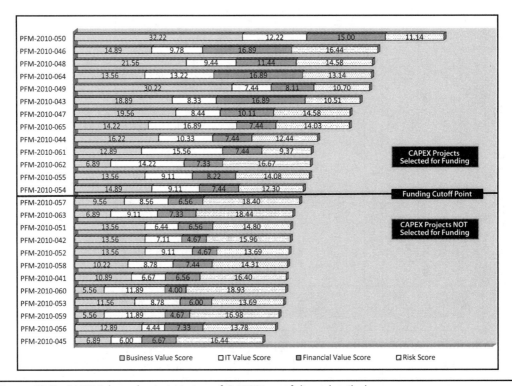

Figure 10-5 MODA-based prioritization of CAPEX portfolio—detailed scores

Table 10-14 CAPEX IT portfolio prioritization report

Description	Funding Amount	Count	% of Total Funding	Desired Funding
All Selected Capital Investments	$116,740,000	14	–	–
Strategic	$30,157,500	4	25.8%	20.0%
Informational	$10,450,000	3	9.0%	10.0%
Transactional	$38,452,500	3	32.9%	30.0%
Infrastructure	$37,680,000	4	32.3%	40.0%
Total MODA Score for Selected Investments	727.39			

organizations select a set of investments from a portfolio of new projects, the result is usually a sub-optimal portfolio of recommended investments.

10.2.3.2 *Prioritization of OPEX Investments*

As with the CAPEX IT portfolio, the utility values for each of the OPEX IT investments have been consolidated in a single spreadsheet to facilitate the prioritization of the OPEX investments. This is illustrated in Table 10-15, which shows all the OPEX investments that have been ranked and selected on the basis of their MODA scores and the available OPEX IT funding for 2010, which is $296M.

MODA-based prioritization has resulted in the selection of 33 OPEX investments to be fully funded. These are ranked 1 to 33 in Table 10-15 and have the 33 highest aggregate MODA scores. The investment cutoff occurs at the 34th investment, the inclusion of which in the category of fully funded OPEX investments would set the total OPEX funding to $297.738M, higher than the OPEX funding cutoff limit of $296M. Any OPEX investment that has been selected as a result of prioritization receives full funding (i.e., allocated funding = requested funding in Table 10-15), while an unselected investment is not funded (i.e., allocated funding = $0 in Table 10-15). The graphical representation of OPEX investment selection based on prioritization is shown in Figures 10-6 and 10-7.

The prioritization of OPEX investments fulfills the objective that the total cost of the funded OPEX investments should be limited to a maximum of $296M. Thirty-three investments were selected, while seven investments were not. Every OPEX investment that was selected is to be fully funded, while every investment that was not selected will not receive any funding. For non-selected investments, the funding allocation is $0, in order to meet the OPEX budgetary constraint. Zero funding for unapproved OPEX investments is not a viable choice in the real world because IT organizations have to fulfill obligations based on contractual agreements with vendors and service level agreements with business units among others, all of which necessitate a minimum level of funding for every OPEX investment, regardless of whether or not it has been selected by the prioritization process.

Further, prioritization fails to meet the decision criteria imposed by management in terms of its inability to incorporate inter-project dependencies into the selection of

Table 10-15 MODA-based prioritization of SIRC OPEX investments

ID	Sub-Portfolio Group	Business Value	IT Value	Cost	Risk	Total Score	Rank	Investment Amount ($)	Cumulative Amount ($)	Selected (Y/N)	Allocated Funding ($)
PFM-2010-001	Application Preservation	13.56	9.78	7.86	14.38	45.57	37	$15,402,000	$322,354,000	N	$0
PFM-2010-002	Application Preservation	22.22	13.11	11.33	14.98	61.64	7	$11,492,000	$50,864,000	Y	$11,492,000
PFM-2010-003	Application Preservation	13.56	7.67	11.11	14.14	46.48	35	$6,052,000	$303,790,000	N	$0
PFM-2010-004	Application Preservation	9.56	4.67	16.33	16.07	46.62	33	$3,672,000	$291,516,000	Y	$3,672,000
PFM-2010-005	Application Preservation	15.56	11.33	12.67	13.78	53.33	21	$6,732,000	$221,000,000	Y	$6,732,000
PFM-2010-006	Application Preservation	11.56	7.11	16.11	12.40	47.18	32	$3,672,000	$287,844,000	Y	$3,672,000
PFM-2010-007	Application Preservation	24.22	12.89	16.33	12.83	66.28	3	$4,012,000	$15,096,000	Y	$4,012,000
PFM-2010-008	Application Preservation	6.89	7.44	16.33	12.38	43.04	38	$3,502,000	$325,856,000	N	$0
PFM-2010-009	Application Preservation	14.89	9.11	11.33	11.28	46.61	34	$6,222,000	$297,738,000	N	$0
PFM-2010-010	Application Preservation	16.22	10.44	11.11	11.98	49.76	30	$5,882,000	$280,262,000	Y	$5,882,000
PFM-2010-011	Application Preservation	12.22	5.67	14.11	18.13	50.13	29	$4,352,000	$274,380,000	Y	$4,352,000
PFM-2010-012	Application Preservation	13.56	6.11	16.11	17.24	53.02	22	$4,352,000	$225,352,000	Y	$4,352,000
PFM-2010-013	Application Preservation	16.22	8.11	15.83	17.47	57.63	13	$3,672,000	$82,688,000	Y	$3,672,000
PFM-2010-014	Application Preservation	24.89	13.11	14.00	14.61	66.61	2	$4,692,000	$11,084,000	Y	$4,692,000
PFM-2010-015	Application Preservation	6.22	4.67	17.00	14.38	42.27	39	$4,012,000	$329,868,000	N	$0
PFM-2010-016	Application Preservation	25.56	11.22	14.00	14.48	65.26	4	$7,922,000	$23,018,000	Y	$7,922,000
PFM-2010-017	Application Preservation	24.89	11.22	12.17	15.64	63.92	5	$8,092,000	$31,110,000	Y	$8,092,000
PFM-2010-018	Application Preservation	18.89	11.11	13.33	16.18	59.51	11	$4,692,000	$76,806,000	Y	$4,692,000
PFM-2010-019	Application Preservation	24.22	12.89	11.42	14.61	63.14	6	$8,262,000	$39,372,000	Y	$8,262,000
PFM-2010-020	Application Preservation	18.67	4.33	9.94	7.06	40.01	40	$10,132,000	$340,000,000	N	$0
PFM-2010-021	Application Preservation	28.22	10.33	12.67	16.44	67.67	1	$6,392,000	$6,392,000	Y	$6,392,000
PFM-2010-022	Application Preservation	15.56	7.44	15.00	13.17	51.17	27	$3,672,000	$258,128,000	Y	$3,672,000
PFM-2010-023	Application Preservation	15.56	6.56	17.00	12.50	51.61	25	$2,992,000	$235,416,000	Y	$2,992,000
PFM-2010-024	Application Preservation	15.56	9.11	14.33	13.17	52.17	24	$4,182,000	$232,424,000	Y	$4,182,000
PFM-2010-025	Application Preservation	10.22	6.78	16.33	12.28	45.61	36	$3,162,000	$306,952,000	N	$0

PFM-2010-026	Service Management	6.89	15.00	20.00	15.78	57.67	12	$2,210,000	$79,016,000	Y	$2,210,000
PFM-2010-027	Service Management	10.22	16.89	12.67	16.98	56.76	15	$7,820,000	$102,068,000	Y	$7,820,000
PFM-2010-028	Service Management	5.56	15.00	20.00	15.78	56.33	17	$2,210,000	$112,438,000	Y	$2,210,000
PFM-2010-029	Service Management	13.56	14.33	14.83	17.24	59.97	10	$10,880,000	$72,114,000	Y	$10,880,000
PFM-2010-030	Technology Preservation	8.22	8.33	16.33	15.71	48.60	31	$3,910,000	$284,172,000	Y	$3,910,000
PFM-2010-031	Technology Preservation	13.56	11.11	14.17	17.78	56.61	16	$8,160,000	$110,228,000	Y	$8,160,000
PFM-2010-032	Technology Preservation	16.22	10.44	12.92	17.78	57.36	14	$11,560,000	$94,248,000	Y	$11,560,000
PFM-2010-033	Technology Preservation	18.89	15.11	5.28	15.41	54.69	18	$66,640,000	$179,078,000	Y	$66,640,000
PFM-2010-034	Technology Preservation	12.89	16.89	7.86	16.01	53.65	19	$28,560,000	$207,638,000	Y	$28,560,000
PFM-2010-035	Technology Preservation	9.56	15.33	9.11	17.34	51.34	26	$19,040,000	$254,456,000	Y	$19,040,000
PFM-2010-036	Technology Preservation	13.56	12.22	11.17	14.08	51.02	28	$11,900,000	$270,028,000	Y	$11,900,000
PFM-2010-037	Technology Preservation	10.22	12.22	15.00	15.91	53.36	20	$6,630,000	$214,268,000	Y	$6,630,000
PFM-2010-038	Technology Preservation	6.89	10.89	18.00	16.60	52.38	23	$2,890,000	$228,242,000	Y	$2,890,000
PFM-2010-039	Technology Preservation	11.56	15.56	15.67	17.28	60.06	9	$6,800,000	$61,234,000	Y	$6,800,000
PFM-2010-040	Technology Preservation	14.22	14.00	17.67	15.21	61.10	8	$3,570,000	$54,434,000	Y	$3,570,000

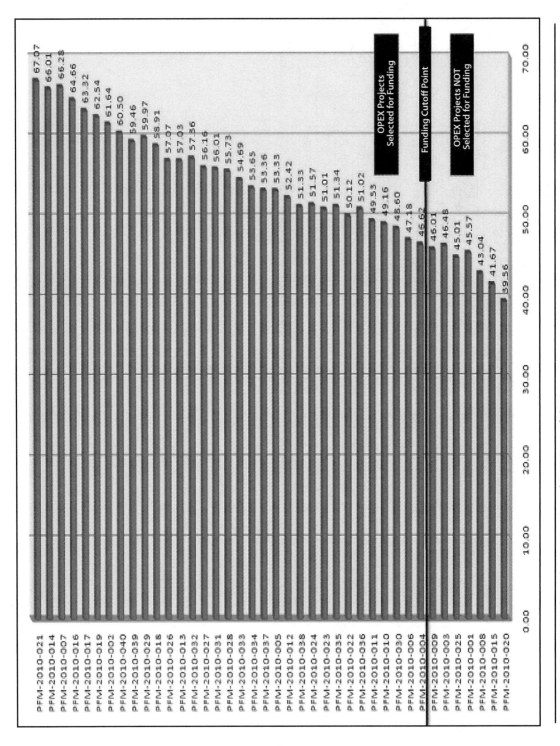

Figure 10-6 MODA-based prioritization of OPEX portfolio—summary scores

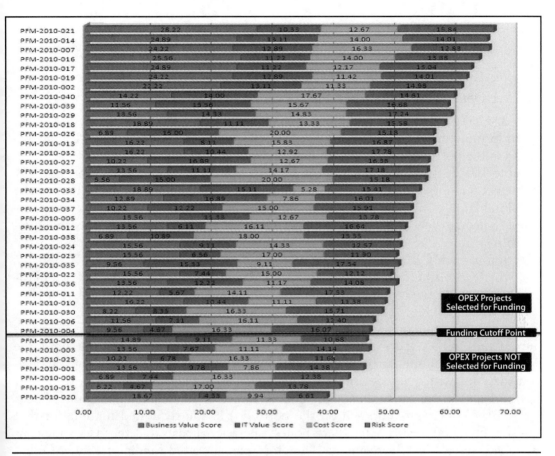

Figure 10-7   MODA-based prioritization of OPEX portfolio—detailed scores

investments for funding. In summary, prioritization of OPEX IT investments is not a viable portfolio selection technique for SIRC.

10.2.4 Portfolio Selection by Optimization

Next, portfolio selection will be accomplished using binary integer linear programming. As also covered in Appendix B, a binary integer linear programming problem can be expressed as:

$$\text{MAX (or MIN) } c_1 X_1 + c_2 X_2 + \ldots + c_n X_n$$

subject to:

$$a_{11}X_1 + a_{12}X_2 + \ldots + a_{1n}X_n \leq k_1$$

$$\ldots$$

$$a_{j1}X_1 + a_{j2}X_2 + \ldots + a_{jn}X_n \geq k_j$$

$$\ldots$$

$$a_{m1}X_1 + a_{m2}X_2 + \ldots + a_{mn}X_n = k_m$$

where X_1, X_2 ... X_n are binary integers. The symbols c_1, c_2, ..., c_n in the objective function are called the *objective function coefficients*, and may represent the marginal profit or cost or utility value associated with the decision variables X_1, X_2 ... X_n, respectively.

10.2.4.1 *Optimization Problem Formulation*

A binary integer linear programming problem is formulated for the case study. As an aid to formulating the problem, let us examine the list of OPEX and CAPEX investments in the portfolio, as shown in Table 10-16.

Table 10-16 lists the utility values (MODA scores) for each OPEX and CAPEX investment, along with the requested funding amount, the names and values of the decision variables, as well as whether the investment has been selected (column labeled "Selected Y/N") as a result of portfolio optimization based on maximization of utility value. The decision variables are binary integers that correspond to the selection of each OPEX and CAPEX investment and are represented by X_1, X_2, ..., X_{65}, which correspond to the investments PFM-2010-001, PFM-2010-002, ..., PFM-2010-065, respectively. Of these, X_1, X_2, ..., X_{40} correspond to the OPEX investments, while X_{41}, X_{42}, ..., X_{65} correspond to the CAPEX investments.

The objective function is to maximize the total utility value, which is the aggregate sum of the MODA scores for each IT investment under consideration. It should be noted that the column labeled "Variable Value" corresponds to the value of the decision variables, with every decision variable having an initial value of 0 prior to finding an optimal solution. Every OPEX investment has to be funded at a minimum of 50% (one of the constraints imposed on the portfolio) of the requested funding for that investment, based on estimated "bare-bones" operational costs to cater to existing contracts and service level agreements. Therefore, the allocated funding for each OPEX investment is set at 50% of the requested amount, even prior to finding an optimal solution.

In contrast, every CAPEX investment is funded at $0 prior to finding an optimal solution, as indicated by the values in the column for "allocated funding" in Table 10-16. The optimization of the combined portfolio is an exercise to determine which of the 40 OPEX and 25 CAPEX investments are to be fully funded, subject to all the constraints given earlier in this chapter.

The objective function for this linear programming (LP) problem can be expressed as:

MAX: Total utility value
where total utility value = $\Sigma\ U_i X_i$ for i = 1, 2, ..., 40, 41, 42, ..., 65

U_i is the incremental MODA score for the ith investment and X_i is the binary integer decision variable corresponding to the ith investment.

Table 10-16 IT portfolio of OPEX and CAPEX investments before optimization

ID	Portfolio Type	Portfolio Sub-Group	Utility Value	Requested Funding ($)	Variable Name	Variable Value	Selected (Y/N)	Allocated Funding ($)
PFM-2010-001	OPEX	Application Preservation	45.57	$15,402,000	X_1	0	N	$7,701,000
PFM-2010-002	OPEX	Application Preservation	61.64	$11,492,000	X_2	0	N	$5,746,000
PFM-2010-003	OPEX	Application Preservation	46.48	$6,052,000	X_3	0	N	$3,026,000
PFM-2010-004	OPEX	Application Preservation	46.62	$3,672,000	X_4	0	N	$1,836,000
PFM-2010-005	OPEX	Application Preservation	53.33	$6,732,000	X_5	0	N	$3,366,000
PFM-2010-006	OPEX	Application Preservation	47.18	$3,672,000	X_6	0	N	$1,836,000
PFM-2010-007	OPEX	Application Preservation	66.28	$4,012,000	X_7	0	N	$2,006,000
PFM-2010-008	OPEX	Application Preservation	43.04	$3,502,000	X_8	0	N	$1,751,000
PFM-2010-009	OPEX	Application Preservation	46.01	$6,222,000	X_9	0	N	$3,111,000
PFM-2010-010	OPEX	Application Preservation	49.16	$5,882,000	X_{10}	0	N	$2,941,000
PFM-2010-011	OPEX	Application Preservation	49.53	$4,352,000	X_{11}	0	N	$2,176,000
PFM-2010-012	OPEX	Application Preservation	52.42	$4,352,000	X_{12}	0	N	$2,176,000
PFM-2010-013	OPEX	Application Preservation	57.03	$3,672,000	X_{13}	0	N	$1,836,000
PFM-2010-014	OPEX	Application Preservation	66.01	$4,692,000	X_{14}	0	N	$2,346,000
PFM-2010-015	OPEX	Application Preservation	41.67	$4,012,000	X_{15}	0	N	$2,006,000
PFM-2010-016	OPEX	Application Preservation	64.66	$7,922,000	X_{16}	0	N	$3,961,000
PFM-2010-017	OPEX	Application Preservation	63.32	$8,092,000	X_{17}	0	N	$4,046,000
PFM-2010-018	OPEX	Application Preservation	58.91	$4,692,000	X_{18}	0	N	$2,346,000
PFM-2010-019	OPEX	Application Preservation	62.54	$8,262,000	X_{19}	0	N	$4,131,000
PFM-2010-020	OPEX	Application Preservation	39.56	$10,132,000	X_{20}	0	N	$5,066,000
PFM-2010-021	OPEX	Application Preservation	67.07	$6,392,000	X_{21}	0	N	$3,196,000
PFM-2010-022	OPEX	Application Preservation	50.12	$3,672,000	X_{22}	0	N	$1,836,000
PFM-2010-023	OPEX	Application Preservation	51.01	$2,992,000	X_{23}	0	N	$1,496,000
PFM-2010-024	OPEX	Application Preservation	51.57	$4,182,000	X_{24}	0	N	$2,091,000
PFM-2010-025	OPEX	Application Preservation	45.01	$3,162,000	X_{25}	0	N	$1,581,000

(continues)

Table 10-16 *(Continued)*

ID	Portfolio Type	Portfolio Sub-Group	Utility Value	Requested Funding ($)	Variable Name	Variable Value	Selected (Y/N)	Allocated Funding ($)
PFM-2010-026	OPEX	Service Management	57.07	$2,210,000	X_{26}	0	N	$1,105,000
PFM-2010-027	OPEX	Service Management	56.16	$7,820,000	X_{27}	0	N	$3,910,000
PFM-2010-028	OPEX	Service Management	55.73	$2,210,000	X_{28}	0	N	$1,105,000
PFM-2010-029	OPEX	Service Management	59.97	$10,880,000	X_{29}	0	N	$5,440,000
PFM-2010-030	OPEX	Technology Preservation	48.60	$3,910,000	X_{30}	0	N	$1,955,000
PFM-2010-031	OPEX	Technology Preservation	56.01	$8,160,000	X_{31}	0	N	$4,080,000
PFM-2010-032	OPEX	Technology Preservation	57.36	$11,560,000	X_{32}	0	N	$5,780,000
PFM-2010-033	OPEX	Technology Preservation	54.69	$66,640,000	X_{33}	0	N	$33,320,000
PFM-2010-034	OPEX	Technology Preservation	53.65	$28,560,000	X_{34}	0	N	$14,280,000
PFM-2010-035	OPEX	Technology Preservation	51.34	$19,040,000	X_{35}	0	N	$9,520,000
PFM-2010-036	OPEX	Technology Preservation	51.02	$11,900,000	X_{36}	0	N	$5,950,000
PFM-2010-037	OPEX	Technology Preservation	53.36	$6,630,000	X_{37}	0	N	$3,315,000
PFM-2010-038	OPEX	Technology Preservation	51.33	$2,890,000	X_{38}	0	N	$1,445,000
PFM-2010-039	OPEX	Technology Preservation	59.46	$6,800,000	X_{39}	0	N	$3,400,000
PFM-2010-040	OPEX	Technology Preservation	60.50	$3,570,000	X_{40}	0	N	$1,785,000
PFM-2010-041	CAPEX	Informational	42.84	$7,500,000	X_{41}	0	N	$0
PFM-2010-042	CAPEX	Transactional	42.82	$6,250,000	X_{42}	0	N	$0
PFM-2010-043	CAPEX	Strategic	58.82	$3,755,000	X_{43}	0	N	$0
PFM-2010-044	CAPEX	Strategic	47.98	$6,752,500	X_{44}	0	N	$0
PFM-2010-045	CAPEX	Informational	40.20	$3,126,000	X_{45}	0	N	$0
PFM-2010-046	CAPEX	Informational	62.20	$3,950,000	X_{46}	0	N	$0
PFM-2010-047	CAPEX	Transactional	56.89	$3,452,500	X_{47}	0	N	$0
PFM-2010-048	CAPEX	Strategic	61.22	$2,650,000	X_{48}	0	N	$0
PFM-2010-049	CAPEX	Transactional	56.59	$22,500,000	X_{49}	0	N	$0
PFM-2010-050	CAPEX	Strategic	72.92	$17,000,000	X_{50}	0	N	$0

PFM-2010-051	CAPEX	Transactional	42.89	$4,500,000	X_{51}	0	N	$0
PFM-2010-052	CAPEX	Transactional	42.56	$4,500,000	X_{52}	0	N	$0
PFM-2010-053	CAPEX	Transactional	44.22	$2,500,000	X_{53}	0	N	$0
PFM-2010-054	CAPEX	Transactional	45.28	$12,500,000	X_{54}	0	N	$0
PFM-2010-055	CAPEX	Informational	48.17	$3,000,000	X_{55}	0	N	$0
PFM-2010-056	CAPEX	Transactional	43.44	$2,500,000	X_{56}	0	N	$0
PFM-2010-057	CAPEX	Infrastructure	45.40	$5,430,000	X_{57}	0	N	$0
PFM-2010-058	CAPEX	Infrastructure	43.09	$8,500,000	X_{58}	0	N	$0
PFM-2010-059	CAPEX	Infrastructure	40.62	$11,000,000	X_{59}	0	N	$0
PFM-2010-060	CAPEX	Infrastructure	41.91	$7,500,000	X_{60}	0	N	$0
PFM-2010-061	CAPEX	Infrastructure	46.79	$24,750,000	X_{61}	0	N	$0
PFM-2010-062	CAPEX	Informational	49.31	$3,500,000	X_{62}	0	N	$0
PFM-2010-063	CAPEX	Infrastructure	45.98	$2,000,000	X_{63}	0	N	$0
PFM-2010-064	CAPEX	Infrastructure	61.81	$2,000,000	X_{64}	0	N	$0
PFM-2010-065	CAPEX	Infrastructure	54.92	$5,500,000	X_{65}	0	N	$0

For the SIRC IT portfolio under consideration, the objective function is:

MAX: $45.57X_1 + 61.64X_2 + 46.48X_3 + 46.62X_4 + 53.33X_5 + 47.18X_6 + 66.28X_7$
$+ 43.04X_8 + 46.01X_9 + 49.16X_{10} + 49.53X_{11} + 52.42X_{12} + 57.03X_{13} + 66.01X_{14}$
$+ 41.67X_{15} + 64.66X_{16} + 63.32X_{17} + 58.91X_{18} + 62.54X_{19} + 39.56X_{20} + 67.07X_{21}$
$+ 50.12X_{22} + 51.01X_{23} + 51.57X_{24} + 45.01X_{25} + 57.07X_{26} + 56.16X_{27} + 55.73X_{28}$
$+ 59.97X_{29} + 48.60X_{30} + 56.01X_{31} + 57.36X_{32} + 54.69X_{33} + 53.65X_{34} + 51.34X_{35}$
$+ 51.02X_{36} + 53.36X_{37} + 51.33X_{38} + 59.46X_{39} + 60.50X_{40} + 42.84X_{41} + 42.82X_{42}$
$+ 58.82X_{43} + 47.98X_{44} + 40.20X_{45} + 62.20X_{46} + 56.89X_{47} + 61.22X_{48} + 56.59X_{49}$
$+ 72.92X_{50} + 42.89X_{51} + 42.56X_{52} + 44.22X_{53} + 45.28X_{54} + 48.17X_{55} + 43.44X_{56}$
$+ 45.40X_{57} + 43.09X_{58} + 40.62X_{59} + 41.91X_{60} + 46.79X_{61} + 49.31X_{62} + 45.98X_{63}$
$+ 61.81X_{64} + 54.92X_{65}$

- The applicable constraints are:
  - OPEX and CAPEX budgetary constraints.
  - Constraints mandating that certain OPEX investments be fully funded.
  - Inter-investment dependencies within the OPEX portfolio.
  - Funding restrictions imposed by management on groups of OPEX investments.
  - CAPEX portfolio balance constraints.
  - Inter-project dependencies within the CAPEX portfolio.
  - Cross-portfolio investment dependencies.
  - Cross-portfolio resource constraints (mutual exclusivity between investments).
- The *OPEX budgetary constraint* is based on the following rules that will help formulate a mathematical expression for this constraint:
  - Every OPEX investment that is selected as a result of optimization will be fully funded.
  - Every OPEX investment that is *not* selected will experience a drastic reduction in funding and will be funded based on the CIO's discretion in order to provide "bare-bones" maintenance service as required by contractual obligations and service level agreements, i.e., to keep the lights on, legally.
  - All unselected OPEX investments will be uniformly funded up to a maximum of b% of the full funding amount requested for each investment, where $0 \le b \le 100$. For SIRC's OPEX portfolio, b has been set at 50%, i.e., an unselected OPEX investment will only be funded at 50% of the requested funding amount.
  - Therefore, for any one OPEX investment, the funding equation can be expressed as $C_iX_i + (1 - X_i)bC_i$, which can be simplified as $(1 - b)C_iX_i + bC_i$; for $i = 1, 2, \ldots 40$, where C_i is the funding requested for i^{th} OPEX investment and X_i is the binary integer decision variable corresponding to the ith OPEX investment. Basically, if an investment is selected, the allocated funding is C_iX_i, and if it is not selected, the allocated funding is $(1 - X_i)bC_i$.

- ○ Therefore, the budgetary constraint for all the OPEX investments can be expressed as:

  $\Sigma\,(1 - b)\,(C_iX_i + bC_i) \leq Y$, i.e., $(1 - b)\,\Sigma\,C_iX_i \leq Y - b\,\Sigma\,C_i$, for $i = 1, 2, \dots, 40$, where Y is the amount that the total OPEX budget cannot exceed. This can be simplified further and expressed as $\Sigma\,C_iX_i \leq (Y - b\,\Sigma\,C_i)/(1 - b)$, for $i = 1, 2, \dots, 40$.

- ○ For the SIRC OPEX portfolio, this equation becomes:

  $15,402,000X_1 + 11,492,000X_2 + 6,052,000X_3 + 3,672,000X_4$
  $+ 6,732,000X_5 + 3,672,000X_6 + 4,012,000X_7 + 3,502,000X_8$
  $+ 6,222,000X_9 + 5,882,000X_{10} + 4,352,000X_{11} + 4,352,000X_{12}$
  $+ 3,672,000X_{13} + 4,692,000X_{14} + 4,012,000X_{15} + 7,922,000X_{16}$
  $+ 8,092,000X_{17} + 4,692,000X_{18} + 8,262,000X_{19} + 10,132,000X_{20}$
  $+ 6,392,000X_{21} + 3,672,000X_{22} + 2,992,000X_{23} + 4,182,000X_{24}$
  $+ 3,162,000X_{25} + 2,210,000X_{26} + 7,820,000X_{27} + 2,210,000X_{28}$
  $+ 10,880,000X_{29} + 3,910,000X_{30} + 8,160,000X_{31} + 11,560,000X_{32}$
  $+ 66,640,000X_{33} + 28,560,000X_{34} + 19,040,000X_{35} + 11,900,000X_{36}$
  $+ 6,630,000X_{37} + 2,890,000X_{38} + 6,800,000X_{39} + 3,570,000X_{40}$
  $\leq (296,000,000 - 0.5 * 340,000,000)/(1 - 0.5)$

  which can be simplified as:

  $15,402,000X_1 + 11,492,000X_2 + 6,052,000X_3 + 3,672,000X_4$
  $+ 6,732,000X_5 + 3,672,000X_6 + 4,012,000X_7 + 3,502,000X_8$
  $+ 6,222,000X_9 + 5,882,000X_{10} + 4,352,000X_{11} + 4,352,000X_{12}$
  $+ 3,672,000X_{13} + 4,692,000X_{14} + 4,012,000X_{15} + 7,922,000X_{16}$
  $+ 8,092,000X_{17} + 4,692,000X_{18} + 8,262,000X_{19} + 10,132,000X_{20}$
  $+ 6,392,000X_{21} + 3,672,000X_{22} + 2,992,000X_{23} + 4,182,000X_{24}$
  $+ 3,162,000X_{25} + 2,210,000X_{26} + 7,820,000X_{27} + 2,210,000X_{28}$
  $+ 10,880,000X_{29} + 3,910,000X_{30} + 8,160,000X_{31} + 11,560,000X_{32}$
  $+ 66,640,000X_{33} + 28,560,000X_{34} + 19,040,000X_{35} + 11,900,000X_{36}$
  $+ 6,630,000X_{37} + 2,890,000X_{38} + 6,800,000X_{39} + 3,570,000X_{40}$
  $\leq 252,000,000$

- • The *CAPEX budgetary constraint* can be expressed as follows:
  - ○ $\Sigma\,A_{i1}X_i \leq k_1$, for $i = 41, 42, \dots, 65$, where A_{i1} is the requested capital investment in year 1 for the ith CAPEX investment and k_1 is the board-mandated CAPEX funding amount in year 1, i.e., $k_1 = \$118,400,000$. The budgetary constraint for this portfolio is:

    $7,500,000X_{41} + 6,250,000X_{42} + 3,755,000X_{43} + 6,752,500X_{44}$
    $+ 3,126,000X_{45} + 3,950,000X_{46} + 3,452,500X_{47} + 2,650,000X_{48}$
    $+ 22,500,000X_{49} + 17,000,000X_{50} + 4,500,000X_{51} + 4,500,000X_{52}$
    $+ 2,500,000X_{53} + 12,500,000X_{54} + 3,000,000X_{55} + 2,500,000X_{56}$
    $+ 5,430,000X_{57} + 8,500,000X_{58} + 11,000,000X_{59} + 7,500,000X_{60}$
    $+ 24,750,000X_{61} + 3,500,000X_{62} + 2,000,000X_{63} + 2,000,000X_{64}$
    $+ 5,500,000X_{65} \leq 118,400,000$

- The *mandatory investment constraints* pertain to OPEX *investments* that have to be fully funded in order for the IT division to serve the critical needs of the business units. These can be expressed as:
  - SCM: Transportation Management (PFM-2010-012) is to be fully funded, i.e., $X_{12} = 1$.
  - SCM: Order Fulfillment (PFM-2010-016) is to be fully funded, i.e., $X_{16} = 1$.
  - SCM: Manufacturing (PFM-2010-017) is to be fully funded, i.e., $X_{17} = 1$.
  - SCM: Demand and Supply Planning (PFM-2010-018) is to be fully funded, i.e., $X_{18} = 1$.
  - CRM: Siebel Call Center Operations (PFM-2010-021) is to be fully funded, i.e., $X_{21} = 1$.
  - ITSM: Service Operation (PFM-2010-027) is to be fully funded, i.e., $X_{27} = 1$.
  - ITSM: Service Design — Business Continuity Plan and Disaster Recovery (PFM-2010-029) is to be fully funded, i.e., $X_{29} = 1$.
  - INFR: Security Management (PFM-2010-032) is to be fully funded, i.e., $X_{32} = 1$.
  - INFR: Platform Management (PFM-2010-033) is to be fully funded, i.e., $X_{33} = 1$.
  - INFR: Network Management (PFM-2010-034) is to be fully funded, i.e., $X_{34} = 1$.
  - INFR: Data Center & Facilities Management (PFM-2010-035) is to be fully funded, i.e., $X_{35} = 1$.
  - IT LCM: IT Resource Planning (PFM-2010-039) is to be fully funded, i.e., $X_{39} = 1$.
- The inter-investment dependencies within the OPEX portfolio can be expressed as:
  - Enterprise Asset Management Operations (PFM-2010-003) may be fully funded only if Financial Operations (PFM-2010-002) is fully funded, i.e., $X_3 - X_2 \leq 0$.
  - ERP Cross-Functional Operations (PFM-2010-005) may be fully funded only if Financial Operations (PFM-2010-002) is fully funded, i.e., $X_5 - X_2 \leq 0$.
  - SRM Purchasing Governance Operations (PFM-2010-008) may be fully funded only if SRM Indirect Procurement Operations (PFM-2010-009) is fully funded, i.e., $X_8 - X_9 \leq 0$.
- The funding restrictions imposed by management on groups of OPEX investments can be expressed as:
  - PLM: At most only Product Management (PFM-2010-022), Product Dev. and Collaboration (PFM-2010-023), or Foundational Components Operations (PFM-2010-025) can be fully funded, i.e., $X_{22} + X_{23} + X_{25} \leq 1$.
  - ITSM: At most only Service Transition (PFM-2010-026) or Service Management Tools Operations (PFM-2010-028) can be fully funded, i.e., $X_{26} + X_{28} \leq 1$.

- ○ INFR: At most only one of Unstructured Data Management (PFM-2010-030), Data Access Management (PFM-2010-036), or Application Middleware Operations (PFM-2010-037) can be fully funded, i.e., $X_{30} + X_{36} + X_{37} \leq 1$.
- ○ IT LCM: At most only Systems Development Lifecycle Operations (PFM-2010-038) or Enterprise Architecture Operations (PFM-2010-040) can be fully funded, i.e., $X_{38} + X_{40} \leq 1$.
- CAPEX portfolio balance constraints: The portfolio balance constraints can be mathematically expressed as:
  - ○ $\sum A_{ip}X_i \leq Y_p$, for i = 41, 42, ..., 65; $p \in$ {Infrastructure, Transactional, Informational, Strategic}, where A_{ip} is the capital investment required for i^{th} project belonging to the pth portfolio sub-group and X_i is a binary integer decision variable corresponding to the ith project.
  - ○ The desired CAPEX portfolio balance, as stated in Chapter 2, is such that the approved CAPEX investments should not exceed the following proportions within acceptable limits:
    - Infrastructure = 40%
    - Transactional = 30%
    - Strategic = 20%
    - Informational = 10%
  - ○ Therefore, the portfolio balance constraints can be expressed as:

    Infrastructure: $5,430,000X_{57} + 8,500,000X_{58} + 11,000,000X_{59} + 7,500,000X_{60} + 24,750,000X_{61} + 2,000,000X_{63} + 2,000,000X_{64} + 5,500,000X_{65} \leq 47,360,000$

    Transactional: $6,250,000X_{42} + 3,452,500X_{47} + 22,500,000X_{49} + 4,500,000X_{51} + 4,500,000X_{52} + 2,500,000X_{53} + 12,500,000X_{54} + 2,500,000X_{56} \leq 35,520,000$

    Strategic: $3,755,000X_{43} + 6,752,500X_{44} + 2,650,000X_{48} + 17,000,000X_{50} \leq 23,680,000$

    Informational: $7,500,000X_{41} + 3,126,000X_{45} + 3,950,000X_{46} + 3,000,000X_{55} + 3,500,000X_{62} \leq 11,840,000$

- Inter-project dependencies within the CAPEX portfolio can be expressed as:
  - ○ PLM program dependencies: The PLM program comprises four CAPEX initiatives, the decision variables corresponding to which are X_{52}, X_{53}, X_{54}, and X_{55}. X_{54} corresponds to the primary project in this program, the Product Data Management Project. X_{52}, X_{53}, and X_{55} are dependent on X_{54} and can be started only if X_{54} is started; the dependent projects can only be approved if X_{54} is approved. These constraints can be expressed as:
    - $X_{52} - X_{54} \leq 0$
    - $X_{53} - X_{54} \leq 0$
    - $X_{55} - X_{54} \leq 0$

- Service Parts project dependencies: Decision variables X_{47} and X_{48} correspond to Service Parts Order Fulfillment and Service Parts Planning, respectively. The latter cannot be started unless the Order Fulfillment Project is started. This constraint can be expressed as:
  - $X_{48} - X_{47} \le 0$

- The cross-portfolio investment dependencies are:
  - CAPEX RFID Asset Tagging Project (PFM-2010-042) cannot start unless OPEX Enterprise Asset Management Operations (PFM-2010-003) is fully funded, i.e., $X_{42} - X_3 \le 0$.
  - CAPEX RFID Asset Tagging Project (PFM-2010-042) cannot start unless OPEX ERP Cross-Functional Operations (PFM-2010-005) is fully funded, i.e., $X_{42} - X_5 \le 0$.
  - CAPEX Siebel Marketing and Analytics Project (PFM-2010-050) cannot start unless OPEX Legacy Marketing Operations (PFM-2010-020) is fully funded, i.e., $X_{50} - X_{20} \le 0$.
  - CAPEX Siebel Marketing and Analytics Project (PFM-2010-050) cannot start unless OPEX INFR Structured Data Management Operations (PFM-2010-031) is fully funded, i.e., $X_{50} - X_{31} \le 0$.
  - CAPEX Siebel Marketing and Analytics Project (PFM-2010-050) cannot start unless OPEX INFR Application Middleware Operations (PFM-2010-037) is fully funded, i.e., $X_{50} - X_{37} \le 0$.
  - CAPEX ITSM Service Design Implementation (PFM-2010-065) cannot start unless OPEX ITSM Service Management Tools Operations (PFM-2010-028) is fully funded, i.e., $X_{65} - X_{28} \le 0$.

- The *cross-portfolio resource constraints* are based on the assumption that the organization can only support the full funding request of either the investments within the OPEX PLM Operations (PFM-2010-022, PFM-2010-023, PFM-2010-024, and PFM-2010-025) or the projects within the CAPEX PLM program (PFM-2010-052, PFM-2010-053, PFM-2010-054, and PFM-2010-055), owing to resource constraints and limited subject matter expertise in the organization. Therefore, exactly one of each of the corresponding initiatives within each set must be fully funded:
  - Either OPEX Legacy PLM Product Management Operations (PFM-2010-022) or CAPEX Oracle Product Management (PFM-2010-052) must be fully funded, i.e., $X_{22} + X_{52} = 1$.
  - Either OPEX Legacy PLM Product Development and Collaboration (PFM-2010-023) or CAPEX Oracle Product Management Integration (PFM-2010-053) must be fully funded, i.e., $X_{23} + X_{53} = 1$.
  - Either OPEX Legacy PLM Product Data Management Operations (PFM-2010-024) or CAPEX Oracle Product Data Management (PFM-2010-054) must be fully funded, i.e., $X_{24} + X_{54} = 1$.
  - Either OPEX Legacy PLM Foundational Components (PFM-2010-025) or CAPEX Oracle Product Analytics (PFM-2010-055) must be fully funded, i.e., $X_{25} + X_{55} = 1$.

Therefore, the LP problem for the joint portfolio optimization can be summarized as follows:

MAX: $45.57X_1 + 61.64X_2 + 46.48X_3 + 46.62X_4 + 53.33X_5 + 47.18X_6 + 66.28X_7$
$+ 43.04X_8 + 46.01X_9 + 49.16X_{10} + 49.53X_{11} + 52.42X_{12} + 57.03X_{13} + 66.01X_{14}$
$+ 41.67X_{15} + 64.66X_{16} + 63.32X_{17} + 58.91X_{18} + 62.54X_{19} + 39.56X_{20} + 67.07X_{21}$
$+ 50.12X_{22} + 51.01X_{23} + 51.57X_{24} + 45.01X_{25} + 57.07X_{26} + 56.16X_{27} + 55.73X_{28}$
$+ 59.97X_{29} + 48.6X_{30} + 56.01X_{31} + 57.36X_{32} + 54.69X_{33} + 53.65X_{34} + 51.34X_{35}$
$+ 51.02X_{36} + 53.36X_{37} + 51.33X_{38} + 59.46X_{39} + 60.5X_{40} + 42.84X_{41} + 42.82X_{42}$
$+ 58.82X_{43} + 47.98X_{44} + 40.20X_{45} + 62.20X_{46} + 56.89X_{47} + 61.22X_{48} + 56.59X_{49}$
$+ 72.92X_{50} + 42.89X_{51} + 42.56X_{52} + 44.22X_{53} + 45.28X_{54} + 48.17X_{55} + 43.44X_{56}$
$+ 45.40X_{57} + 43.09X_{58} + 40.62X_{59} + 41.91X_{60} + 46.79X_{61} + 49.31X_{62} + 45.98X_{63}$
$+ 61.81X_{64} + 54.92X_{65}$

subject to:

$15,402,000X_1 + 11,492,000X_2 + 6,052,000X_3 + 3,672,000X_4 + 6,732,000X_5$
$+ 3,672,000X_6 + 4,012,000X_7 + 3,502,000X_8 + 6,222,000X_9 + 5,882,000X_{10}$
$+ 4,352,000X_{11} + 4,352,000X_{12} + 3,672,000X_{13} + 4,692,000X_{14} + 4,012,000X_{15}$
$+ 7,922,000X_{16} + 8,092,000X_{17} + 4,692,000X_{18} + 8,262,000X_{19} + 10,132,000X_{20}$
$+ 6,392,000X_{21} + 3,672,000X_{22} + 2,992,000X_{23} + 4,182,000X_{24} + 3,162,000X_{25}$
$+ 2,210,000X_{26} + 7,820,000X_{27} + 2,210,000X_{28} + 10,880,000X_{29} + 3,910,000X_{30}$
$+ 8,160,000X_{31} + 11,560,000X_{32} + 66,640,000X_{33} + 28,560,000X_{34}$
$+ 19,040,000X_{35} + 11,900,000X_{36} + 6,630,000X_{37} + 2,890,000X_{38} + 6,800,000X_{39}$
$+ 3,570,000X_{40} \le 252,000,000$ (OPEX budgetary constraint)

$7,500,000X_{41} + 6,250,000X_{42} + 3,755,000X_{43} + 6,752,500X_{44} + 3,126,000X_{45}$
$+ 3,950,000X_{46} + 3,452,500X_{47} + 2,650,000X_{48} + 22,500,000X_{49} + 17,000,000X_{50}$
$+ 4,500,000X_{51} + 4,500,000X_{52} + 2,500,000X_{53} + 12,500,000X_{54} + 3,000,000X_{55}$
$+ 2,500,000X_{56} + 5,430,000X_{57} + 8,500,000X_{58} + 11,000,000X_{59} + 7,500,000X_{60} +$
$24,750,000X_{61} + 3,500,000X_{62} + 2,000,000X_{63} + 2,000,000X_{64} + 5,500,000X_{65}$
$\le 118,400,000$ (CAPEX budgetary constraint)

$5,430,000X_{57} + 8,500,000X_{58} + 11,000,000X_{59} + 7,500,000X_{60} + 24,750,000X_{61}$
$+ 2,000,000X_{63} + 2,000,000X_{64} + 5,500,000X_{65}$
$\le 47,360,000$ (CAPEX infrastructure portfolio balance constraint)

$6,250,000X_{42} + 3,452,500X_{47} + 22,500,000X_{49} + 4,500,000X_{51} + 4,500,000X_{52}$
$+ 2,500,000X_{53} + 12,500,000X_{54} + 2,500,000X_{56}$
$\le 35,520,000$ (CAPEX transactional portfolio balance constraint)

$3,755,000X_{43} + 6,752,500X_{44} + 2,650,000X_{48} + 17,000,000X_{50}$
$\le 23,680,000$ (CAPEX strategic portfolio balance constraint)

$7,500,000X_{41} + 3,126,000X_{45} + 3,950,000X_{46} + 3,000,000X_{55} + 3,500,000X_{62}$
$\le 11,840,000$ (CAPEX informational portfolio balance constraint)

$$\left.\begin{array}{l} X_{52} - X_{54} \leq 0 \\ X_{53} - X_{54} \leq 0 \\ X_{55} - X_{54} \leq 0 \\ X_{48} - X_{47} \leq 0 \end{array}\right\} \text{CAPEX project}$$

$$\left.\begin{array}{l} X_3 - X_2 \leq 0 \\ X_5 - X_2 \leq 0 \\ X_8 - X_9 \leq 0 \end{array}\right\} \text{OPEX inter-investment}$$

$$\left.\begin{array}{l} X_{22} + X_{23} + X_{25} \leq 1 \\ X_{26} + X_{28} \leq 1 \\ X_{30} + X_{36} + X_{37} \leq 1 \\ X_{38} + X_{40} \leq 1 \end{array}\right\} \text{Management-imposed funding restrictions on OPEX}$$

$$\left.\begin{array}{l} X_{12} = 1 \\ X_{16} = 1 \\ X_{17} = 1 \\ X_{18} = 1 \\ X_{21} = 1 \\ X_{27} = 1 \\ X_{29} = 1 \\ X_{32} = 1 \\ X_{33} = 1 \\ X_{34} = 1 \\ X_{35} = 1 \\ X_{39} = 1 \end{array}\right\} \text{Mandatory OPEX}$$

$$\left.\begin{array}{l} X_{22} + X_{52} = 1 \\ X_{23} + X_{53} = 1 \\ X_{24} + X_{54} = 1 \\ X_{25} + X_{55} = 1 \end{array}\right\} \text{Cross-portfolio resource constraints (mutual exclusivity)}$$

$$\left.\begin{array}{l} X_{42} - X_3 \leq 0 \\ X_{42} - X_5 \leq 0 \\ X_{50} - X_{20} \leq 0 \\ X_{50} - X_{31} \leq 0 \\ X_{50} - X_{37} \leq 0 \\ X_{65} - X_{28} \leq 0 \end{array}\right\} \text{Cross-portfolio investment}$$

where

$$X_1, X_2, \ldots, X_{65} \text{ are binary integers}$$

This LP problem is characterized by 65 decision variables and 39 constraints (not including the 65 binary integer constraints on the decision variables) and will be solved in the subsequent section.

10.2.4.2 *Results of IT Portfolio Selection by Optimization*

The LP has been formulated in Excel Premium Solver[5] and solved as a standard LP simplex problem, for which an optimal solution has been found; a summary is provided in Table 10-17.

Table 10-18 displays the values of the decision variables after the optimization. The decision variables with a value of 1 correspond to OPEX and CAPEX investments selected from the optimization methodology, while those with a value of 0 correspond to the ones that were not selected for funding approval as a result of the optimization. Both CAPEX and OPEX investments selected by the optimal solution will be fully funded (i.e., allocated funding = requested funding). Unselected OPEX investments will be funded at 50% of the requested funding amount for the corresponding OPEX

Table 10-17 IT portfolio optimization (utility maximization) summary

OPEX Investments				
Description	**Funded Amount ($)**	**Count**	**% OPEX Budget**	
OPEX Investments Selected (i.e., Fully Funded)	$250,070,000	25	84.76%	
OPEX Investments not Selected (i.e., Partially Funded)	$44,965,000	15	15.24%	
Total Operational Budget (OPEX Budget)	$295,035,000	N/A	N/A	
CAPEX Investments				
Description	**Funded Amount ($)**	**Count**	**% CAPEX Budget**	**Variance**
CAPEX Strategic	$20,755,000	2	20.30%	0.30%
CAPEX Informational	$9,626,000	3	9.41%	−0.59%
CAPEX Transactional	$29,952,500	6	29.29%	−0.71%
CAPEX Infrastructure	$41,930,000	7	41.00%	1.00%
All Selected Capital Investments (CAPEX)	$102,263,500	18	N/A	
Total NPV of Selected CAPEX Investments	$9,109,411	N/A	N/A	
Summary Information				
Total IT Budget (OPEX and CAPEX)	$397,298,500			
Management-imposed OPEX Budget Limit	$296,000,000			
Management-imposed CAPEX Budget Limit	$118,400,000			
Management-imposed Total Budget Limit	$414,400,000			

---

[5]Excel Premium Solver, a spreadsheet-based optimization tool from Frontline Systems, is easy to install and use. Trial copies can be downloaded from http://www.solver.com/xlspremsolv.htm and information on purchasing fully licensed copies is also available on this site.

Table 10-18 SIRC IT portfolio after optimization (utility value maximization)

ID	Portfolio Type	Portfolio Sub-Group	MODA Score	Requested Funding ($)	Variable Name	Variable Value	Selected (Y/N)	Allocated Funding ($)
PFM-2010-001	OPEX	Application Preservation	45.57	$15,402,000	X_1	0	N	$7,701,000
PFM-2010-002	OPEX	Application Preservation	61.64	$11,492,000	X_2	0	N	$5,746,000
PFM-2010-003	OPEX	Application Preservation	46.48	$6,052,000	X_3	0	N	$3,026,000
PFM-2010-004	OPEX	Application Preservation	46.62	$3,672,000	X_4	1	Y	$3,672,000
PFM-2010-005	OPEX	Application Preservation	53.33	$6,732,000	X_5	0	N	$3,366,000
PFM-2010-006	OPEX	Application Preservation	47.18	$3,672,000	X_6	1	Y	$3,672,000
PFM-2010-007	OPEX	Application Preservation	66.28	$4,012,000	X_7	1	Y	$4,012,000
PFM-2010-008	OPEX	Application Preservation	43.04	$3,502,000	X_8	0	N	$1,751,000
PFM-2010-009	OPEX	Application Preservation	46.01	$6,222,000	X_9	1	Y	$6,222,000
PFM-2010-010	OPEX	Application Preservation	49.16	$5,882,000	X_{10}	1	Y	$5,882,000
PFM-2010-011	OPEX	Application Preservation	49.53	$4,352,000	X_{11}	1	Y	$4,352,000
PFM-2010-012	OPEX	Application Preservation	52.42	$4,352,000	X_{12}	1	Y	$4,352,000
PFM-2010-013	OPEX	Application Preservation	57.03	$3,672,000	X_{13}	1	Y	$3,672,000
PFM-2010-014	OPEX	Application Preservation	66.01	$4,692,000	X_{14}	1	Y	$4,692,000
PFM-2010-015	OPEX	Application Preservation	41.67	$4,012,000	X_{15}	1	Y	$4,012,000
PFM-2010-016	OPEX	Application Preservation	64.66	$7,922,000	X_{16}	1	Y	$7,922,000
PFM-2010-017	OPEX	Application Preservation	63.32	$8,092,000	X_{17}	1	Y	$8,092,000
PFM-2010-018	OPEX	Application Preservation	58.91	$4,692,000	X_{18}	1	Y	$4,692,000
PFM-2010-019	OPEX	Application Preservation	62.54	$8,262,000	X_{19}	0	N	$4,131,000
PFM-2010-020	OPEX	Application Preservation	39.56	$10,132,000	X_{20}	1	Y	$10,132,000
PFM-2010-021	OPEX	Application Preservation	67.07	$6,392,000	X_{21}	1	Y	$6,392,000
PFM-2010-022	OPEX	Application Preservation	50.12	$3,672,000	X_{22}	0	N	$1,836,000
PFM-2010-023	OPEX	Application Preservation	51.01	$2,992,000	X_{23}	0	N	$1,496,000
PFM-2010-024	OPEX	Application Preservation	51.57	$4,182,000	X_{24}	0	N	$2,091,000
PFM-2010-025	OPEX	Application Preservation	45.01	$3,162,000	X_{25}	0	N	$1,581,000
PFM-2010-026	OPEX	Service Management	57.07	$2,210,000	X_{26}	0	N	$1,105,000
PFM-2010-027	OPEX	Service Management	56.16	$7,820,000	X_{27}	1	Y	$7,820,000
PFM-2010-028	OPEX	Service Management	55.73	$2,210,000	X_{28}	1	Y	$2,210,000
PFM-2010-029	OPEX	Service Management	59.97	$10,880,000	X_{29}	1	Y	$10,880,000
PFM-2010-030	OPEX	Technology Preservation	48.60	$3,910,000	X_{30}	0	N	$1,955,000
PFM-2010-031	OPEX	Technology Preservation	56.01	$8,160,000	X_{31}	1	Y	$8,160,000
PFM-2010-032	OPEX	Technology Preservation	57.36	$11,560,000	X_{32}	1	Y	$11,560,000

PFM-2010-033	OPEX	Technology Preservation	54.69	$66,640,000	X_{33}	1	$66,640,000	Y
PFM-2010-034	OPEX	Technology Preservation	53.65	$28,560,000	X_{34}	1	$28,560,000	Y
PFM-2010-035	OPEX	Technology Preservation	51.34	$19,040,000	X_{35}	1	$19,040,000	Y
PFM-2010-036	OPEX	Technology Preservation	51.02	$11,900,000	X_{36}	0	$5,950,000	N
PFM-2010-037	OPEX	Technology Preservation	53.36	$6,630,000	X_{37}	1	$6,630,000	Y
PFM-2010-038	OPEX	Technology Preservation	51.33	$2,890,000	X_{38}	0	$1,445,000	N
PFM-2010-039	OPEX	Technology Preservation	59.46	$6,800,000	X_{39}	1	$6,800,000	Y
PFM-2010-040	OPEX	Technology Preservation	60.50	$3,570,000	X_{40}	0	$1,785,000	N
PFM-2010-041	CAPEX	Informational	42.84	$7,500,000	X_{41}	0	$0	N
PFM-2010-042	CAPEX	Transactional	42.82	$6,250,000	X_{42}	0	$0	N
PFM-2010-043	CAPEX	Strategic	58.82	$3,755,000	X_{43}	1	$3,755,000	Y
PFM-2010-044	CAPEX	Strategic	47.98	$6,752,500	X_{44}	0	$0	N
PFM-2010-045	CAPEX	Informational	40.20	$3,126,000	X_{45}	1	$3,126,000	Y
PFM-2010-046	CAPEX	Informational	62.20	$3,950,000	X_{46}	0	$0	N
PFM-2010-047	CAPEX	Transactional	56.89	$3,452,500	X_{47}	1	$3,452,500	Y
PFM-2010-048	CAPEX	Strategic	61.22	$2,650,000	X_{48}	0	$0	N
PFM-2010-049	CAPEX	Transactional	56.59	$22,500,000	X_{49}	0	$0	N
PFM-2010-050	CAPEX	Strategic	72.92	$17,000,000	X_{50}	1	$17,000,000	Y
PFM-2010-051	CAPEX	Transactional	42.89	$4,500,000	X_{51}	1	$4,500,000	Y
PFM-2010-052	CAPEX	Transactional	42.56	$4,500,000	X_{52}	1	$4,500,000	Y
PFM-2010-053	CAPEX	Transactional	44.22	$2,500,000	X_{53}	1	$2,500,000	Y
PFM-2010-054	CAPEX	Transactional	45.28	$12,500,000	X_{54}	1	$12,500,000	Y
PFM-2010-055	CAPEX	Informational	48.17	$3,000,000	X_{55}	1	$3,000,000	Y
PFM-2010-056	CAPEX	Transactional	43.44	$2,500,000	X_{56}	1	$2,500,000	Y
PFM-2010-057	CAPEX	Infrastructure	45.40	$5,430,000	X_{57}	1	$5,430,000	Y
PFM-2010-058	CAPEX	Infrastructure	43.09	$8,500,000	X_{58}	1	$8,500,000	Y
PFM-2010-059	CAPEX	Infrastructure	40.62	$11,000,000	X_{59}	1	$11,000,000	Y
PFM-2010-060	CAPEX	Infrastructure	41.91	$7,500,000	X_{60}	1	$7,500,000	Y
PFM-2010-061	CAPEX	Informational	46.79	$24,750,000	X_{61}	0	$0	N
PFM-2010-062	CAPEX	Informational	49.31	$3,500,000	X_{62}	1	$3,500,000	Y
PFM-2010-063	CAPEX	Infrastructure	45.98	$2,000,000	X_{63}	1	$2,000,000	Y
PFM-2010-064	CAPEX	Infrastructure	61.81	$2,000,000	X_{64}	1	$2,000,000	Y
PFM-2010-065	CAPEX	Infrastructure	54.92	$5,500,000	X_{65}	1	$5,500,000	Y

investments (i.e., allocated funding = 0.5 * requested funding), while unselected CAPEX investments will not be funded (allocated funding = $0).

Figures 10-8, 10-9, and 10-10 illustrate the results of LP optimization based on maximizing the total utility value of the investments for the SIRC IT portfolio.

The optimization of the combined CAPEX and OPEX portfolios resulted in an optimal solution with the following results:

- Of the 40 OPEX investments under consideration, 25 were selected to be fully funded, while 15 were not selected for full funding, thereby meriting only the "bare-bones" funding required for the minimum acceptable level of service in those operational areas. The total OPEX expense resulting from this solution is $295.035M, which is below the maximum available OPEX funding.
- Of the 25 CAPEX investments under consideration, 18 were selected to be fully funded, and the total CAPEX investment resulting from the solution is $102.2635M, which also satisfies the CAPEX budgetary constraint. All the other constraints were satisfied, inclusive of the CAPEX portfolio balance constraints and the cross-portfolio constraints, within the desired thresholds.

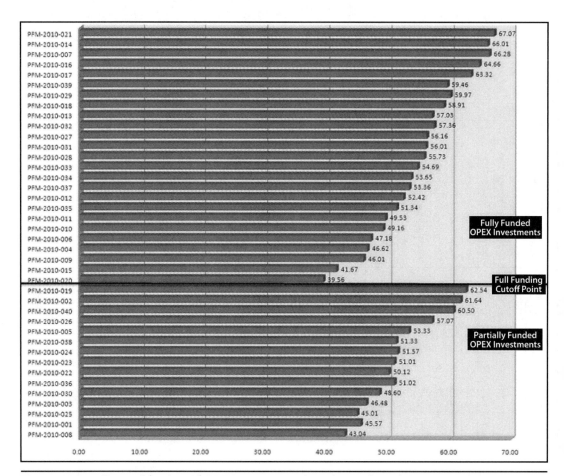

Figure 10-8 Allocated funding of OPEX investments based on utility value maximization

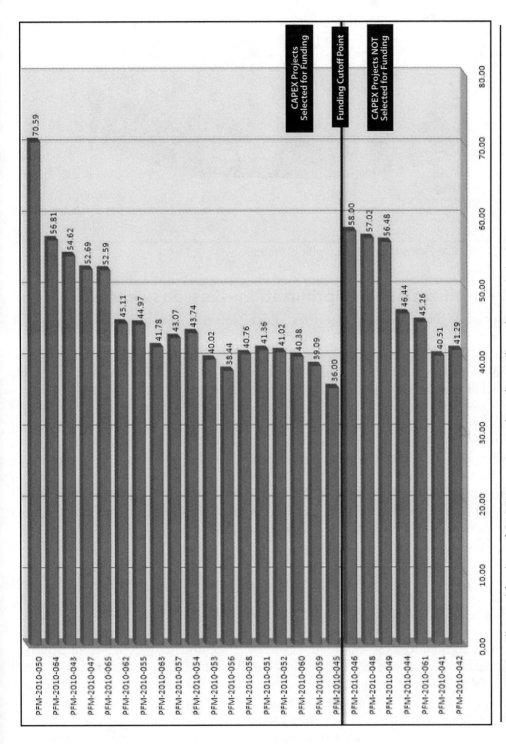

Figure 10-9 Allocated funding of CAPEX investments based on utility value maximization

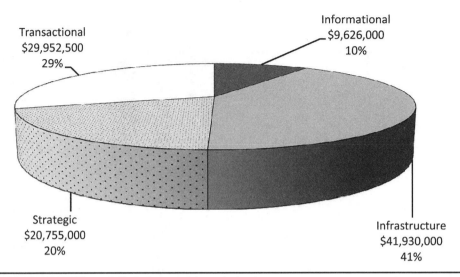

Figure 10-10 CAPEX portfolio balance with optimization

10.3 Prioritization vs. Optimization—Lessons Learned

A comparison of the results of prioritization and optimization is listed in Table 10-19. The comparison highlights the superiority of optimization over prioritization in guiding portfolio selection. For example, all the business requirements (constraints) for portfolio selection, such as cross-portfolio dependencies, and sub-portfolio constraints and portfolio balance, among others, can be satisfied only via optimization.

Moreover, without heroic tinkering and manipulation of the prioritization methodology (often rendering it mathematically indefensible), prioritization cannot account for viable business choices, such as partially funding OPEX investments (since existing IT investments to run the business cannot be unfunded), whereas optimization accounts for these practical considerations. To underscore the superiority of optimization over prioritization, consider the CAPEX investment CRM Marketing—Siebel Marketing and Analytics (PFM-2010-050), which has the highest utility value (72.92) of all the investments in either portfolio. PFM-2010-050 has a cross-portfolio dependency on OPEX Legacy Marketing Operations (PFM-2010-020) and needs PFM-2010-020 to be fully funded as a prerequisite.

However, PFM-2010-020 has not been selected by the prioritization technique (see Table 10-15 or Figure 10-6), despite PFM-2010-050 being dependent on this OPEX investment being fully funded (expressed as a cross-portfolio dependency). This is because, again, without indefensible mathematical tinkering and manipulation, project prioritization cannot account for cross-portfolio dependencies, or other requirements for that matter. On the other hand, optimization ensures that PFM-2010-020 is selected for full funding (see Table 10-18 or Figure 10-8), to accommodate the selection of PFM-2010-050. This example illustrates how optimization can take into consideration all the business requirements and determine, with defensible mathematical rigor, the best set of investments for the organization to pursue, something that simply cannot be matched by prioritization.

Additionally, portfolio optimization results in a higher aggregate utility value from the optimal mix of project investments in the entire portfolio.

Table 10-19 Summary of the results of prioritization and optimization

Feature	Prioritization	Optimization
OPEX Budgetary Constraint	Satisfied	Satisfied
CAPEX Budgetary Constraint	Satisfied	Satisfied
CAPEX Portfolio Balance Constraints	Not Possible	Satisfied
CAPEX Project Dependencies	Not Possible	Satisfied
OPEX Investment Dependencies	Not Possible	Satisfied
OPEX Mandatory Investments	Not Possible	Satisfied
OPEX Management-Imposed Funding Restrictions	Not Possible	Satisfied
Cross-Portfolio Investment Dependencies	Not Possible	Satisfied
Cross-Portfolio Resource Constraints	Not Possible	Satisfied
OPEX Portfolio	1,845	1,763[1]
CAPEX Portfolio	727	823
CAPEX and OPEX Portfolios	2,572	2,586
Funding Allocation ($)	$291,516,000	$295,035,000
Budget Limit ($)	$296,000,000	$296,000,000
Funding Slack ($)	$4,484,000	$965,000
# Fully Funded Investments	33	25
# Partially Funded Investments	0	15
# Unfunded Investments	7	0
Funding Allocation ($)	$106,240,000	$102,263,500
Budget Limit ($)	$118,400,000	$118,400,000
Funding Slack ($)	$12,160,000	$16,136,500
# Approved Investments	14	18
# Rejected Investments	11	7
Infrastructure	37.3%	41.0%
Transactional	24.4%	29.3%
Strategic	28.4%	20.3%
Informational	9.8%	9.4%
Portfolio Balance Summary	Not Achieved	Achieved

[1]The utility value of the OPEX investments is computed as Σ (MODA score of selected OPEX investments) + 0.5 * Σ (MODA score of unselected OPEX investments), since it could be argued with merit that the unselected investments are being utilized at 50% of their total utility value. The actual results of the optimal solution in Excel Premium Solver do not take this into account and instead compute the utility value of the OPEX investments simply as Σ (MODA score of selected OPEX investments). The authors have implemented this extra step in the calculation primarily to reflect an accurate representation of the utility value based on the actual funding allocation.

The focal point of the analysis is that IT portfolio selection through conventional investment prioritization techniques leads almost inevitably to the pursuit of a suboptimal portfolio of investments, whereas the use of programming methodologies leads to a superior portfolio result. IT organizations seeking to improve the value of the portfolio selection process should therefore aspire to achieve competencies in portfolio optimization as a harbinger of success in IT resource planning. Organizational behavior that dictates portfolio selection based on the notion of prioritization as the precursor to or in lieu of optimization should be challenged because prioritization results almost inevitably in the creation of a sub-optimal portfolio.

Further, there is no guarantee that any of the investments chosen as a result of prioritization would be selected in an optimal solution. Therefore, prioritization prior to, or instead of, optimization is a portfolio selection methodology that is guaranteed to submaximize the value of the organization's IT portfolio. This is not to say that prioritization is not a worthwhile activity. It is important to note that while the somewhat qualitative nature of project prioritization renders it inferior to portfolio optimization, prioritization is nevertheless an important aspect of the entire portfolio selection process where temporal resource management considerations are in effect. IT organizations seeking to extract the maximum value from the portfolio selection process should instead exploit the best features of both prioritization and optimization. Therefore, the following step-by-step approach to IT portfolio selection as a best practice for IT organizations is recommended:

- **Step 1:** Develop MODA models for CAPEX and OPEX investments, similar to the models discussed in Chapter 8, Project Prioritization.
- **Step 2:** Compute the utility value of every IT investment in both the CAPEX and OPEX categories.
- **Step 3:** Formulate the optimization problem (using binary integer linear programming logic), with the objective being the maximization of the total utility value of the entire set of investments under consideration, subject to the constraints imposed on the portfolio.
- **Step 4:** Perform portfolio selection by solving the optimization problem formulated in the previous step.
- **Step 5:** Prioritize the resulting portfolio of selected investments to schedule or sequence the investments *in alignment* with the organization's resource allocation plan for the period under consideration.

10.4 Summary

This case study provided a step-by-step illustration of portfolio selection in an enterprise's IT portfolio, taking into consideration all the business requirements (constraints). Further, it clearly demonstrated the superiority of optimization over prioritization as a portfolio selection technique. Optimization using binary integer linear programming was accomplished to select the sets of investments that would maximize the total utility value of the IT portfolio, while adhering to the constraints imposed. The optimal portfolio thus selected can have the underlying projects sequenced based on prioritization in adherence to the organizational resource considerations. Also, a step-by-step approach was provided for IT organizations to adopt for selecting the best set of investments to pursue in an IT portfolio. This approach is not limited to IT portfolios alone, but can be extended to any portfolio of investments in an enterprise. The next case study in Chapter 11, which draws on the pharmaceutical industry, will illustrate even more sophisticated methods of portfolio selection, such as goal programming and stochastic optimization.

11

Case Study in R&D Portfolio Management

11.1 Introduction to the R&D Case Study

In the following case study, Diversified Healthcare, Inc. (DHI) is a healthcare company that is comprised of four business units (BUs): Consumer Goods (CG), Diagnostics (DIA), Medical Devices (MD), and Prescription Drugs (Rx). Each BU has 10 projects, so the company has a total of 40 projects at different stages of research and development across its entire portfolio. The primary challenge to DHI is to decide on which projects to invest in since it is constrained by the size of its budget, as well as the current number of researchers and developers it has on board.

This case study is divided into three parts: (a) portfolio selection predicated on project prioritization that, in turn, is based on multiple and single decision-making attributes, but not accounting for technical and regulatory risk and commercial uncertainty; (b) portfolio selection predicated on deterministic portfolio optimization, based on single and multiple objectives and accounting for technical and regulatory risk; and (c) portfolio selection predicated on stochastic portfolio optimization, based on single objectives and accounting for technical and regulatory risk and commercial uncertainty.

11.2 Portfolio Selection Based on Project Prioritization

DHI's portfolio selection is based on project prioritization, using multiple and single decision-making attributes, but not accounting for technical and regulatory risk and commercial uncertainty. The data that accompanies this case is given in Table 11-1. The overarching intent of the organization is to maximize its strategic and financial goals as measured by strategic value (column 2) and financial value (cumulative, short-term, top line sales, shown in column 3; net present value [NPV] over the life of the product is in column 4).

For each project, there are 11 attributes (columns 2-12) that are used by DHI to assess the level of importance or attractiveness of each project on an ongoing basis within the portfolio. As discussed in Chapter 8, the raw numerical or categorical score for each attribute is converted into a utility score between 0 and 10, using a utility function for

Table 11-1 DHI project data

DIVERSIFIED HEALTHCARE INC.

PROJECT ID	MODA ATTRIBUTE SCORES AND CORRESPONDING WEIGHTS											Aggregate MODA Score	RESOURCE DEMAND		
	Strategic Value (6%)	Top Line Sales (16%)	NPV (12%)	Commercial Uncertainty (6%)	Technical Risk (15%)	Regulatory Risk (9%)	p(Patent Infringement) (6%)	R&D Cost (12%)	S&M Cost (8%)	Time To Launch (7%)	Time To Patent Expiration (3%)		2012 Cost ($M)	2012 Researchers	2012 Developers
Weight	0.06	0.16	0.12	0.06	0.15	0.09	0.06	0.12	0.08	0.07	0.03				
CG1	9.00	2.00	1.00	9.00	9.50	9.50	9.00	10.00	8.00	9.50	1.50	6.89	20.00	0.00	14.00
CG10	4.50	1.00	1.00	8.50	9.00	9.00	9.50	10.00	9.00	9.50	1.00	6.45	14.00	0.00	14.00
CG2	7.50	2.00	1.00	9.50	9.00	9.00	9.00	10.00	8.00	9.00	2.00	6.69	13.00	13.00	12.00
CG3	7.00	3.00	1.00	10.00	8.50	9.00	9.00	10.00	9.00	8.00	2.50	6.80	16.00	15.00	10.00
CG4	3.50	3.00	2.00	10.00	9.50	9.50	9.00	10.00	8.00	8.50	2.00	6.85	18.00	14.00	20.00
CG5	5.00	3.00	2.00	7.50	8.50	9.00	9.50	10.00	9.00	8.50	2.00	6.62	12.00	12.00	13.00
CG6	4.50	4.00	2.00	9.50	9.50	9.00	9.00	10.00	9.00	9.50	1.50	7.16	15.00	0.00	12.00
CG7	3.00	4.00	2.00	8.50	8.50	9.00	9.00	9.00	7.00	9.00	1.00	6.50	14.00	10.00	13.00
CG8	5.00	2.00	1.00	8.00	9.50	9.00	8.50	10.00	7.00	9.00	0.50	6.42	16.00	20.00	13.00
CG9	6.00	2.00	1.00	9.00	9.00	9.50	9.00	10.00	9.00	9.00	0.50	6.65	14.00	10.00	14.00
DIA1	7.00	2.00	1.00	7.50	6.00	8.00	5.00	9.00	8.00	8.00	2.50	5.59	15.00	0.00	22.00
DIA10	1.50	1.00	1.00	8.50	8.00	8.50	5.00	9.00	8.00	7.50	2.00	5.45	32.00	20.00	14.00
DIA2	7.00	3.00	1.00	9.00	9.00	7.50	5.50	10.00	7.00	7.00	3.50	6.27	45.00	14.00	13.00
DIA3	8.00	1.00	1.00	7.00	7.50	8.00	7.50	10.00	8.00	7.50	4.00	5.96	40.00	16.00	13.00
DIA4	5.50	5.00	3.00	8.00	8.00	8.00	8.00	10.00	7.00	8.50	6.50	6.92	40.00	0.00	15.00
DIA5	6.50	2.00	1.00	8.00	7.50	7.00	4.50	10.00	9.00	7.00	5.00	5.97	25.00	12.00	16.00
DIA6	4.50	5.00	1.00	5.00	8.00	7.00	3.50	10.00	8.00	8.00	5.50	6.02	16.00	0.00	16.00
DIA7	5.00	3.00	1.00	6.50	7.50	7.50	3.00	10.00	8.00	8.50	4.50	5.77	32.00	0.00	15.00
DIA8	3.00	1.00	1.00	6.00	6.50	6.50	4.00	10.00	9.00	4.50	6.50	5.05	15.00	10.00	17.00
DIA9	1.00	3.00	1.00	7.00	7.50	7.00	4.00	9.00	8.00	5.00	5.50	5.31	30.00	8.00	0.00
MD1	6.00	4.00	2.00	7.00	6.50	3.00	6.50	8.00	6.00	6.50	2.50	5.27	80.00	8.00	20.00
MD10	3.00	5.00	3.00	6.00	8.00	3.00	7.00	10.00	6.00	6.00	8.00	5.63	45.00	15.00	15.00
MD2	6.00	5.00	3.00	6.00	6.00	3.50	7.50	9.00	4.00	7.00	7.50	5.66	60.00	0.00	16.00
MD3	5.50	3.00	2.00	7.00	7.00	5.50	3.00	9.00	7.00	7.50	6.00	5.54	45.00	0.00	16.00
MD4	6.00	4.00	2.00	4.50	7.50	5.00	5.00	9.00	6.00	4.00	8.50	5.48	60.00	18.00	18.00
MD5	8.50	4.00	3.00	6.50	4.00	6.00	5.00	9.00	5.00	5.00	8.00	5.41	50.00	18.00	18.00
MD6	6.50	2.00	2.00	7.50	3.50	6.50	5.50	9.00	6.00	5.00	6.50	4.95	50.00	16.00	25.00
MD7	2.00	8.00	3.00	8.00	4.00	8.00	6.50	9.00	5.00	5.50	6.50	5.53	45.00	18.00	20.00
MD8	4.00	8.00	5.00	8.50	5.50	7.50	6.00	9.00	5.00	6.50	8.50	6.68	65.00	15.00	18.00
MD9	3.00	4.00	2.00	7.50	5.50	7.50	6.50	9.00	6.00	6.00	7.50	5.61	70.00	15.00	17.00
Rx1	7.00	4.00	4.00	3.00	5.00	8.00	4.00	7.00	5.00	1.00	9.00	5.01	65.00	25.00	20.00
Rx10	10.00	7.00	6.00	2.50	1.50	3.00	5.00	4.00	3.00	2.00	9.50	4.53	175.00	15.00	20.00
Rx2	8.00	5.00	4.00	4.00	2.50	9.00	4.00	4.00	3.00	3.00	8.50	4.61	160.00	20.00	25.00
Rx3	9.50	8.00	7.00	1.00	2.50	5.00	5.00	7.00	3.00	9.00	8.00	5.83	60.00	0.00	15.00
Rx4	6.00	9.00	8.00	1.50	4.00	5.00	7.00	5.00	4.00	6.00	7.50	5.89	75.00	25.00	45.00
Rx5	8.00	6.00	3.00	3.50	3.50	2.00	8.00	5.00	3.00	7.00	8.00	4.77	105.00	0.00	60.00
Rx6	5.00	7.00	6.00	4.50	5.00	4.00	2.00	6.00	2.00	8.00	9.00	5.35	70.00	0.00	55.00
Rx7	7.00	9.00	7.00	6.00	3.50	3.00	2.50	6.00	1.00	5.00	9.00	5.43	80.00	0.00	30.00
Rx8	7.50	10.00	5.00	6.00	2.00	1.00	2.50	4.00	1.00	5.50	10.00	4.50	150.00	25.00	22.00
Rx9	9.00	10.00	8.00	5.50	2.50	4.50	4.00	1.00	1.00	7.50	10.00	5.48	300.00	15.00	47.00

each attribute that reflects the risk tolerance of the organization. The absolute contribution of each of these attributes to the overall importance of each project is expressed in the form of its weight (shown in row 5). These 11 attributes form the basis of a multiple objective decision analysis (MODA) methodology, as described in Chapter 8, which is used routinely to rank order projects (Figure 11-1).

Portfolio management governance at DHI, comprised of executive management, has determined that the absolute weights of its four organizational value drivers are 40% (benefits), 30% (risk), 20% (cost), and 10% (time). These weights were arrived at via the use of an analytic hierarchy process, where it was determined that while cost was twice as important as time and half as important as benefits, risk was 3 times as important as time, and therefore 1.5 times as important as cost and 0.75 as important as benefits.

In column 13 of Table 11-1, the weighted aggregate MODA score for each project is calculated before a rank order is performed. As an example, the weighted aggregate score for Project CG 1 (6.89) is calculated as the sum product of the utility score for each of the 11 attributes and its corresponding weight in row 5. It is important to stress that the data in columns 2-12 represent forecasted values that have been converted to utility values (scale 0-10) using utility functions (not shown) similar to those described in Chapter 8 and in the preceding IT case study in Chapter 10. For example, for Project CG1, the strategic value attribute was scored categorically as "high," which corresponds to a utility value of 9.00. Further, the same project was scored numerically as $110M on cumulative, short-term, top line sales and $500M on long-term NPV; these raw values correspond to utility values of 2.00 and 1.00, respectively. In the final three columns of Table 11-1, the actual forecasted demand for 2012 in terms of cost in $M, researchers, and developers is shown. The data serve to inform DHI of the number of projects it can afford to undertake in 2012 when its budgetary and human

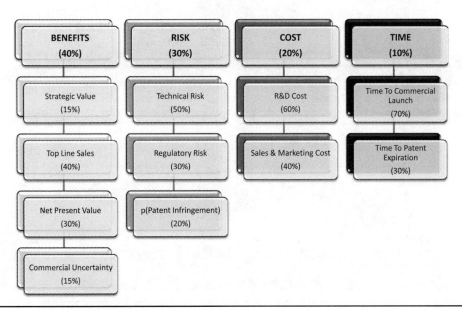

Figure 11-1   MODA model for project prioritization

constraints for the portfolio—$1.5B, 350 researchers, and 650 developers—are taken into account.

On the basis of 3 of the 11 attributes (top line sales, NPV, and overall cost), a comparison of the projects in each of the four BUs is shown in Figure 11-2. Note that in the Consumer Goods BU, projects are clustered in the bottom left of the chart, i.e., displaying relatively low sales and low NPV. Project CG10 is the most unattractive project with respect to both top line sales and NPV, while CG7 is the most attractive project in terms of top line sales, and CG6 is the project with the highest NPV. On the basis of overall R&D cost alone (bubble size), CG10 requires the lowest investment, while CG7 and CG8 are the most expensive projects in this BU. During 2012, costs for projects in this BU range from $12M-$20M.

Within the Diagnostics BU, Project DIA4 outshines all other projects in terms of both sales and NPV, while DIA8 is the least expensive project and DIA10 is the most costly project in the portfolio. The range of lifetime R&D costs for this BU is $25M-$80M, while 2012 costs range from $15M-$45M. Within the Medical Devices BU, the portfolio gravitates markedly away from the relatively low sales and NPV that are seen within the Consumer Goods BU. Here, MD8 is the clear winner in both sales and NPV metrics, while MD6 has the lowest sales and NPV of all projects within this BU. While generally more expensive than both Consumer Goods and Diagnostics, projects within

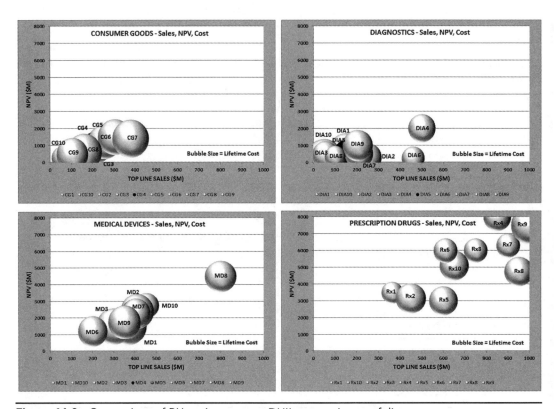

Figure 11-2 Comparison of BU projects across DHI's enterprise portfolio

the Medical Devices BU range from $47M-$105M in lifetime R&D cost, with MD10 being the least expensive and MD1 and MD3 representing the most costly projects.

Within the Prescription Drugs BU, Projects Rx9, Rx8, Rx7, and Rx4 display the highest sales values, while Rx4 and Rx9 possess the highest NPVs. When lifetime R&D cost is considered alone, Rx9 is, by far, the most expensive within a range of $165M-$500M.

It is noteworthy that these lifetime R&D costs represent projected expenditures until the launch of each product; all of the Prescription Drugs and Medical Devices projects require multi-year investments, while the same cannot be stated of projects within both the Consumer Goods and Diagnostics portfolios. Nevertheless, for the purposes of simplicity, this layer of complexity is not addressed in the case study. Suffice it to state, however, that portfolio management should always be conducted on a rolling, multi-period basis so that an organization has a clear understanding of what budgetary and human resources are required to support the continued investment in projects across the portfolio. What makes this difficult, but certainly not unmanageable, is the fact that in both R&D and IT, where project risks predicate that not every project will materialize into a commercial product, careful multi-year analysis is required. Few areas of portfolio management can be as frustrating as initiating projects when there are sufficient budgetary and human resources in a given year, only to have them stalled indefinitely in later years, because of inadequate planning, when there are insufficient resources to continue their progression through the pipeline.

Once the weighted MODA score for each project in the DHI portfolio is calculated, projects can be rank ordered from the most attractive (i.e., highest weighted aggregate utility score) to the least attractive (i.e., lowest weighted utility score). If DHI were interested in portfolio selection based on prioritizing its projects on the strength of their weighted aggregate MODA scores when all 11 attributes are taken into account, it would not be unreasonable for this organization to use the results of the analysis shown in Figure 11-3 to determine which projects it should invest in and support from its budget and human resource pool of researchers and developers in 2012.

Note that of the top 10 projects, 8 belong to the Consumer Goods BU, with one (DIA4) in the Diagnostics BU and one in the Medical Devices (MD8). Interestingly, none of the Prescription Drugs projects is ranked in the top 10. Despite the fact that the majority of the highest sales and NPV scores are found within the Prescription Drugs BU, 6 of the this BU's projects fall within the bottom 10 projects on the prioritized list.

When the budget and human resource constraints are taken into account for 2012, DHI could afford to invest in all of the top 32 projects above the budgetary cutoff line and only 1 of the bottom 8 projects (DIA8) that fall below the budgetary line, yielding a cumulative utility score of 198.81. In addition, the 33 projects for which the organization has sufficient budgetary resources consume $1.467B of the budget and account for 335 researchers and 608 developers.

This is a feasible portfolio of 33 projects since none of the constraints (i.e., $1.50B budget, 350 researchers, and 650 developers) is exceeded in 2012 (Figure 11-4).

Interestingly, if this portfolio was pursued and the risks of each project ignored purely for the purposes of simplicity, DHI is forecasted to earn 21.12 utils in weighted

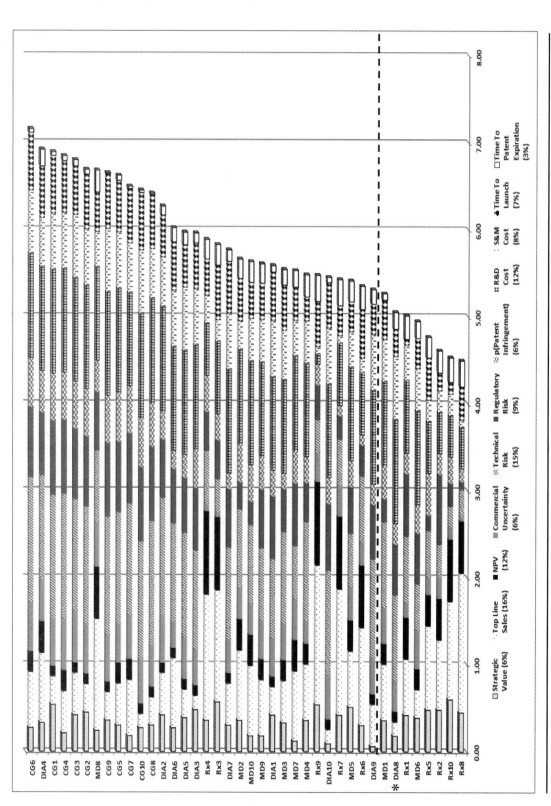

Figure 11-3   Rank order of DHI projects based on weighted MODA scores

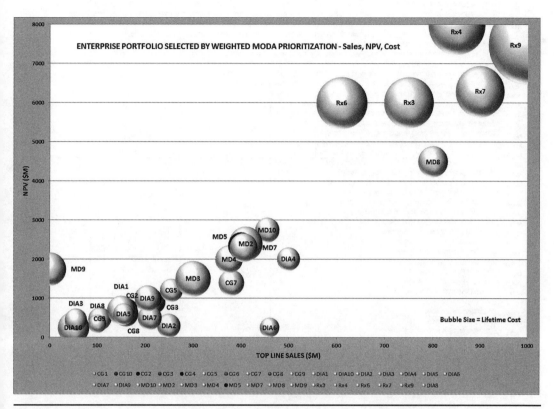

Figure 11-4 Enterprise portfolio based on prioritization of weighted MODA scores

sales and 10.08 utils in weighted NPV. Parenthetically, the unweighted sales and NPV in terms of utils are 133.00 and 85.00, respectively. In terms of forecasted, unweighted, non-risk-adjusted sales and NPVs, the utility values for this portfolio translate into $11.715B in top line sales and $68.400B in NPV.

Although many organizations prioritize their projects on the basis of multiple attributes using weighted aggregate utility scores (and hence use some version of a MODA methodology), they rarely try to maximize the value of utility in their portfolios. Rather, organizations such as DHI strive to maximize a financial value (e.g., sales, NPV, ROI) because they set themselves annual, multi-period goals. So, how different from the results shown in Figure 11-3 would project prioritization by unweighted sales or NPV be? To address this, projects across the DHI enterprise are ranked by forecasted top line sales (raw data not shown), from which utility scores were generated in Table 11-1, and the results of this prioritization are shown in Figures 11-5 and 11-6.

Not surprisingly, based on the relatively high top line sales data for the Prescription Drugs BU (raw data not shown), from which utility scores were generated in Table 11-1, 8 of the top 10 projects are from this BU. On the basis of this analysis, DHI would select only 16 projects, effectively committing itself to a cost of $1.496B along with 186 researchers and 437 developers in 2012. In terms of forecasted sales and

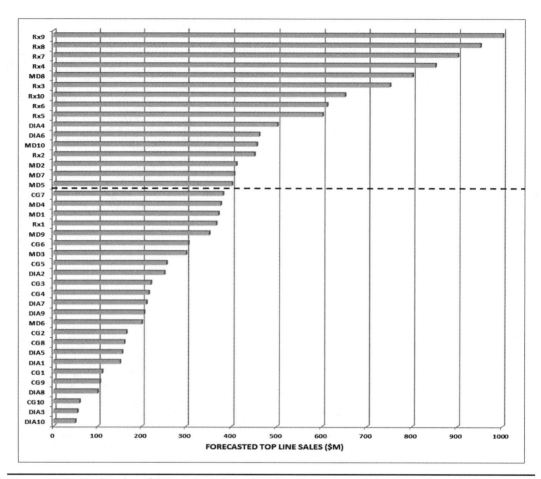

Figure 11-5   Rank order of DHI projects based on forecasted (unweighted) top line sales

NPV, this sales-ranked portfolio could yield $10.190B in top line sales and $66.375B in NPV. Again, this is a feasible portfolio based on sales prioritization because none of the budgetary and human resource constraints are violated. Here, every Prescription Drug project can be undertaken, while none of the Consumer Goods and all but one (DIA4) of the projects within the Diagnostics BU should not be invested in. Within the Medical Devices BU, four projects (MD8, MD10, MD2, and MD7) should be pursued. Of course, DHI may choose to pursue the research and development of far more projects from within the Consumer Goods and Diagnostics BUs, but this would result in an erosion of forecasted sales value as projects from both the Prescription Drugs and Medical Devices BUs would have to be foregone.

At a weight of 12%, NPV is certainly not an unimportant attribute to decision making at DHI. Consequently, it would be helpful to conduct a similar project prioritization analysis on this financial metric alone to ascertain the differences in results between pursuing a purely short-term goal (sales) as opposed to a longer-term goal (NPV). The results of a prioritization analysis based on unweighted NPV alone are shown in Figure

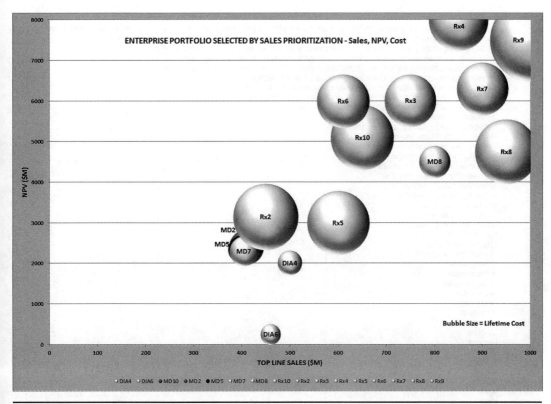

Figure 11-6   Enterprise portfolio based on prioritization of forecasted (unweighted) top line sales

11-7. The analysis of this project prioritization shows that of the 15 projects (14 above the budgetary line and DIA4 below this line) that can be pursued without violating any of the organization's stated constraints, all of the Prescription Drug and four of the Medical Devices projects (MD8, MD10, MD2, and MD5) constitute the top ranked projects. None of the projects from the Consumer Goods and Diagnostics BUs is selected, as shown in Figure 11-8, resulting in a forecasted use of $1.500B of the 2012 budget, along with 193 researchers and 421 developers. If these projects are selected for pursuit in 2012, the portfolio has the potential to yield $9.690B in top line sales and $67.320B in NPV.

The summary results of the different portfolio selection strategies are presented in Table 11-2. When all decision-making attributes for portfolio selection are taken into account, DHI stands to create 198.81 utils in value that translate into $11.715B in short-term, top line sales and $68.400B in NPV over the life of the projects in the portfolio. By comparison, when sales are used as the sole decision-making criterion, the organization stands to realize $10.190B in sales and $66.375B in NPV. Further, when maximization of NPV is considered as the only goal, DHI's portfolio can yield $9.690B in sales and $67.320B in NPV.

Although it is clear from Table 11-2 that project prioritization based on different attributes (or combinations of attributes) yields differing results in terms of (a) project

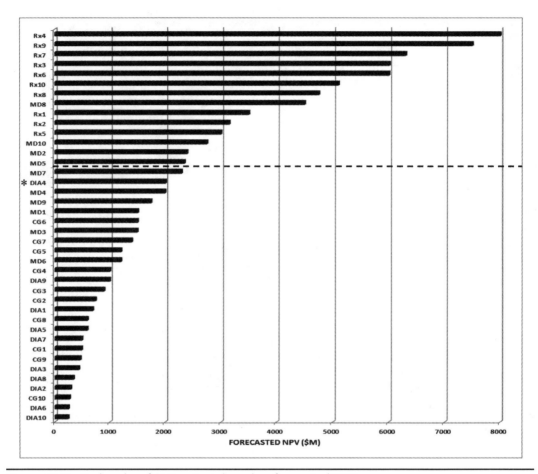

Figure 11-7   Rank order of DHI projects based on forecasted NPV

selection, (b) utility and financial values, and (c) consumption of budgetary and human resources, we cannot be certain that these portfolios, while feasible, are optimal, i.e., they are populated by projects that make the best use of available resources. For each selected attribute or combination of attributes displayed in Table 11-2, therefore, there may be better combinations of projects that would yield greater utility value (and consequently higher top line sales and NPV) or higher direct sales and NPVs without violating budgetary and human resource constraints.

To test this hypothesis, using optimization techniques such as integer linear programming described in Chapter 7, we can search for portfolios that maximize the value of one or more goals, such as top line sales and NPV, across all four BUs within DHI's portfolio subject to the budgetary and human resource constraints already described. The results of this methodological approach are shown in Table 11-3.

To compare, in each of the three optimizations performed, without violating budgetary and human resource constraints, a superior result to prioritization is achieved. In the first optimization strategy, where the objective is to maximize weighted aggregate utility using all of the 11 decision-making MODA values, the optimal portfolio

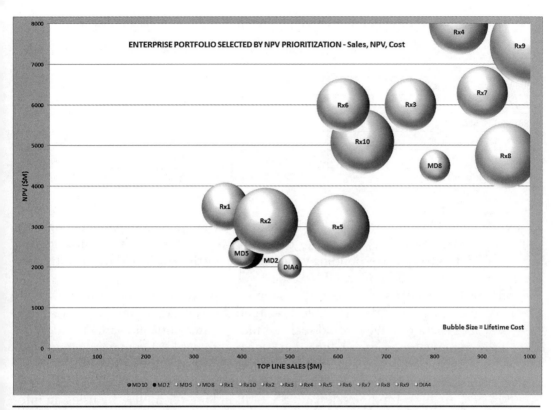

Figure 11-8   Enterprise portfolio based on prioritization of forecasted NPV

Table 11-2 Summary of portfolio characteristics based on different prioritization objectives

	All Attributes	Unweighted Sales	Unweighted NPV
# of Projects Selected	33	16	15
Total Utility Value (Utils)	198.81	—	—
Total Cost ($B) in 2012	1.467	1.496	1.500
Total # of Researchers in 2012	335	186	193
Total # of Developers in 2012	608	437	421
Aggregate Sales ($B)	11.715	10.190	9.690
Aggregate NPV ($B)	68.400	66.375	67.320

is comprised of 35 projects with a total utility value of 207.43, which is superior to that found by prioritization—comprised of 33 projects with a total utility value of 198.81—as was shown in Table 11-2.

However, because the optimization objective is to seek the portfolio that yields the highest value in terms of weighted aggregate utility, it is not surprising that it does not provide higher sales or NPV than the portfolio selected by prioritization (Table 11-3). When maximization of top line sales becomes the short-term objective in the second optimization strategy, the optimal portfolio, comprised of 33 projects with an aggregate value of $12.835B, is clearly superior to that chosen by prioritization (16 projects

Table 11-3 Summary of portfolio characteristics based on different optimization objectives

	All Attributes	Unweighted Sales	Unweighted NPV
# of Projects Selected	35	33	31
Total Utility Value (Utils)	207.43	–	–
Total Cost ($B) in 2012	1.392	1.481	1.497
Total # of Researchers in 2012	344	342	335
Total # of Developers in 2012	641	642	612
Aggregate Sales ($B)	11.400	12.835	12.255
Aggregate NPV ($B)	62.110	72.685	75.490

valued at $10.190B). Likewise, when the portfolio strategy is to maximize long-term gain (i.e., NPV), the optimal portfolio is populated by 31 projects for an aggregate value of $75.490B; the corresponding values for the portfolio selected by prioritization are 15 projects and $67.320B in NPV, respectively.

From this brief analysis, the message is simple yet powerful and consistent: without altering any of the project data in Table 11-1 (and the raw data from which these utility scores are generated), DHI could realize much greater portfolio value by adopting a portfolio optimization methodology that is geared toward value maximization, subject to budgetary and human resource constraints. *Ceteris paribus*, why would DHI, or any rational decision maker, willingly walk away from enterprise value in the form of $0.850B in short-term top line sales and $5.930B in long-term NPV by using an inferior portfolio selection methodology? To put this dilemma into personal terms, if you were the CEO of DHI, would you knowingly forego nearly $1B in sales and almost $6B in NPV? Hopefully not.

Often, organizations such as DHI may have several objectives in mind and wish to pursue the maximization of multiple financial values while paying attention to different sector or BU resource investment strategies. First, let us deal with maximizing multiple financial objectives, in this case top line sales and NPV. Recall that each decision-making attribute was weighted at 16% and 12%, respectively. If these weights were unchanged and without inclusion of any of the other nine decision-making attributes, the portfolio prioritized by these weighted attributes alone would be comprised of 15 projects that yield a cumulative utility of 81.79 before budgetary constraints are exceeded (Figure 11-9).

In addition to all of the Prescription Drug projects, there are four projects from the Medical Devices BU (MD8, MD10, MD2, and MD7) and one (DIA4) from the Diagnostics BU. If pursued, this portfolio could yield $9.695B in top line sales and $67.270B in NPV, while utilizing $1.485B of budget along with 193 researchers and 423 developers.

11.3. Portfolio Selection Based on Deterministic Optimization

This next section will illustrate portfolio selection based on deterministic portfolio optimization that accounts for technical and regulatory risk, but not for commercial

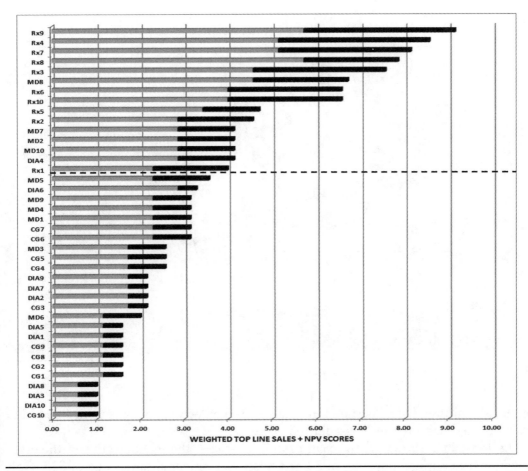

Figure 11-9   Rank order of DHI projects based on weighted top line sales and NPV scores

uncertainty. Thus far, we have considered different portfolio valuations that are based on projects for which the following two parameters have been ignored: (a) technical and regulatory risk and (b) commercial uncertainty. As shown in Tables 11-2 and 11-3, aggregate utility scores, sales, and NPVs are determined from project data for which technical and regulatory risk and commercial uncertainty have not been accounted for. In reviewing DHI's portfolio on the basis of technical and regulatory risk, NPV, and sales, it can be seen that there is a wide spread of project risks—as measured by a joint probability of technical and regulatory success for each project—across the four BUs (Figure 11-10).

Although generally high in both sales and NPV, projects within the Prescription Drugs BU carry the highest risk load. Conversely, the Consumer Goods BU is populated by projects that bear comparatively low risk, along with modest sales and NPVs. Unless these risks are accounted for in the integrated evaluation of each project, DHI would have little understanding of how its potential, non-risk-adjusted portfolio value could be impacted in both the short and long terms. Therefore, for the remainder of this case, we will turn our attention to examining how to maximize portfolio value

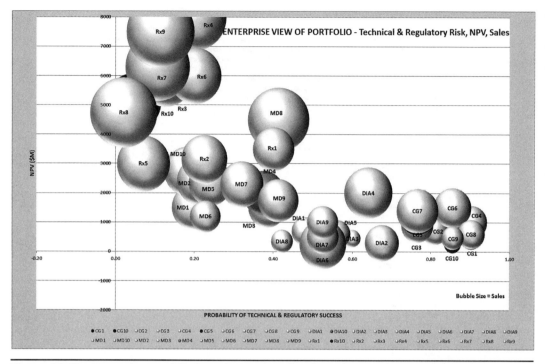

Figure 11-10   Enterprise portfolio based on technical and regulatory risk, NPV, and top line sales

on a risk-adjusted basis. As stated in Chapter 5, the decision analysis term "expected" value is used to represent "risk-adjusted" value.

As Table 11-3 shows, when maximization of sales is the sole objective of the organization, the optimal portfolio of 33 projects yields potential sales value of $12.835B and potential NPV of $72.685B. Likewise, when maximization of NPV is the objective, the optimal portfolio promises $75.490B in NPV and $12.255B in sales. On a risk-adjusted basis, these potential values translate into optimal portfolios with the characteristics described in Table 11-4. When maximization of expected sales is the objective, the optimal portfolio yields $4.703B and results in an expected NPV (ENPV) of $23.300B. On the other hand, when maximization of ENPV is the objective, the optimal portfolio yields $23.367B and results in expected sales of $4.568B.

Note that the portfolio optimized for expected sales does indeed have the highest expected sales value ($4.703B) while possessing a lower ENPV ($23.300B) than the portfolio optimized for ENPV ($23.367B). The converse is true in that the portfolio optimized for ENPV has a lower sales value ($4.568B) than that optimized for sales ($4.703B). While these differences in expected portfolio values may appear to be marginal, it is worth noting from Table 11-3 that the difference in NPV on a non-risk-adjusted basis between portfolios optimized for sales and NPV separately is nearly $3B.

As presented in Chapter 7, when there are two competing goals, it is not possible to attain a state where the optimal portfolio yields the highest value for both goals. In fact, the more a portfolio achieves on one goal (e.g., short-term, top line sales), the less

Table 11-4 Summary of portfolio characteristics based on risk-adjusted optimization objectives

	Unconstrained Portfolio	Optimization for Expected Sales	Optimization for ENPV
# of Projects Selected	40	33	33
Expected Sales ($B)	5.015	4.703	4.568
ENPV ($B)	25.266	23.300	23.367
Total Cost ($B) in 2012	2.252	1.435	1.430
Total # of Researchers in 2012	444	343	345
Total # of Developers in 2012	800	607	607
Excluded Projects	–	DIA3, DIA8, DIA10; Rx5, Rx8, Rx9, Rx10	DIA2, DIA8, DIA10; Rx5, Rx8, Rx9, Rx10

it does on another (e.g., long-term NPV). This is the basis for a more complex form of portfolio optimization referred to as *goal programming* (GP), using linear programming where iterative optimization solutions that allow for trade-offs in value between competing goals, such as expected sales and ENPV, are required before a satisfactory solution can be found for the decision makers at DHI.

Parenthetically, trade-offs between goals often require decision makers to relax the nature of their constraints, and in this case, DHI may decide that its 2012 budget of $1.500B and human resources of 350 researchers and 650 developers represent *targets* that may be violated slightly, rather than *hard constraints* that cannot be exceeded. With GP, iterative portfolio optimization scenarios provide insights into the trade-offs between value gained or lost on multiple, competing objectives as target constraints are exceeded to a limited extent.

It is not unreasonable for DHI to want to maximize both short-term value in the form of top line sales as well as long-term value in the form of NPV. In fact, this is the substance of perennial debate in many organizations regarding whether to invest disproportionately higher in projects that yield greater short-term value than in opportunities that promise longer-term value creation. Let's make DHI's value creation goals explicit in the following form:

- **Goal A:** On a risk-adjusted basis, the portfolio should provide expected short-term top line sales of approximately $4.703B.
- **Goal B:** On a risk-adjusted basis, the portfolio should provide long-term ENPV of approximately $23.367B.

Goals A and B can be referred to as X_1 and X_2, respectively. As described in detail in Appendix B, deviational, non-negative, underachievement and overachievement variables, d_i^- and d_i^+, can be created to represent the amount by which Goals A and B deviate from their target values of $4.703B in expected sales and $23.367B in ENPV.

Likewise, deviational variables can be generated for DHI's budgetary and human resource constraints in 2012. Parenthetically, if the organization mandated that the 2012 budget of $1.500B could not be exceeded, this would represent a *hard constraint*

$$X_1 + d_1^- - d_1^+ = \$4.703B$$

rather than a *goal constraint*. Assuming only goal constraints, DHI's GP optimization problem can be formulated as follows:

Expected Sales: $X_1 + d_1^- - d_1^+ = \$4.703B$

ENPV: $X_2 + d_2^- - d_2^+ = \$23.367B$

2012 Budget: $X_3 + d_3^- - d_3^+ = \$1.500B$

2012 Researchers: $X_4 + d_4^- - d_4^+ = 350$

2012 Developers: $X_5 + d_5^- - d_5^+ = 650$

GP can now be employed to search for the portfolio that maximizes expected sales and ENPV by minimizing the weighted percentage deviation from each goal (see Appendix B). As an example, DHI may wish to consider the following preferences related to each of the five goals:

- **Expected Sales:** Undesirable to underachieve $4.703B but indifferent to overachievement of this goal.
- **ENPV:** Undesirable to underachieve $23.367B but indifferent to overachievement of this goal.
- **2012 Budget:** Undesirable to overachieve $1.500B but indifferent to underachievement of this goal.
- **2012 Researchers:** Undesirable to overachieve 350 but indifferent to underachievement of this goal.
- **2012 Developers:** Undesirable to overachieve 650 but indifferent to underachievement of this goal.

DHI's objective is to find an optimal solution that minimizes the weighted percentage deviation from each goal in the form expressed by the following objective:

MIN = $(w_1^-/4.703) * d_1^- + (w_2^-/23.367) * d_2^- + (w_3^+/1.500) * d_3^+ + (w_4^+/350) * d_4^+ + (w_5^+/650) * d_5^+)$

where w_i^- and w_i^+ represent numeric constants that can be assigned weights to the various deviational variables d_i^- and d_i^+.

Subject to the five goal constraints:

Expected Sales: $X_1 + d_1^- - d_1^+ = \$4.703B$

ENPV: $X_2 + d_2^- - d_2^+ = \$23.367B$

2012 Budget: $X_3 + d_3^- - d_3^+ = \$1.500B$

2012 Researchers: $X_4 + d_4^- - d_4^+ = 350$

2012 Developers: $X_5 + d_5^- - d_5^+ = 650$

Using integer linear programming (ILP) and GP, several optimization scenarios can be investigated to determine which portfolios result in minimization of the weighted aggregate percentage deviation from the five goals (Table 11-5).

Consider scenario 1, where DHI finds it undesirable to underachieve its expected sales and ENPV goals, thereby assigning weights of 1, but is indifferent about

Table 11.3 Summary of optimization scenarios based on weighted preferences to portfolio goals

DIVERSIFIED HEALTHCARE INC.

TARGET Values for 2012: Expected Sales = $4,703B, ENPV = $23,367B, Cost = $1,500B, # Researchers = 350, # Developers = 650

SCENARIO	BASE CASE	Scenario #1	Scenario #2	Scenario #3	Scenario #4	Scenario #5	Scenario #6	Scenario #7	Scenario #8	Scenario #9	Scenario #10	Scenario #11
WEIGHT	NONE	0	ALL WEIGHTS = 1									
GOAL CONSTRAINTS		SALES 1+, NPV 1+, COST 1+, RESEARCHERS 1+, DEVELOPERS 1+, Other WEIGHTS =		SALES 10+, Other WEIGHTS = 1	NPV 10+, Other WEIGHTS = 1	COST 10+, Other WEIGHTS = 1	RESEARCHERS 10+, Other WEIGHTS = 1	DEVELOPERS 10+, Other WEIGHTS = 1	SALES 10, NPV 10, COST 10+, RESEARCHERS 10+, DEVELOPERS 10+, Other WEIGHTS = 1	SALES 16, NPV 12+, COST 10+, RESEARCHERS 10+, DEVELOPERS 10+, Other WEIGHTS = 1	RESEARCHERS 10+, DEVELOPERS 20+, Other WEIGHTS = 1	COST 5+, RESEARCHERS 10+, DEVELOPERS 20+, Other WEIGHTS = 1
CONSTRAINTS	NONE	ALL CONSTRAINTS	ALL CONSTRAINTS	ALL CONSTRAINTS	ALL CONSTRAINTS	ALL CONSTRAINTS	ALL CONSTRAINTS	ALL CONSTRAINTS	ALL CONSTRAINTS	ALL CONSTRAINTS	ALL CONSTRAINTS	ALL CONSTRAINTS
# OF PROJECTS	40	33	34	34	34	34	34	34	34	34	33	34
OBJECTIVE	N/A	0.289%	2.390%	2.390%	2.390%	2.390%	2.860%	3.031%	7.226%	7.337%	3.901%	3.973%
RESULTING EXPECTED SALES ($B)	$5,015	$4,703	$4,706	$4,706	$4,706	$4,706	$4,675	$4,695	$4,703	$4,703	$4,683	$4,654
RESULTING EXPECTED NPV ($B)	$25,266	$23,300	$23,485	$23,485	$23,485	$23,485	$23,031	$23,382	$23,360	$23,360	$23,171	$22,929
ALLOCATED COST ($B)	$2,252	$1,435	$1,500	$1,500	$1,500	$1,500	$1,501	$1,482	$1,465	$1,465	$1,508	$1,500
ALLOCATED RESEARCHERS	444	343	351	351	351	351	349	355	345	345	347	349
ALLOCATED DEVELOPERS	800	607	660	660	660	660	653	649	652	652	642	645
	DECISION VARIABLES	DECISION VARIABLES	DECISION VARIABLES	DECISION VARIABLES	DECISION VARIABLES	DECISION VARIABLES	DECISION VARIABLES	DECISION VARIABLES	DECISION VARIABLES	DECISION VARIABLES	DECISION VARIABLES	DECISION VARIABLES
CG1	1	1	1	1	1	1	1	1	1	1	1	1
CG10	1	1	1	1	1	1	1	1	1	1	0	1
CG2	1	1	1	1	1	1	1	1	1	1	1	1
CG3	1	1	1	1	1	1	1	1	1	1	1	1
CG4	1	1	1	1	1	1	1	1	1	1	1	1
CG5	1	1	1	1	1	1	1	1	1	1	1	1
CG6	1	1	1	1	1	1	1	1	1	1	1	1
CG7	1	1	1	1	1	1	1	1	1	1	1	1
CG8	1	1	1	1	1	1	1	1	1	1	1	1
CG9	1	1	1	1	1	1	1	1	1	1	1	1
DIA1	1	1	1	1	1	1	1	1	1	1	1	1
DIA10	1	0	0	0	0	0	0	0	0	0	1	0
DIA2	1	1	1	1	1	1	1	1	1	1	1	1
DIA3	1	0	1	1	1	1	1	1	1	1	0	1
DIA4	1	1	1	1	1	1	1	1	1	1	1	1
DIA5	1	1	1	1	1	1	1	1	1	1	1	1
DIA6	1	1	1	1	1	1	1	1	1	1	1	1
DIA7	1	1	1	1	1	1	1	1	1	1	1	1
DIA8	1	1	1	1	1	1	1	0	1	1	1	1
DIA9	1	1	1	1	1	1	1	1	1	1	1	1
MD1	1	1	0	0	0	0	0	0	0	0	1	1
MD10	1	1	1	1	1	1	1	1	1	1	1	1
MD2	1	1	1	1	1	1	1	1	1	1	1	1
MD3	1	1	1	1	1	1	1	1	1	1	1	1
MD4	1	1	1	1	1	1	1	1	1	1	1	1
MD5	1	1	1	1	1	1	1	1	1	1	1	1
MD6	1	1	1	1	1	1	1	1	1	1	1	1
MD7	1	1	1	1	1	1	1	1	1	1	1	1
MD8	1	1	1	1	1	1	1	1	1	1	1	1
MD9	1	1	1	1	1	1	1	1	1	1	1	1
Rx1	1	1	1	1	1	1	1	1	1	1	1	1
Rx10	1	0	0	0	0	0	0	0	0	0	0	0
Rx2	1	1	0	1	1	1	1	1	1	1	1	1
Rx3	1	0	1	1	1	1	1	1	1	1	1	1
Rx4	1	1	1	1	1	1	1	1	1	1	1	1
Rx5	1	0	1	1	1	1	1	1	1	1	1	1
Rx6	1	1	1	1	1	1	1	1	1	1	1	1
Rx7	1	1	1	1	1	1	1	1	1	1	1	1
Rx8	1	0	0	0	0	0	0	0	0	0	0	0
Rx9	1	0	0	0	0	0	0	0	0	0	0	0

overachieving them, thereby assigning weights of 0. Further, the organization has decided that it is undesirable to overachieve its 2012 cost, researchers, and developers goals, thereby assigning weights of 1, but is indifferent about underachieving them (thereby assigning weights of 0). A synopsis of this portion of the ILP GP model is shown in Table 11-6, where the objective cell represents the sum product of the percentage deviations and assigned weights for the deviational variables.

The optimal portfolio from the conditions laid out in scenario 1 shows no deviation from the goal of $4.703B in expected sales, while an underachievement of approximately $68M from the ENPV goal is observed. This underachievement in ENPV is equivalent to a deviation from the target goal of 0.29%, which, being weighted at 1, results in a weighted percentage deviation of 0.29%. When the remaining goal constraints are taken into account, cost is underachieved by $65M, researchers by 7, and developers by 43. Although underachievement of these three goals is equivalent to 4.33%, 2.00%, and 6.62% deviation from their respective target values, they do not contribute to the overall weighted percentage deviation, as they are each weighted by decision makers at DHI at 0. The overall result is that the aggregate weighted percentage deviation is 0.29% where 33 projects are selected, yielding expected sales of $4.703B and ENPV of $23.300B, while consuming $1.435B in budget along with 343 researchers and 607 developers (Table 11-5, column 3).

Note in Table 11-5 that three projects from the Diagnostics BU (DIA3, DIA8, and DIA10) and four projects from within the Prescription Drugs BU (Rx5, Rx8, Rx9,

Table 11-6 Summary of ILP GP portfolio optimization model parameters

TOTAL	$15,300	$90,610		18		
Goal Constraints	**Sales**	**NPV**		**Cost**	**# Researchers**	**# Developers**
Actual Amount	$4,703.46	$23,299.60		$1,435	343	607
+ Under	$0	$68		$65	7	43
- Over	$0	$0		$0	0	0
= Goal	$4,703.46	$23,367.10		$1,500	350	650
Target Value	$4,703.46	$23,367.10		$1,500	350	650
Percent Deviation						
Under	0.00%	0.29%		4.33%	2.00%	6.62%
Over	0.00%	0.00%		0.00%	0.00%	0.00%
Weights						
Under	1	1		0	0	0
Over	0	0		1	1	1
Objective	0.289%					

Rx10) are excluded from the optimal portfolio. On the basis of the weighted preferences to the goal constraints and optimization results from scenario 1, should DHI proceed with the execution of the selected portfolio of 33 projects? It depends. If the decision makers at DHI are satisfied with both the extent of the deviations from the five goal constraints and the projects selected, the portfolio selected from scenario 1 can be pursued. On the other hand, if DHI wishes to investigate what it may gain or forego by minimizing the deviation from one or another goal, it should examine other scenarios. As shown in Table 11-5, 10 additional scenarios are investigated in which different weights are applied to the deviational variables and the portfolio re-optimized, so that decision makers may judge which scenario provides them with the greatest degree of satisfaction.

In scenario 2, where it is equally undesirable to underachieve or overachieve any of the five goals (thereby assigning weights of 1), the optimal portfolio is comprised of 34 projects, providing roughly the same expected sales value and yielding $185M greater in ENPV than in scenario 1. However, while the cost target goal for 2012 of $1.500B is not exceeded, both target goals for researchers and developers are exceeded by 1 and 10, respectively. The aggregate weighted percentage deviation is now 2.390%, with an overachievement in ENPV of $118 when compared to the ENPV target goal of $23.367B. Exceeding the target ENPV goal of $23.367B resulted in the worsening of two other goals in that both targets for researchers and developers are exceeded.

Further, DIA3 and Rx5, which were not selected in scenario 1, are now included in scenario 2, while MD1, which was selected in scenario 1, is now excluded from the optimal portfolio in scenario 2. A cursory review of Table 11-5 reveals that increasing the penalty for underachievement of expected sales (scenario 3) and ENPV (scenario 4) separately does not alter the optimal portfolio solution found in scenario 2. Similarly, increasing the penalty for overachievement of cost (scenario 5) does not result in a different optimal portfolio. In scenarios 6 and 7, where the penalty for overachievement of target goals for researchers and developers is increased separately, expected sales and ENPV are underachieved in scenario 6 and expected sales are underachieved in scenario 7. The remaining scenarios 8-11 allow decision makers at DHI to determine the extent to which deviations from target goals can be tolerated by altering weights to the deviational variables associated with expected sales, ENPV, cost, researchers, and developers. Although it may be tempting to compare the results of the GP scenarios on the basis of their objective function values where a lower weighted aggregate value represents a smaller deviation from the goals, it is far more important to compare the results from each GP solution in terms of their individual deviation from goals.

To complete this section on deterministic optimization using multiple goals, it may be helpful for DHI to consider a special type of GP formulation that involves multiple objective linear programming (MOLP), where it is necessary to determine target values for each goal or objective, one or more of which (e.g., budget) may be hard constraints. Here, the use of an objective function—the MINIMAX objective Q—is helpful in GP when there is a need to find an optimal portfolio solution that minimizes the maximum deviation from any of the goals. On a technical note (described in detail in Appendix B), the optimization approach requires the creation of one additional constraint for each of the five deviational variables, where:

$$d_i^- \leq Q$$
$$d_i^+ \leq Q$$

Because the objective is to minimize the variable Q, and since Q must be greater than or equal to the values of all of the deviational variables, it will always be set to the maximum value of the deviational variables (Ragsdale, 2008). Concurrently, the *objective function* searches for a solution where the maximum deviational variable is as small as possible. This allows the search for a solution which results in the minimization of the maximum deviation from all of the goals.

DHI's challenge is to find an optimal solution that maximizes expected sales and ENPV in the form expressed by the following objective:

$$\text{MAX:} \quad \text{Sum}(\text{ESales}_i \text{Project}_i)$$

$$\text{MAX:} \quad \text{Sum}(\text{ENPV}_i \text{Project}_i)$$

where $\text{ESales}_i \text{Project}_i$ and $\text{ENPV}_i \text{Project}_i$ represent the expected sales and ENPV for each project subject to the three constraints:

  2012 Budget: $\text{Sum}(\text{Cost}_i \text{Project}_i) \leq \$1.500\text{B}$
  2012 Researchers: $\text{Sum}(\text{Researchers}_i \text{Project}_i) \leq 350$
  2012 Developers: $\text{Sum}(\text{Developers}_i \text{Project}_i) \leq 650$

Using ILP and MOLP, several optimization scenarios can be investigated to determine which portfolios result in minimization of the maximum percentage weighted deviation from the two goals (Table 11-7).

From the ILP analyses conducted earlier (Table 11-4), DHI knows, given its 2012 constraints of $1.500B in budget, 350 researchers, and 650 developers, that the maximum it can achieve in expected sales is $4.703B, while $23.367B is the maximum it can attain in ENPV. These latter two values are generated by optimal portfolios that

Table 11-7 Summary of ILP MOLP portfolio optimization model parameters

MOLP Constraints	Resulting Expected Sales ($B)	Resulting ENPV ($B)
Actual Amount	$4.703	$23.300
Target Value	$4.703	$23.367
% Deviation	0.00%	0.29%
Weight	1	1
% Weighted Deviation	0.00%	0.29%

Objective	
MiniMax Var. Q	0.29%

are similar but not identical in project composition, while an optimal portfolio where both maximum values in expected sales and ENPV are achieved does not exist.

The approach to finding an optimal portfolio that gets close to both maximization values is therefore very similar to the GP methodology used previously, where improving the value of expected sales results in foregoing ENPV and vice versa. However, knowing the maximum target values for expected sales and ENPV allows DHI to compute the percentage deviation from each goal, as follows:

Expected Sales: (Target Value – Actual Value)/(Target Value)

$$= (\$4.703B - Sum(ESales_iProject_i))/\$4.703B$$

ENPV: (Target Value – Actual Value)/(Target Value)

$$= (\$23.367B - Sum(ENPV_iProject_i))/\$23.367B$$

Because these percentage deviation calculations are linear functions of the project decision variables, an objective function can be formulated as a weighted combination of these percentage deviation functions to yield:

$$MAX: w_1 (\$4.703B - Sum(ESales_iProject_i))/\$4.703B + w_2 (\$23.367B - Sum(ENPV_iProject_i))/\$23.367B$$

and using the MINIMAX variable Q:

$$w_1 (\$4.703B - Sum(ESales_iProject_i))/\$4.703B \le Q$$

$$w_2 (\$23.367B - Sum(ENPV_iProject_i))/\$23.367B \le Q$$

By adjusting the weights w_1 and w_2 of expected sales and ENPV, DHI can explore several optimization solutions until the organization achieves the highest level of satisfaction from the chosen portfolio (Table 11-8).

In scenario 1, where both objectives are equally weighted at 1, the optimal portfolio is comprised of 33 projects that yield aggregate expected sales of $4.703B and ENPV of $23.300B. Increasing the weight of expected sales from 1 to 10 in scenario 2 has no impact on the optimal solution, since the maximum expected sales value has already been attained at $4.703B. On the other hand, increasing the weight of the ENPV objective from 1 to 10 results in a similar but non-identical optimal portfolio where ENPV reaches its maximum value of $23.267B, while foregoing $135M in expected sales. Note that DIA2 and DIA3 trade places between the two dominant, Pareto optimal portfolios. If DHI is not satisfied with the trade-off in value between the gain in ENPV and loss in expected sales, it should investigate other scenarios by further altering the weights of each objective.

11.4 Portfolio Selection Based on Stochastic Optimization

Portfolio selection can also be based on stochastic portfolio optimization that accounts for technical and regulatory risk and for commercial uncertainty. Thus far, DHI has explored ways of finding optimal portfolio based on (a) single objectives such as expected sales and (b) multiple objectives, e.g., expected sales and ENPV. In both cases, and as

Table 11-8 Summary of optimization scenarios based on weighted preferences to expected sales and ENPV

DIVERSIFIED HEALTHCARE INC.

TARGET Values for 2012: Sales = $4.703B, NPV = $23.367B, Cost = $1.500B, # Researchers = 350, # Developers = 650

SCENARIO WEIGHT	BASE CASE	Scenario # 1	Scenario # 2	Scenario # 3
CONSTRAINTS	NONE	ALL CONSTRAINTS	ALL CONSTRAINTS	ALL CONSTRAINTS
CONSTRAINTS	NONE	SALES = 1, NPV = 1	SALES = 10, NPV = 1	SALES = 1, NPV = 10
# OF PROJECTS	40	33	33	33
OBJECTIVE (Minimax Q)	N/A	0.290%	0.290%	2.890%
RESULTING EXPECTED SALES ($B)	$5.015	$4.703	$4.703	$4.568
RESULTING EXPECTED NPV ($B)	$25.266	$23.300	$23.300	$23.367
ALLOCATED COST ($B)	$2.252	$1.435	$1.435	$1.430
ALLOCATED RESEARCHERS	444	343	343	345
ALLOCATED DEVELOPERS	800	607	607	607
	DECISION VARIABLES	DECISION VARIABLES	DECISION VARIABLES	DECISION VARIABLES
CG1	1	1	1	1
CG10	1	1	1	1
CG2	1	1	1	1
CG3	1	1	1	1
CG4	1	1	1	1
CG5	1	1	1	1
CG6	1	1	1	1
CG7	1	1	1	1
CG8	1	1	1	1
CG9	1	1	1	1
DIA1	1	1	1	1
DIA10	1	0	0	0
DIA2	1	1	1	0
DIA3	1	0	0	1
DIA4	1	1	1	1
DIA5	1	1	1	1
DIA6	1	1	1	1
DIA7	1	1	1	1
DIA8	1	0	0	0
DIA9	1	1	1	1
MD1	1	1	1	1
MD10	1	1	1	1
MD2	1	1	1	1
MD3	1	1	1	1
MD4	1	1	1	1
MD5	1	1	1	1
MD6	1	1	1	1
MD7	1	1	1	1
MD8	1	1	1	1
MD9	1	1	1	1
Rx1	1	1	1	1
Rx10	1	0	0	0
Rx2	1	1	1	1
Rx3	1	1	1	1
Rx4	1	1	1	1
Rx5	1	0	0	0
Rx6	1	1	1	1
Rx7	1	1	1	1
Rx8	1	0	0	0
Rx9	1	0	0	0

discussed in Chapter 5, it was posited that it is good business practice to incorporate risk—in the form of technical and regulatory risk—into the optimization objectives. However, a crucial element discussed in Chapter 6, that has not yet been accounted for, is commercial uncertainty, which can be expressed as ranges of values for sales and NPV and, when coupled with risk, results in ranges of values for expected sales and ENPV. As an example, can DHI be absolutely certain that short-term sales for project CG1 are exactly $110M and that long-term NPV is precisely $525M? One should argue against such belief in certainty and further argue that +/– 25% (a suspiciously popular range estimate!) could account for the judgmental spread in project values.

To reflect the fact that DHI is uncertain about its forecasted sales and NPVs, the company has incorporated range estimates for short-term sales and NPV, using a beta-PERT distribution that requires knowledge of a minimum, likeliest, and maximum value for each project. Using the methodology of stochastic optimization, as described in Chapter 7, DHI can incorporate both the risk of failure (measured by a probability of technical and regulatory success) and commercial uncertainty (measured by a beta-PERT distribution) for each project in its portfolio to more accurately determine the viability of its portfolio toward meeting its goals under defined budgetary and human resource constraints. Recall from Table 11-4 that DHI's unconstrained portfolio has the potential to yield $5.015B in expected sales and $25.266B in ENPV. When uncertainty in sales and NPV are taken into account, a simulation of DHI's unconstrained portfolio shows that it has the potential to deliver expected sales of between $2.139B and $9.729B with a mean of $5.024B (Figure 11-11a) and ENPV with a distribution of $8.836B and $59.334B with a mean of $25.844B (Figure 11-11b). Because both risk and uncertainty are assumed to be largely uncontrollable, DHI should be aware of the potential for both downside and upside value in its portfolio, both of which would be missed under purely deterministic conditions.

In consideration of budgetary and human resource constraints in 2012, it is necessary to find the portfolio that DHI should pursue which maximizes the value of its financial objectives, i.e., expected sales and ENPV. When the portfolio objective is maximization of expected sales, a stochastic optimization is performed where project combinations are evaluated to find the optimal portfolio while simulating across each project's distribution of sales and NPV. The results of this simulation and optimization are shown in Figure 11-12, where an optimal portfolio that yields approximately $3.9B in expected sales is found.

Upon close inspection of the range of expected sales associated with this stochastic optimization, the distribution results from a minimum of $1.464B and a maximum of $7.072B with a mean of $3.877B (Figure 11-13a). Note that there is only an 18.4%

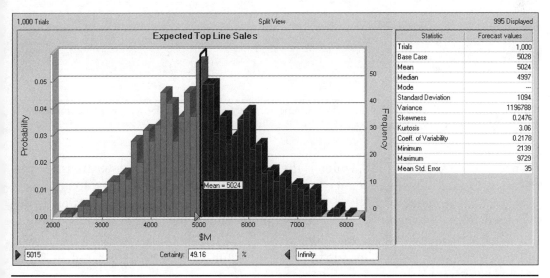

Figure 11-11a Simulation of unconstrained enterprise portfolio accounting for technical and regulatory risk and commercial uncertainty—distribution of expected sales

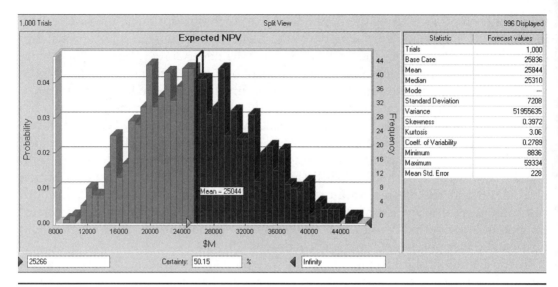

Figure 11-11b   Simulation of unconstrained enterprise portfolio accounting for technical and regulatory risk and commercial uncertainty—distribution of ENPV

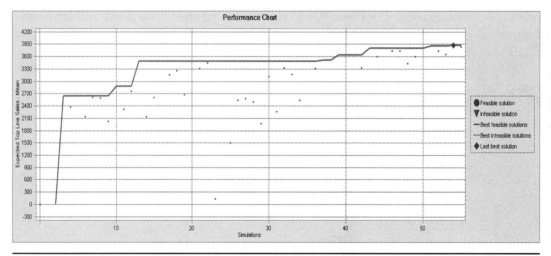

Figure 11-12   Stochastic optimization accounting for technical and regulatory risk and commercial uncertainty—objective: expected sales

chance of exceeding $4.703B, which is the value obtained from the deterministic optimization in Table 11-4, where no commercial uncertainty was accounted for.

Similarly, the range of ENPVs associated with this stochastic optimization is determined to lie between $6.191B and $44.093B with a mean of $20.029B. There is roughly a 28% likelihood of exceeding $23.300B, the value observed from the deterministic optimization in Table 11-4, where no commercial uncertainty was incorporated (Figure 11-13b).

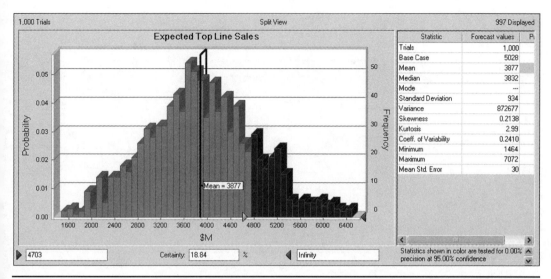

Figure 11-13a   Stochastic optimization accounting for technical and regulatory risk and commercial uncertainty—objective: expected sales; display: range of expected sales

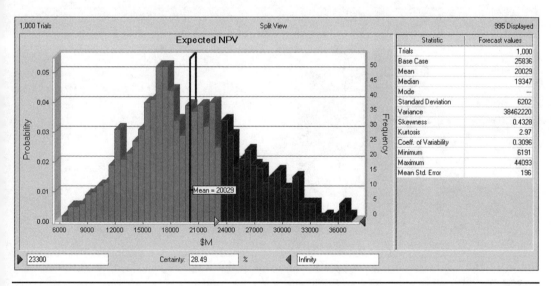

Figure 11-13b   Stochastic optimization accounting for technical and regulatory risk and commercial uncertainty—objective: expected sales; display: range of ENPV

When DHI's portfolio objective is switched from maximization of expected sales to maximization of ENPV, the results of the stochastic optimization reveal that the optimal portfolio yields approximately $20B in ENPV (Figure 11-14).

The full distribution of ENPVs that results from this optimization reveals that ENPV could be as low as $5.842B or as high as $55.769B with a mean of $19.824B (Figure 11-15a). Note that the deterministic value of $23.367B in ENPV, shown in

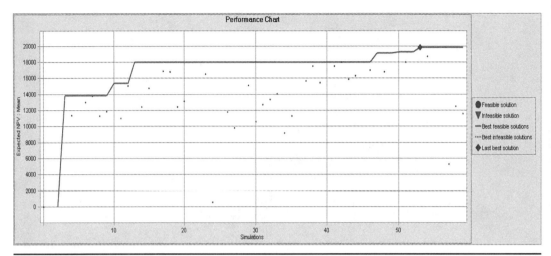

Figure 11-14   Stochastic optimization accounting for technical and regulatory risk and commercial uncertainty—objective: ENPV

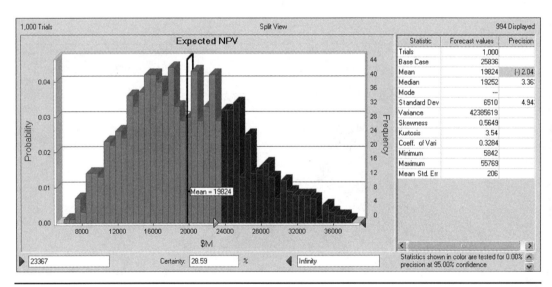

Figure 11-15a   Stochastic optimization accounting for technical and regulatory risk and commercial uncertainty—objective: ENPV; display: range of ENPV

Table 11-4, is exceeded with a probability of only 28.59%. Similarly, the distribution of expected sales values, resulting from a portfolio that is optimized for ENPV, yields a range of $1.204B-$8.830B with a mean of $3.873B. This optimal portfolio has a 23.29% probability of exceeding $4.568B (Figure 11-15b), which resulted from the search for the optimal portfolio under deterministic conditions (Table 11-4).

The consolidated results of the two stochastic optimizations based on maximization of (a) expected sales and (b) ENPV are shown in Table 11-9. Note that although both optimal portfolios result from the selection of 27 projects that yield almost identical

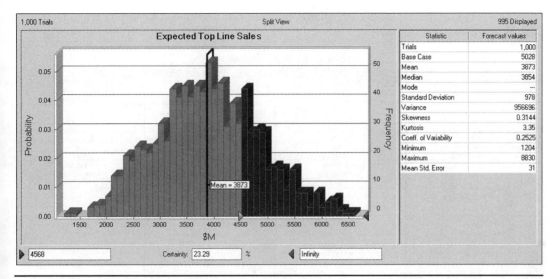

Figure 11-15b Stochastic optimization accounting for technical and regulatory risk and commercial uncertainty—objective: ENPV; display: range of expected sales

values in terms of expected sales and ENPV, there are marked differences between the projects that are selected. When maximization of expected sales is the portfolio objective, nine projects from Consumer Goods, four projects from Diagnostics, seven from Medical Devices, and seven from Prescription Drugs constitute the optimal portfolio.

On the other hand, when ENPV is the value maximization objective, eight projects from Consumer Goods, seven projects from Diagnostics, seven from Medical Devices, and five from Prescription Drugs constitute the optimal portfolio.

To minimize or avoid the anxiety associated with projects being included or excluded from optimal portfolios under different scenarios, organizations are advised to pay judicious attention to the C in CREOPM™, in that once a category of truly non-discretionary projects is agreed to, these projects should be "fixed" (i.e., given a value of 1), before any optimization analysis is conducted. As discussed in Chapter 7, a viable alternative is to exclude these projects from the optimization analysis, but only after accounting for their resource requirements.

11.5 Summary

In the face of impending budgetary and human resource constraints, DHI employed three methods of portfolio selection, based on:

(A) Project prioritization, using multiple and single decision-making attributes where the underlying currency is utils.
(B) Deterministic portfolio optimization, using single and multiple financial objectives and accounting for technical and regulatory risk.
(C) Stochastic portfolio optimization, using single financial objectives and accounting for technical and regulatory risk and commercial uncertainty.

Table 11-9 Comparison of results of stochastic optimizations accounting for technical and regulatory risk and commercial uncertainty

DIVERSIFIED HEALTHCARE INC.			
TARGET Values for 2012: Sales = $4.703B, NPV = $23.367B, Cost = $1.500B, # Researchers = 350, # Developers = 650			
SCENARIO WEIGHT	BASE CASE	Scenario # 1	Scenario # 2
CONSTRAINTS	NONE	ALL CONSTRAINTS	ALL CONSTRAINTS
OBJECTIVE	NONE	MAXIMIZE ESALES	MAXIMIZE ENPV
# OF PROJECTS	40	27	27
RESULTING EXPECTED SALES ($B)	$5.015	$3.877	$3.876
RESULTING EXPECTED NPV ($B)	$25.266	$20.029	$19.817
ALLOCATED COST ($B)	$2.252	$1.361	$1.295
ALLOCATED RESEARCHERS	444	318	295
ALLOCATED DEVELOPERS	800	525	498
	DECISION VARIABLES	DECISION VARIABLES	DECISION VARIABLES
CG1	1	1	1
CG10	1	1	1
CG2	1	1	1
CG3	1	1	1
CG4	1	1	1
CG5	1	1	1
CG6	1	1	1
CG7	1	1	1
CG8	1	1	0
CG9	1	0	0
DIA1	1	0	1
DIA10	1	0	0
DIA2	1	0	0
DIA3	1	1	1
DIA4	1	1	1
DIA5	1	0	1
DIA6	1	1	1
DIA7	1	1	1
DIA8	1	0	0
DIA9	1	0	1
MD1	1	1	1
MD10	1	0	1
MD2	1	0	0
MD3	1	0	0
MD4	1	1	1
MD5	1	1	1
MD6	1	1	1
MD7	1	1	1
MD8	1	1	1
MD9	1	1	0
Rx1	1	1	1
Rx10	1	1	0
Rx2	1	0	0
Rx3	1	1	1
Rx4	1	1	1
Rx5	1	0	0
Rx6	1	1	0
Rx7	1	1	1
Rx8	1	1	0
Rx9	1	0	1

The organization has shown that when deterministic optimization is utilized, this methodology generates a Pareto optimal portfolio that dominates the best portfolio created by project prioritization. Further, when technical and regulatory risk is taken into account, portfolios can be optimized deterministically on the basis of single or multiple objectives. Finally, when both technical and regulatory risk and commercial uncertainty are accounted for, stochastic portfolio optimization reveals the ranges of financial values associated with optimal portfolios, thereby informing decision makers at DHI of both upside and downside potential of its optimal portfolios.

12

Epilogue

It is difficult to find an industry or organization that has not been impacted in one way or another by the effects of globalization, mergers and acquisitions, restructuring, downsizing, cost cutting, outsourcing, and change management, all of which have placed a greater burden on portfolio management to create and deliver sustainable organizational value. Organizations that appear to be the most affected by these changes are those that are of relatively large size, where economies of scale and scope are of paramount importance to maintaining healthy global profit margins.

Nowhere are the impacts of these changes more pronounced than in the pharmaceutical and biotechnology industry, where, after a protracted period of annual, double-digit, top line growth, patent expiration of blockbuster drugs has forced many successful corporations to reexamine and alter their business models. Today, an increasing amount of drug discovery and preclinical research continues to be outsourced to companies whose business model is to serve precisely this purpose, and clinical development has become the forte of contract research organizations that are able to offer significant cost savings that cannot be matched by the internal engines of most pharmaceutical and biotechnology companies.

By themselves, cost efficiencies do not necessarily create additional value. Rather, they improve productivity per unit of cost. Only if they enable increased investments to be diverted back into R&D is additional value really created. On the other hand, when used effectively, portfolio management methodologies such as CREOPM™ are capable, at best, of maximizing value creation to an enterprise or, at worst, minimizing value left on the table that was caused by inferior portfolio management practices. A brief review of the six facets of CREOPM™ consists of:

- **Categorization**—Enables a clear separation between non-discretionary and discretionary project and program investments to the extent that the focus of an active portfolio should primarily be on discretionary investments.
- **Risk Analysis**—Facilitates an understanding of which risk elements are controllable (and therefore can be mitigated) and those that are not, so that the appropriate due diligence and analysis can be applied to uncontrollable factors.
- **Evaluation**—Allows for the integration of the four value drivers (benefit, risk, cost, and time) into a risk-adjusted or expected value metric that can be used for trade-off analysis between investments.

- **Optimization**—Provides a technically reproducible understanding of which combination of project and program investments yields the highest enterprise value, subject to the organization's resource constraints (primarily budgetary, human, and manufacturing).
- **Prioritization**—Allows an organization to create rules for rank ordering investments in projects and programs within the context of the optimized portfolio and without the subjective bias that creeps into unstructured decision making.
- **Management**—Enables proactive risk, resource, and stakeholder management along with the ability to measure an enterprise's capability maturity level in portfolio management.

To be sure, CREOPM™ is not an algorithm or panacea to be applied to portfolio value creation. When applied consistently in organizations with the cultural orientation and discipline to adhere to its tenets, this portfolio management framework is capable of providing organizations with transparent choices between optimal and sub-optimal portfolios, given certain prerequisites or obligations. In fact, of the sub-optimal portfolios available to an organization from which to choose, CREOPM™ can assist in the selection of the best. In the case of the pharmaceutical and biotechnology industry, rather than view a pipeline of drug discovery and development opportunities as "random shots on goal," organizations can improve their performance by making clear and consistent choices regarding how their constrained budgetary and human resources are utilized. As opposed to the singularly flawed act of prioritizing projects for portfolio selection, CREOPM™ offers a disciplined framework that can be utilized to make clear policy and strategic decisions regarding which projects and programs to pursue and why.

No good portfolio management framework, including CREOPM™, removes judgment entirely from project and program selection. Rather, the methodology allows decision makers at all levels of an organization to understand the trade-offs in value (more correctly, *expected* value) between optimal and sub-optimal portfolios, so that transparent and defensible choices can be made.

CREOPM™ does not escape an often asked question: "How can you prove that the adoption of this or any other formal portfolio management methodology adds enterprise value?" Perhaps the best and only way to answer this question (or more appropriately, criticism of naysayers) is to compare the delta in value between the portfolio choices recommended by the use of CREOPM™ and those that are devoid of the aid of the methodology over a protracted period of time. In effect, without the aid of a "controlled portfolio" as a frame of comparative reference, it is almost impossible to prove that any portfolio management framework, including CREOPM™, adds enterprise portfolio value.

Of course, on theoretical grounds alone, such a comparison can be made almost instantaneously when one examines the value gained by such a formal portfolio management methodology and one based largely on prioritization methods, heuristics, and judgment. In practical terms, since every selected project or program within a portfolio cannot lead to a successful outcome, i.e., a product, it has to be argued that

CREOPM™, like all other portfolio management methodologies, should really be judged on the basis of portfolio selection and not on the outcomes of such portfolio selection. This seems a rather defensive statement, but to believe otherwise, is akin to folly. If the lack of a formal portfolio management methodology leads to a portfolio selection for which value can be bettered by the presence and adoption of the principles and practices of a formal methodology such as CREOPM™, it can be argued that portfolio value is being destroyed by its absence.

For even the most successful of organizations, it is this book's contention that "good enough is no longer good enough." Stated otherwise, portfolio selection that leaves value on the table is indistinguishable from value that is being destroyed. While the mantra of much of today's business literature stresses "the need to create enterprise value," we argue for the "the need to maximize enterprise value." It is our fervent belief that enterprise portfolio value can be created in at least one of two primary ways: (a) optimal or superior portfolio selection as measured by risk-adjusted or expected value and (b) good portfolio selection from amongst a collective set of sub-optimal alternatives. Based on experiences from a plethora of organizational practices in portfolio management (or the lack thereof), there are many opportunities for improvement in such practices that can lead to greater enterprise value creation. We therefore implore organizations to seek ways of enhancing enterprise value by adopting formal portfolio management practices and principles, one of which, CREOPM™, forms the basis of this book.

Appendix A

A Primer in Decision Analysis

A.1 Introduction to Decision Analysis and Its Utility in Decision Making

Decision analysis is a quantitative discipline that follows a structured process to enable the identification and assessment of a range of alternative solutions to a problem after which a dominant solution may emerge. It is best utilized under the following conditions:

- The problem has several potential solutions, none of which may appear to be readily dominant.
- The problem can be decomposed into a series of sequential investments during which time information may be gathered to enable better informed downstream decisions.
- The entire problem requires relatively high investments over a protracted time horizon for which there may be significant uncontrollable risks and uncertain outcomes.

In many organizations, traditional decision making has been based largely on a combination of experience, judgment, heuristics, advocacy, and of course analysis. The extent to which quantitative analysis has shaped informed decision making has ranged from its use as the principal guide to its relegation to the role of no more than a supporting data point. Far too often, qualitative decision criteria (e.g., brand image, strategic positioning) are commingled with quantitative attributes (e.g., gross profit, ROI), creating the perception of a holistic decision when, in fact, quantitative value is foregone. A decision that leads to acceptable value creation tends to be made and all parties feel satisfied that, after an appropriate investment of time and energy for discussion and deliberation, a good decision has been rendered.

Because intuition is difficult to audit for completeness and logical consistency and defensibility of thought (Skinner, 1999), it is not evident that better decisions created by superior intuition could have emerged from the existing information. Taken to its logical extreme, while a good decision may lead to value creation, only the *best* decision can lead to value maximization. The challenge for decision makers is, therefore, where to use the discipline of decision analysis to make decisions that could maximize value to the organization. It is noteworthy that modern decision analysis does not profess to always yield optimal decisions; rather, as Keeney (1982) suggests, its purpose is to produce insight and creativity to enable better decisions.

The best solution generated by decision analysis to a problem can be described as *conditionally prescriptive* in that it is subject to the judgments that occur during the course of the analysis as well as the rationality (and risk preferences) of the decision makers (Goodwin & Wright, 2010). Nevertheless, even if the best solution proposed by the decision analysis process differs from the collective best judgment of the decision makers, a foundation is provided for understanding why such a difference exists. Further dialogue and cogent extractions from the analysis often reveal where the apparent gaps lie.

The use of decision analysis does not imply that once the best decision is made, the highest value will be realized. Why is this so? First and foremost, decision analysis is synonymous with decision control, but should not be mistaken for outcome control. Stated otherwise, while decision analysis allows the best decision amongst a spectrum of alternatives to be evaluated, the discipline cannot control the outcome of any such decision. Consider the following examples:

- **Decision alternative A:** Invest \$10M to create product A, which, according to the best available market research, will yield \$100M in sales in year 1.
- **Decision alternative B:** Invest \$10M to create an alternative product B, which, according to the best available market research, will yield \$95M in sales in year 1.

At an ROI of 10, decision alternative A dominates decision alternative B. However, can you control for or guarantee that either outcome (i.e., sales of product A and product B in year 1) *will be exactly* \$100M and \$95M, respectively? What happens if, because of uncertain competitive forces, year 1 sales for product A could be between \$80M and \$105M, while corresponding sales for product B could be between \$90M and \$120M? Using a simple PERT formula, the estimated mean sales for product A are \$97.5M while those of product B are \$98.3M. Upon closer inspection, alternative B dominates alternative A.

The best decisions, defined as superior to all others while adhering to the tenets of logical consistency and actionability, do not guarantee or always result in the best outcomes because such outcomes cannot be controlled. In fact, some poor decisions can result in favorable or even the best outcomes but, on average, they yield inferior or bad outcomes. Nevertheless, there are certain factors associated with superior decision making (Figure A-1) which, if refined over a protracted period of time, result in more favorable outcomes to the most complex of problems.

While the use of decision analysis can be time consuming, it frequently uncovers hidden courses of action that yield compelling alternatives to the solution of a problem. Sometimes, project teams are blinded to possible development and commercial alternatives and present an illusory "best alternative" which does represent good thinking but not necessarily their best thinking. Consequently, while logical consistency and actionability are fulfilled, the project team has no way of knowing how much

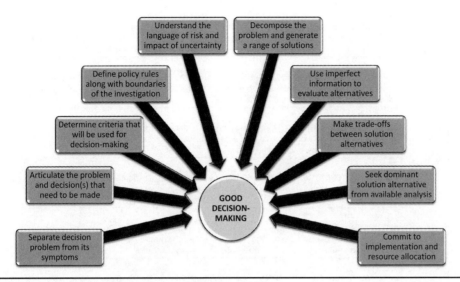

Figure A-1   Factors associated with good decision making

better its decision could have been and, consequently, how much value may have been unintentionally foregone or destroyed.

Moreover, decision analysis enables complex decisions to be decomposed into smaller, phased decisions where the relevant focus is placed on what is important and needs to be decided on now, as opposed to what needs refinement and may be decided on at a later point in time. Perhaps just as important, decision analysis allows a project team to know when sufficient analysis has been done to enable a decision. Several decision analysis processes have been proposed over the years, a combination of which, founded on the principles of the Dialogue Decision Process (Strategic Decisions Group, 2005) and the Decision Analysis Cycle (Skinner, 1999) has been used by one of the authors for more than a decade in the pharmaceutical and biotechnology industry (Figure A-2).

In the first step of the decision analysis process, the decision frame is established by asking a handful of fundamental questions that include the following:

- What problem needs to be solved?
- Which decisions (i.e., higher level policy and lower level operational) will not be impacted by the analysis?
- What are the boundaries of the investigation?

Although these questions may appear to be self-explanatory, an understanding of the answers on the part of every member of a team is necessary before an analysis gets underway. When addressed in the order shown above, the questions help to:

(a) Prevent the investment of time and analysis on generating good solutions to the wrong problem.

(b) Avoid commingling strategic decisions that need to be made as a consequence of the investigation with policy and operational decisions.

(c) Focus the team on the solution space that will be assessed in search of the best solution.

Figure A-2   The six-step decision analysis process

During step 1 of decision making, it is helpful to raise issues that may impact the quality of the ensuing analysis and recommended solution. Without this, a team may be limited by its own thinking and biases, resulting in constrained creativity and missed opportunities. A conceptual model of the problem is often helpful at this stage of the decision analysis process (Strategic Decisions Group, 2005).

In step 2, a strategy table is often used to generate solution alternatives that are mutually exclusive and actionable by the organization. While there is a theoretical maximum to the number of alternatives that can be generated by this table, it is most helpful to teams to restrict their solution set to a handful of solutions that includes hybrid alternatives.

Based on decision criteria established early on in the process, step 3 focuses on gathering information and data that are relevant to decision making. Because required information and data may not reside within an organization, it is necessary to decide what additional knowledge needs to be secured externally and at what cost. A guiding principle is to use value of information calculations to determine the maximum one would pay to gain additional knowledge from which to make a more informed decision and without which the lure of additional information can often prove to be a wasteful use of resources.

During the evaluation phase in step 4, alternatives are subjected to risk-adjusted assessments using decision trees in search of a solution that dominates all others on the basis of expected value or expected utility. It is often insightful to conduct sensitivity analyses to risk and uncertainty to gain a good understanding of the data and which analysis is most susceptible to shifting the dominant decision. If this is found to be the case, the team is advised to conduct a more granular analysis of appropriate risk and uncertainty parameters that are identified from the sensitivity analysis. If it is not, it serves to inform the team that further analysis and deliberation add no value to the decision problem.

In step 5, assuming risk neutrality, the best solution alternative is recommended to decision makers. However, depending on the risk tolerance of the organization, additional alternatives should be presented for discussion of trade-offs in values so that a decision that resonates with the risk preferences of the organization's decision makers is rendered. This often ensures a successful completion to the decision analysis process in step 6, where endorsement for the required investment of budgetary and human resources is gained. Additionally, a communication package that describes the outcome of the decision analysis process should be made available, at a minimum, to stakeholders affected by the project decision.

The vast majority of us try to repeat the processes that have led us to successful outcomes and to avoid those that resulted in poor outcomes. This includes making decisions, especially on complex, risky, and uncertain ventures. However, without an audit trail, and especially if some decision makers leave an organization, it is difficult to replicate those processes that led to successful outcomes or investigate the ones that led to unfavorable outcomes. This is an area where decision analysis has tremendous utility because it serves as a bedrock for traceability.

While decision analysis is not recommended for minor decisions with small investments, those with minimal risk and little uncertainty, or where a clearly dominant decision exists, it can be of enormous value to organizations that are trying to make major investment decisions under conditions of high risk and uncertainty, as well as over lengthy time horizons. Nevertheless, organizations that have excelled in the use of decision analysis have done so through a protracted investment in its use by training and education of personnel tasked with performing various aspects of this discipline. It results infrequently in immediate gratification and requires an investment of time, resources, and commitment in order to achieve superior results. Several applications of decision analysis have been detailed by many different authors. The reader is encouraged to review the work of Goodwin and Wright (2010) for a synopsis of its applications by companies that include DuPont, ICI Americas, Phillips Petroleum Company, and the U.S. military.

A.2 Risk—The Language of Probability

"Project A is *most likely* to succeed," while "project B is *highly unlikely* to succeed." Assuming that those statements originated from an informed individual, what can we infer from them? *Ceteris paribus*, one could deduce, with little or no argument from others, that project A has a higher chance of success than does project B. However, the statements do not suggest that if both projects were undertaken today, A would succeed while B would fail. Rather, they imply that if project A were undertaken a sufficiently large number of times and project B conducted an equal number of times, on the average or in the long term, project A would succeed more often than would project B. The issue at hand, therefore, is not whether project A succeeds more frequently than project B, but rather, given the belief that the long-term averages favor success in project A more than in project B, how could this be represented quantitatively if both projects were undertaken just once?

This quantitative representation of success can be embodied in a probability of success estimate, which serves as the cornerstone of decision analysis in trying to represent the likelihood of occurrence of a future event. An objective probability estimate is simple to arrive at: for a total number of historical events Y, if a particular event is observed to occur X number of times, the probability of its occurrence is X/Y.

On the other hand, a subjective probability is dependent, not on merely historical observations, but on a person's beliefs, knowledge, data, and experience (Skinner, 1999). Probabilities are measured by values ranging from 0 to 1.0, where 0 represents certainty that an event will not occur, while 1.0 represents certainty that an event will occur. Probability judgments, therefore, establish a quantitative basis for a discussion between individuals in regard to their beliefs about the occurrence of future events, and avoid the ambiguous nature of everyday statements such as "project A is *most likely* to succeed." To an optimist, *most likely* could mean a probability (p) of 0.9 or higher, while to a pessimist, the same phrase could mean any number greater than 0.5 but less than 1.0. The conversion of judgmental estimates to a numerical representation between 0 and 1.0 is an unnatural and, in many cases, uncomfortable act for most people.

Why is this so? We believe there are several major issues that create discomfort in quantifying probability estimates. First, people are much more comfortable articulating uncertainty of the future in language that is ambiguous. Second, placing a numerical value on a judgmental estimate can convey the impression of greater certainty when, in fact, such certainty does not exist. Third, if a subject matter expert provides a probability of success estimate of 0.9 for a project and it fails, there is the fear of the backlash of a tarnished reputation. Fourth, since several data points and assumptions are taken into account when generating a probability estimate, a subject matter expert will often state that there is insufficient information on which to provide an accurate estimate. Last, unlike objective probabilities, people are generally reluctant to offer a subjective probability estimate between 0 and 1.0, which for one chance event cannot be correct. This is because of two underlying reasons: (a) a subjective probability is not a property of the event; rather, it is a person's interpretation of the likelihood of occurrence of the event, and (b) for a single occurrence, the event will either occur (with a probability of 1.0) or not occur (with a probability of 0) (Skinner, 1999). Unlike objective probabilities therefore, subjective probabilities cannot be correct; based on a person's state of knowledge, they may only be judgmentally defensible.

Using the five-step process described by Kirkwood (1997) in Chapter 5, probability estimates can be elicited from subject matter experts in a manner that reflects their underlying knowledge and with a minimum of bias. While such elicitation techniques do not profess to ensure nullification of bias, they are capable of enabling defensible estimates that are consistent with the fundamentals of probability theory.

Fundamentals of Probability Theory

According to Goodwin and Wright (2010, adapted with permission), some of the terms involved with probability theory are:

- **Mutual exclusivity**—Two events are mutually exclusive if the occurrence of one of the events precludes the simultaneous occurrence of the other. For example, if peak sales for a product are greater than $1M, sales in its peak year cannot also be less than $1M.
- **Collective exhaustiveness**—Represents the range of possible events associated with a course of action or outcome. For example, one may invest a high amount, a moderate amount, or a low amount in a new financial instrument or one may invest in a new financial instrument that may yield high, moderate, or low returns.

Kolmogorov's Axioms

Kolmogorov's axioms are used to assess the probability or likelihood of occurrence of events.

- **Positiveness**—The probability of occurrence of an event must be non-negative.
- **Certainty**—The probability of occurrence of a certain event is 1.0, and the probability of non-occurrence of a certain event is 0; consequently, the probability of occurrence of an uncertain event must be greater than 0 but less than 1.0.
- **Unions**—If two events A and B are mutually exclusive, then:

$$p(A \text{ or } B) = p(A) + p(B)$$

The Addition Rule

If two events A and B are mutually exclusive, the addition rule is:

$$p(A \text{ or } B) = p(A) + p(B)$$

For example, since clinical drug development is a lengthy and uncertain process, a drug may launch in 5, 6, or 7 years from the time it is first administered in human subjects. If the probability of a drug being launched in each of these years is 0.2, 0.5, and 0.3, respectively, the probability that a drug will launch in 5 or 6 years can be calculated as:

$$p(\text{Launch in 5 or 6 years}) = p(\text{Launch in 5 years}) + p(\text{Launch in 6 years})$$
$$= 0.2 + 0.5 = 0.7$$

However, if two events A and B are *not* mutually exclusive, the addition rule is:

$$p(A \text{ or } B) = p(A) + p(B) - p(A \text{ and } B)$$

Consider the hypothetical information in Table A-1, showing the relationship between insults to the brain (caused, for example, by professional boxing and leading to neu-

Table A-1 Frequency of Alzheimer's Disease in 1,000 retired professional boxers

	Low Level of Insults	High Level of Insults	Total
Alzheimer's Disease	50	350	400
No Alzheimer's Disease	400	200	600
Total	450	550	1,000

ronal destruction that can be measured by brain imaging techniques) and Alzheimer's Disease in 1,000 retired professional boxers:

Faced with a decision to enter the sport of professional boxing and a concern about its possible health implications, one may calculate the probability of enduring a high level of brain insults or Alzheimer's Disease during a professional career as follows:

p(High number of insults or Alzheimer's Disease) = p(High number of insults) + p(Alzheimer's Disease) – p(High number of insults and Alzheimer's Disease)

$$= (550/1,000) + (400/1,000) - (350/1,000) = 0.60$$

Complementary Events

If A is an event, the event "A does not occur" is referred to as the *complement* of the event A, shown as A bar (Ā):

$$p(\bar{A}) = 1 - p(A)$$

For example, if the probability of technical and regulatory success of a drug is 0.2, the probability of technical and regulatory failure = 1.0 – 0.2 = 0.8.

Marginal and Conditional Probabilities

Consider Table A-2 in which a diagnosis of 1,000 hypothetical patients, some of whom have a family history of Alzheimer's Disease, was conducted. These patients were categorized on the basis of whether or not they have a family history of the disease and if they had been subsequently diagnosed with the disease.

From Table A-2, the probability of a patient being diagnosed with Alzheimer's Disease, irrespective of whether or not he/she has a family history of the disease, can be calculated as:

p(Patient diagnosed with Alzheimer's Disease) = 55/1,000 = 0.055

Table A-2 Results of a diagnosis of hypothetical patients for Alzheimer's Disease

	Patients Diagnosed with Disease	Patients not Diagnosed with Disease	Total Number of Patients
Family history of disease	40	400	440
No family history of disease	15	545	560
Total number of patients	55	945	1,000

This is an *unconditional or marginal probability* because it is not influenced by whether or not a patient has a family history of the disease. On the other hand, one may calculate the probability that a patient who has a family history of Alzheimer's Disease is, in fact, diagnosed with the disease as:

p(Patient diagnosed with Alzheimer's Disease | Family history of disease)
= 40/440 = 0.091

This probability is referred to as *conditional* in that it is influenced (or conditioned) by whether or not a patient has a family history of the disease. It is noteworthy that this conditional probability (0.091) is higher than the marginal probability (0.055) of being diagnosed with Alzheimer's Disease, implying that having a family history of the disease predisposes a patient to contracting the disease more so than if a patient has no family history of the disease. Given this information, the converse is also true: one would expect that a patient with no family history of the disease would have a lower probability of being diagnosed with Alzheimer's Disease than if she/he had a family history of the disease. Consequently:

p(Patient diagnosed with Alzheimer's Disease | No family history of disease)
= 15/560 = 0.027

Revising Conditional Probabilities in Light of New Information

Consider the following hypothetical state of knowledge where 10% of adults aged 65 or older have mild cognitive impairment (MCI). If an individual with MCI is given a positron emission tomography (PET) diagnostic brain imaging test, there is a 0.9 probability that the test will indicate the presence of MCI. This is termed a "true positive" state. On the other hand, if an individual who does not have MCI is given the same diagnostic test, there is a 0.95 probability that the test will indicate that the individual does not have MCI. This is termed a "true negative" state. If an individual 65 years or older visits a neurologist with symptoms of repeated, short-term memory loss and a PET test is administered which turns out to be positive, what is the probability that the person actually has MCI? This same data can be represented in an uncertainty tree in Figure A-3.

The probability of a positive PET test result, irrespective of whether or not an individual has MCI, can be calculated as:

p(Positive PET) = p(Positive PET | MCI) * p(MCI) + p(Positive PET | No MCI) *
p(No MCI)

= (0.90 * 0.10) + (0.05 * 0.90) = 0.135

Using the condition of a complementary event, the probability of a negative PET test result, irrespective of whether or not an individual has MCI, can be calculated as:

p(Negative PET) = 1 − p(Positive PET) = 1 − 0.135 = 0.865

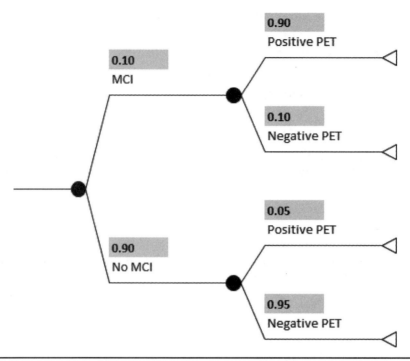

Figure A-3 Uncertainty tree for probability of occurrence of MCI and PET diagnoses

The probability that an individual has MCI, given that the PET test is positive, can be calculated as:

$$p(\text{MCI} \mid \text{Positive PET}) = p(\text{Positive PET} \mid \text{MCI}) * p(\text{MCI})/p(\text{Positive PET})$$

$$= (0.90 * 0.10)/(0.135) = 0.667$$

Alternatively, one may use Bayes' theorem, which was introduced in Chapter 5:

$$p(\text{MCI} \mid \text{Positive PET}) = [p(\text{Positive PET} \mid \text{MCI}) * p(\text{MCI})]/[[p(\text{Positive PET} \mid \text{MCI}) * p(\text{MCI})] + [p(\text{Positive PET} \mid \text{No MCI}) * p(\text{No MCI})]]$$

$$= (0.90 * 0.10)/(0.90 * 0.10) + (0.05 * 0.90) = (0.90)/(0.135) = 0.667$$

Using the condition of a complementary event, the probability that an individual does not have MCI given that the PET test is positive = $1 - 0.667 = 0.333$. The same logic can be applied to determine the probability that an individual has (or does not have) MCI given that the PET test is negative.

Independent and Dependent Events

Two events A and B are independent if the probability of occurrence of event A is unaffected by the occurrence or non-occurrence of event B. If events A and B are independent:

$$p(\text{A} \mid \text{B}) = p(\text{A})$$

Stated otherwise, although event B has occurred, the probability of occurrence of A remains unaffected. For example, since no clinical relationship has been found between Alzheimer's Disease and male pattern baldness, the probability that a patient will contract Alzheimer's Disease is independent of whether or not the patient will develop male pattern baldness.

Likewise:

$$p(B \mid A) = p(B)$$

Stated otherwise, although event A has occurred, the probability of occurrence of B remains unaffected.

However, there appears to be a relationship between a patient developing diabetes if she/he is clinically obese. These two events are therefore dependent in the same way as previously demonstrated by the example in Table A-2, where the probability of a patient being diagnosed with Alzheimer's Disease was affected by whether or not she/he had a family history of the disease.

The Multiplication Rule

If two events A and B are independent, the probability of occurrence of both events is the multiple of the events:

$$p(A \text{ and } B) = p(A) \times p(B)$$

For example, a drug that works for the treatment of Alzheimer's Disease is unlikely to work for the treatment of male pattern baldness. Therefore, the probability that a drug will work for both diseases can be calculated as:

$$p(\text{Drug success in Alzheimer's Disease and Male Pattern Baldness}) = p(\text{Drug success in Alzheimer's Disease}) \times p(\text{Drug Success in Male Pattern Baldness})$$

If two events A and B are not independent, the probability of occurrence of both events is the multiple of the probability of the first event and the probability of the second event, given that the first event has occurred (or vice versa):

$$p(A \text{ and } B) = p(A) \times p(B \mid A)$$

For example, since many patients who develop MCI go on to develop Alzheimer's Disease, a drug that works for Alzheimer's Disease may also work for MCI. In this case, the probability that a drug will work for both diseases can be calculated as:

$$p(\text{Drug success in Alzheimer's Disease and MCI}) = p(\text{Drug success in Alzheimer's Disease}) \times p(\text{Drug success in MCI} \mid \text{Drug success in Alzheimer's Disease})$$

Likewise:

$$p(B \text{ and } A) = p(B) \times p(A \mid B)$$

If the rules of probability theory are adhered to closely, risks for unique events, although subjective, can be carefully elicited from subject matter experts and used in decision analysis to aid decision making.

A.3 Uncertainty—The Language of Outcomes

Once a course of action is decided on or taken, the results of such an action lead to consequences or outcomes, which, though they may be influenced, are largely uncontrollable. Such outcomes can manifest themselves in varying degrees of success (or failure) as exemplified by high, moderate, and low product share of the market. A company that has decided to launch a new product may, depending on the nature of the competitive landscape for similar products, invest heavily in advertising and promotion to increase customer awareness of the attributes of the product. To an extent, therefore, the company can influence customer awareness, but cannot control their responsiveness to buying the product. Likewise, while smart and seductive advertising campaigns may increase customer knowledge and interest in a product, the extent to which competitors respond to the introduction of the new product cannot be controlled. Taken together, controllability in decision making does not lend itself to controllability in the outcomes of such decisions; these outcomes are therefore uncertain.

While "risk management" has been popularized, and justifiably so, through the discipline of project management for several decades, the term *uncertainty management* has emerged relatively recently to describe the process of achieving a balance between risk reduction and value creation (Goodwin & Wright, 2010). Decision analysis can play a pivotal role in achieving this balance by examining the potential impact of risks and various uncertainties on the risk-adjusted value created by the pursuit of one course of action or another.

In most businesses, while it is understood that outcomes are uncertain, it is common practice to pretend that the future can be accurately depicted by a "base case" estimate. However, what do these estimates really represent? Is the *base case* the mean, median, or mode of an uncertain distribution of outcomes, or is it the "best guess" of the outcome? In either event, the base case represents a deterministic estimate of a future outcome and could therefore be termed a prediction (implying no uncertainty) rather than an estimate (implying uncertainty).

Consider the following statement: *In 2020, sales in the U.S. for this new product are estimated to be $100M.* The following questions immediately come to mind:

- What level of confidence does this sales estimate represent? Is it the highest (100th percentile), lowest (0th percentile), or median (50th percentile) estimate, and what does the distribution of outcomes look like (e.g., symmetric, skewed)?
- On the basis of what assumptions (e.g., price, advertising, and promotional investment) is this estimate generated? What does this assume about the competitors' response?
- If the company's product share of the market is estimated to be $100M, what does it assume about the estimates for its competitors?
- If sales in 2020 were weighted to account for their uncertainty, how far from $100M would the weighted estimate be, and would the company still consider this level sufficiently attractive to maintain the product on the market?

While these questions appear to require labor-intensive analysis to answer—and they probably do—the key to informed decision making is knowing how much imperfect information is required to make a good, defensible decision. This becomes of paramount importance when making decisions where large, staged investments are necessary in an environment of high risk and uncertainty.

A common response to the questions posed above is another question: "Why should we do further analysis that merely serves to layer one assumption over another, as all it does is introduce greater subjectivity?" The authors' response to this is: "All estimates, whether quantitative (e.g., sales forecasts) or qualitative (e.g., customer satisfaction), are subjective." What is important is not whether uncertain estimates are subjective; rather, the focus should be on their level of logical consistency, traceability, and defensibility for the purposes of informed decision making.

Consider the following investment opportunities, each of which costs $1,000, as shown in Figure A-4a:

- Invest in A, with an average payoff of $10,000.
- Invest in B, with an average payoff of $10,000.

Knowing nothing more of either investment opportunity, a risk-neutral decision maker would be indifferent between these choices of investments. But, what if the outcomes of each investment were reflected by a range of uncertainty, where each outcome was equally likely to occur? This could be represented in Figure A-4b.

Again, on the basis of expected value (EV) alone, a risk-neutral decision maker would be indifferent between these two investment alternatives. However, on closer inspection, investment A yields no possible downside while investment B does, as evidenced by 50% probability of a payoff of zero. If you were making a one-time investment, which investment alternative would you choose? Would your decision change if you were making this decision a fixed number of multiple times, but with your own personal savings?

Paradoxically, many project teams in successful R&D and IT organizations believe that under conditions of high risk and uncertainty (e.g., at the beginning of a project

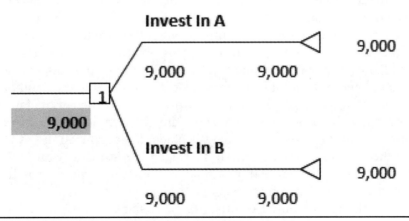

Figure A-4a   Investment opportunities with the same EV, version I

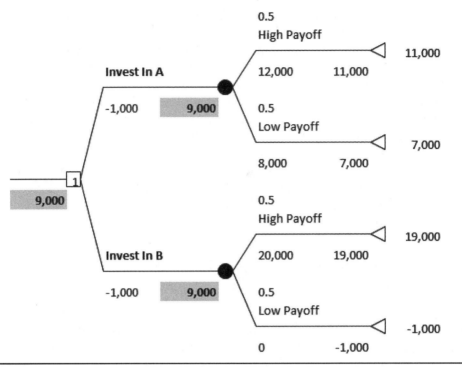

Figure A-4b　Investment opportunities with the same EV, version II

lifecycle), a business case that harbors no more than "high-level estimates" of the four value drivers—benefit, risk, cost, and time—is necessary to justify the first investment in a project. As the project matures and more information is gained, these high-level estimates assume a more granular state for decision making. This approach should be reversed. Stated otherwise, before the first investment in a project is made, a team should strive to represent its lack of knowledge of these value drivers by generating defensible estimates of the uncertainty surrounding benefit, cost, and time.

Furthermore, a systematic approach to uncertainty should be adopted where, at a minimum, estimates that reflect a defined confidence interval (e.g., 80%) are generated. In many organizations, projects may often not realize the forecasted benefit, cost more than estimated initially, and take much longer to complete. While this may appear to be the norm for many organizations, this practice is value destructive at the portfolio level, meaning that as some projects require more constrained resources and time to be completed, they inhibit other projects from realizing their full potential.

More importantly, many projects are often presented in their most favorable light (i.e., high benefit, low risk, low cost, and short time to completion) in order to secure their first investment; once this investment is made, the organization has tremendous emotional difficulty in not making the next, staged investment. A business case that defensibly reflects the uncertainty of potential outcomes in terms of benefit, cost, and time is the best guide to decision making under high uncertainty.

In addition, although an initial estimate of the riskiness of a project is fully warranted, as information is gained, the risk assessment should be updated. As a project matures, the business case should become more refined—not necessarily more granular—in that uncertainty estimates should become narrower with the same level of defined confidence.

What are the characteristics of a good business case, and where should project uncertainties be captured? The primary elements of a robust business case are:

(A) Understanding of the industry as well as current and future market environment

(B) Uniqueness of the business opportunity

(C) Key strategies for success

(D) Alignment with strategic objectives

(E) Estimated contribution to financial goals

(F) Estimated resources required to attain benefits

(G) Major risks and estimated uncertainties

(H) Estimated timeline necessary to attain benefits

(I) Project team and key sponsor(s)

Clearly, uncertainties should be reflected in the estimates provided in items E-H.

The impact of uncertain outcomes to decision making is shown in the next section with the application of tornado and spider analyses to a decision problem of whether or not to invest in one or two diseases. In the case of a tornado analysis that shows the impact of a range of uncertain values to a dominant decision, the decision maker is provided with a guide as to which uncertainties warrant further consideration (and may require an investment of resources) to provide greater clarity before committing to a decision.

A.4 Decision Making Under Conditions of Risk and Uncertainty

In the world of drug discovery, development, and commercialization, investment options are seldom straightforward, rendering decision making difficult. Consider the case of Drugs 'R Us, a corporation that is trying to decide between the following options:

- Strategy A—Invest the lead compound in Alzheimer's Disease (AD) alone at a cost of $350M.

- Strategy B—Invest the lead compound in AD and the promising backup compound in general anxiety disorder (GAD) at a combined cost of $625M.

While there are technical and regulatory risks associated with the successful development of both compounds, commercial uncertainties manifest themselves as a consequence of the competitive environment.

Information and data regarding (a) the probabilities of technical and regulatory success of the various outcomes of each strategy, (b) the probabilities of high and low commercial success, and (c) the commercial values associated with high and low commercial success are provided in Table A-3.

Table A-3 Risks and uncertainties associated with different strategies in drug development

STRATEGY A			STRATEGY B		
Technical & Regulatory Outcome	High Commercial Success	Low Commercial Success	Technical & Regulatory Outcome	High Commercial Success	Low Commercial Success
p(Lead succeeds in AD)	p(Success) = 0.75 Payoff = $1,000M	p(Success) = 0.25 Payoff = $800M	p(Lead succeeds in AD; Backup fails in GAD) = 0.60 * 0.80 = 0.48	p(Success) = 0.50 Payoff = $1,000M	p(Success) = 0.50 Payoff = $800M
p(Lead fails in AD)			p(Lead fails in AD; Backup succeeds in GAD) = 0.40 * 0.20 = 0.08	p(Success) = 0.50 Payoff = $1,750M	p(Success) = 0.50 Payoff = $1,250M
			p(Lead succeeds in AD; Backup succeeds in GAD) = 0.60 * 0.20 = 0.12	p(Success) = 0.50 Payoff = $2,750M	p(Success) = 0.50 Payoff = $2,050M
			p(Lead fails in AD; Backup fails in GAD) = 0.40 * 0.80 = 0.32		

On the basis of the information and data from Table A-3, a decision tree (Figure A-5) can be used to map the two strategic options facing Drugs 'R Us.

The rolled back EV from the decision tree reveal that strategy A (invest the lead compound in AD) is the dominant strategy, where EV = $220M. Note, however, that strategy A is marginally dominant over strategy B (EV = $215M). Such a decision, involving large committed investments, high technical and regulatory risks, and significant commercial uncertainties, requires a detailed exploration into the parameters that could influence decision making. In this regard, it may be helpful to conduct a sensitivity analysis to one or more risks to determine which are likely to be most impactful to the dominant decision.

In strategy A, the probability of high commercial success given the technical and regulatory success of the lead compound in AD is estimated at 0.75. If this probability is lowered, at what point would the decision maker be indifferent between both strategies? While one can conduct a manual analysis, it is much easier to use Excel's solver function to determine the break point probability at which the EVs for both strategies are the same. The results of such a sensitivity analysis (Figure A-6) reveal that if the probability of high commercial success, given technical and regulatory success of the lead compound in AD, is lowered to roughly 0.71, a risk-neutral decision maker would be indifferent between both strategies.

Given the sensitivity of the dominant decision to the probability of high commercial success if the lead compound succeeds in AD, what other risks may the dominant decision be most sensitive to? With the use of Excel's data table function, one may examine concomitantly the impact of the probability of high commercial success—estimated at 0.50—given the technical and regulatory success of the lead and backup

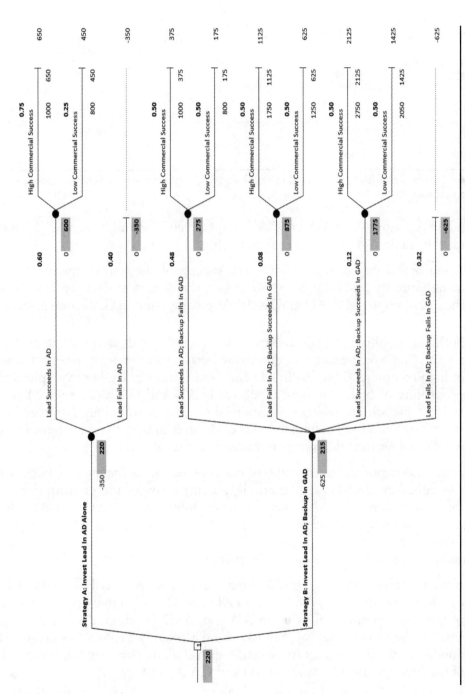

Figure A-5 Decision tree of investment strategies related to lead compound in AD alone or lead and backup compounds in AD and GAD, respectively

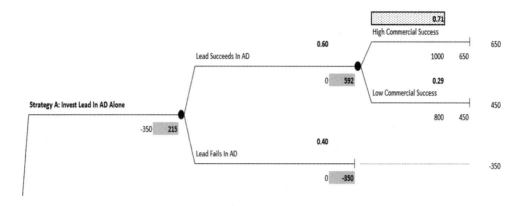

Figure A-6   One-way sensitivity analysis to the probability of high commercial success if the lead compound succeeds in AD

compounds in AD alone or in AD and GAD, respectively. The results of such an analysis are shown in Table A-4 and reveal the following:

- If the probability of high commercial success of the lead compound in AD alone (strategy A) is roughly 0.30 or less, the dominant decision is to invest the lead compound in AD and the backup compound in GAD, irrespective of the probability of high commercial success in AD and GAD (strategy B).
- If the probability of high commercial success in AD alone (strategy A) is roughly 0.30 or greater, the dominant decision depends on the probability of high commercial success in AD and GAD (strategy B). For example, if the probability of high commercial success in AD and GAD (strategy B) is 0.5 and the probability of high commercial success in AD alone (strategy A) is roughly 0.8 or greater, the dominant decision is to invest in AD alone. Otherwise, the dominant decision is to pursue strategy B.

One may also interrogate the sensitivities of commercial values (payoffs) of both strategies to the dominant decision. For example, a comparison of the concomitant sensitivities of high commercial value, ranging from $850M to $1,250M in AD alone (strategy A) and ranging from $2,500M to $3,500M in AD and GAD (strategy B), is shown in Table A-5.

The results of the data table show the following:

- If high commercial value in AD alone (strategy A) is roughly $900M or less, the dominant decision is to invest in AD and GAD (strategy B), irrespective of the high commercial value in AD and GAD (strategy B). On the other hand, if the commercial value in AD alone is roughly $1,200M or greater, the dominant decision swings to investing in AD alone (strategy A), irrespective of the high commercial value in AD and GAD (strategy B).
- If the high commercial value in AD alone (strategy A) is roughly $900M or greater, the dominant decision depends on the high commercial value in AD and GAD (strategy B). For example, if the high commercial value in AD and GAD (strategy B) is $2,700M and the high commercial value in AD alone

Table A-4 Two-way sensitivity analysis to the probability of high commercial success if the lead compound succeeds in AD and the lead and backup compounds succeed in AD and GAD, respectively

	PROBABILITY OF HIGH COMMERCIAL SUCCESS IN AD ALONE										
AD Alone	0	0.1	0.2	0.3	0.4	0.5	0.6	0.7	0.8	0.9	1
0	AD & GAD	AD & GAD	AD & GAD	AD & GAD	AD Alone	AD Alone	AD Alone	AD Alone	AD Alone	AD Alone	AD Alone
0.1	AD & GAD	AD & GAD	AD & GAD	AD & GAD	AD & GAD	AD Alone	AD Alone	AD Alone	AD Alone	AD Alone	AD Alone
0.2	AD & GAD	AD & GAD	AD & GAD	AD & GAD	AD & GAD	AD Alone	AD Alone	AD Alone	AD Alone	AD Alone	AD Alone
0.3	AD & GAD	AD & GAD	AD & GAD	AD & GAD	AD & GAD	AD & GAD	AD Alone	AD Alone	AD Alone	AD Alone	AD Alone
0.4	AD & GAD	AD & GAD	AD & GAD	AD & GAD	AD & GAD	AD & GAD	AD & GAD	AD Alone	AD Alone	AD Alone	AD Alone
0.5	AD & GAD	AD & GAD	AD & GAD	AD & GAD	AD & GAD	AD & GAD	AD & GAD	AD & GAD	AD Alone	AD Alone	AD Alone
0.6	AD & GAD	AD & GAD	AD & GAD	AD & GAD	AD & GAD	AD & GAD	AD & GAD	AD & GAD	AD Alone	AD Alone	AD Alone
0.7	AD & GAD	AD & GAD	AD & GAD	AD & GAD	AD & GAD	AD & GAD	AD & GAD	AD & GAD	AD & GAD	AD Alone	AD Alone
0.8	AD & GAD	AD & GAD	AD & GAD	AD & GAD	AD & GAD	AD & GAD	AD & GAD	AD & GAD	AD & GAD	AD & GAD	AD Alone
0.9	AD & GAD	AD & GAD	AD & GAD	AD & GAD	AD & GAD	AD & GAD	AD & GAD	AD & GAD	AD & GAD	AD & GAD	AD Alone
1	AD & GAD	AD & GAD	AD & GAD	AD & GAD	AD & GAD	AD & GAD	AD & GAD	AD & GAD	AD & GAD	AD & GAD	AD & GAD

The left axis is labeled PROBABILITY OF HIGH COMMERCIAL SUCCESS IN AD & GAD.

Table A-5 Two-way sensitivity analysis to the value of high commercial success if the lead compound succeeds in AD and the lead and backup compounds succeed in AD and GAD, respectively

	HIGH COMMERCIAL VALUE IN AD ALONE								
AD Alone	850	900	950	1000	1050	1100	1150	1200	1250
2500	AD & GAD	AD & GAD	AD Alone	AD Alone	AD Alone	AD Alone	AD Alone	AD Alone	AD Alone
2600	AD & GAD	AD & GAD	AD Alone	AD Alone	AD Alone	AD Alone	AD Alone	AD Alone	AD Alone
2700	AD & GAD	AD & GAD	AD & GAD	AD Alone	AD Alone	AD Alone	AD Alone	AD Alone	AD Alone
2800	AD & GAD	AD & GAD	AD & GAD	AD Alone	AD Alone	AD Alone	AD Alone	AD Alone	AD Alone
2900	AD & GAD	AD & GAD	AD & GAD	AD & GAD	AD Alone	AD Alone	AD Alone	AD Alone	AD Alone
3000	AD & GAD	AD & GAD	AD & GAD	AD & GAD	AD Alone	AD Alone	AD Alone	AD Alone	AD Alone
3100	AD & GAD	AD & GAD	AD & GAD	AD & GAD	AD & GAD	AD Alone	AD Alone	AD Alone	AD Alone
3200	AD & GAD	AD & GAD	AD & GAD	AD & GAD	AD & GAD	AD & GAD	AD Alone	AD Alone	AD Alone
3300	AD & GAD	AD & GAD	AD & GAD	AD & GAD	AD & GAD	AD & GAD	AD Alone	AD Alone	AD Alone
3400	AD & GAD	AD & GAD	AD & GAD	AD & GAD	AD & GAD	AD & GAD	AD & GAD	AD Alone	AD Alone
3500	AD & GAD	AD & GAD	AD & GAD	AD & GAD	AD & GAD	AD & GAD	AD & GAD	AD Alone	AD Alone

The left axis is labeled HIGH COMMERCIAL VALUE IN AD & GAD.

(strategy A) is roughly $1,000M or greater, the dominant decision is to invest in AD alone. Otherwise, the dominant decision is to pursue strategy B.

Finally, one can examine the sensitivity of technical and regulatory risk as well as commercial uncertainty to the dominant decision. For example, comparing the probability of technical and regulatory success in AD alone (strategy A) alongside the high commercial value in AD and GAD (strategy B) enables an informed decision to be rendered (Table A-6).

The results of the data table show the following:

- If the probability of technical and regulatory success in AD alone (strategy A) is roughly 0.70 or greater, the dominant decision is to invest in AD alone (strategy A), irrespective of the high commercial value in AD and GAD (strategy B). On the other hand, if the probability of technical and regulatory success in AD alone (strategy A) is roughly 0.50 or less, the dominant decision swings

Table A-6 Two-way sensitivity analysis to the probability of high commercial success if the lead compound succeeds in AD, and the value of high commercial success if the lead and backup compounds succeed in AD and GAD, respectively

	AD Alone	0	0.1	0.2	0.3	0.4	0.5	0.6	0.7	0.8	0.9	1
						PROBABILITY OF SUCCESS IN AD ALONE						
HIGH COMMERCIAL VALUE IN AD & GAD	2500	AD & GAD	AD & GAD	AD & GAD	AD & GAD	AD & GAD	AD & GAD	AD Alone	AD Alone	AD Alone	AD Alone	AD Alone
	2600	AD & GAD	AD & GAD	AD & GAD	AD & GAD	AD & GAD	AD & GAD	AD Alone	AD Alone	AD Alone	AD Alone	AD Alone
	2700	AD & GAD	AD & GAD	AD & GAD	AD & GAD	AD & GAD	AD & GAD	AD Alone	AD Alone	AD Alone	AD Alone	AD Alone
	2800	AD & GAD	AD & GAD	AD & GAD	AD & GAD	AD & GAD	AD & GAD	AD Alone	AD Alone	AD Alone	AD Alone	AD Alone
	2900	AD & GAD	AD & GAD	AD & GAD	AD & GAD	AD & GAD	AD & GAD	AD & GAD	AD Alone	AD Alone	AD Alone	AD Alone
	3000	AD & GAD	AD & GAD	AD & GAD	AD & GAD	AD & GAD	AD & GAD	AD & GAD	AD Alone	AD Alone	AD Alone	AD Alone
	3100	AD & GAD	AD & GAD	AD & GAD	AD & GAD	AD & GAD	AD & GAD	AD & GAD	AD Alone	AD Alone	AD Alone	AD Alone
	3200	AD & GAD	AD & GAD	AD & GAD	AD & GAD	AD & GAD	AD & GAD	AD & GAD	AD Alone	AD Alone	AD Alone	AD Alone
	3300	AD & GAD	AD & GAD	AD & GAD	AD & GAD	AD & GAD	AD & GAD	AD & GAD	AD Alone	AD Alone	AD Alone	AD Alone
	3400	AD & GAD	AD & GAD	AD & GAD	AD & GAD	AD & GAD	AD & GAD	AD & GAD	AD Alone	AD Alone	AD Alone	AD Alone
	3500	AD & GAD	AD & GAD	AD & GAD	AD & GAD	AD & GAD	AD & GAD	AD & GAD	AD Alone	AD Alone	AD Alone	AD Alone

  to investing in AD and GAD (strategy B), irrespective of the high commercial value in AD and GAD (strategy B).

- If the probability of technical and regulatory success in AD alone (strategy A) is 0.60, the dominant decision depends on the high commercial value in AD and GAD (strategy B). If the high commercial value in AD and GAD (strategy B) is roughly $2,900M or greater, the dominant decision is to invest in AD and GAD (strategy B). Otherwise, the dominant decision is to pursue strategy A.

The analyses presented above satisfy much more than an inquisitive need. Rather, they help to inform decision makers, under conditions of high investment, risk, and uncertainty, of the data points—and underlying assumptions—that are most impactful to the dominant decision. With analyses and insights in hand, decision makers are able to focus their investigations into areas of further analysis, if necessary, before committing to a major investment for a given strategy.

The use of data tables to conduct sensitivity analyses in decision trees can be complemented by the conversion of deterministic commercial values into uncertainty estimates by using probability distributions. As shown in Figure A-7, an asymmetric triangular distribution is assigned to each of the commercial value outcomes (AD; GAD; AD and GAD) in the stochastic decision tree.

Upon inspection, it can be seen that the dominant strategy changes from A to B. This is, of course, dependent on the choice of parameters used for each distribution. Because the mode of each distribution is chosen, the rolled back EVs from the decision tree show strategy B to be superior at $259M. The next step is to determine the distribution of EVs that results from a simulation through the decision tree.

For strategy A, the range of EVs is $135M-$248M, with a mean of $201M (Figure A-8). More important is a roughly 25% probability of exceeding $220M, the deterministic EV generated from the decision tree in Figure A-5.

The corresponding range of EVs for strategy B is $141M-$303M, with a mean of $229M (Figure A-9). For this strategy, there is an approximate 70% likelihood of exceeding $215M, the deterministic EV generated from the decision tree in Figure A-5.

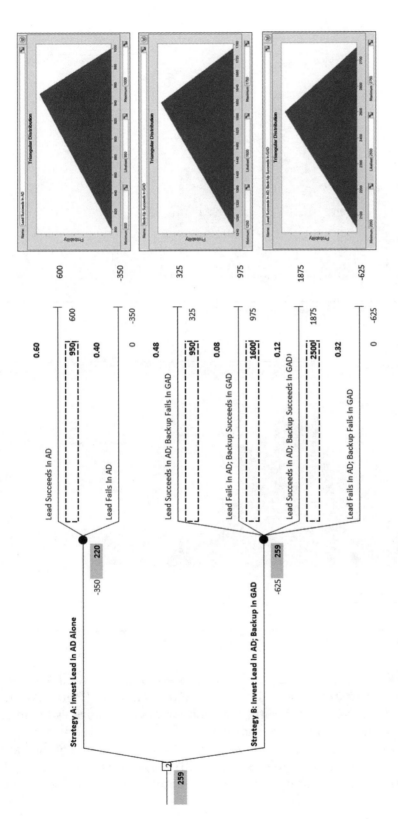

Figure A-7 Conversion of deterministic decision tree to a stochastic tree, using range estimates to represent uncertain commercial values

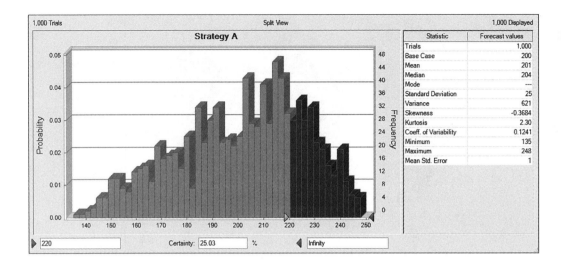

Figure A-8   Results for strategy A of decision tree simulation

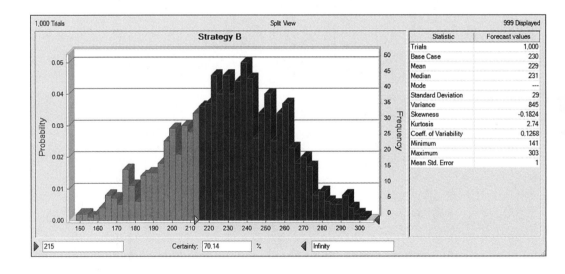

Figure A-9   Results for strategy B of decision tree simulation

Using Crystal Ball™, a tornado analysis can be utilized to investigate the impact or sensitivity of uncertainties to the risk-adjusted value of strategy A (Figure A-10). In this case, using the 1st and 99th percentiles of each commercial range estimate used for the simulation of the decision tree from Figure A-10, one can see that the most impactful uncertainty is success of the lead compound in AD and failure of the backup compound in GAD. If the 1st percentile estimate ($817M) of this range is used, with all other uncertainties held at their base (modal) estimate, the EV of this strategy is as

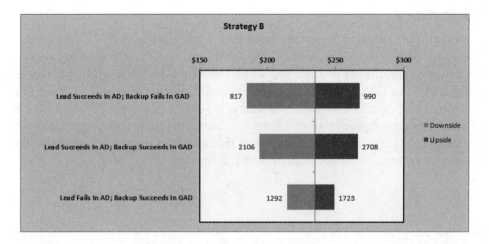

Figure A-10   Tornado sensitivity analysis of commercial uncertainties to the EV of strategy B

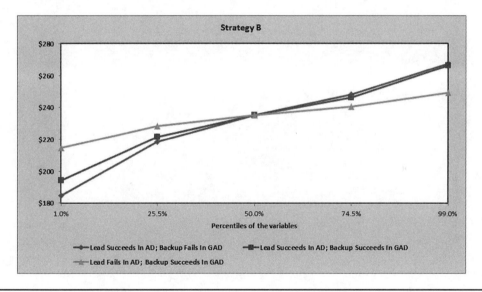

Figure A-11   Spider sensitivity analysis of commercial uncertainties to the EV of strategy B

low as $185M. If swung to its 99th percentile estimate ($990M), with all other un-certainties held at their base (modal) estimate, the EV rises to $267M. The EV of this strategy is least sensitive to the commercial uncertainty represented by the failure of the lead compound in AD and success of the backup compound in GAD.

An alternative way of displaying this information is with the use of a spider analysis that accompanies a tornado sensitivity analysis from the decision tree using Crystal Ball™ (Figure A-11).

A.5 Summary

As demonstrated, decision trees are powerful tools with which to utilize decision analysis in the evaluation of strategic options where large investments are required to be made under conditions of high technical and regulatory risk and commercial uncertainty. With the aid of data tables, deterministic decision trees generate significant insight into the impact of risk and uncertainty on dominant decisions. In addition, the use of simulation techniques allows for a full range of uncertainty inputs to be used in the analysis; in turn, a full distribution of risk-adjusted outcomes for each strategic option can be created to better inform decision making.

Appendix B

A Primer in Mathematical Programming

An overview of the basic concepts of mathematical programming is provided in this appendix. Specifically, the theories behind linear programming, goal programming, multiple objective linear programming, and stochastic optimization are addressed.

This appendix is not an in-depth treatise on mathematical programming; there are several books that provide a fuller treatment of linear and non-linear programming that can serve as excellent references for the same concepts. Practitioners interested in a broad coverage of practical concepts in mathematical programming are encouraged to peruse the works of Ragsdale (2008) and Winston and Albright (2007).

In essence, this appendix provides an overview of typical optimization techniques used in project portfolio management and serves as a supplement to Chapter 7, Portfolio Optimization.

B.1 Mathematical Programming

Mathematical programming (MP) is a branch of management science devoted to finding the optimal or most efficient way of using constrained resources (e.g., budget, people) to achieve objectives (e.g., top line sales growth, cash flow) of an individual or a business (Ragsdale, 2008). Mathematical programming is often also referred to as *optimization*, which can be described as:

- A system (e.g., portfolio) to make the most effective use of something (e.g., budget)
- A methodology of making something (e.g., manufacturing plant capacity) as fully perfect, functional, or effective as possible
- A method to attain the highest degree (e.g., productivity) under implied or specified conditions (e.g., availability of machinery and equipment)

There are several applications of optimization, including but not limited to R&D and financial investment planning, resource allocation, manufacturing, and logistics. MP or optimization problems are characterized by three components: (a) objectives, (b) decisions, and (c) constraints.

An *objective* is a desire to maximize (e.g., sales revenues) or minimize (e.g., cost) a business goal. A *decision* is an allocation of resources, for a specific phase or part of a project, and is more often than not irrevocable in nature. A *constraint* is a restriction placed on the decision alternatives available to the decision makers; examples of constraints include budget, functional full time equivalents, and manufacturing capacity.

A particular form of constraint—a *requirement* (e.g., annual new product launches)—can be regarded as a "soft" restriction. If the requirement is violated, the organization could still conduct its business affairs without any form of penalty. On the other hand, "hard" constraints, such as a budget, often cannot be violated in most organizations without a penalty to the business. Simply restated, from the perspective of a business, a constraint is a limited resource that can either be fungible (e.g., budget) or non-fungible (e.g., functionally trained personnel), which needs to be taken into consideration in the determination of any actionable solution to an organization's portfolio goals. From the perspective of a mathematical model, the decisions in an MP or optimization problem can be represented by the symbols $X_1, X_2, \ldots, X_n$. These are commonly referred to as *decision variables* in the model. The constraints in an optimization problem are generally represented in three ways:

A less than or equal to constraint: $f(X_1, X_2, \ldots, X_n) \leq k$

A greater than or equal to constraint: $f(X_1, X_2, \ldots, X_n) \geq k$

An equal to constraint: $f(X_1, X_2, \ldots, X_n) = k$

In each case, the constraint is a function of the decision variables $X_1, X_2, \ldots, X_n$ that must be (a) less than or equal to, (b) greater than or equal to, or (c) equal to a specific value (represented by k). The objective in a mathematical programming problem is represented by an objective function in a general format:

$$\text{MAX (or MIN)} = f(X_1, X_2, \ldots, X_n)$$

The objective function identifies a function (e.g., values, combination) of the decision variables required by the decision maker in order to MAXimize (e.g., top line sales revenue) or MINimize (e.g., operating cost) a specific goal. The objective function can be represented in the general format:

$$\text{MAX (or MIN)} f_0(X_1, X_2, \ldots X_n)$$

subject to:

$$f_1 X_1, X_2, \ldots, X_n) \leq k_1$$

$$f_j(X_1, X_2, \ldots, X_n) \geq k_j$$

$$f_m(X_1, X_2, \ldots, X_n) = k_m$$

The objective function format describes the objective function that needs to be maximized or minimized and the constraints that cannot be violated. The goal in optimization is to find the values of the decision variables $X_1, X_2, \ldots, X_n$ that maximize or minimize the objective function while satisfying all of the constraints (Ragsdale, 2008).

B.2 Linear Programming

Linear programming (LP) is a type of mathematical modeling that involves creating and solving optimization problems with linear objective functions and constraints. This technique is strictly applicable only when there is direct proportionality between objectives and constraints; for example, a 5% increase in an input (e.g., person hours) leads to a 5% increase in productivity (e.g., widgets). LP has tremendous utility in solving business problems, including R&D and IT project portfolio selection.

As demonstrated in Chapters 10 and 11, although project prioritization currently serves as the basis for much of the portfolio selection across a wide range of industries, LP is a superior technique that serves to find the "best solution" to portfolio selection. When some or all of the decision variables in an LP problem are restricted to assuming only integer values, the resulting problem is referred to as an integer linear programming (ILP) problem. For example, if an organization is trying to decide how many buses to buy or lease for transporting workers to and from sites, it must obtain an integer solution since the company cannot buy or lease fractional numbers of buses. This is an example of a pure ILP problem, since the business solution contains decision variables that can only assume integer values.

Not surprisingly, if the business solution involves both integer and non-integer decision variables, the problem is of a *mixed integer linear programming* (MILP) variation. In certain situations, a further restriction may be imposed on the decision variables in that they will need to be binary integer variables (i.e., can assume one of two integer values: 0 and 1). Binary variables are useful in many practical modeling situations, including project portfolio selection (i.e., optimization) problems. In fact, every project portfolio optimization problem is based on binary integer decision variables corresponding to the selection or otherwise of projects in the portfolio. (The fact that a project may be selected for a partial investment does not preclude its inclusion in the previous statement; the project must first either be selected for investment or not.) Detailed explanations of optimization and the applicability of this technique are elaborated in Chapter 7 and Chapter 11.

For now, consider the mathematical expression for a *binary integer linear programming* (BILP) problem, which can be stated as:

$$\text{MAX (or MIN)} \; c_1X_1 + c_2X_2 + \dots + c_nX_n$$

subject to:

$$a_{11}X_1 + a_{12}X_2 + \dots + a_{1n}X_n \le k_1$$

$$\dots$$

$$a_{j1}X_1 + a_{j2}X_2 + \dots + a_{jn}X_n \ge k_j$$

$$\dots$$

$$a_{m1}X_1 + a_{m2}X_2 + \dots + a_{mn}X_n = k_m$$

where $X_1, X_2 \dots X_n$ are binary integers. The symbols $c_1, c_2, \dots, c_n$ in the objective function are the *objective function coefficients* and may represent the marginal profit or cost associated with the decision variables $X_1, X_2, \ldots, X_n$, respectively. The key to portfolio optimization with BILP lies in formulating the LP problem correctly and can be enhanced by adopting a systematic approach, outlined as follows:

Step 1. Understand the scope of the problem and what is being requested by the decision maker(s); the importance of clearly understanding the *frame* (What problem are we trying to solve?) and *scope* (What are the boundaries of the analysis?) of the problem cannot be overstated.

Step 2. Identify the decision variables, i.e., what decisions need to be made and which ones, at least according to definition, have already been made. In particular, if some project investments (e.g., Must Do projects) are not discretionary in nature, they are clearly not "'variables" and should be treated accordingly by fixing their selection in the portfolio (as described in Chapter 11). While this may appear to be a rather trivial qualifier at this step, identifying decision variables can avoid unnecessary debates during portfolio selection meetings where there is disagreement over which projects are non-discretionary in nature, as well as avoid the resulting degeneration of the discussion without any binding decision making.

Step 3. State the objective function as a linear combination of the decision variables.

Step 4. State the constraints as linear combinations of the decision variables. In addition, identify any decision requirements that may need to be classified as soft or hard constraints. This is an important step because once an optimal solution is generated, it is easy to track the impact the solution has on soft constraints.

If, for example, the optimal solution (e.g., highest value creation) results in an unacceptable number of new product launches (a soft constraint), a decision-making body may wish to pursue a sub-optimal solution (i.e., less-than-maximum value creation) that results in an acceptable number of new product launches. Note: *Optimization only informs decision making; it should not dictate what decisions must be made*.

Step 5. Identify any upper or lower bounds on the decision variables (e.g., invest no less than $W in business sector X; do not exceed $Y in funding for business sector Z). This is particularly important when attempting to "balance" a portfolio with respect to resource allocation, risk, and reward. Otherwise, in the pursuit of one or more portfolio objectives, an optimal solution that does not *a priori* take into account boundaries on investment sectors may result in the type of disproportionate allocation of resources that quickly starves a core capability within an organization (Ragsdale, 2008).

For all optimization problems, we recommend this systematic five-step process as our experience shows that several minefields can be avoided by seeking to understand the frame of decisions that need to be taken before an analysis gets underway. In short, a technically sound analysis conducted on an inappropriately structured portfolio problem is often of less value than a poorly done analysis on a correctly scoped problem.

B.3 Goal Programming and Multiple Objective Linear Programming

The LP techniques (LP, ILP, MILP, and BILP) are based on the assumption that organizational constraints which dictate largely how an LP model is constructed are hard constraints or constraints that are not to be violated. While hard constraints (e.g., manufacturing capacity) are appropriate in many business situations, there are often situations where, in the absence of any flexibility to these constraints, finding an acceptable portfolio solution becomes difficult as the feasible region or solution space provided by an optimization frame is far too restrictive.

The concept of the *feasible region* is well-described by Ragsdale (2008); in short, since many goals tend to compete with each other, trade-offs need to be made between such goals in order to find one or more acceptable optimization solutions. Further, organizations can unknowingly compromise the quality of an optimization solution by placing too many goals on a portfolio problem. For example, an attempt to maximize revenues *and* cash flow *and* ROI, while minimizing cost *and* risk *and* time to market, can result in a restricted feasible region within which lies only a handful of possible solutions. Yet, this is the basis on which portfolio selection via project prioritization is conducted, often without any assessment of the value created or destroyed, by adopting a multiple objective prioritization selection technique.

Organizations often desire the attainment of certain goals or targets (e.g., annual new product launches) which may be more accurately viewed as soft constraints, i.e., constraint violation does not necessarily spell the demise of the entity. There are a multitude of organizational problems that can be modeled by relaxing hard constraints and converting them into goals or targets. Such problems may not have a single objective function that needs to be maximized or minimized; rather, the objectives are stated as a collection of goals, some of which may be in conflict with each other (e.g., increasing reward and reducing risk at the same time). These types of problems are known as *goal programming* (GP) problems; rather than attempting to maximize or minimize a single objective function, GP seeks to minimize the deviations among the desired goals and actual results according to certain levels of importance or priority. The steps in formulating an LP model for a GP problem (Ragsdale, 2008) are outlined as:

Step 1. Identify the decision variables; again, if a variable (e.g., project) falls into the non-discretionary investment category, assign the integer 1 to it so as to ensure that it is always a part of the collection of variables that constitutes the optimal solution. In the authors' experience, few portfolio discussions are more distracting than those where decision makers wish to first include and then exclude non-discretionary projects from a portfolio selection.

Step 2. Identify the hard constraints (if any exist) in the problem and formulate them as one would for a standard LP problem.

Step 3. State the goals or targets of the problem together with their desired target values.

Step 4. Create constraints using the decision variables that enable the exact achievement of these goals.

Step 5. Transform the hard constraints from Step 4 into goal constraints by including deviational variables. In other words, create a goal constraint for each goal in the problem. A goal constraint enables the decision maker to evaluate how close an optimization solution comes to achieving a specific goal. A typical goal constraint for an LP problem takes the following form:

$$a_{j1}X_1 + a_{j2}X_2 + \ldots + a_{jn}X_{jn} + d_j^- - d_j^+ = k_j$$

where $X_1, X_2 \ldots X_n$ are the decision variables, and if there are m goals for the LP problem, then j takes values from 1, 2, ... , m.

Basically, the *right-hand side value* of the equation for each goal constraint (i.e., k_j) is the target value for the goal, while the variables d_j^- and d_j^+ are termed *deviational* or *perturbation variables* because they represent the amount by which each goal is either underachieved or overachieved. As stated, they do not yet represent a penalty for deviating from the target value of each goal. It is noteworthy that deviational or perturbation variables can only have non-negative values.

Step 6. Determine which deviational variables represent truly undesirable deviations from the goals (as opposed to marginally more or less than the desired targets).

Step 7. Formulate an objective that would penalize any decidedly undesirable deviations. Typically, the objective function in a GP problem is formulated by assigning weights to each deviational variable based on the importance of each goal, such that the weights assigned to each deviational variable appropriately reflect the importance and desirability of deviations, represented as:

Minimize the weighted sum of the deviations: MIN: $\Sigma\,(w_j^- d_j^- + w_j^+ d_j^+)$

or

Minimize the weighted sum of the percentage
deviations: MIN: $\Sigma\,(w_j^- d_j^- + w_j^+ d_j^+)/t_j$

In these weighted objective functions, w_j^- and w_j^+ represent numeric constants that can be assigned values to weight the deviational variables for the jth goal in the problem, while t_j represents the target value for the jth goal. If there are m goals for the problem, then j takes values from 1, 2, ... , m.

A variable that represents a highly undesirable deviation from a specific goal is assigned a relatively large weight, making it highly undesirable for that variable to assume a value larger than 0 and, in essence, converting that variable into more or less (but not exactly) a hard constraint. This type of weighting in optimization is referred to as *preemptive GP*, which involves a hierarchy of priority levels for goals, such that goals of primary importance receive first order attention, while those of secondary importance receive lower attention, and so on. A variable that represents a neutral or desirable deviation from a specific goal is assigned a weight of 0 or a value lower than 0 to reflect that it is acceptable for the variable to assume a value greater than 0.

Step 8. Create appropriate weights for the objective. This is, not surprisingly, an often contentious issue since stakeholders seldom agree, *a priori*, to the weights for one or another objective. A recommendation is to use the analytic hierarchy process described in Chapter 8 to enable the assignment of weights to objectives.

Step 9. Solve the problem, then analyze the solution to the problem. If the solution is unacceptable, return to Step 8 to revise the weights of one or another objective where necessary, and rerun the optimization in search of a better solution. Note that, unlike previous LP problems, there is no straightforward optimal solution. Rather, because of the flexibility introduced by the deviational variables in GP, decision makers have an opportunity to discuss what objectives are more or less important and which solutions are better or worse. This is most helpful because both desirability and undesirability in the context of achievement of target goals are phenomena that do not easily lend themselves to quantitative resolution. Nevertheless, optimality is now effectively replaced by satisficing.

As stated by Ragsdale (2008), different GP solutions should not be compared simply on the basis of the values of their optimal objective functions, since the weights in the objective functions change in an iterative manner, depending on the wishes of the decision maker; this would be akin to comparing the rank order of projects in a portfolio selection exercise based on different weights to objectives or attributes in one MODA analysis versus another (Chapter 8). Therefore, the different solutions to the problem should be compared until decision makers are content that the best solution fulfills, more or less, their objectives and target goals without creating dissatisfactory undesirability. It is also worth noting that in a GP problem, hard constraints can be placed on deviational variables to limit the amount by which one can deviate from a goal. These can assume one of three possible states:

1. A lower, one-sided goal that places a lower limit on the value of a goal that the solution should not fall under while exceeding that limit is acceptable
2. An upper, one-sided goal that places an upper limit on the value of a goal that the solution should not exceed while falling under that limit is acceptable
3. A two-sided goal that sets a specific target that should neither be overachieved nor underachieved on either side of the goal

Finally, another type of objective function, the *MINIMAX function*, is useful to incorporate in GP problems, especially when a decision maker wishes to minimize the maximum a solution may deviate from any goal. To accommodate the MINIMAX objective, an additional constraint needs to be created for each deviational variable, where Q is the MINIMAX variable, and the objective is to minimize the value of Q, which can be stated as *MIN:Q*:

$$d_1^- \leq Q$$
$$d_1^+ \leq Q$$
$$d_2^- \leq Q \ldots$$

Q is always set equal to the maximum value of the deviational variables because Q is, by definition, greater than or equal to the values of all the deviational variables. This objective function simultaneously tries to find a solution where the maximum value of

Q is as small as possible. This type of objective is especially valuable if a GP problem has hard lower or upper constraints (Ragsdale, 2008).

A special type of GP technique used to solve LP problems with multiple objective functions is called *multiple objective linear programming* (MOLP). MOLP problems can be viewed as special types of GP problems, where as part of solving the problem one must also determine target values for each goal or objective. Analyzing such problems effectively also requires the use of the MINIMAX objective, Q, described previously. In MOLP, a decision alternative is dominated if there is another alternative that produces a better solution for at least one objective without worsening the values of the other objectives. A summary of optimization of multiple objectives, using MOLP, is as follows:

Step 1. As with GP, identify the decision variables in the problem. Ensure that non-discretionary investments are assigned an integer value of 1.

Step 2. Identify the objectives and formulate them as a collection of different LP problems with single objectives.

Step 3. Identify the constraints in the problem and formulate them as one would for an LP problem.

Step 4. Run an optimization once for each of the objectives to determine the maximum or minimum value for each objective.

Step 5. Restate the objectives as goals, using the optimal value for each objective identified in Step 4 as the target values.

Step 6. Create a deviation function for each goal that measures the amount by which any solution overachieves or underachieves the goal.

Step 7. Assign a weight to each deviation function and create a constraint that forces the value of the weighted deviation function to be less than the *MINIMAX* Q variable.

Step 8. Solve the problem by minimizing the value of Q and determine if the solution satisfies the goals of the decision makers. As with GP, if the solution is not acceptable, revise the weights of one or another deviation function and rerun the optimization in search of a more acceptable solution (Ragsdale, 2008).

Chapter 11 includes a case study in optimizing an R&D portfolio, providing an illustration of how GP can be leveraged in project portfolio selection.

So far, no discussion has been entered into regarding the other major form of deterministic optimization, namely, *non-linear programming* (NLP). NLP problems present themselves in such a way that they possess non-linear objective functions and/or non-linear constraints and include economic order quantity, location, and non-linear network problems. While NLP models are often more realistic than linear models, they are difficult to solve. The works of Ragsdale (2008) and Winston and Albright (2007) are highly recommended for more detailed descriptions of how real-world problems can be solved with the use of NLP techniques.

B.4 Stochastic Optimization

Stochastic programming is a methodological approach to solving optimization problems that involve uncertainty. Thus far, various optimization approaches to solving deterministic LP problems were discussed, where parameters (e.g., project value, functional full-time equivalents) are known (or believed to be known) with certainty. In reality, many organizational problems, including project portfolio management, involve parameters that are *not known with certainty* when a decision is to be made.

The term *not known with certainty* is stressed, as opposed to *unknown*, primarily because organizations have a remarkable tendency to predominantly use heuristics for decision making simply because data are not known with certainty. Rather than apply uncertainty to the structure of the problem set, some decision makers tend to fixate on the average of a historical data set or to override uncertainty by pretending that a "base value" represents the mode or most likely value of a parameter. Needless to state, both practices can lead to flawed decision making, because if history were a perfect predictor of the future, the need for programming of any sort would quickly be obsolete.

When parameters are uncertain but there is sufficient data or a belief that they lie within a distribution of possible values (i.e., the probability distributions are known or can be estimated with significant confidence), a solution that optimizes a given objective function and is feasible for the entire distribution of possible values can be sought (Shapiro et al., 2009). Stochastic programming can be applied not only to solving repetitive problems (e.g., minimization of delivery distance between stops in response to random online orders) where the objective is to arrive at a solution which results in the best possible outcome on the average or in the long term. However, since one or another parameter is uncertain, the best possible solution may result in a sub-optimal outcome, as a single outcome is governed by the law of averages only in the long term.

Stochastic programming can also be applied to organizational problems in which one-off decisions must be made, e.g., the selection of a portfolio of R&D or IT projects, some or all of which have unique risks (as defined by their elicited probabilities of success) and uncertain elements (e.g., competitive success in a dynamically changing commercial environment). In such cases, it becomes somewhat contentious to make one-off decisions based on expected value or expected utility, meaning that the subjective component of the decision makers' risk attitudes must be taken into account.

While many stochastic programming techniques are available for solving optimization problems, the IT (Chapter 10) and R&D (Chapter 11) case studies involved computer simulation, which is a widely used and well-accepted technique. Specifically, the case studies both used the Monte Carlo and Latin hypercube methods of sampling to perform the random simulations. Computer simulation employs the use of models that imitate real life or help make projections to assist decision making. When, for example, an Excel spreadsheet model is created, there exist a certain number of input parameters and a few equations that use those inputs to produce a series of outputs (or *response variables*). A model that uses response variables is usually deterministic or harbors fixed point parametric estimates, meaning that one gets the same results no matter how many times the problem is solved.

Simulation is also a technique for iteratively evaluating a deterministic model, using sets of random numbers as inputs where, if a sufficiently large number of simulations are not undertaken, one may not reproducibly generate the same solution. This method is often used when the model is complex, non-linear, or involves more than just a few uncertain parameters. The Monte Carlo technique is one of a few methods for analyzing uncertain inputs, where the goal is to determine how variation in random selection, imperfect knowledge, or error affects the sensitivity, performance, or reliability of the system that is being modeled prototypically.

Monte Carlo simulation is categorized as a sampling method because the inputs are randomly generated from probability distributions to simulate the process of sampling from an actual population. The aim is to try to choose a distribution for the inputs that most closely matches data already available or best represents the decision-maker's current state of knowledge. The data generated from the simulation can be represented as probability distributions or histograms or converted to error bars, reliability predictions, tolerance zones, and confidence intervals.

The basic steps in implementing a Monte Carlo simulation model in a spreadsheet are:

Step 1. Create a parametric model, $Y = f(X_1, X_2, \ldots , X_q)$.

Step 2. Generate a set of random inputs, $X_{i1}, X_{i2}, \ldots , X_{iq}$.

Step 3. Evaluate the model and store the results as Y_i.

Step 4. Repeat Steps 2 and 3 for $i = 1$ to n.

Step 5. Analyze the results using histograms, confidence intervals, and other statistical representations.

For certain classes of problems, there is a need to address the impact of uncertainties on decision variables. Consider variable Y, which is a function of other variables $X_1, X_2, \ldots , X_k$. If uncertainties exist in determining the value of $X_1, X_2, \ldots , X_k$, then relevant questions to be investigated are:

- How does Y vary when the Xs vary according to an assumed joint probability distribution?
- What is the expected value of Y?
- What is the jth percentile of Y?

A conventional approach to these questions is to apply Monte Carlo sampling. By sampling repeatedly from the assumed joint probability density function of X, and evaluating Y for each sample, the distribution of Y, along with its mean and other characteristics, can be estimated. A disadvantage of Monte Carlo sampling with n repetitions is that if n is a large number, then a large number of computations are required from the function or program of interest, which is potentially a very large computational exercise, given the relatively greater degree of randomness of the values of the variables generated by the Monte Carlo sampling.

An alternative approach, which can yield more precise estimates with limited sampling, is to use a constrained Monte Carlo sampling technique. This scheme, developed by McKay, Beckman, and Conover (1979), is *Latin hypercube sampling (LHS)*, which uses a technique known as *stratified sampling without replacement* (Wyss & Jorgensen 1998). The probability distribution is split into n intervals of equal probability, where n is the number of samples that are to be performed on the model. As the simulation progresses, each of the n intervals is sampled once. Basically, LHS selects n different values from each of the k variables $X_1, X_2, \ldots , X_k$ in the following steps:

Step 1. The range of each variable is divided into n non-overlapping intervals on the basis of equal probability.

Step 2. One value is selected from each interval at random with respect to the probability density of the interval.

Step 3. The n values obtained for X_1 are then paired in a random manner (equally likely combinations) with the n values for X_2.

Step 4. These n pairs are then combined in a random manner with the n values of X_3 to form triplets, and so on, until n k-tuplets are formed.

It is convenient to think of this Latin hypercube sampling (or any random sample of size n) as forming an $(n \times k)$ matrix where the ith row contains the specific values for each of the k input variables to be used in the ith run of the computer model. LHS has the advantage of generating a set of samples that more precisely reflect the shape of a sampled distribution than pure random (Monte Carlo) samples. The general effect is that the *mean* of a set of simulation results more quickly approaches the "true" value, particularly for models that are simply adding or subtracting a number of variables.

While the manual compilation of Monte Carlo sampling or LHS-based simulation models is feasible for simple problems in a spreadsheet, there are considerable advantages to using software packages that enable the construction of computer-generated models for large, complex problems such as those under consideration in portfolio selection. One type of software that integrates well with Excel spreadsheets is Oracle Corporation's Crystal Ball™. The case study on an R&D portfolio described in Chapter 11 illustrates the application of stochastic programming to portfolio selection using Crystal Ball™.

Appendix C
MODA Models for
IT Investment Prioritization

MODA models for prioritizing CAPEX and OPEX investments are described in Tables C-1 and C-2. Each model lists all the attributes in the corresponding utility hierarchy, weights for the objectives, attributes and sub-attributes, the score description, raw scores, and weighted scores.

Table C-1 MODA model with raw and weighted scores for IT CAPEX investments

Objective	Objective Weight	Attribute	Attribute Weight	Sub-Attribute	Sub-Attribute Weight	Score Description	Score Levels	Raw Score	Weighted Score
Business Value	40%	Strategic Fit	15%	N/A	100%	Little to none—May indirectly impact stated objectived (SOs) of business unit (BU)	N/A	0	0.00
						Low—Indirectly impacts company SOs	Low	2	1.33
						Medium—Directly impacts BU SOs	Medium	5	3.33
						High—Directly impacts company SOs	High	9	6.00
		Customer Need	15%	N/A	100%	N/A—IT initiated project	N/A	0	0.00
						Low—Work group manager of company BU	Low	2	1.33
						Medium—Head of BU	Medium	5	3.33
						High—Multiple BUs clamoring for this capability	High	9	6.00
		Compliance	15%	N/A	100%	Not required from a legal or regulatory compliance standpoint	N/A	0	0.00
						Required for the long term (2-3 years)	Low	2	1.33
						Required for the medium term (1-2 years)	Medium	5	3.33
						Required immediately (within 1 year)	High	9	6.00
		Revenue Impact	15%	N/A	100%	None/Unknown at this time	N/A	0	0.00
						Indirect link to additional incremental revenue	Low	2	1.33
						Intellectual property rights generation/ directly prevent future loss	Medium	5	3.33
						Directly generates revenue for the company	High	9	6.00
		Performance Improvement	15%	N/A	100%	None	N/A	0	0.00
						<5%	<5%	2	1.33
						>5% but <10%	>5% but <10%	5	3.33
						>10%	>10%	9	6.00

					Description	Level		Value
IT Value 20%	Level of Innovation	10%	N/A	100%	Potential for degradation in competitive advantage	Poor	0	0.00
					No change in competitive advantage	Low	2	0.89
					Moderate enhancement in competitive advantage	Medium	5	2.22
					New innovation—Dramatic improvement in competitive advantage	High	9	4.00
	Issues Resolution	15%	N/A	100%	No change in resolving customer issues	N/A	0	0.00
					Slight improvement in resolving customer issues	Low	2	1.33
					Moderate improvement in resolving customer issues	Medium	5	3.33
					Significant improvement in resolving customer issues	High	9	6.00
	Internal Demand	15%	N/A	100%	Little to none	N/A	0	0.00
					Low—IT middle management request	Low	2	0.67
					Medium—IT senior management request	Medium	5	1.67
					High—CIO request	High	9	3.00
	IT Stated Objectives Alignment	20%	N/A	100%	Little to none	N/A	0	0.00
					Low—Indirectly aligned.	Low	2	0.89
					Medium—Directly aligned with IT BU's SOs	Medium	5	2.22
					High—Directly aligned with enterprise IT SOs and goals	High	9	4.00
	Productivity Improvement	15%	N/A	100%	None	N/A	0	0.00
					<5%	Low	2	0.67
					>5% but <10%	Medium	5	1.67
					>10%	High	9	3.00
	Learning & Innovation	5%	N/A	100%	Little to none	N/A	0	0.00
					Low—Departmental level	Low	2	0.22
					Medium—Enterprise level	Medium	5	0.56
					High—Industry level	High	9	1.00

(continues)

Table C-1 *(Continued)*

Objective	Objective Weight	Attribute	Attribute Weight	Sub-Attribute	Sub-Attribute Weight	Score Description	Score Levels	Raw Score	Weighted Score
		Unit Cost Reduction	15%	N/A	100%	None	N/A	0	0.00
						<5%	Low	2	0.67
						>5% but <10%	Medium	5	1.67
						>10%	High	9	3.00
		Impact on Future Investments	10%	N/A	100%	No impact	N/A	0	0.00
						Potential impact or optional building block	Low	2	0.44
						Necessary but replaceable building block	Medium	5	1.11
						Necessary—Irreplaceable building block	High	9	2.00
IT Value *(continued)*	20% *(continued)*	Quality and Reliability	10%	N/A	100%	Degradation	Poor	0	0.00
						No impact	N/A	2	0.44
						Necessary to maintain current level of service	Good	5	1.11
						Necessary to restore current level of service	Excellent	9	2.00
		Component Reuse	10%	N/A	100%	No opportunity to create or consume assets	N/A	0	0.00
						Minor opportunities to create or consume assets	Low	2	0.44
						Significant opportunities to create or consume assets	Medium	5	1.11
						Significant opportunities to create and consume assets	High	9	2.00
Financial Value	20%	Net Present Value	20%	N/A	100%	<$100K	Low	0	0.00
						≥$100K but <$1M	Medium	2	0.89
						≥$1M but <$5M	High	5	2.22
						≥$5M	Very High	9	4.00

Category	Criterion	Weight	Sub-criterion	Sub-weight	Description	Rating	Score	Value
	Payback Period	15%	N/A	100%	≥5 Years	Low	0	0.00
					≥3 Years but <5 Years	Medium	2	0.67
					≥1 Year but <3 Years	High	5	1.67
					<1 Year	Very High	9	3.00
	Internal Rate of Return	15%	N/A	100%	<15%	Low	0	0.00
					≥15% but <25%	Medium	2	0.67
					≥25% but <40%	High	5	1.67
					≥40%	Very High	9	3.00
	Return on Investment	20%	N/A	100%	<0%	Low	0	0.00
					≥0% but <10%	Medium	2	0.89
					≥10% but <25%	High	5	2.22
					>25%	Very High	9	4.00
	Level of Investment	30%	N/A	100%	>10% of overall IT budget	Low	0	0.00
					≤10% but >5% of overall IT budget	Medium	2	1.33
					≤5% but >1% of overall IT budget	High	5	3.33
					<1% of overall IT budget	Very High	9	6.00
Risk 20%	Business Risk	30%			All of the following are true: 1) Executive management commitment is lukewarm at best 2) End-user community is skeptical about this initiative 3) Business and IT need to put in more effort (over and above day jobs)	High	0	0.00
			Organizational Change Risk	25%	Two of the following are true: 1) Executive management commitment is lukewarm at best 2) End-user community is skeptical about this initiative 3) Business and IT need to put in more effort (over and above day jobs)	Medium	2	0.33

(continues)

Table C-1 *(Continued)*

Objective	Objective Weight	Attribute	Attribute Weight	Sub-Attribute	Sub-Attribute Weight	Score Description	Score Levels	Raw Score	Weighted Score
				Organizational Change Risk *(continued)*	25%	One of the following is true: 1) Executive management commitment is lukewarm at best 2) End-user community is skeptical about this initiative 3) Business and IT need to put in more effort (over and above day jobs)	Low	5	0.83
						None of the following is true: 1) Executive management commitment is lukewarm at best 2) End-user community is skeptical about this initiative 3) Business & IT need to put in more effort (over and above day jobs)	N/A	9	1.50
Risk *(continued)*	20%	Business Risk	30%	Management Risk	25%	Company may acquire another organization or be acquired, division may be sold off, or organizational redesign underway—High likelihood of management change	High	0	0.00
						Organizational redesign anticipated—Some likelihood of management change	Medium	5	0.83
						No organizational redesign anticipated—Very low likelihood of management change	Low	9	1.50
				External Risk	25%	Very dynamic marketplace, high level of competitive threat, or sweeping industry changes likely from government regulators	High	0	0.00
						Some changes in market likely or some level of competition exists that may cause reprioritization or potential new regulations (along the lines of SOX,	Medium	5	0.83

			Description	Rating	Value	Score
Technical Risk	40%	Strategic Risk	25%	Fairly stable external environment or little impact of external changes on this IT investment	Low	9	1.50
				IT investment directly impacts organization's strategic goals and objectives	High	0	0.00
				IT investment indirectly impacts organization's strategic goals and objectives	Medium	5	0.83
				Little to no impact on organization's strategic goals and objectives	Low	9	1.50
		Complexity Risk	25%	New technology requiring hardware, software, application, or infrastructure components that are not present in the organization currently or significant specialized expertise required in technical competencies	High	0	0.00
				Hardware exists but not operations tested, software requires significant advances, or some amount of specialized expertise required in technical competencies	Medium	5	1.11
				Low complexity by virtue of existing organizational resources and competencies that make the complexity risk manageable	Low	9	2.00
		Feasibility Risk	15%	Brand new innovation—High likelihood of infeasibility, owing to significant design complexity	High	0	0.00
				Step change in capabilities requiring some innovation; there is a reasonable chance that the desired solution may be infeasible	Medium	5	0.67
				Low degree of uncertainty on feasibility of solution	Low	9	1.20
		Integration Risk	25%	Significant integration required, necessitating architecture redesign; development of a number of new interfaces is required	Very High	0	0.00

(continues)

Table C-1 *(Continued)*

Objective	Objective Weight	Attribute	Attribute Weight	Sub-Attribute	Sub-Attribute Weight	Score Description	Score Levels	Raw Score	Weighted Score
Risk *(continued)*	20%	Technical Risk	40%	Integration Risk *(continued)*	25%	Some degree of integration required, does not require architecture redesign; however a number of new interfaces need to be developed	High	2	0.44
						Low degree of integration, few new interfaces and/or modifications to existing interfaces	Medium	5	1.11
						Minimal integration required, mostly minor tweaks to existing interfaces	Low	9	2.00
				Lifecycle Stage Risk	15%	Technology has risk of obsolescence—No longer supported by vendor	Very High	0	0.00
						Legacy or declining technology	High	2	0.27
						Niche or special use technology	Medium	5	0.67
						Mature technology	Low	9	1.20
				Security Risk	20%	Limited security model—Rudimentary, difficult to configure, no role-based access	Very High	0	0.00
						Embedded security model with some configuration capabilities, role-based access	High	2	0.36
						Security model in alignment with organization's security standards, practices, and policies	Medium	5	0.89
						New paradigm in IT security, the adoption of which is redefining the IT industry (not yet in organization, but will significantly improve organization's security standards)	Low	9	1.60

			Description	Rating	Score	Value
Operational Risk	30%	Business Continuity Plan (BCP) Risk	30%	No BCP/Disaster Recovery (DR) Plan in place	Very High	0	0.00
			Class C Plan—DR within 5 business days	High	2	0.40
			Class B Plan—DR within 2 business days	Medium	5	1.00
			Class A Plan—DR within 2 hours of failure	Low	9	1.80
		Project Risk	40%	All of the following are true: 1) Project encountering slippage in cost, schedule 2) Project is dependent on the success of other initiatives 3) Project scope change is likely during implementation	Very High	0	0.00
			Two of the following are true: 1) Project encountering slippage in cost, schedule 2) Project is dependent on the success of other initiatives 3) Project scope change is likely during implementation	High	2	0.53
			One of the following is true: 1) Project encountering slippage in cost, schedule 2) Project is dependent on the success of other initiatives 3) Project scope change is likely during implementation	Medium	5	1.33
			None of the following is true: 1) Project encountering slippage in cost, schedule 2) Project is dependent on the success of other initiatives 3) Project scope change is likely during implementation	Low	9	2.40

(continues)

Table C-1 *(Continued)*

Objective	Objective Weight	Attribute	Attribute Weight	Sub-Attribute	Sub-Attribute Weight	Score Description	Score Levels	Raw Score	Weighted Score
Risk *(continued)*	20%	Operational Risk	30%	Vendor Risk	30%	Small company with niche product, regional vendor with no national presence, limited sales, support, and delivery model; vendor has <25 customers with live implementations	Very High	0	0.00
						Vendor with national presence, good product strategy/vision, multiple channels of sales and implementation support; potential for being acquired by competitor exists; vendor has >25 and <100 customers with live implementations	High	2	0.40
						Vendor with international presence, excellent product strategy, multiple channels of sales and implementation support; products have >100 customers with live implementations	Medium	5	1.00
						Global leader in multiple products/solutions, excellent product strategy and vision, multiple channels of sales and implementation support; products have >500 customers with live implementations	Low	9	1.80

Table C-2 MODA model with raw and weighted scores for IT OPEX investments

Objective	Objective Weight	Attribute	Attribute Weight	Sub-Attribute	Sub-Attribute Weight	Score Description	Score Levels	Raw Score	Weighted Score
Business Value	40%	Strategic Fit	15%	N/A	100%	Little to none—May indirectly impact SOs of business unit	N/A	0	0.00
						Low—Indirectly impacts company SOs	Low	2	1.33
						Medium—Directly impacts BU SOs	Medium	5	3.33
						High—Directly impacts company SOs	High	9	6.00
		Customer Need	15%	N/A	100%	N/A—IT initiated project	N/A	0	0.00
						Low—Work group manager of company BU	Low	2	1.33
						Medium—Head of BU	Medium	5	3.33
						High—Multiple BUs clamoring for this capability	High	9	6.00
		Compliance	15%	N/A	100%	Not required from a legal or regulatory compliance standpoint	N/A	0	0.00
						Required for the long term (2-3 years)	Low	2	1.33
						Required for the medium term (1-2 years)	Medium	5	3.33
						Required immediately (within 1 year)	High	9	6.00
		Revenue Impact	15%	N/A	100%	None/Unknown at this time	N/A	0	0.00
						Indirect link to additional incremental revenue	Low	2	1.33
						Intellectual property rights generation/ directly prevent future loss	Medium	5	3.33
						Directly generates revenue for the company	High	9	6.00
		Performance Improvement	15%	N/A	100%	None	N/A	0	0.00
						<5%	<5%	2	1.33
						>5% but <10%	>5% but <10%	5	3.33
						>10%	>10%	9	6.00

(continues)

Table C-2 *(Continued)*

Objective	Objective Weight	Attribute	Attribute Weight	Sub-Attribute	Sub-Attribute Weight	Score Description	Score Levels	Raw Score	Weighted Score
Business Value *(continued)*	40%	Level of Innovation	10%	N/A	100%	Potential for degradation in competitive advantage	Poor	0	0.00
						No change in competitive advantage	Low	2	0.89
						Moderate enhancement in competitive advantage	Medium	5	2.22
						New innovation—Dramatic improvement in competitive advantage	High	9	4.00
		Issues Resolution	15%	N/A	100%	No change in resolving customer issues	N/A	0	0.00
						Slight improvement in resolving customer issues	Low	2	1.33
						Moderate improvement in resolving customer issues	Medium	5	3.33
						Significant improvement in resolving customer issues	High	9	6.00
		IT Stated Objectives Alignment	20%	N/A	100%	Little to none	N/A	0	0.00
						Low—Indirectly aligned	Low	2	0.67
						Medium—Directly aligned with IT BU's SOs	Medium	5	1.67
						High—Directly aligned with enterprise IT SOs and goals	High	9	3.00
IT Value	20%	Productivity Improvement	15%	N/A	100%	None	N/A	0	0.00
						<5%	Low	2	0.44
						>5% but <10%	Medium	5	1.11
						>10%	High	9	2.00
		Learning & Innovation	10%	N/A	100%	Little to none	N/A	0	0.00
						Low—Departmental level	Low	2	0.67
						Medium—Enterprise level	Medium	5	1.67
						High—Industry level	High	9	3.00

Category		Criterion	Weight	Sub	Sub Wt	Level Description	Rating	Score	Value
		Unit Cost Reduction	15%	N/A	100%	None	N/A	0	0.00
						<5%	Low	2	0.44
						>5% but <10%	Medium	5	1.11
						>10%	High	9	2.00
		Impact on Future Investments	10%	N/A	100%	No impact	N/A	0	0.00
						Potential impact or optional building block	Low	2	0.44
						Necessary but replaceable building block	Medium	5	1.11
						Necessary—Irreplaceable building block	High	9	2.00
		Quality and Reliability	10%	N/A	100%	Degradation	Poor	0	0.00
						No impact	N/A	2	0.44
						Necessary to maintain current level of service	Good	5	1.11
						Necessary to restore current level of service	Excellent	9	2.00
		Component Reuse	10%	N/A	100%	No opportunity to create or consume assets	N/A	0	0.00
						Minor opportunities to create or consume assets	Low	2	0.44
						Significant opportunities to create or consume assets	Medium	5	1.11
						Significant opportunities to create and consume assets	High	9	2.00
		IT Employee Satisfaction	10%	N/A	100%	N/A	N/A	0	0.00
						Low	Low	2	0.44
						Medium	Medium	5	1.11
						High	High	9	2.00
Cost	20%	Direct Costs	75%	Staffing	25%	>40 full-time equivalents (FTEs)	Very High	0	0.00
						>20 FTEs but ≤40 FTEs	High	2	0.83
						>5 FTEs but ≤20 FTEs	Medium	5	2.08
						≤5 FTEs	Low	9	3.75

(continues)

Table C-2 *(Continued)*

Objective	Objective Weight	Attribute	Attribute Weight	Sub-Attribute	Sub-Attribute Weight	Score Description	Score Levels	Raw Score	Weighted Score
Cost *(continued)*	20%	Direct Costs *(continued)*	75% *(continued)*	Infrastructure	30%	>$10M	Very High	0	0.00
						>$5M but ≤$10M	High	2	1.00
						>$1M but ≤$5M	Medium	5	2.50
						≤$1M	Low	9	4.50
				Administrative	10%	>$2M	Very High	0	0.00
						>$1M but ≤$2M	High	2	0.33
						>$250K but ≤$1M	Medium	5	0.83
						≤$250K	Low	9	1.50
				Development	20%	>$5M	Very High	0	0.00
						>$2M but ≤$5M	High	2	0.67
						>$500K but ≤$2M	Medium	5	1.67
						≤$500K	Low	9	3.00
				Operations	15%	>$5M	Very High	0	0.00
						>$2M but ≤$5M	High	2	0.50
						>$500K but ≤$2M	Medium	5	1.25
						≤$500K	Low	9	2.25
		Indirect Costs	25%	End User	30%	>$2M	Very High	0	0.00
						>$1M but ≤$2M	High	2	0.33
						>$250K but ≤$1M	Medium	5	0.83
						≤$250K	Low	9	1.50
				Outages	60%	>$2M	Very High	0	0.00
						>$1M but ≤$2M	High	2	0.67
						>$250K but ≤$1M	Medium	5	1.67
						≤$250K	Low	9	3.00
				Miscellaneous	10%	>$1M	Very High	0	0.00
						>$500K but ≤$1M	High	2	0.11
						>$100K but ≤$500K	Medium	5	0.28
						≤$100K	Low	9	0.50

Risk		Business Risk							
Risk	20%	Business Risk	30%	Organizational Change Risk	25%	All of the following are true: 1) Executive management commitment is lukewarm at best 2) End-user community is skeptical about this initiative 3) Business and IT need to put in more effort (over and above day jobs)	High	0	0.00
						Two of the following are true: 1) Executive management commitment is lukewarm at best 2) End-user community is skeptical about this initiative 3) Business and IT need to put in more effort (over and above day jobs)	Medium	2	0.33
						One of the following is true: 1) Executive management commitment is lukewarm at best 2) End-user community is skeptical about this initiative 3) Business and IT need to put in more effort (over and above day jobs)	Low	5	0.83
						None of the following is true: 1) Executive management commitment is lukewarm at best 2) End-user community is skeptical about this initiative 3) Business and IT need to put in more effort (over and above day jobs)	N/A	9	1.50
				Management Risk	25%	Company may acquire another organization or be acquired, division may be sold off, or organizational redesign underway—High likelihood of management change	High	0	0.00
						Organizational redesign anticipated—Some likelihood of management change	Medium	5	0.83
						No organizational redesign anticipated—Very low likelihood of management change	Low	9	1.50

(continues)

Table C-2 *(Continued)*

Objective	Objective Weight	Attribute	Attribute Weight	Sub-Attribute	Sub-Attribute Weight	Score Description	Score Levels	Raw Score	Weighted Score
Risk *(continued)*	20%	Business Risk *(continued)*	30%	External Risk	25%	Very dynamic marketplace, high level of competitive threat, or sweeping industry changes likely from government regulators	High	0	0.00
						Some changes in market likely or some level of competition exists that may cause reprioritization or potential new regulations (along the lines of SOX, FDA, HIPAA, etc.)	Medium	5	0.83
						Fairly stable external environment or little impact of external changes on this IT investment	Low	9	1.50
				Strategic Risk	25%	IT investment directly impacts organization's strategic goals and objectives	High	0	0.00
						IT investment indirectly impacts organization's strategic goals and objectives	Medium	5	0.83
						Little to no impact on organization's strategic goals and objectives	Low	9	1.50
		Technical Risk	45%	Scalability Risk	20%	At maximum level—Cannot scale any further	Very High	0	0.00
						Up to 100% scalable	High	2	
						100% to 200% scalable	Medium	5	1.00
						>200% scalable	Low	9	1.80
				Customization Risk	30%	Custom-developed solution	Very High	0	0.00
						Packaged solution with 31% to 50% customization	High	2	0.60
						Packaged solution with 10% to 30% customization	Medium	5	1.50
						Packaged solution with <10% customization	Low	9	2.70

Criterion	Weight	Description	Rating	Value	Score
Integration Risk	20%	Significant integration required, necessitating architecture redesign; development of a number of new interfaces is required	Very High	0	0.00
		Some degree of integration required, does not require architecture redesign; however, a number of new interfaces need to be developed	High	2	0.40
		Low degree of integration, few new interfaces and/or modifications to existing interfaces	Medium	5	1.00
		Minimal integration required, mostly minor tweaks to existing interfaces	Low	9	1.80
Lifecycle Stage Risk	15%	Technology has risk of obsolescence—No longer supported by vendor	Very High	0	0.00
		Legacy or declining technology	High	2	0.30
		Niche or special use technology	Medium	5	0.75
		Mature technology	Low	9	1.35
Security Risk	15%	Limited security model—Rudimentary, difficult to configure, no role-based access	Very High	0	0.00
		Embedded security model with some configuration capabilities, role-based access	High	2	0.30
		Security model in alignment with organization's security standards, practices, and policies	Medium	5	0.75
		New paradigm in IT security, the adoption of which is redefining the IT industry (not yet in organization, but will significantly improve organization's security standards)	Low	9	1.35

(continues)

Table C-2 (Continued)

Objective	Objective Weight	Attribute	Attribute Weight	Sub-Attribute	Sub-Attribute Weight	Score Description	Score Levels	Raw Score	Weighted Score
Risk (continued)	20%	Operational Risk	25%	BCP Risk	30%	No BCP/Disaster Recovery Plan in place	Very High	0	0.00
						Class C Plan—DR within 5 business days	High	2	0.33
						Class B Plan—DR within 2 business days	Medium	5	0.83
						Class A Plan—DR within 2 hours of failure	Low	9	1.50
				Supportability Risk	40%	Only vendor can support	Very High	0	0.00
						Contractors supporting this solution (no in-house staff)	High	2	0.44
						Both in-house personnel and contractors for support	Medium	5	1.11
						Supported wholly by in-house staff	Low	9	2.00
				Vendor Risk	30%	Small company with niche product, regional vendor with no national presence, limited sales, support and delivery model; vendor has <25 customers with live implementations	Very High	0	0.00
						Vendor with national presence, good product strategy/vision, multiple channels of sales and implementation support; potential for being acquired by competitor exists; vendor has >25 and <100 customers with live implementations	High	2	0.33
						Vendor with international presence, excellent product strategy, multiple channels of sales and implementation support, products have >100 customers with live implementations	Medium	5	0.83
						Global leader in multiple products/solutions, excellent product strategy and vision, multiple channels of sales and implementation support, products have >500 customers with live implementa-	Low	9	1.50

Appendix D

SIRC's Enterprise IT Portfolio

Descriptions of each investment in the IT portfolio are provided in Tables D-1 and D-2.

Table D-1 SIRC IT OPEX portfolio

ID	Investment Name	Asset Class	IT Domain	IT Segment	Description of Proposed IT Investment	Requested Funding ($)
PFM-2010-001	PeopleSoft HCM OpEx	Application	ERP	Human Capital Management	PeopleSoft HRMS commercial off-the-shelf (COTS) solution has been implemented globally for: 1) Workforce Deployment (Employee Administration, Organizational Management, Benefits Management, Time & Attendance, Payroll, Employee Self-Service/Manager Self-Service, etc.). 2) Talent Management (Competency Management, Recruiting, Employee Performance Management, Employee Development, Compensation Mgmt, etc). 3) Travel Management (Travel Request & Approval, Travel Planning & Booking, Travel & Expense Management, etc.). The OpEx Costs are for ongoing support of this solution.	$15,402,000
PFM-2010-002	SAP ERP FI OpEx	Application	ERP	Financials	SAP COTS solution has been implemented globally; the whole effort was a seven-year program that cost approx. $180M to implement, which included: 1) ERP (Financials, Enterprise Asset Management, Direct Procurement, Cross-Functional Operations). 2) SCM (Demand & Supply Planning, SCM Procurement, Warehousing, Manufacturing, Order Fulfillment, Transportation, Supply Chain Visibility & Collaboration). 3) SAP Tools (NetWeaver, BW). This is the OpEx cost for SAP ERP's financials solution.	$11,492,000
PFM-2010-003	SAP ERP EAM OpEx	Application	ERP	Enterprise Asset Management	See note for PFM-2010-002. This is the OpEx cost for SAP ERP's Enterprise Asset Management solution.	$6,052,000
PFM-2010-004	SAP ERP DP OpEx	Application	ERP	Direct Procurement	See note for PFM-2010-002. This is the OpEx cost for SAP ERP's Direct Procurement solution.	$3,672,000
PFM-2010-005	SAP ERP XFO OpEx	Application	ERP	Cross-Functional Operations	See note for PFM-2010-002. This is the OpEx cost for SAP ERP's solutions to enable cross-functional operations.	$6,732,000
PFM-2010-006	Ariba SRM SBM OpEx	Application	SRM	Supply Base Management	Ariba Procurement & Supplier Management COTS solutions were initially implemented in 2001-2002, during the ".com bubble" era. This has since been upgraded and supported by the Procurements Information Services department. Ariba's Supplier Contract Management was implemented in 2007. This is the OpEx cost of	$3,672,000

PFM-2010-007	Ariba SRM SC OpEx	Application	SRM	Supplier Collaboration	See note for PFM-2010-006. This is the OpEx cost of Ariba SRM's Supplier Collaboration solution.	$4,012,000
PFM-2010-008	Ariba SRM PG OpEx	Application	SRM	Purchasing Governance	See note for PFM-2010-006. This is the OpEx cost of Ariba SRM's Purchasing Governance solution.	$3,502,000
PFM-2010-009	Ariba SRM IP OpEx	Application	SRM	Indirect Procurement	See note for PFM-2010-006. This is the OpEx cost of Ariba SRM's Indirect Procurement solution.	$6,222,000
PFM-2010-010	Ariba SRM CM OpEx	Application	SRM	Contract Management	See note for PFM-2010-006. This is the OpEx cost of Ariba SRM's Contract Management solution.	$5,882,000
PFM-2010-011	SAP SCM WH OpEx	Application	SCM	Warehousing	See note for PFM-2010-002. This is the OpEx cost of SAP SCM's Warehousing solution.	$4,352,000
PFM-2010-012	SAP SCM TP OpEx	Application	SCM	Transportation	See note for PFM-2010-002. This is the OpEx cost of SAP SCM's Transportation solution.	$4,352,000
PFM-2010-013	SAP SCM SNC OpEx	Application	SCM	Supply Network Collaboration	See note for PFM-2010-002. This is the OpEx cost of SAP SCM's Supply Network Collaboration solution.	$3,672,000
PFM-2010-014	SAP SCM SCV OpEx	Application	SCM	Supply Chain Visibility	See note for PFM-2010-002. This is the OpEx cost of SAP SCM's Supply Chain Visibility solution.	$4,692,000
PFM-2010-015	SAP SCM PR OpEx	Application	SCM	Procurement	See note for PFM-2010-002. This is the OpEx cost of SAP SCM's Procurement solution.	$4,012,000
PFM-2010-016	SAP SCM OF OpEx	Application	SCM	Order Fulfillment	See note for PFM-2010-002. This is the OpEx cost of SAP SCM's Order Fulfillment solution.	$7,922,000
PFM-2010-017	SAP SCM MF OpEx	Application	SCM	Manufacturing	See note for PFM-2010-002. This is the OpEx cost of SAP SCM's Manufacturing solution.	$8,092,000
PFM-2010-018	SAP SCM DSP OpEx	Application	SCM	Demand & Supply Planning	See note for PFM-2010-002. This is the OpEx cost of SAP SCM's Demand & Supply Planning solution.	$4,692,000
PFM-2010-019	Siebel Sales OpEx	Application	CRM	Sales	Siebel SFA was implemented in 2004. Siebel Center and associated Customer Service solutions were implemented in 2006. These solutions are supported by the Sales & Marketing Information Services Department. This is the OpEx cost of the Siebel Sales solution.	$8,262,000
PFM-2010-020	Legacy Marketing OpEx	Application	CRM	Marketing	A number of small, tightly coupled home-grown solutions were implemented more than 10 years back to enable marketing planning and operations. The marketing division maintains its own customer repository, customer segmentation, and list management based on IT intensive efforts every time that a small change needs to be made. This is the annual M&O for IT Services to support marketing planning, brand management, and operations.	$10,132,000

(continues)

Table D-1 (Continued)

ID	Investment Name	Asset Class	IT Domain	IT Segment	Description of Proposed IT Investment	Requested Funding ($)
PFM-2010-021	Siebel Call Center OpEx	Application	CRM	Customer Service	See note for PFM-2010-019. This is the OpEx cost of Siebel's CRM solution.	$6,392,000
PFM-2010-022	Legacy PLM PM OpEx	Application	PLM	Product Management	Legacy home-grown solution for product management called GPR (Global Product Repository). This is the OpEx cost of GPR.	$3,672,000
PFM-2010-023	Legacy PLM PDC OpEx	Application	PLM	Product Development & Collaboration	Patchwork of home-grown solutions integrated with the legacy product management and product data management. This is the OpEx cost of the custom solutions for Product Development & Collaboration.	$2,992,000
PFM-2010-024	Legacy PLM PDM OpEx	Application	PLM	Product Data Management	See note for PFM-2010-022. This is the OpEx cost of custom-developed PDM solution.	$4,182,000
PFM-2010-025	Legacy PLM FC OpEx	Application	PLM	Foundational Components	See note for PFM-2010-022. This is the OpEx cost of the custom-developed solutions for PLM foundational components.	$3,162,000
PFM-2010-026	ITSM ST OpEx	Technology	ITSM	Service Transition	OpEx cost for Release Management & Configuration Management implemented with ITIL v2.	$2,210,000
PFM-2010-027	ITSM SO OpEx	Technology	ITSM	Service Operation	OpEx cost for Incident Management, Problem Management, Service Desk, and Change Management implemented with ITIL v2.	$7,820,000
PFM-2010-028	ITSM SMT OpEx	Technology	ITSM	Service Mgmt. Tools	OpEx cost for Service Management Tools inclusive of upgrade from HP Service Desk to HP Service Manager, associated training, testing, and rollout.	$2,210,000
PFM-2010-029	ITSM SD OpEx	Technology	ITSM	Service Design	OpEx cost for Business Continuity & Disaster Recovery Support, i.e., IT Service Design.	$10,880,000
PFM-2010-030	INFR UDM OpEx	Technology	INFR	Unstructured Data Management	OpEx cost for Content Mgmt. (Microsoft SharePoint, Interwoven), Document Management (SharePoint), Document Generation (DocSciences), and Records Retention (IMR, Symantec Enterprise Vault). Supported by Global Infrastructure's Data Management team.	$3,910,000
PFM-2010-031	INFR SDM OpEx	Technology	INFR	Structured Data Management	OpEx cost for Structured Data Management (Oracle EE, MS SQL Server, associated tools, utilities, and administration). Supported by Global Infrastructure's Data Management team.	$8,160,000
PFM-2010-032	INFR SM OpEx	Technology	INFR	Security Management	OpEx cost for Security Management—Identity, Access & Content Security is handled by a combination of prepackaged security components within COTS solutions, OAM for authentication, SIRC's home-grown authorization framework for custom application development, enterprise anti-virus, encryption, password synchronization solutions. Supported by the Security & Risk Management department within Information Services.	$11,560,000

		Technology	INFR	Platform Management	OpEx cost for Desktop Hardware (Windows), Distributed Hardware (HP-UX Servers, Sun UNIX Servers, IBM AIX Servers), Print & Fax Servers, associated Operating Systems, Storage Management from EMC, Archival & Retrieval (COLD), Backup & Recovery (NetBackup). Supported by the Global Infrastructure department in Information Services.	$66,640,000
PFM-2010-033	INFR PM OpEx					
PFM-2010-034	INFR NM OpEx	Technology	INFR	Network Management	Supported by Network Operations within Global Infrastructure—OpEx for: 1. LAN, MAN, Campus/MAN, Remote Access, Business Partner Connectivity, Internet Access—CISCOWorks, OPNET 2. Voice/Video Networks—CISCO, Avaya, or GeniSys Global 3. Performance Enhancement—Coradiant 4. Quality of Service (QOS)—NetQoS 5. Protocols—TCP/IP 6. File Management—Windows, SAMBA 7. Email/Calendaring—Microsoft Exchange Server, IBM Lotus Notes 8. Collaboration/Groupware—Microsoft SharePoint, SaaS based Collaboration Tools, MS Instant Messenger, IBM SameTime, MS LiveMeeting, etc. 9. Voice Services/Call Recording—NICE, Witness 10. Audio/Video Distribution—VBRICK 11. Directory—Active Directory, LDAP 12. Address Management—DHCP	$28,560,000
PFM-2010-035	INFR DC OpEx	Technology	INFR	Data Center & Facilities Mgmt.	OpEx cost for managing SIRC's 29 existing data centers and IT facilities supported by Network Operations within Global Infrastructure.	$19,040,000
PFM-2010-036	INFR DAM OpEx	Technology	INFR	Data Access Management	Data Access Management is the responsibility of the Enterprise Informatics group within Information Services. OpEx cost for Data Warehouse, BI, Reporting & Analysis, Data Discovery, Data Mining, & Enterprise Search. 1. Data Warehouse—Oracle EE RDBMS, inclusive of COTS solutions DWs and Data Marts, including SAP BW 2. BI, Reporting, & Analysis—SAS, MS SSRS, Oracle BI EE, Cognos ReportNet, and PowerPlay 3. Data Discovery—IBM (Exeros) Data Discovery, Trillium Software 4. eDiscovery—Metalogix 5. Data Mining—SAS Enterprise Miner 6. Enterprise Search—Google Search, Microsoft SharePoint Enterprise Search	$11,900,000

(continues)

Table D-1 *(Continued)*

ID	Investment Name	Asset Class	IT Domain	IT Segment	Description of Proposed IT Investment	Requested Funding ($)
PFM-2010-037	INFR AM OpEx	Technology	INFR	Application Middleware	The Integration Shared Services (ISS) team, a CoE for Application Middleware, is responsible for the development, administration, and support of all middleware related activities in the organization. This team uses a combination of charge-back and base costs to support middleware operations in the organization. They are not responsible for managing SAP NetWeaver, which is under the purview of the SAP CoE. This is the OpEx cost for: 1. Application Server—IBM WAS, Microsoft Internet Information Server 2. Portal Infrastructure—IBM WAS, Microsoft SharePoint 3. Business Process Management Systems—PegaSystems SmartBPM™ Suite 4. Business Rules Engine—PegaSystems SmartBPM™ Suite, FairIssac 5. Extract, Transform & Load (ETL)—Informatica PowerCenter 6. Enterprise Application Integration (EAI)—IBM Websphere Business Integrator, IBM DataStage TX 7. WILY Middleware Monitoring Solution 8. B2B Integration—DataPower (Appliance) 9. Web Services Infrastructure—Logic Library, IBM WSRR 10. DB Middleware/Gateway—IBM DB2Connect, Oracle MVS Client 11. Transaction Processing—CICS 12. Messaging Middleware—IBM WPS, IBM MQSeries 13. EDI Solutions & Utilities—Sterling Commerce EDI Solution, IBM WTX	$6,630,000

	SDLC OpEx			Development Lifecycle	... of the Application Architecture Services team within the EA group. OpEx includes: 1. Requirements Management—IBM Rational Requisite Pro 2. Analysis/Design—IBM Rational Software Architect, ERWin 3. Engineering/Configuration—IBM RAD, Microsoft Visual Studio, etc. 4. Testing—HP Quality Center, IBM Rational Suite of Testing Tools, etc. 5. Deployment—InstallShield, Vendor IDEs, Ant 6. Software Configuration Management—IBM Rational ClearCase, PVCS 7. Programming Languages—Java, COBOL, C#, PL/SQL, etc. 8. Data Modeling—CA ERWin 9. Markup—XMLSpy, Dreamweaver, etc. 10. Design Patterns—Industry Standard Design Patterns, Custom (in-house) 11. Reusable Assets—Apache SW EJB, J2EE Common Components, etc. 12. Software Development Frameworks—J2EE, Struts, Spring, .NET, etc. 13. Software Development Process—IBM Rational Unified Process	$2,000,000
PFM-2010-039	IT LCM RP OpEx	Technology	IT LCM	IT Resource Planning	OpEx costs in IT Resource Planning include: 1. Portfolio Management—Oracle Prosight, Tree Plan, Oracle Crystal Ball 2. Project Management—Microsoft Project Server 3. Application Services Support (CoE for Tools & Technologies for COTS solutions)—SAP NetWeaver, SAP BW, Services, etc.)—this is the biggest spend component for IT Resource Planning, inclusive of licenses for tools and technologies and technical staff in support of ALM for COTS solutions	$6,800,000
PFM-2010-040	IT LCM EA OpEx	Technology	IT LCM	Enterprise Architecture (EA)	OpEx cost for Enterprise Architecture in support of: 1. Architecture Consulting overhead for EA to work with business and IT teams to create, maintain, & update EA blueprints in support of business needs, using TOGAF's ADM 2. Tools—Troux Technologies suite of modeling tools 3. Funds for anticipated prototyping and proofs of concepts, for innovative, forward-looking ideas in an e-lab environment	$3,570,000

Table D-2 SIRC IT CAPEX portfolio

ID	Investment Name	Asset Class	IT Domain	IT Segment	Description of Proposed IT Investment	Requested Funding ($)	New Initiative Category
PFM-2010-041	ERP HCM—e-Learning	Application	ERP	Human Capital Management	Proposal to implement an e-learning, i.e., Learning Management System, based on SumTotal's SaaS Solution (ResultsOnDemand), and integrate with the PeopleSoft HRMS suite. This initiative aims to achieve cost savings in training a field sales force of 6000, using e-learning as opposed to instructor-led training to achieve cost savings by reducing operational costs and improving efficiency.	$7,500,000	Informational
PFM-2010-042	ERP EAM—RFID Asset Tagging	Application	ERP	Enterprise Asset Management	Initiative aims to significantly improve asset tracking capabilities by implementing a project to tag assets with active wi-fi enabled RFID tags for all assets at corporate headquarters, and then to extend these capabilities throughout the organization. The initiative aims to improve operational efficiencies and achieve cost savings by reducing time to locate assets, increasing asset utilization and reducing asset theft and damage.	$6,250,000	Transactional
PFM-2010-043	SRM SC—Supplier Collaboration	Application	SRM	Supplier Collaboration	Initiative aims to implement improved supplier collaboration capabilities to enable web-based supplier interaction, direct document exchange, and supplier network management.	$3,755,000	Strategic
PFM-2010-044	SRM SC—Sourcing	Application	SRM	Sourcing	Initiative aims to improve sourcing capabilities by implementing new systems to enable a global central sourcing hub, RFP/RFQ & auctioning, and rules-based bid evaluation & awarding.	$6,752,500	Strategic
PFM-2010-045	SRM SC—Spend Analytics	Application	SRM	Purchasing Governance	Initiative aims to implement integrated Global Spend Analysis solution to provide greater insight into spend management and consolidated global spend reporting.	$3,126,000	Informational
PFM-2010-046	SCM SCV—SAP Supply Chain Design & Analytics	Application	SCM	Supply Chain Visibility	Implement improved capabilities with SAP's COTS solution for Strategic Supply Chain Design powered by comprehensive Supply Chain Analytics in order to respond better to market pressures and customer demands.	$3,950,000	Informational

PFM-2010-047	SCM OF— Service Parts Order Fulfillment	Application	SCM	Order Fulfillment	New investment to extend current Order Fulfillment capabilities to enable Service Parts Order Fulfillment. Goes hand-in-hand with PFM-2010-048.	$3,452,500	Transactional
PFM-2010-048	SCM DSP— Service Parts Planning	Application	SCM	Demand & Supply Planning	New investment to extend Demand & Supply Planning functionality to incorporate improved Service Parts Planning capabilities. Goes hand-in-hand with PFM-2010-047.	$2,650,000	Strategic
PFM-2010-049	CRM Sales— Contracts & Pricing Management	Application	CRM	Sales	SIRC Corp.'s current Contract & Pricing management business processes and underlying supporting systems are unable to adequately support the dynamic needs of the business in rebates management and up-front discount sales schemes driven by complex marketing innovations, with potential contractual violations resulting in fines or overpayment. The underlying infrastructure and procedures are unable to support informed decision making and reporting requirements. This initiative aims to implement a new COTS Contract Management System which will integrate with ERP & SCM systems and considerably reduce profit leakage, loss of financial controls, and channel conflicts and improve customer service.	$22,500,000	Transactional
PFM-2010-050	CRM Marketing— Siebel Marketing and Analytics	Application	CRM	Marketing	SIRC needs to improve its current marketing capabilities and implement new systems for Marketing Resource Management (MRM), Campaign Management, Customer Segmentation, List Management, Loyalty Management and Real-Time Offer Management, the latter two seeking to significantly exploit web 2.0 capabilities to bring in additional revenue among other benefits. The integration between Marketing, Sales, and Customer Service is limited such that multi-stage Campaign Management capabilities are rudimentary. Further, Lead Management and Loyalty Management capabilities are virtually non-existent. The company's products were blockbusters which sold without the need for tremendous marketing efforts, so	$17,000,000	Strategic

(continues)

Table D-2 (*Continued*)

ID	Investment Name	Asset Class	IT Domain	IT Segment	Description of Proposed IT Investment	Requested Funding ($)	New Initiative Category
PFM-2010-050 (*continued*)	CRM Marketing—Siebel Marketing and Analytics	Application	CRM	Marketing	the emphasis on improving marketing capabilities was not recognized. However, with the aggressive marketing push by competitors to enter the consumer goods sector, among others, SIRC's Chief Marketing Officer wants to revamp the entire suite of marketing applications and has entrusted the Director of Marketing & the Director of Marketing Information Systems with the joint responsibility of doing so. After considerable effort, the two directors have proposed a program called Multi-Channel Management, involving a combination of Siebel Marketing and custom development for enhanced web and mobile apps marketing capabilities.	$17,000,000	Strategic
PFM-2010-051	CRM CS—Service Contracts Integration	Application	CRM	Customer Service	New initiative aspires to improve Customer Support with new integration capabilities around Service Contracts & Agreement functionality as well as with Service Sales and Marketing.	$4,500,000	Transactional
PFM-2010-052	PLM—Oracle Product Management	Application	PLM	Product Management	PLM Program: Integration of new Product Data Management solution with existing Product Management capabilities. Dependence on PFM-2010-054.	$4,500,000	Transactional
PFM-2010-053	PLM—Oracle Product Management Integration	Application	PLM	Product Development & Collaboration	PLM Program: Integration of new Product Data Management solution with existing Product Development & Collaboration capabilities. Dependence on PFM-2010-054.	$2,500,000	Transactional
PFM-2010-054	PLM—Oracle Product Data Management	Application	PLM	Product Data Management	PLM Program: Implement new global Product Data Management with COTS solution for integrated global Product Master & Structure Management, Specification & Recipe Management, Service & Maintenance Structure Management, and Configuration Management aimed at reducing redundancies in product data across various business units and underlying systems in the organization. The new Product Data Management suite will serve as the authoritative source of product data throughout the organization.	$12,500,000	Transactional

ID	Name	Type	Code	Component	Description	Cost	Category
PFM-2010-055	PLM—Oracle Product Analytics	Application	PLM	PLM Foundational Components	PLM Program: Implement new Product Intelligence (Analytics) solution to leverage global product master data capabilities enabled by PFM-2010-054.	$3,000,000	Informational
PFM-2010-056	INFR SDM—Trillium Data Cleansing	Technology	INFR	Structured Data Management	Initiative to bring in new data cleansing, standardization, and data quality tool such as Trillium or Initiate in order to improve the quality of customer data, supplier data, as well as some reference data quality improvement as the data makes its way across from operational systems to the Enterprise Data Warehouse (EDW). The aim is to improve the quality of the core data in the EDW to enable better customer and supplier analytics that have suffered due to poor quality data.	$2,500,000	Transactional
PFM-2010-057	INFR SM—Risk Monitoring Tools	Technology	INFR	Security Management	Implement new Risk Monitoring & Control tools to enhance Security Management capabilities. A niche player, eEye Digital Security Solutions seems to offer a comprehensive suite of Risk Monitoring and control tools.	$5,430,000	Infrastructure
PFM-2010-058	INFR PM—Thin Computing Wyse & VMWare	Technology	INFR	Platform Management	This infrastructure project aims to bring Green computing into the organization through a desktop virtualization strategy. This project will replace all desktops in SIRC's Call Centers and Global Support Operations Desktop Replacement (more than 1000 desktops) with Thin Computing devices based on Wyse V90L client terminals, Wyse Virtualization Software, and VMWare View. This infrastructure upgrade is expected to generate significant savings, while taking the company on the path toward positive environmental impact.	$8,500,000	Infrastructure
PFM-2010-059	INFR NM—Unified Messaging System	Technology	INFR	Network Management	Unified Messaging System—Global e-mail consolidation from disparate e-mail systems across different geographic regions, borne as a result of SIRC Corp. acquiring other companies. This effort aims to improve organization-wide productivity with improved collaboration as a result of a global Microsoft Exchange based e-mail, calendars, instant messaging, and other collaborative features.	$11,000,000	Infrastructure

(continues)

Table D-2 (Continued)

ID	Investment Name	Asset Class	IT Domain	IT Segment	Description of Proposed IT Investment	Requested Funding ($)	New Initiative Category
PFM-2010-060	INFR NM— Corp. HQ Wireless	Technology	INFR	Network Management	Upgrade Network Infrastructure at corporate head-quarters to wireless network infrastructure. This initiative, sponsored by the CTO (head of GIS), is aimed at achieving cost savings from both direct benefits (reduced cost of future wiring, reduction in cost of moves, associated savings, etc.) and intangible benefits from improved productivity and worker mobility.	$7,500,000	Infrastructure
PFM-2010-061	INFR DC— Data Center Consolidation	Technology	INFR	Data Center	As a result of SIRC's acquisitions and distributed growth in the past 10 years, a number of legacy data centers have remained in existence in multiple locations (29 DCs and 14 different networks world-wide), many of which are redundant. The CTO (head of Global Infrastructure Services) has put forth a Data Center Consolidation proposal to consolidate to four data centers and shift the company network to a virtual private network (VPN) managed by a telecom provider, for improved reliability and qual-ity of service. This would be a major undertaking for global infrastructure, one that is expected to consume a significant amount of GIS resources for 12-15 months.	$24,750,000	Infrastructure
PFM-2010-062	INFR DAM— Reporting Tools Consolidation	Technology	INFR	Data Access Management	A number of disparate reporting and BI tool sets exist across the organization at various stages of tools maturity, including some declining and unsup-ported tool sets. This initiative aims to provide a unified suite of BI, Analysis and Reporting tools that can work seamlessly with both custom develop-ment efforts and integrate with SIRC's packaged implementation of ERP, SCM, SRM, and CRM capa-bilities. The chosen solution is Microsoft Enterprise SQL Server Reporting Services (SSRS). Existing reports in disparate technologies are to be con-verted to SSRS, the non-SSRS reporting tools and technologies are to be decommissioned, and staff will be consolidated across development and sup-port teams into SSRS CoE to achieve cost savings.	$3,500,000	Infrastructure

PFM-2010-063	INFR AM—WPS Upgrade	Technology	INFR	Application Middleware	Enterprise-wide implementation of IBM's Websphere Process Server (WPS), a business process automation engine to help form processes that meet business goals. SIRC's existing application middleware is built on the IBM platform (except for SAP NetWeaver for the ERP and SCM components), which provide the necessary foundation (WAS & WS ESB) for WPS. WPS is built on open standards; it deploys and executes processes that orchestrate services within SIRC's service-oriented architecture (SOA) or non-SOA infrastructure.	$2,000,000	Infrastructure
PFM-2010-064	IT LCM—EA Reference Models	Technology	IT LCM	Enterprise Architecture (EA)	Effort aimed at developing holistic set of reference models such as Process Reference Model (PRM), Data Reference Model (DRM), and Technical Reference Model (TRM) in an effort to improve process and data quality throughout the enterprise. Includes purchase of Troux Technologies' suite of EA solutions to serve as the EA repository and integrate with IT strategy & portfolio management efforts.	$2,000,000	Infrastructure
PFM-2010-065	IT LCM— Service Design Implementation	Technology	ITSM	Service Design	SIRC has implemented ITIL v2 capabilities for Release Mgmt., Configuration Mgmt., Incident Mgmt., Problem Mgmt., Service Desk, Change Mgmt., and Service Mgmt. Foundational Components, leveraging HP Service Manager. Additional capabilities are to be implemented to improve the quality of service offered by Global IT in support of SIRC's business needs. These new solutions seek to significantly improve capabilities in Availability Mgmt., Capacity Mgmt., and Service Level Mgmt. to further augment existing Service Mgmt. capabilities.	$5,500,000	Infrastructure

References

Abraham, S. C. (2006). *Strategic Planning: A Practical Guide for Competitive Success*. Thomson South-Western; Mason, OH.

Apfel, A. L., & Smith, M. (2003). *TVO Methodology: Valuing IT Investments via the Gartner Business Performance Framework*. Stamford: The Gartner Group.

Ariely, D. (2008). *Predictably Irrational—The Hidden Forces that Shape Our Decisions*. Harper Collins.

Balanced Scorecard Institute. (2009). Balanced Scorecard Basics. Retrieved May 2009, from Balanced Scorecard Institute: http://www.balancedscorecard.org/BSCResources/About theBalancedScorecard/tabid/55/Default.aspx.

Carnegie Mellon University. (2007). https://buildsecurityin.us-cert.gov/daisy/bsi/articles/ knowledge/business/684-BSI.html. Retrieved 2009, from https://buildsecurityin.us-cert .gov/daisy/bsi/articles/knowledge/business/684-BSI.html.

Carr, N. (2004). Does IT Matter? Information Technology and the Corrosion of Competitive Advantage. HBS Press, 81 (5), Vol. 81, Issue 5.

Celona, J., & McNamee, P. (2005). Decision Analysis for the Professional. Strategic Decisions Group (Editions 1 & 2) and SmartOrg (Editions 3 & 4).

Chatterjee, S. (2008, May). Applied Information Architecture (AIE): Not Just Calculate, Scientifically MEASURE IT. Retrieved April 2009, from www.CIOIndex.com: http://www .cioindex.com/nm/templates/MainPage.aspx?articleid=68754&zoneid=4.

Cooper, R., Edgett, S., & Kleinschmidt, E. (2001). *Portfolio Management for New Products*. Cambridge: Perseus Books Group; New York.

DiMasi, J. A., Hansen, R. W., & Grabowski, H. G. (2003). The price of innovation: new estimates of drug development costs. *Journal of Health Economics*. Vol. 22, 151–185.

DuBrin, A. J. (2007). *Fundamentals of Organizational Behavior*. Thomson South-Western; Mason, OH.

Gido, J., & Clements, J. P. (2009). *Successful Project Management*. Thomson South-Western; Mason, OH.

Gilbert, J., Henske, P., & Singh, A. (2003). Rebuilding big pharma's business model in vivo. Windhover Information Inc., Vol. 21, #10.

Gliedman, C. (2008). *The Total Economic Impact Methodology: A Foundation for Sound Technology Investments*. Cambridge: Forrester Research.

Goodwin, P., & Wright, G. (2010). *Decision Analysis for Management Judgment*. John Wiley & Sons Ltd; Hoboken, NJ.

Hammond, J., Keeney, R., & Raiffa, H. (2002). *Smart Choices—A Practical Guide to Making Better Life Decisions*. Broadway.

Hertz, D. P., & Dowse, C. (2009, May). http://www.cioinsight.com/c/a/IT-Management/Does-CIO-Behavior-Derail-Intentions-526614/. Retrieved May 2009, from CIOInsignt.com: http://www.cioinsight.com/c/a/IT-Management/Does-CIO-Behavior-Derail-Intentions -526614/.

Hill, C. W., & Jones, G. R. (2010). *Strategic Management: An Integrated Approach*. South-Western Cengage Learning; Mason, OH.

Intel Corporation. (2001). Managing IT Investments: Intel's IT Business Value Metrics Program. Retrieved 2009, from www.intel.com: http://premierit.intel.com/community/ipip.

ISACA. (2006). VAL IT Overview. Retrieved from Information Systems Audit and Control Association (ISACA): http://www.isaca.org/Content/ContentGroups/Val_IT1/Val_IT.htm.

Keeney, R. L. (1982). Decision analysis: an overview. *Operations Research*, Vol. 30, 803–838.

Kirkwood, C. W. (1997). *Strategic Decision Making: Multiobjective Decision Analysis with Spreadsheets*. Brooks/Cole; Belmont, CA.

Kodukula, P., & Papudesu, C. (2006). *Project Valuation Using Real Options: A Practitioner's Guide*. J. Ross Publishing; Ft. Lauderdale, FL.

Lewis, J. P. (2003). *Project Leadership*. McGraw-Hill; New York.

Letavec, C. (2006). *The Program Management Office: Establishing, Managing and Growing the Value of a PMO*. J. Ross Publishing; Ft. Lauderdale, FL.

Maizlish, B., & Handler, R. (2005). *IT Portfolio Management Step-by-Step*. John Wiley and Sons, Inc.; Hoboken, NJ.

McClure, B. (2003). http://www.investopedia.com/articles/fundamental/03/031203.asp. Retrieved 2009.

McKay, M. D., Beckman, R. J., & Conover, W. J. (1979). *A Comparison of Three Methods for Selecting Values of Input Variables in the Analysis of Output from a Computer Code*. Technometrics (American Statistical Association), 239–245.

Merkhofer, L. (2008). Keys to Implementing Project Portfolio Management. Retrieved from www.prioritysystem.com.

Mintzberg, H., Ahlstrand, B., & Lampel, J. (1998). *Strategy Safari—A Guided Tour through the Wilds of Strategic Management*. The Free Press; New York.

Office of Government Commerce (OGC). (2008). Portfolio, Programme and Project Offices. The Stationery Office.

Ragsdale, C. T. (2008). *Spreadsheet Modeling & Decision Analysis—A Practical Introduction to Management Science, 5e*. Thomson—South Western; Mason, OH.

Rang, H. P. (2006). *Drug Discovery and Development—Technology in Transition*. Churchill Livingstone Elsevier.

Shapiro, A., Dentcheva, D., & Ruszczyski, A. (2009). Lectures on stochastic programming: modeling and theory.

Skinner, D. C. (1999). *Introduction to Decision Analysis: A Practitioner's Guide to Improving Decision Quality*. Probabilistic Publishing.

Software Engineering Institute (SEI). (2010). Retrieved April 2010, from http://www.sei.cmu.edu/cmmi/.

Strategic Decisions Group. (2005). See Celona & McNamee.

Taleb, N. N. (2007). *The Black Swan: The Impact of the Highly Improbable*. Random House.

Tufte, R. E. (2001). *The Visual Display of Quantitative Information*. Graphic Press.

United States Food and Drug Administration. (2012). Investigational New Drug (IND) Application. Retrieved from Development & Approval Process (Drugs): http://www.fda.gov/drugs/developmentapprovalprocess/howdrugsaredevelopedandapproved/approvalapplications/investigationalnewdrugindapplication/default.htm.

Winston, W., & Albright, C. (2007). *Practical Management Science*. Thomson South-Western; Mason, OH.

Wyss, G. D., & Jorgensen, K. H. (1998, February). A User's Guide to LHS: Sandia's Latin Hypercube Sampling Software. Retrieved from A User's Guide to LHS: Sandia's Latin Hypercube Sampling Software.

Index